Mister Providence College

Mister Providence College

*The Selected Writings of
Rev. Joseph L. Lennon, O.P.*

Edited by
Russell J. DeSimone

Introduction by
Patrick T. Conley
Rhode Island Historian Laureate

The Rhode Island Publications Society
Providence ♦ 2019

Copyright 2019 Rhode Island Publications Society

All rights reserved. No part of this book may be reproduced in any form whatsoever without permission in writing from the publisher, except for brief passages in connection with a review.

For information write:
The Rhode Island Publications Society
1445 Wampanoag Trail, Suite #201
East Providence, RI 02915
Tel: (401) 273-1776
Fax: (401) 273-1791

Printed in the United States of America
ISBN: 978-1-930483-07-1

Typeset in Adobe Jenson Pro
Book design and production by Clifford Garber

Contents

PREFACE   xi

INTRODUCTION — MISTER PROVIDENCE COLLEGE   xiii

1   EDUCATION

Thinking: The Main Job of Formal Education   3
The True Function of the Nation's School Systems   6
Home and School: A Cooperative Enterprise   10
The Value of a Liberal Education   16
The Pleasures and Pains of Learning   19
Blaming Teachers Allows the Real Culprit to Escape   24
Have Faith In Your Teacher   27
Teachers Should Grow On The Job   30
Teacher's Task In Education Is To Build Upon Authority   33
Striking a Balance Between Discipline, Freedom   36
Crisis in Public School Teaching   38
Pros and Cons of Public Education   40
Parents Have Rights in Classroom   42

2   THE LAW

Law: The Magic Mirror   44
There Oughta Be a Law   52
Please Don't Kill The Lawyers   59
What Is Legal Is Not Always Moral   62
Screening Those Future Judges   65
Cops Can Only Do So Much   68

3 Politics

Politics and the Common Good 71
Challenge of Getting Out the Vote 74
Spoils System and Political Cronyism 76
Politics and Ethics in an Imperfect World 79
Public Service and Ethics in Government 82
The Kind of Leadership We Deserve 88
Public Behavior of Private Officials 91
No Cure for Bureaucracy 94

4 Ethics and Morals

Be Smart: Be Good: Be Wise 97
The Evanescence of Honor 100
Has Greed Come to Define the New American Spirit? 102
Honor and Cheating 104
Ethics in Business... The Good & The Bad 107
Here We Are—Rationalizing Sin 110
Pensions and Milking the System —
    Legal, Yes, But Is It Moral? 113
"Right to Privacy" Pushes Aside Common Sense 116

5 Religion and the Modern World

What Is Religion? 118
What Can God and Religion Do for Me? 121
How Religiously Mature Are You? 124
Intellect Still Has Its Place 127
Do Jews Belong in the Ecumenical Movement? 129
Sound Doctrine Lacking in Uplift Literature 132
Religion Possesses Revolutionary Spirit 136
Religion, Secularism, and American Polity 140
The Devil Is Thriving in American Society 144

6 Catholicism and the Catholic Church

Call Me Catholic *First* 146
Catholic Identity and the Second Vatican Council 149
Ignoring the Saints Is a Sad Commentary
  on Modern Culture 159
Catholics Obligated to Become a Political Force 162
The Clerical Line Separating Church and State 165
Catholic Intellectuals: The Need of the Church 167
Criticism of Pope Shows Ignorance of Church's Mission 170
Vocations. A Need to Address the Vocations Crisis 173
Professor Says Kennedy Needs Brush-up Courses 178
Noble Celibacy Is Never Out of Date 181

7 The Right to Life

The God Squad 184
Politics and the Pro-life Voter 191
Catholics Must Maximize Their Voting Power 194
Anti-Catholic Bigotry Again 196
The Bloodiest War in Human History 199
Single-Issue Voting Is OK 200
Our Desacralized Society Can Spawn a Mengele 202
Exercising Our Right to Influence Congress 204

8 The Family

The Family—The Basic Unit of Civilization 207
Pressures Influencing Family Stability 213
First, Let Our Children Be Children 226
Where Lies Parental Responsibility? 229
Delinquency Is a Product of Our Own Homes 231

9 Gender

American Womanhood: An Untapped Source of Power   233
The Status of Women in Business and Professions   238
The Catholic Woman as an Intellectual   240
Sex Discrimination and Ordination of Women
   in the Catholic Church   247
Role of Women Religious Is Changing   250

10 Sexuality

Lust Permeates, Grows, Rooted in Our Culture   253
American Culture Nurtures Promiscuity   256
Viagra, Sex, and Spiritual Impotence   259
Christianity and the Sexual Revolution   261
Women's Clothes Can Betray Silent Intent   263
Sex, Even Between Spouses, Can Be a Sin   266
Cohabitation Stance Ignores Original Sin   268
Reservations About Dispensing Contraceptives to Teens   270
It's Not a Street of Joy   272
Imbue Teens with a Proper Sense of Sexual Morality   274
Preach Abstinence; Youths Need to Hear It   276
Pope John Paul vs. Ann Landers on Solitary Sex   279

11 Temper of the Times

The 'Geriatric' Divorce   282
Competitive Spirit and the Highway   285
TV's Stunting Impact on Growing Minds   286
Technology and Today's Society   288
Homosexual Orientation a Matter of Choice   291
Demotion of Grieving Leads to Greater Loss   293
Drug Control Necessary in a Thrill-Seeking Society   296
Case of the Narcissistic Philanthropist   298
How Far Can Tolerance Go?   301

12 Sundry Subjects

George Washington Admonishes Americans of Today   304
How to Break Out of Prison   312
Free? In Prison?   319
The Spirit of Providence College   322
The Meaning of Being Irish   325
Poor Entitled to 'American Dream'   328
A Cult of Mediocrity Is a Danger to Be Avoided   331
The Lottery Craze and Lady Luck   334
Sports and the Whole Man: First Things First   337
Holy 9-Irons!   340
Where'syoursenseofhumor?   342
Ecclesiastical Jokes Needed   348

Preface

Growing up as I did in Rhode Island in the 1950s, Father Lennon was somewhat of a celebrity. Not only was he the public face of Providence College, he seemed to be everywhere—on television, the radio and in the newspapers. He seemed to be the unofficial moralist for Rhode Islanders, not just for Roman Catholics but non-Catholics as well. In the early 1960s I entered Providence College where Father Lennon was the Dean of the College. I only knew him from a distance as college administrators didn't necessarily "rub elbows" with the student body. In fact, I don't think I ever spoke to him until many years later, near the end of his life, when I had a pleasant conversation with him at one of Patrick and Gail Conley's famous Constitution Day celebrations held at their home in Bristol. While that conversation was brief and for me memorable, I can't say I really got to know the man until recently when I was asked to select and edit Father's writings in preparation for this book. In reading the nearly three hundred essays that were handed to me in a large box it soon became evident that Father Lennon was a true humanist. His essays reveal a man that was a theologian, philosopher, educator, moralist, sociologist, priest, man of faith, public speaker, humorist and avid golfer. While I can't say I knew him in life, however, through his writings, I think I got to know the man quite well and I hope the essays selected for this book will allow the reader to get to know him too.

This book has its genesis in a conversation between Patrick Conley and Father Lennon in 2005 when Pat suggested to Father that a book of his essays be published for posterity. A year later the essays appeared at Conley's law office in two boxes. Over time the essays were sorted, and some were professionally edited; however, due to funding issues the book was set aside and never published. In June 2011, Father Lennon died but Pat's commitment to publishing the book of essays did not die. In 2017 Pat and I devised a plan to use Rhode Island Heritage Harbor Foundation funds to publish several books of local interest under the imprint of the Rhode Island Publications Society. Pat as President of both the Society and the Foundation and I as a board of directors' member of both organizations presented the plan to publish to both boards which was whole-heartedly approved. In a sense the publication of this book ends a fifteen-year journey. I hope Father Lennon would be pleased with the results.

Father wrote for numerous newspapers and journals. Oftentimes he would reuse or repurpose his essays to meet the needs of his target audience. Often the same essay would appear several times over a span of several years under different titles. Quite frequently he would appropriate sentences, paragraphs or even pages from previous essays and weave them into new essays. As the reader looks over these essays he will notice where this occurs. While somewhat redundant it was thought proper to keep some of these examples as it provides some insight into Father's thinking and wordsmithing skills. It should be noted that most of these essays were written before political correctness made its impact on American discourse.

No publication is the accomplishment of just one person, certainly without Father Lennon there would be no book, but also the vision and long-term commitment by Patrick Conley must be recognized as well as his faith in me to produce this book. Russell Franks and Robin Rancourt at Providence College's Phillips Memorial Library's special collections department were most helpful in locating images of Father Lennon. And lastly to my family, especially my wife Linda, who endured my time away from family events while this book was in development.

Russell J. DeSimone
Middletown, Rhode Island

Mister Providence College

Reverend Joseph L. Lennon has been called the "ubiquitous Father Lennon," the versatile Father Lennon, and "Mister Providence College."

Joseph Luke Lennon was a native Rhode Islander and maintained a lifelong connection with the Elmhurst section of Providence. He was born on September 21, 1919, a son of John J. Lennon and Marjorie (McCabe) Lennon. He had six brothers, John, James, Frederick, Robert, Ralph, and Bernard, and two sisters, Marjorie and Mary. He graduated from LaSalle Academy in 1936 and earned his B.A. from Providence College in 1940 without having to leave his cherished Elmhurst neighborhood. At PC he majored in the classics and enrolled in a pre-ecclesiastical program. Lennon then entered the Dominican Order's novitiate at St. Rose Priory in Springfield, Kentucky choosing the religious name Luke, in honor of the Evangelist who contributed more text to the New Testament than anyone else. Considering his future literary output, Lennon's choice of Luke as his saintly patron was both appropriate and prophetic.

Postulant Lennon then studied for two years at St. Joseph Priory in Somerset, Ohio and then earned his bachelor's and licentiate degrees in sacred theology at the Dominican House of Studies in Washington, D.C. On June 5, 1947 he was ordained a priest in Washington, and in 1949, Father Lennon joined the Providence College faculty where he taught education, theology, and philosophy until he retired from regular teaching in 1968 to assume the college's vice presidency of community affairs. At the outset of his teaching career he added to his already impressive academic credentials by earning his Master of Arts and Ph.D. degrees at the University of Notre Dame in 1949 and 1952, respectively.

Lennon has been described as ubiquitous, because he blanketed the State of Rhode Island with his preaching, teaching, lecturing, and priestly ministrations. He was everywhere, even in retirement, visiting the sick in hospitals and nursing homes, talking to service clubs, counseling the bereaved at wakes and funerals, presiding at weddings, and joining the celebrations of first communion, confirmation, anniversaries, testimonials, and other social events. A twenty-five year Providence Rotary Club member, Father Lennon was actively engaged in a wide spectrum of humanitarian and community services.

Lennon was called versatile because of his multi-faceted personality and talents; he did many things and he did them well. He is the author of three books and over 500 articles, published in the *Providence Visitor*, the *Providence Journal-Bulletin*, and such scholarly periodicals as the *Thomist*,

New Scholasticism, Modern Schoolman, Catholic Education Review, Rhode Island Medical Journal, Columbia, Harvard Educational Review, Catholic Educator, Delta Epsilon Sigma Bulletin, and other learned journals. Over one hundred of those varied essays are reprinted in this memorial volume marking the centennial of his birth.

Father Lennon was heard for four years on weekly radio talks and lectured for fifteen years on WJAR-TV in a weekly program entitled, "Psychology in Everyday Life." He was often referred to as Rhode Island's Fulton J. Sheen, a reference to a monsignor (later bishop), who was a very popular national TV personality in the 1950s. Lennon also conducted seminars in Europe for the U. S. Air Force Educational Program, was a featured Lenten preacher at St. Patrick's Cathedral in New York City, was keynote speaker at several annual state educational conferences, and was a popular lecturer along the Eastern seaboard. This member of the Order of Preachers (O.P.) was unrivaled as an orator.

Father Lennon was also a familiar figure in the Rhode Island golfing community. A low-handicap golfer for many years, he was a thirty-year member of the Board of Directors and the Selection Committee of the John Burke Caddy Scholarship Foundation. When he was chairman of the Rhode Island Heart Fund Campaign, Father Lennon cooperated with businessmen William Carroll and Christopher Antonelli to start the Father Lennon Golf Tournament for the Heart Fund Campaign. Since its inception this charitable athletic enterprise has raised over a half-million dollars.

Father Lennon was hailed as a keen competitor on the links. He won the Rhode Island Golf Association Senior Golf championship in 1980 and the Rhode Island State Seniors Golf Association championship in 1981, 1982, and 1984.

The ubiquitous and versatile Father Lennon was also known as "Mister Providence College" because of his involvement in the community as a Dominican priest. He became the most recognizable cleric, professor, and administrator at Providence College. Wherever he went people said "That's the Providence College priest." His efforts in promoting the name of PC and exemplifying in his personal life the ideals it espouses has accounted in no small measure for the favorable reputation Providence College enjoys in the Rhode Island community.

In a professional career dedicated to the education of youth, Father Lennon always stressed the intellectual and moral virtues which produce well-informed Catholics, staunch family men and women, and socially-conscious citizens. At Providence College, Father Lennon joined the faculty in 1949, became Dean of Men in 1956, Dean of the College in August 1957, and Vice President for Community Affairs in August 1968.

While serving in an administrative capacity, Father Lennon represented Providence College as Vice President of the American Association of University and College Deans, member of the Association of Vice Presidents for Community Affairs, Vice President of the New England Association of Affirmative Action Officers, and president for three years of Delta Epsilon Sigma, the national honor society for Catholic colleges and universities.

This Dominican dynamo was awarded an honorary Doctor of Letters by Bradford Durfee College in 1963 and by the University of Southeastern Massachusetts (now UMass Dartmouth) in 1975. In 1980, Roger Williams University conferred upon him an honorary Doctor of Humane Letters. Camden Avenue Playground in the Smith Hill neighborhood was renamed Father Lennon Park in his honor in 1997 to recognize his fiftieth anniversary as a priest.

Among Lennon's local civic services are his thirty-year membership on the Board of Directors of Rhode Island Blue Cross and Blue Shield; member of the Board of Directors and campaign chairman of the Rhode Island Heart Association; member of the Trustees and chairman of the Rhode Island Chapter of the Easter Seal Society; arbitrator for the Rhode Island State Board of Labor; and Chairman of the Scholarship Committee of the Laborers International Union of North America. In addition, Father Lennon was a director, trustee, or member of more than two dozen additional organizations, primarily those concerned with health care and disease prevention.

A resume of Father Lennon's life and work may be found in *Who's Who in America* and *Who's Who Among American Educators*. However, a mere recitation of his accomplishments and civic involvements does not capture his relentless and indefatigable spirit, his sharp Irish wit, his spellbinding oratory, or the exuberance of his personality.

Father Lennon lost his long and courageous battle with cancer on June 21, 2011 at the age of ninety-one, and he was buried in the Dominican cemetery on the PC campus. All of his eight siblings pre-deceased him. Appropriately, he died on that day of the year called the Summer Solstice when the sun shines the longest, a symbolic tribute to his brilliance and his warmth.

✥

Father Lennon (left), who would eloquently deliver most of the Constitution Day invocations, is shown in September 2000 as he, hostess Gail Conley, and Pat Conley prepare to greet the guests at the entrance to Gale Winds, the Conleys' Bristol home, on the first Constitution Day observance.

On a personal level, Father Lennon and I did not become close friends until late in our lives, even though we shared a Providence College experience. When I was a student (Class of 1959), I did not have him as a professor. During my thirty years of teaching at PC (1963–1993) we interacted only in a cursory manner. Not until 1999 when, as Hall of Fame director, I nominated and inducted Lennon into the Rhode Island Heritage Hall of Fame did we become close friends.

After Father Lennon's induction—where he joined his Dominican colleagues, Fathers Dore, Begley, and Forster—he often gave spirited and humorous invocations at several of the Hall's annual banquets, and, from 2000 through 2010, he performed the same function for the Constitution Day observances that I conducted in collaboration with my wife Gail. His invocations and supplementary remarks were always eloquent and witty.

In 2005, after reading one of his enlightening, common sense essays in the *Providence Journal*, I told Father Lennon that his body of literary works ought to be preserved in book form. I made this suggestion because I had just completed my own anthology in a volume called *Rhode Island in Rhetoric and Reflection* (2004). Father Lennon promptly agreed and brought two cartons of his various writings to my office for editing and publication by the Rhode Island Publications Society. I gave this literary treasure to the Society's editor Dr. Hilliard Beller who worked on it for several months. Unfortunately when the manuscripts were returned, money to publish them was unavailable. The only subsidy the Society received after a limited appeal was a $1,000 gift from the author's sister Marjorie. Then came the Great Recession, and Father Lennon's prospective opus languished in the cartons that he had used to deliver them.

However, in 2016 a large fund of money became available to the Publications Society for projects such as this when I created the Heritage Harbor Foundation with help from Al Klyberg, Tony Marandola, and Richard Licht. In concert with Grants Committee Chairman, Russell DeSimone, we secured the approval of the Foundation to embark upon a project to publish or reprint important works pertaining to Rhode Island's history and culture. To date the partnership between the Foundation and the Society has produced fifteen pamphlets and two booklets, but this is the first book-length production. The indefatigable DeSimone painstakingly edited, sorted, and organized this anthology into its final topical form. Father Lennon's lustrous legacy has been preserved and a promise has been kept.

After a careful reading of these essays, drawing as they do, upon the wisdom of a vast array of philosophers, theologians, scientists, poets, scholars, social critics, historians, jurists, statesmen, and *literati*, I have come to the belief that this volume could also be titled *Father Lennon's Mother Lode*, because it is a goldmine of insights and contains rich veins of practical, intellectual, and spiritual guidelines for life, both here and hereafter.

       (Dr.) Patrick T. Conley
       Historian Laureate of Rhode Island
       President, Heritage Harbor Foundation
       and Rhode Island Publications Society

Mister Providence College

(1)
Education

Thinking: The Main Job of Formal Education
(The Cowl, October 28, 1987)

Schools risk losing their identity when they fritter away time on tasks only remotely connected with the job of forming the minds of students.

Thinking, Aristotle tells us, is what makes man distinctively human and education succeeds or fails on how well it allows the rational faculty dominance and full play.

"Sweet reasonableness," the fruit of worthwhile education, springs from the belief that reason can be trusted, that it ought to prevail in dealings among human beings. "If Not Reason, What?" asks Yale's one time president, Dr. Kingman Brewster.

Schools will be judged not on how they amuse, condition, pacify, or keep youth busy, but on how successful they are in implanting the sway of the mind. At a time when man's very rationality is being questioned or downplayed, there can be no higher calling. Dissemination of psychoanalytical theory has led to an overstatement of the case for the primacy of the unconscious and the irresistibility of irrational impulse. Consequently, a spreading disbelief in the power, and even the desirability, of impersonal thinking has taken root.

Freud, near the end of his life wrote: "I am only sure of one thing, that the judgments of value made by mankind . . . are attempts to prop up their illusions with arguments." Exultantly English writer and poet D. H. Lawrence declared: "My great religion is a belief in the blood, the flesh, as being wiser than the intellect."

What makes this doctrine so dangerous is the breadth of its acceptance. Leaders who appeal to emotion gain the most followers. Voices vibrant with passion are most bewitching in time of crisis.

Yet, the control of emotion in the interest of truth ought to be part of the Freemasonry of educated people, a natural by-product of a good education.

Intellectual integrity has always been the mark of a cultured mind and enlightened heart. It embraces a passion for truth, a refined conscience that makes one feel that he befouls himself if he descends to name-calling, or judges another in anger or envy, or subscribes to underhanded practices, or argues *ad hominem*, or generalizes from insufficient facts, or dogmatizes without ground.

A hundred years ago, people agreed, more or less, on certain fundamental propositions. Victorians were convinced that much of what they believed could be explained and defended, and those who disagreed with them had the task of demonstrating, by logic and evidence, why they disagreed. Faith itself had to be rationally credible. St. Paul said, "Give reason for the faith that is in you."

This reliance on reason was thought a great advance; indeed, it was the essence of the idea of progress, if by progress is meant something besides inventions and manufactures. Unlike today, man formerly exhibited confidence in the power of mind to control idiotic imaginings, resist the promptings of passion, and restrain the surge of primitive impulse.

This insistence on the primacy of intellect in education, in no way belittles the importance of feeling. Passionless education lacks the verve to inspire. Thought needs the heat of desire as much as desire needs the light of thought.

Reason without emotion is lifeless, while emotion without reason is blind. Moreover, reasonableness in thought ought to be balanced by reasonableness in feeling. The golfer who blows his stack over a missed putt, or the prom date who panics over a blossoming pimple, have allowed their feelings to dominate their common sense. Cause and effect are incommensurate; the outburst and the incident do not jibe.

But we live in a sensation-seeking age where feeling is king. Americans chase relentlessly after the physical and emotional high. Self-styled swingers, effete middle-agers, and bored housewives are persuaded or have convinced themselves that any thrill-producing activity is itself worth pursuing.

Purveyors of transporting experience exploit this yen for kicks. The appeal of much in the encounter movement—from the "let-it-all-hang-out" of the primal scream to the goofiness of the nude marathon—can be ascribed to the heady excitement aroused in the client. The frenzy evoked by punk rock music accounts for its Pied Piper attraction.

But enthusiasms can be reasonable or unreasonable. A new discovery, invention, or artistic production can send the *cognoscenti* into a tizzy. But much of what we find in today's mass culture is shoddy and scarcely worth getting excited about. Feeling, in itself, and apart from the worth of the object, is hardly a rational end for human beings; if it were, the manic case in the hospital should be the envy of us all.

What matters is whether we get excited about the right things. In Plato's Phaedrus, Socrates asks a young man with whom he has been pursuing a discussion of ultimate truth, whether they should go on with the inquiry. "Should we continue, do you say?" replies the youth. "Are there any pleasures worth living for like these?" Such a display of delight in learning is not only gratifying to teachers but also bolsters faith in the value of man's unique faculty: reason.

The True Function of the Nation's School Systems
(The Providence Evening Bulletin, date not known)

We are often told that the main function of the school is to produce good citizens. How acceptable is this statement? Since a normal life means a life lived in society, including political society, education for citizenship is undoubtedly a valuable and even a necessary aim. But is it adequate as the sole aim, or even as the main aim of education?

Before we can say what the primary aim of education should be, we must find out what we are educating. We are educating a human person, a free rational being, capable of knowledge and love through the spiritual principle of his or her nature, transcending the determined material order, possessing an intrinsic liberty, having a destiny beyond the temporal world, an independent whole and not merely a part of nature, an end, and not merely a means.

A Social Animal

Because he is what he is, man is naturally a social animal. Hereafter, I will use traditional, generic masculine pronoun to express my views, fully mindful they embrace women as well. He tends to society, both domestic and civil, because he is a man. It is true that society is natural to man because it satisfies his material needs through making possible the division of labor, and because it satisfies his intellectual needs through making possible the office of teaching. But society is also natural to man because it allows greater scope for his specifically human powers of knowledge and love; it allows him to communicate his thoughts to his fellows and to express his natural generosity and love to them. Society exists to enable man to give, as well as to take, and thus to reach a fuller degree of human development.

Society then is human society, erected by the free consent of human persons and having as its aim the common good of its members, the providing of the conditions of the good life through which they can most completely develop their human potentialities. A citizen, then, must first be a man before he can be a citizen, and the better man he is, the better citizen he will make. Those schools which aim only, or even first, at making a citizen are motivated by a false view of the nature of man and of society. They are putting the cart before the horse.

Good citizenship is best achieved by aiming at something else. An education that aims at making the student first a fully developed man, by stressing his intellectual and moral training, also will make him a good citizen; an education that aims first at making him a citizen by stressing exclusively or even chiefly, his social training will only make him a slave by stunting the growth of his intellectual powers. It will make him the slave of inhuman forces by regarding and training him as a being whose role is to adapt himself to his environment rather than to form his environment by the free exercise of his human intellect and will.

This leads to another and even more serious criticism of the conception of citizenship as the sole or the primary aim of education. This conception implies that man is a means and society, his end; it denies in effect, if not in intention, the fundamental liberties of the human person, and sees in him only a tool of the state. And if education is for citizenship, then the state of which the student is a citizen quickly will become the power that decides what type of education its citizens shall have. Education for citizenship will come in practice to mean education of the type that a particular state demands, a type subservient to its desires in lending itself to its particular aims. This is what happened in Mussolini's Italy and Hitler's Germany, and what is still happening in Russia and China today.

Consciously or unconsciously, education for citizenship implies the totalitarian conception of man and of the state. It is based on the tenet that the state has given the individual everything he has, and consequently, that it rightly may demand all in return. If citizenship is allowed to become the sole aim, or even the primary aim of education, it will lead inevitably to the totalitarian state. Was it not Mussolini who said: "Nothing above the state, nothing beyond the state, nothing outside the state."

A Matter of Giving

By this, I do not mean to derogate from the importance of good citizenship as an aim of education, even though it is a partial and subordinate aim, a by-product, as it were, of more universal objectives. Let me explain. The purpose of citizenship is the common welfare of the state in which citizenship is enjoyed. A state is its citizens; rulers and ruled, united in the pursuance of a common social peace and well-being. It is to be conceived in terms of motion; it is a directed movement aimed at a goal. It is the common good which gives reason for citizenship and is the determinant of the goodness of the citizen. He is a good citizen who is well disposed in regard to the common good. In conformity with the nature of the citizen as he is a man, this disposition must be rational and voluntary; in order that it be constant and efficacious, it must be a virtuous attachment—a habitual inclination to meet the demands of the common good.

"Unselfish love of the common good," says Thomas Aquinas, "makes a good citizen." The common good is in some degree an actuality, and at the same time it is an ideal, a good to be achieved by organized cooperative activity on the part of the citizens. Both as an actuality and as an ideal, it is a good, and consequently an object of love.

Only a By-Product

An unselfish love means no more than a constant effective desire to do good to another. It is not a matter of getting for one's self; it is a matter of giving, of spending one's self for another. He who truly loves the good of the state does not wish to control or corner it. He is not looking to receive. He desires to preserve it in all its integrity and to advance it as much as it is within his power to do so. His attitude and attachment is the direct opposite of that of the tyrants, big, and small, who, bent solely on personal advantage, and void of all vision and generosity, would absorb the common good. President John F. Kennedy expressed it eloquently when he said: "Ask not what your country can do for you; ask what you can do for your country."

This love of the citizen must, of course, like all love, be preceded by knowledge. It is here that our schools can be most helpful. The citizen has to be profoundly conscious of his dependence upon society; he has to recognize himself as incomplete, as insufficient unto himself. He has to see civil society as it is, a unity of men like himself who desire to live the good life and who join for the purpose of offering mutual help toward the realization of a common social and cultural well-being in which all may participate. The student has to be taught that the progress which has been made is the product, in no small degree, of the efforts of men who have gone before, men who have left their achievements as a heritage, not to be squandered or lost, but to be appreciated and enhanced. We are all indebted to these men. They are, in a very real sense, our heroes. Every citizen should be acquainted with the great men and women of his land, should know the history, the traditions and the ideals of his country. To impart this knowledge is a fundamental duty of the schools.

Moreover, it is important for the citizen to understand that dependence upon society does not mean personal helplessness. A society entirely or even largely comprised of dependents would have little upon which to depend. The development of one's own abilities and resources is bound up with the furtherance of the good of society, for unless one can help himself, there is little hope of his helping others. In other words, the citizen should realize that there is a true individualism which means social progress. The commonwealth is fostered by private works. Each man's job, however seemingly insignificant it is, assumes importance when it is seen in its relation to the whole. One's private vocation, whatever it may be, as long as it is within the law and consequently good, is not only a private work, it is a post of public duty. To be a good citizen one must realize the element of public good in what he does.

The Russians perhaps have succeeded more than we have in impressing upon the individual the larger significance of his job, no matter how menial it might be. Being conscious of the meaning and worth of his work, and its connection with the progress of his country, the worker is willing to labor with might and main, happy in the thought that he is contributing to the success of Communist objectives.

A Major Task

A society that gauges the worth of an individual according to the scale of jobs—the less worthy the man, the more menial the job—makes it more difficult for the worker to determine the true value of himself and his work in relation both to the common good of society and the end for which he was created. A different criterion is needed. As former Secretary of Health, Education and Welfare John W. Gardner states in his book *Excellence*: "Human dignity and worth should be assessed only in terms of those qualities of mind and spirit that are within the reach of every human being." A good plumber is just as necessary to our society as a good philosopher; we need both. In order to get both, the plumber must be as convinced of the worth of his plumbing as the philosopher is of his philosophizing.

By reason of his status as a part of the whole, the positive influence of the private citizen in the procuring of the common good is only partial. Nevertheless, it is important. It is so important that consciousness of it should not be left to chance. One of the major tasks of the school in our democratic society is to impress constantly upon the student the active role he plays, indeed must play, in achieving the common good of his country.

Home and School: A Cooperative Enterprise
(Talk delivered to Rhode Island Congress of Parents and Teachers, April 26, 1979)

There is no greater stimulant to the advice gland of an educator than to be invited to give a speech at a P.T.A. meeting. Here is a golden opportunity to air a few gripes, to "tell it like it is" to parents and teachers, to view with alarm, warn of dangerous academic trends, or point to ominous clouds on the educational horizon.

But talk is cheap! Perhaps that is why we have so much of it. Self-improvement guru Dale Carnegie assures us that "anyone may easily become a good speaker if he acquires the art of diluting a two-minute idea with a two-hour vocabulary." But if volubility and intelligence went together, back fence gossipers would be veritable Einsteins. No less an authority than educator John Dewey states, "Long-windedness and glibness are quite compatible with moving round and round in a circle of moderate radius."

Let me state at once that a lifetime as a pedagogue has made it perfectly plain to me that I do not understand education. This sad fact has never made me especially melancholy, because I am convinced that my fellow-educators, especially administrators, do not understand it either. But I do not understand nuclear fission and fusion either, but I am satisfied that I should know a nuclear missile if I should be hit by one. By the same token, I am hardy enough to think that I would still know an educated man when I met him.

Much fun has been poked at education. Will Rogers once described "college bred" as a "four-year-old loaf made with the flavor of youth and the old man's dough." The late Dr. Robert Hutchins, founder of the Center for the Study of Democratic Institutions, explained, "The reason we give sheepskins to college graduates is in order to cover up their intellectual nakedness." One pundit noted, "You can lead a horse to water but you can't make him drink. You can send a boy to college, but you can't make him think."

In spite of this twitting of education, the public revered its schools, looked upon formal learning as a golden opportunity to climbing the ladder of socio-economic success, and thought that education would solve society's problems (open a school; close a jail). That is why Americans willingly voted a general fund budget in which 50% went for education. Novelist H. G. Wells said civilization was a race between education and catastrophe and everyone preferred education. God bless our children.

Now, however, education is foundering in a sea of troubles—blackboard jungles in the cities, truancy, vandalism, anarchy, dropping scores, rising costs, sagging standards, incompetent teachers, and penny-pinching legislatures. And the public is asking: Are we getting our money's worth?

Since the public is fond of questioning the schools, perhaps it's about time teachers and administrators started questioning the public. One question that should be asked is: what is a school for? What do you, the public, want it to do and what can it rightfully be expected to do?

Because this question is never asked of the public, the public uses education as a sort of trash can in which to dump all the odds and ends of social living.

Doesn't Johnny know how to wipe his nose? The teacher will show him. Is Johnny shy? School will take care of that. Is Susie too aggressive? The teacher will curb her tantrums. Can Jimmy dance? Let the school be his Arthur Murray. Should Joe learn to drive a car? Then let's have driving instruction. Is Fred a poor citizen? The teacher will cultivate his civic virtues. Is his body under-developed? School will make a man out of him.

The school becomes an omnium-gatherum of everything that needs doing and that no one else wants to do. The demands become staggering. White House conferences on education, foundations encouraging educational research, governmental agencies, and school departments provide detailed lists of educational objectives. Too frequently, these lists lose all contact with reality. They expect the teacher to be a scholar, a humanist, a social director, a psychiatrist, a coach, a prophet, a moral leader, an artist, an entertainer, a high priest, and a magician.

It may be said in rebuttal that these are merely goals. Goals most often exceed a person's grasp, but everybody should aim as high as he can. Granted, but there is a vast difference between ambition and wishful thinking. Our goals should be high, but they must be in the realm of achievability; otherwise, we are living a fantasy life. And I strongly suggest that the present grab-bag idea of education is a neurotic fantasy.

Because the public requires teachers to equip the "total child," they are attempting to do so at the cost of neglecting the one thing teachers do best, namely, teaching. When pupil performance suffers, we have scapegoating down the line. The colleges blame the high schools. The high schools blame the upper grades in the primary schools, the upper grades blame the intermediate grades and the intermediate grades blame the beginning grades—and I am sure the beginning grades complain that kindergartens aren't turning out the sort of children they used to.

This calls to mind a cartoon I saw recently in which a little boy says to his teacher as he is leaving the classroom: "You're afraid of the principal, the principal is afraid of the superintendent, the superintendent is afraid of the school board, the school board is afraid of the voters, but I'm not afraid of anybody!"

This infinite regression of responsibility is laughable, but it is also pathetic and more than a little ominous. I venture the opinion that everyone is mistaken in blaming the lower for what's wrong at the higher. The responsibility—as it does everywhere, in business or in government—rests squarely at the top. Let's blame the right people.

What do I mean by this? I mean it is manifestly impossible to start at the lowest grades because even by the age of five or six, the child has already been imbued with an attitude toward life and is emotionally saturated with an atmosphere at home.

The place to check and reverse this terrible trend toward ignorance is not in the first grade but in the college and among young, married adults generally. If our colleges inculcated in their students a decent respect for learning, these students on graduation and marriage would then begin to rear families in an atmosphere that was conducive to learning. And if, in addition, we supported a nationwide program of adult education, we might also change the complexion and the slant of American homes today where small children are growing up with a wholly distorted sense of values.

This is the only way to cut the Gordian knot of education. We must start with the people who already have or are about to have families. It is an absolute psychological fact—attested to by such powerful and divergent groups as the Communists, the Freudians, the Catholic Church, and most recently by the Thomas Coram Research Institute of Education at London University—that by the time a child is six years old, his deepest attitudes have already formed themselves into a rigid structure. And a few hours of schooling a day, under conditions not always ideal, cannot make much of a dent in this structure. The late Harvard University president James Conant once said, "I have become more and more convinced that it is the home which, to a large degree, determines the nature of the school." Failure to recognize this fact invalidates much of the criticism of our public schools.

All teachers know that the one intangible, but essential, element in learning is motivation. The *I Will* is far more important than the *I.Q.* We provide excellent facilities, counseling, and encouragement, but these are not enough. How can we motivate these young people to want to learn?

How can we strike the spark of ambition? What is the key to the transformation of an unresponsive, apathetic pupil into one who is actively motivated to achieve? How do we generate drive? The answer to these questions is found more in the home than in the classroom.

The home environment supplies not only the attitude but many of the essential skills for achievement. The cultural resources of the home give some children an excellent start in academic life. If the parents are uneducated, seldom read, and use only a limited vocabulary, children are apt to have more than usual difficulty with reading, spelling, and oral or written expression. Parents who use extensive and discriminating vocabulary, who provide books, art, and music as well as toys for their children make it much easier for those pupils to do well in school.

Incidentally, this cruciality of the home in learning is recognized in such programs as the Benton Harbor Home Education Learning Project, the Brookline Early Education Project, several programs of HEW and the parent-as-educator programs of the Home & School Institute at Trinity College, Washington, D.C.—all which acknowledge the fact that learning in the classroom does not necessarily happen, particularly when home support is lacking.

The growth of programs like these is a healthy sign that responsibility for learning must be shared by parents. A survey conducted by Gallup for the Institution for the Development of Educational Activities indicates that most Americans would like to see the parents of school-age children try to do something about their own shortcomings in order to improve the schools. Indeed, seventy-seven percent of those polled said they believed that it would be a good idea as a regular part of the public-school systems to offer courses for parents to help them aid their children.

In emphasizing the importance of the home in motivating the child to learn, I do not mean to minimize the power of the teacher. Good teachers make good schools. The sage advises: "If you would be learned, attach yourself to the wise." *Nemo dat quod no habet*—no one gives what he hasn't got. Teachers who are themselves living examples of intellectual force and refinement, make it impossible even for less gifted students to have other than profound respect for the intellectual interests they represent—a respect which often becomes a life-long attitude toward fine things of the mind.

On the other hand, teachers who are not admired and loved drive children to hate school and learning. Indeed, motivation to stay in school is weakest among those pupils who have frequently had to contend with teachers they dislike. Often, the dislike has been mutual and both teacher and pupil have vied in efforts to make life uncomfortable for the other. The vicious circle of attack-resentment-counterattack brings mounting hatred. Each longs to escape the endless frustrating struggle with the other. It's the kind of battle which nobody wins, and any learning that takes place is purely accidental.

In the final analysis, the most important, and probably the most difficult, part of a teacher's job is to inspire in students a love for learning. This can only be done when the teacher has a deep love for learning himself. A lamp can never light another lamp unless it continues to burn its own flame. No teacher can inspire students who merely repeats his lessons and has no living traffic with his field of study. If ideas are important and exciting to the teacher, that enthusiasm will be communicated to the students through the teacher's obvious concern that they learn and learn well.

What nobler mission can exist than that of dispersing the darkness and superstition of his times by an apostolate of study and teaching. As an unknown poet expresses it:

The Builders

A builder builded a temple
He wrought it with grace and skill;
Pillars and groins and arches
All fashioned to work his will.
And men said, as they saw its beauty
"It never shall know decay.
Great is they skill, O builder,
Thy work shall endure for aye."
A teacher builded a temple
With loving and infinite care;
Planning each arch with patience
Laying each stone with a prayer.
None saw the unceasing effort,
None knew of the wondrous plan
For the temple the teacher builded
Was unseen by the eye of man.
Gone is the builder's temple
Crumped into the dust.
Low lies each stately pillar
Food for consuming rust.

*But the temple the teacher builded
Will last while the ages roll,
For the beautiful unseen temple
Was a youth's immortal soul.*

The Value of a Liberal Education
(*The Echo*, March 13, 1975)

How do you measure the worth of a college education? Quantitively? Let's try it. Imagine the college as a big factory. The student is the raw product who must pass along the assembly line of the factory. There are certain standard parts which must be affixed to him; other parts may be chosen so as to produce the several models of college education. One part is the course, with a certain quantitative value in credits. The course is a neatly packaged unit of knowledge, complete in itself, duly fastened to the student's mind, inspected, passed—and forgotten. Once it is on, it is on, and he does not have to worry about it anymore. When a student has all the courses bolted on, he is examined to see if anything has been omitted; the credits (coin of the realm) are totaled, and if what is found agrees with the specifications in the catalogue, he is given a degree. This signifies he is an educated man.

But this description does not seem to ring true. If this is all a college education amounts to—a quantitive result, then it is merely an expensive way of wasting four years. It would mean that education is nothing but a depersonalized and mechanical process, a triumph of filing cabinet and adding machine over mind.

The Dollar Value of Education

Why not try applying the "bread and butter" standard? The U.S. Office of Education delights in publishing statistics about the cash value of higher education. The college graduate earns more than the non-graduate. He lives in a better house, travels more, owns more cars, reads more books, frequents the theater more often, and is more likely to own his own home. This may be because the type of man who is going to make a lot of money anyway happens to go to college. Still there does seem to be a high correlation between higher learning and higher income.

Nevertheless, the dollar-and-cents argument seems incomplete. A sneaky suspicion remains that college should give something more than earning power, something deeper than a diploma. And it does. It generates a deep-rooted passion for knowledge, a life-long love of truth, and an ever-increasing intellectual power.

College is truly a place of beginnings, a genuine "commencement" of a self-education which endures until death. The thought that education stops with the awarding of a diploma is enough to horrify anyone who takes learning seriously. Truly, if, with the end of schooling a man's education is finished, he is finished. Not a thousandth part of what you know was gained, or ever could be gained, in any classroom. To paraphrase the remarks of Winston Churchill made in another context: Graduation is not the end; it is not even the beginning of the end. It is just the end of the beginning. All that you can hope for from college is a certain amount of familiarity with some, not all, of the basic tools or ways of learning. But this should be enough to whet your appetite for one thing: truth.

Love of Truth

The truth may not have any applications in practice: that is not the test of its value. "To love the truth for its own sake," said English philosopher John Locke, "is a principal part of human perfection in this world." The utter devotion to truth, without any apologetic intentions, without being the least preoccupied with the consequences, is a quality beyond price. In the classrooms of a college, truth is not simply revered: it is deified. Truth is worshipped literally, since all truths are adumbrations of the First Truth which is God—and the very word "Veritas" (the motto of Providence College) is engraved on the hearts of the professors who teach you. In college halls you learn that the worst enemy of mankind is not the tyrant or the merely greedy or lustful man. He is rather the irrationalist, the enemy of truth, whether a philosopher attacking the foundations of metaphysics or a demagogue twisting issues and distorting facts by "loaded" language and subtle appeals to emotion.

The devotion to truth can be a perilous piety. It will make you forever discontented and dissatisfied—discontented with the glib and the superficial, dissatisfied with shallow reasoning, shoddy conclusions, and sham scholarship. The *Book of Ecclesiastes* states: "In much wisdom is much grief; and he who increases knowledge increases sorrow." Even so, would you, if you had the choice, prefer a joyful life to a harsh truth? Would you for the sake of assurance and peace of mind, choose to live by happy illusion than by bitter reality? Verily, "a gloomy truth is better than a cheerful falsehood."

If, as a result of your college experience, you have acquired a genuine love of objective truth, no matter in what domain—scientific, historical, theological or any other—then you have received a return of more than a hundredfold for the price of your tuition. The mind that has escaped the strait-jacket of prejudice, superstition, and ignorance, the mind that knows the truth about itself, its world and its God, and by knowing the truth has been made free, is itself the highest value a college can confer.

The Pleasures and Pains of Learning
(*The Echo*, December 19, 1974)

Where study is concerned, there is a vast difference between the attitude of the college man and the school boy. The schoolboy's attitude toward study is his attitude toward school. This is captured somewhat in the following verse:

> *If there is a vile, pernicious*
> *Wicked and degraded rule,*
> *Tending to debase the vicious*
> *And corrupt the harmless fool,*
> *If there is a hateful habit*
> *Making man a senseless tool*
> *With the feelings of a rabbit*
> *And the wisdom of a mule,*
> *It's the rule which inculcates*
> *It's the habit that dictates*
> *The wrong and sinful practice of*
> *Going into school.*

And so at the end of the year children sing the ditty: "No more pencils, no more books, no more teacher's dirty looks." It was only last year that I heard some boys singing these lines to the tune of "Glory, Glory, Hallelujah":

> *Mine eyes have seen the glory of the*
> *Burning of the school;*
> *We have tortured every teacher and*
> *We have broken every rule;*
> *We have smacked the lousy principal and*
> *Called him a big fool;*
> *As we go marching on.*

The juvenile attitude towards study, then, looks upon it as a chore to be ducked as soon as possible. At best it is an unpleasant duty. It is begun under constraint, continued under duress, and escaped whenever it is possible to do so. The mark of truly adult learning, on the other hand, is that it is done with no thought of labor or work at all, with no sense of being forced. It is entirely voluntary and performed with a keen sense of enjoyment.

Ask yourself, then, how do you apply yourself? Do you have to chain yourself to your desk? Do you go to the library "like a quarry slave scourged to his dungeon" or like a lover seeking his beloved? Study demands long continued effort. What is there to keep you at it? Will you obey like slaves under the bondage of the law? Out of the grim sense of duty? Will you study because you have a perverse appetite for harsh distasteful work? Or will it be in the hope of attaining some general and remote purpose?

Liking to Learn While Learning to Learn

Learning requires a proximate stimulus, a more limited objective. Human nature being what it is, no one is going to spend his mental energy on something that does not vitally interest him, on something out of which he is getting no pleasure; nor will a person go on learning when he is not forced to do so, when formal schooling is ended, when he has left college, unless he enjoys his work, unless he likes to study.

William Wadsworth, poet and observer of human nature, understood this joy of the scholar. His words support the "pleasure principles drawn from the contemplation of particular facts but what has been built up by pleasure and exists in us by pleasure alone". The man of science, chemist, and mathematician, whatever difficulties and disgust they may have to struggle with, know and feel this. However painful may be the objects which the anatomist's knowledge may be connected, he feels that his knowledge is pleasure and when he has no pleasure he has no knowledge.

The Adventure of Learning

The well-known mathematician, Bertrand Russell, when he was well into his nineties, and still producing writings on philosophy, political science, and pacifism, stated: "The same love of adventure that takes men to the South Pole, the same passion for a trial of strength that leads some men to welcome war, can be found in study and creative work. To give this joy in a greater or less measure to all who are capable of it, is the supreme end for which the education of the mind is to be valued."

This joy of mental adventure is the same initial sense of wonder of which Aristotle and St. Thomas speak, as being the source of philosophy and the cause of attraction and pleasure to the searcher. Martin Luther in the 16th century held the same opinion. He thought that students should take as much pleasure in study as in playing ball all day.

But life, unfortunately, is not all a ballgame (or a ball), and neither is study or learning, in spite of all this talk about delight in learning. Satirist Finley Peter Dunne's inimitable Mr. Dooley says: "Childhern shuddn't be sint to school to larn, but to larn how to larn. I don't care what you larn thim as long as 'tis onpleasant to thim." Of course, study does not always have to be unpleasant. It is not a form of penance and mortification. But Mr. Dooley does recognize the harsh fact that study is not, and cannot, ever be made amusing. A "carnival" attitude toward study is more fatal than coerced effort—forcing the student to go through motions without putting himself into it. Learning demands from the student a moral effort as well as an intellectual effort.

Is Learning Fun?

It is fun to play the violin, but it is not fun to practice the violin. And no matter how attractive you make the approach to the business of practicing, no matter how ingenious your methods for easing this task of practicing, all pleasure evaporates the instant you actually tackle it. Any attempt from the outside to disguise the truth that the job is painfully tedious will always be futile.

Every domain of learning presents the operation of the same principle; recognize the unpleasant, but inevitable, truth that during your life on this earth, your body gradually dies; your emotions become dull; but your mind continues to live, and even grows more lively and active. The pleasures of the mind are sweeter, more precious, more lasting, and leave no bitter aftertaste. But there is another side to the story; sensible pleasures, especially when you are young, are more vehement. They clamor for attention; they are closer to you, more familiar, more importunate, more seductive, and call for less effort. And that is why, says Aquinas, the majority of men seek sensible pleasures more than spiritual pleasures, why they prefer to read the funnies than to read a book, why they would rather stare blindly at television than engage in an exchange of ideas. I do not deny, then, that playing pin-ball machines may give more satisfaction than reading poetry. It does for a day, for a week, for a month; but then the pleasures dies; whereas, if you live for 80 years, you can never exhaust the pleasures of poetry and music.

"The more peril there is in the battle," says St. Augustine, "the greater the joy in the triumph." So also, other things being equal, the more one has to struggle to learn, so much the more will be delight in the knowledge obtained.

Exercise Your Mental Muscles

Of one thing you can be sure: the unexercised mind, like the unexercised body, soon deteriorates. Left to lie fallow, the mind is reduced to solitude or to the deadly company of similarly unexercised minds, dependent on strong external stimulation and increasingly difficult to stimulate except by increasing the strength and dosage of the stimulant. You come to college to learn how to exercise your minds. The joy you experience in the process will be commensurate to the effort you put into it.

Understand, moreover that the road to the castle of knowledge is slippery and studded with obstacles—"physical evils that afflict the body, laziness, unruly passions of the soul, error and deception, ignorance of what we desire to know, uncertainty, and mere opinion where we would have wished for certainty:" so says Thomas Aquinas. Still, the prize is worth the effort and the effort itself becomes enjoyable when the love of learning is a strong bright flame. As St. Augustine said: "where there is love there is no labor, or where there is labor it is a labor of love."

Apply yourself with enthusiasm to your studies and you will find this generous application of energy aids concentration and increases pleasure. As the poet Tim Bovee says: "Mind unemployed is mind unenjoyed." If the Angelic Doctor could enjoy dwelling on a problem to such an extent that he did not even feel his leg being cauterized, then you, of lesser intellectual ability, should find study at least as pleasurable as playing bridge, watching a third-rate movie, or seeing a sloppily-played ballgame.

Intertest Makes Learning Easy

Upon consideration, you will find, I think, that no one succeeds in any job unless that job is interesting either in itself or is made interesting by reason of some future objective. Only when such interest is aroused is energy possible. As a rule, the most successful men are those for whom work has the greatest attractions. You are not eager to give yourself up to the treatment of a doctor who considers the study of disease a mere drudgery, nor do you care, ordinarily, to be shriven by a priest who showed an active repugnance to hearing confessions.

No doubt the skilled man in every pursuit has to go through a great deal of drudgery. But he has a general interest in the subject which extends partially, at least, to its most wearisome details; his energy, too, is excited by the desire of what the drudgery will gain for him. As the ancient Greek poet Hesiod states: "Before the gates of excellence the high Gods have placed sweat. Long and steep is the road to it and rugged at the beginning." Because all learning is rugged, especially at the beginning, no student should let this discourage him. The enjoyment and excellence in performance will come with time and with application.

College, however, is no place for the student who is not willing to work. As stern schoolteacher Bartle Massey says in George Eliot's novel *Adam Bede*: "But the long and short of it is—I'll have nobody in my school that doesn't strive to learn what he came to learn, as hard as if he was striving to get out of a dark hole into broad daylight. I'll send no man away because he is stupid; if Bill Taft, the idiot, wanted to learn anything, I'd not refuse to teach him. But I'll not throw away good knowledge on people who think they can get it by the sixpenn'orth, and carry it away as they would an ounce of snuff. So never come to me again, if you can't show that you have been working with your own heads, instead of thinking you can pay mine to work for you. That's the last word I've got to say to you."

Blaming Teachers Allows the Real Culprit to Escape
(*The Providence Visitor*, October 2, 2003)

Harsh things are being said about teachers today. By urging the de-schooling of America, the late Croatian-Austrian philosopher and priest Ivan Illich would make a teacher's job unnecessary. John Holt in his book, *Instead of Education*, goes so far as to indict teachers for being criminals and mind-maimers who impose education on captive innocent children. Indeed, schools, in his view, are a form of slavery—a tyranny and atrocity against the human mind and spirit.

An acerbic remark such as this calls to mind, the jesting aside, of that terrible-tempered newspaperman, H. L. Mencken, who scoffed, "The average schoolmaster is and always must be essentially an ass, for how can one imagine an intelligent man engaging in so puerile an avocation?"

This sneer echoes the jeering complaint in the pupil's sidewalk chant:

> God made the bees,
> The bees made honey;
> We do the work,
> The teacher gets the money.

Then there's the anecdote ascribed to an old-timer who was reminiscing about his school days. He said: "When I was six years old, I started my formal education at a one-teacher schoolhouse including several grades. The only thing I can remember from that first year at school is that one of the pupils knocked the teacher down with a book. Although I was perhaps not as bright as the average six-year-old, I knew that was no way to treat a book."

More moderate critics are also voicing concern. Evidence is mounting that the output of schools lags behind the input; that despite increasing expenditure of money, schools, judged by the least stringent criterion, are teaching less and less; that there has been a dip in college board scores and in such basic skills as the ability to read, write, and solve simple mathematical problems. Recent studies about primary and secondary education corroborate this view.

This dismal record of declining achievement is aggravated by the problem of wholesale grade inflation. As and Bs are supplanting the Cs and Ds which were once the lot of mythical average student.

Why, if students are doing so poorly, are grades getting better? Don't teachers and administrators give a damn anymore? Are they rebelling against the whole grading system? Do they simply lack the fortitude to tell Johnny he's not as smart as he or his parents think he is?

Whatever the case, John Q. Public is not bashful in telling the teacher what he thinks of him or her. He grades the teachers F or puts them down with the miserable mark of D. Parents pull no punches in blaming low pupil achievement on teacher laziness, lack of classroom discipline, and the fad of relevance.

Americans like to think that every person should get just what's coming to him. If teachers merit lumps for incompetence, then don't spare them. However, the current roasting of teachers smacks of scapegoatism. Hounding the educators is a perennial recreation in which parents, politicians, and newspaper columnists like to have their merry fling. When projects go snafu, citizens seldom beat their breasts and say *mea culpa*. No, they tend to shrug their shoulders and exclaim, "Who? Me?" then look for a villain.

Youths are delinquent; youths are ignorant; youths are discourteous and rude. Who's at fault? Teachers. They are freeloaders, with soft nine-month jobs, who feel little or no obligation to the society that feeds them, who often breach the life of good citizens with a barrage of subversive ideas. What nonsense!

The truth is that educators do not have subversive ideas; indeed, they do not have ideas at all. They are a channel for the ideas of society, often hidden ideas which they carry into the flexible scholastic form.

Teachers and school administrators are no more than agents of a view of life to which our culture is deeply committed, and we cannot wipe out the agents without cleaning up the view of life.

If parents complain about ineffective teaching of reading, writing, and arithmetic, they engage in self-deception; they hardly provide examples of devoted reading which might make young observers regard it as a built-in human activity. If parents find schools becoming trade schools, it is because trades are their real article of faith—a means for getting-on in the world that they really believe in. If parents find schools teaching self-esteem rather than training minds, it is because they feel that emotional fulfillment is better than developing one's own genius. Society will compel the schools to do those things which society wants, values, or feels that it needs.

Teachers need no whitewashing. They are instruments of society, and reflect and interpret rather than originate the values and ideals society prizes. Still, agents are not guiltless. No one is compelled to become resigned to underachievement and mediocrity, and such resignation is more ignoble in a profession entrusted with a special role in the strengthening of society.

So flaying the educators may be worthwhile, if it is understood as a preparation for, and a part of, a larger task of public self-examination of conscience about a second-rate view of life that settles for the mean and the mediocre. If the public institutionalizes and takes delight in kitsch, why should it decry the fact that the schools do not promote Culture with a capital C.

Again, one is vexed over the carping frame of mind which displays resentment against, indeed, shows disdain for those who run our schools and which brands teachers as charlatans and villains. It paints (smears) with a broad brush and leads to what logicians call the "Fallacy of the Imperfect Minister": the vulgar supposition that flaws of the pedagogue establish hollowness in the creed.

Education ranks highly as an American creed, a faith ranking just below belief in the Deity. Cicero, that wise old Roman, states: "What greater gift can we offer the republic than to teach and instruct youths." Schools and good citizenship are correlative terms, English statesman Lord Brougham believed, that "Education makes a people easy to lead, but difficult to drive; easy to govern, but impossible to enslave." Thomas Jefferson put it succinctly, "If a nation expects to be ignorant and free…it expected what never was and never will be."

From the early days of the republic, our forefathers accepted the principle that every citizen should be given the chance to be educated as far as his talents permit. This is a great moral achievement. It would be tragic if valid trust in the value of schooling were diminished because the public found teachers to be less than perfect.

Have Faith In Your Teacher
(*The Echo*, January 2, 1974)

No man has mind, time, or strength enough to know the solutions to the thousand problems which arise in his affairs. The complex life of the civilization in which we find ourselves compels us to seek advice and help from others. If a person has common sense he consults a specialist; if he has uncommon sense he consults two.

While modern man quantitatively knows more than did his ancestors, what he knows is smaller proportionately to the total amount of existent knowledge. Hence, in fields other than his own, he needs to believe what other men tell him. The day of the scholar who took all knowledge for his province is past.

Indeed, in order to make up for the feelings of inadequacy engendered by ignorance, man tends to seek shortcuts to the understanding of subjects out of his line. He grasps at simple explanations, "definitions of situations," as the social psychologist calls them. That accounts for the popularity of outlines and stories of philosophy, history, chemistry, and all other subjects; news reviews and digest magazines; inside-dope newsletters and political precis; how-to books on making love, making friends and making the boss's daughter; book digests of books and books on reading other books.

Dangers of Dependence on Teacher

In this very dependence there are dangers which lie in wait for the unwary. The average person, like the beginning pupil, is liable to be more impressed by the prestige of the expert or writer than by the truth of what he says. This may result in a habit of uncritical acceptance. After all, it is easier, less work, and less trouble merely to take the word of another than to search out the truth for yourself. Because of this mental inertia many a person is duped into giving credence to some of the most ridiculous fantasies:

American showman P. T. Barnum stated in the 19th century that "there is a sucker born every minute." We have no reason to believe, in spite of the growth of literacy and formal education, that there has been a decrease rather than an increase in gullibility in our modern era. Indeed, we need only remember the Martian invasion broadcast of 1938 by Orson Welles, the relatively recent stories about sea serpents, prehistoric animals, missing links, and phony feral children to realize that man is taken in by more than the tall tales related in science fiction. Teachers, moreover, run up against a mental stonewall when they try to disabuse people of these preconceptions, because such ideas are induced by suggestion and circumvent critical intellectual functions by an appeal to the pronouncements of pundits and pros.

Trust the Teacher

This does not mean that you should abandon belief in the words of true teachers or bona fide experts. The fact is that the best educated people rely on the expert, but the less intelligent never do. Docility demands that you begin to learn by placing faith in your mentor. All learning takes off from an assumption and the ideas proposed by the teacher to give you your start. At the same time, St. Thomas Aquinas warns you against clothing any teacher in the mantle of divine infallibility. It would be silly, nay, blasphemous to accord to your teacher the unqualified assent you give to the words of your Maker. This would be slavish subservience. God wants you to use the mind that He gave you.

Statements or arguments should be weighed on their own merits, never on the merits of the person who utters them. This admonition has pertinence today, when respect for the expert is sometimes transferred to whatever he says, even about matters outside the field of his specialty. When a man spreads the cloak of authority over areas alien to his training, where he is either a stranger, a novice, or a desultory dabbler, you should no more listen to him than you should pay heed to an Eskimo if he tries to discourse on the intricacies of Homoiousian doctrine or the differences in Micronesian dialects. French historian Jacques Barzun remarks somewhere that when Einstein's misguided friends published his non-scientific essays, thereby exposing his intellectual inadequacy therein, they helped to lessen the glory that should be rightfully his by reason of his great scientific accomplishments.

To my mind no sorrier spectacle of misplaced trust in the words of an expert was ever paraded before the eyes of the nation that when renowned authorities on sand crabs, scarabs and atoms were induced to express themselves in the Sunday newspaper supplements about their notions of God and religion. The easiest way to win a booby prize is to pontificate on subjects of which you know little or nothing. When your piping breaks down in body or home you call a physician or plumber not an astronomer or economist.

Knowledge and Belief

In any event, knowledge and belief, or even opinion and belief, cannot exist in the same person at the same time under the same aspect. In belief you know that a thing is; in knowledge you know the what and the why of a thing. Belief is related to knowledge as the imperfect to the perfect, as the obscure to the clear, as the dusk to the daylight. It depends, then, on what you want. In professing divine faith you receive merit because you accept the truth you do not see clearly on the word of God Himself; in human faith there is little merit in accepting the word of the teacher when you have developed your mental muscles and have the power and opportunity to see clearly for yourself. Bishop John Lancaster Spalding, a co-founder of the Catholic University of America, stated the matter in this fashion. "They who content themselves with what others have uttered, learn nothing. The blind need a guide, but they who are able to see should look for themselves." In short, it takes a stout heart deliberately to leave the path of least resistance of faith in the teacher and enter the rocky road of toil in the pursuit of knowledge on your own.

Teachers Should Grow On The Job
(*The Providence Sunday Journal*, December 11, 1983)

The supply of new teachers is down. Fewer college students are majoring in education than in the past; the quality of those entering teaching is low.

Furthermore, Albert Shanker, head of the American Federation of Teachers, informs us that almost 50 percent of those who start teaching will leave the profession by the end of the 10th year. If even mediocre college students sneer at teaching and good teachers continue to abandon the classrooms at the current rate, all talk of educational improvement or reform will be meaningless.

Low salary, professional "burn-out," poor working conditions, and an unattractive public image may account for much of the brain-drain from teaching, but failure to grow on the job and derive satisfaction from helping children to learn are also key factors in career discontent.

In this context, in-service development becomes a pressing priority. Mind you, we are not talking about the advantage of adding one more degree to a teacher's name. Rather, we are stressing the necessity of upgrading knowledge and sharpening awareness. Educator Robert Hutchins once suggested that every American should be given a bachelor's degree at birth, so that those who wanted no more than a diploma would not have to go to college.

Plainly put, the problem is this: If I hold the same views at 40 that I held at 20, then I was either exceptionally precocious at 20 or terribly retarded at 40. Or as a physician friend remarked: "If I were to practice medicine with the knowledge I had when I became a doctor, I should be put in jail for malpractice."

Opportunity has an uncanny habit of favoring those who have paid the price of ceaseless preparation. Zeal does not go bail for lack of expertise. The golfer, Gary Player, exclaimed: "It's amazing: the harder I practice, the luckier I get!" If the man who graduated yesterday stops learning today, he'll be uneducated tomorrow.

Formation years are admittedly sheltered and idealistic; life is wide open and real. The times demand that teachers keep up to date and fill the gaps of early learning.

Nobody can truly teach unless he is still learning himself. The teacher who merely repeats his lessons and has no living traffic with his field of study cannot inspire in students a love for learning. He lacks this love himself. *Nemo dat quod non habet.* (No one gives what he does not have.)

A story is told of a teacher seeking advancement. He was passed over in favor of a colleague and wanted to know the reason why. "After all," he said, "I've had 20 years of teaching experience." "That's not the way we looked at it," he was told. "In your case, the board felt you've had one year's experience repeated 20 times."

Much that passes for in-service teacher training is of doubtful quality. Workshops, and night and summer courses for teachers are frequently taken to earn more pay under a system that rewards logging credits of any kind.

Education is not measurable in purely—or even primarily—quantitative terms. The stockpile approach to learning dulls native curiosity and loads the power of observation with a mass of unrelated materials.

Philip Phenix, author of *Realms of Meaning*, points out that "poor education piles fact upon fact, only making certain that each contribution falls within the subject being pursued. Good education, by contrast, chooses facts with the deliberate purpose of giving substance to certain basic concepts and principles that are distinctive of the discipline studied."

The teacher should be a scholar. But scholarship is only a *conditio sine qua non* of good teaching, nothing more. Learning, as such, is no guarantee of teaching skill. The problem of classroom competency is not solved merely by putting teachers through so many credit hours of graduate study, just as processing students through 115 semester credits is no safe index that they are really "students" at all.

Performance skills must go hand in hand with subject-area mastery. That teacher who cannot get across what he knows is pedagogically musclebound. Yet many colleges are dismantling their education departments at the very time they are most needed to acquaint aspirants with the techniques and complexities of effective teaching.

A teacher's talent, literacy, enthusiasm, articulateness, love of children, and sacrificial dedication to teaching count more than anything else in helping pupils to learn. In the classroom, teachers lays more than subject matter before students; they lays themselves. Pupils find out not only what a teacher teaches, but they also come to know why he or she teaches at all.

There is no quick-fix for poor teaching. What we need is a nationwide effort to develop, on a systematic basis, opportunities for quality in-service training at every level.

Urging lifelong learning, John Dewey tells us: "Education is not just to develop responsibility as a mother or a father or a teacher or a worker or a citizen. It is to keep on growing and developing as a human being."

Teacher's Task In Education Is To Build Upon Authority
(*The Providence Visitor*, May 17, 1984)

President Ronald Reagan's remarks about lack of discipline in our schools has sparked discussion about the abuse of obedience and authority in education.

All power groups—political, ecclesiastical, or others—are equally exposed to the temptation of demanding more and more obedience. Meanwhile, the modern media make it possible for officials to extend commands into private lives so that citizens are persuaded to obey unwittingly.

The problem is complicated by a tendency to confuse rightful authority with authoritarianism—wielding power to subjugate or lord it over others. This, in turn, causes Americans to distrust authority as being undemocratic and un-American.

So teachers cede the authority of knowledge and maturity to the ignorance and immaturity of their charges. The "non-directive" teacher is hailed as the "more democratic" teacher. Parents tremble that children will rebel when they enforce a reasonable curfew or restrict the use of the family car.

But the "big stick," shut-up-and-do-as-you're-told kind of authority is a caricature of *bona fide* authority, just as a corpse-like, slavish, blind, passive, police-enjoined obedience is a pathological distortion of authentic obedience.

School and community life cannot thrive without authority and obedience. Where people live together in a community, there must be order. That there be order; the power to command must be present. Not everyone can do as he pleases, and moreover, not everyone can discover for himself just what is required by the total whole.

Command, however, implies obedience. When the pupil understands authority as a rationally prescribed function of order for the life of the school and for the coordination of human effort toward the common goal of learning, he then begins to appreciate what obedience is and why he should obey. Even a society of saints, Aquinas observes, could not flourish without authority and obedience.

Rules, in this context, are seen as liberating rather than repressive. Their ultimate purpose is to help students reach a stage where they can rule themselves. But two extremes ought to be shunned. First, rules should never be so rigid and minute as to leave little scope for individual initiative; otherwise they degenerate into mere formalism—a going through the motions without reason or enthusiasm.

The other extreme is to remove all rules so that the young are left without standards needed to stabilize them in a changing environment. They thus become prey to their own emotions, whims, and fancies. Insist on rules, but hold to them flexibly, imaginatively, and progressively.

Difficulty occurs when school and home exact different standards of behavior regarding drugs, drinking, use of the auto, curfews, wearing apparel, etc. Too much is at stake for school officials to allow parental leniency to wreck young lives. If parents abdicate their responsibility to guide children, the school has to do all that it can to make up for parental dereliction.

Simply "laying down the law" makes young people more discontented, more disinclined to listen or obey. Teachers sense this. Teenagers are no longer children who trust implicitly and obey without question. Even a small child deserves as much explanation as he can comprehend. A demand to obey should never replace the effort to clarify and give reasons for the obedience required.

French author Louis Georges Bernanos warns us that "Men who are trained to obey blindly will suddenly disobey just as blindly. To obey without objection is different from obeying without understanding, and total submissiveness is not so far removed from total revolt as one thinks."

The teacher's task is not merely to maintain, but to build up authority. Two ways are open to him: by educating students to value and esteem authority or by winning over students through sheer force of personality or friendship.

Obedience obtained by personal attraction is short-lived. Emotional factors or accidental circumstances may disturb or destroy even the most firmly established personal relationship; then the authority connected with it vanishes. The teacher who says, "Obey me or I won't like you," is asking for trouble.

On the other hand, the pupil who has been taught the meaning of authority and the ethical obligation of obedience has a certainty that is independent of time, circumstance, or personality. Undoubtedly, it is not easy to get this idea across. A child usually identifies authoritative rank with the person who holds it. That's why authority is weakened by those who abuse it, who use it for selfish ends rather than for the good of those over whom they are placed. Yet when children see the value of respecting and obeying lawful authority, regardless of subjective likes or dislikes, they are left free to do what they should in achieving the goals of the school.

Perhaps the highest conception of authority is embodied in the title of the Pope, "The Servant of the Servants of God." The purpose of all authority, even the highest, is to serve. An educational authority which projects an image of altruistic service and concern will evoke from students a free and filial response of obedience.

Striking a Balance Between Discipline, Freedom
(*The Providence Journal*, March 9, 1984)

Lack of discipline is only a symptom and not a cause of what is wrong with American schools. Nevertheless, President Ronald Reagan's call for stricter discipline is refreshing.

Discipline is necessary to freedom. Educational philosopher John Dewey wrote, "The child who does as he likes is not a free child. He is apt to become the slave of bad habits, selfish, and quite unfit for community life."

Youth who have never been controlled can never control themselves. And there is no insecurity like being unable to control oneself. The Id can be a much more terrible despot than the Superego.

A good part of youthful misbehavior stems from an unwillingness of adults to play their proper roles.

Teachers must believe in the office of teaching. The office of the President of the United States deserves respect whether the holder of the office is a good president or a bad president, a Republican or Democrat. The office of teacher deserves respect whether the teacher is good or bad, interesting or dull. If the teacher has to run for office in the classroom, students will learn only that it is better to be popular than to be wise.

Pupils resent the autocratic Captain Bligh type of teacher. His expectations in conduct and learning are unrealistically high. Driven too hard, the child balks.

But the too-indulgent teacher is resented and despised even more. Indulgence sometimes is, and usually is taken for, a lack of concern or weakness; better the teacher who roars than the teacher who shrugs. At least the former cares.

Some teachers try to teach midst turmoil and confusion; others control students with a word and a stare. Not a few lack the strength of personality and authoritative mien that discourage troublemaking.

The charisma needed to control a class is unrelated to the teacher's physical size, intelligence, or other qualities that one usually thinks important. I recall a 100-pound, four-foot-eleven math teacher in junior high who regulated her class with no-nonsense firmness, whereas the civics class of a six-foot-four, 230-pound coach was a pit of chaos and anarchy.

Students ought to be given as much freedom as they can handle. But limits are essential. Educators who set limits with unambiguous determination find that pupils respond positively. Youth have to be habituated to see the merit of obeying because authority commands.

The fish ball and the sugar cube get better results than the lash and chains, and so parents and teachers nowadays are horrified about using force or threats to make a child do anything. They would rather manipulate the child's desires. Not only is the school to adapt itself to his desires, but a balanced diet must somehow be made more desirable than crackerjacks; medicine must be tasty; and everything that is good for him must be fun for him.

One result of this is that the child learns to consult his desires as guides to action. Another is that he never learns to tolerate the least cessation in the steady stream of gratifications which he is used to. Someday, of course, life forces him to see that duty is not a marshmallow.

Young people have always tried to probe the structure of authority for softness; have always tried, usually good naturedly, to see where parents and teachers are vulnerable. Today's kids have found that adults love peace—or rather, they feel incapable of dealing with the strife that sometimes comes with saying, "No." So they concede, compromise, and give in to youthful demands.

But there is an exquisite cruelty in yielding, yielding, and always yielding; tolerating, tolerating, and always tolerating; understanding, understanding, and always understanding. The child wants the respect of serious and heartfelt resistance. He wants his rebellion opposed; his sins acknowledged for what they are. The permissive fallacy is that children can learn good things from bad experiences.

Some parents let children run wild because they fear the dreaded words: I hate you. Others egg-on their offspring to defy authority.

Boycotts, sit-ins, occupations, slow-downs, and strikes were not invented by the kiddies. If young people think the way to get what you want is to raise hell or defy or intimidate authority, they have learned it from their elders.

When teachers thumb their noses at the law and close the schools by resorting to illegal strikes, they should not be surprised if pupils catch the contagion and decide that the way to get their way is to try a little intimidation.

Our schools are engaged in the noble enterprise of building character as well as training minds. To do so, we have to strike a proper balance between authority and freedom. The enforcement of discipline is not an adult conspiracy against children. It's part of the moral responsibility one generation owes another.

Crisis in Public School Teaching
(*The Providence Journal*, Monday, March 1, 1982)

The Warwick teachers' strike focuses attention on the plight of teachers. The profession faces a crisis. Teachers are not replenishing themselves from the supply of better students. Gifted veterans are leaving; the newcomers are mediocre.

That good teachers make good schools, no one will deny. The sage advises: "If you would be learned, attach yourself to the wise." Teachers who are themselves living examples of intellectual force and refinement, make it impossible for even less gifted pupils to have other than profound respect for the intellectual interests they represent—a respect which often becomes a lifelong attitude toward fine things of the mind.

The key to the quality of the whole educational enterprise lies in the intellectual growth of teachers, their competence in the subjects they teach, their grasp of the learning process, and the purposes of education—their teaching skills sharpened through method courses and practice teaching.

Competence in subject matter takes top priority, or should. Yet it is precisely in this area that teachers are weakest. In 1976, of 16 groups of students with various majors, the education majors placed 14th in the verbal test and 15th on the mathematics exam. The situation has deteriorated to the point where many systems have inaugurated minimum competency testing for teachers.

The crucial factors in enticing more able teachers are: career opportunities, high public prestige, salary commensurate to other professions, and good working conditions.

Today, a low morale prevails. Teachers' pay has not kept up with the cost of living, a hodgepodge of specific and unbalanced certification requirements discourages worthwhile candidates, and teachers are disheartened by a public that refuses to reward and esteem a profession so vital to democracy.

This parlous state is exacerbated by the prevalence among younger teachers of a civil service mentality—a trade union pattern of thought and action: Do as little as you have to; get paid for everything you do. Thus, the line between profession and trade swiftly erodes.

Meanwhile, the burnt-out cases multiply. Teachers suffer from the same malaise afflicting workers in America: alienation. Vexed by an unappreciative public, they no longer feel good about themselves and their work.

Remedies have been proposed: financial aid to education majors, honors programs for bright potential teachers; beefing up course-content requirements; more extensive use of the M.A.T.; greater emphasis on teaching for creativity and productive thinking; greater use of machine procedures for reporting to parents, pupil attendance, and schedule making.

Experts agree that in-service training is presently a more pressing priority than pre-service teacher education. Unfortunately, much that now passes for in-service training is of doubtful quality.

Americans are convinced that better schools make better people and better people make a stronger nation. That is why flaying the educators is a popular pastime. It is a kind of left-handed compliment to teachers and teaching. Such strictures are all for the good if they are part of the larger task of public self-examination of conscience about a second-rate view of life that delights in kitsch and settles for the mean and mediocre.

Gene Maeroff, author of *Don't Blame the Kids*, a study dealing with what's wrong with America's schools, contends that those who work in the schools have probably done more than others to keep a bad condition from getting a lot worse.

The crucial question is whether citizens really want to support their schools in such a way and to such an extent that they create the most salubrious climate for excellent teaching and learning. Americans spend about 3.5 percent of their gross national product on formal education at all levels. To do the job right, the national investment in education ought to be doubled.

The first step, despite tight budgets and retrenchment policies, would be to pay teachers what they're worth. A farmer, so the story goes, was a member of the school board in a rural town. He resented the teachers' request for a raise. "The work is easy," grumbled the farmer. "I don't imagine you people teach more than five or six hours a day." "Sir," replied a faculty spokesman, "we teachers are a lot like one of your prize bulls. It's not the amount of time we spend. It's the importance of what we do."

If civilization is a race between education and catastrophe, to use the Wellsian cliché, then it behooves Americans to speed up efforts to obtain talented teachers for their children.

Pros and Cons of Public Education
(*The Providence Visitor*, March 21, 1985)

Home schooling is the choice of a growing number of families that prefer to teach their children at home rather than accept the materials and values presented in public schools. Rhode Island law permits this so long as parents comply with all the requirements laid down by the school system.

Home schooling is not new. Necessity forced pioneer parents and homesteaders to teach children the "3 R's" at home. Early American leaders—Thomas Jefferson, Benjamin Franklin, John Quincy Adams—were home-tutored, as were twentieth century political leaders, "Winston Churchill, Franklin Roosevelt and German Chancellor Konrad Adenauer.

A rash of articles and books, e.g., John Holt's *Teach Your Own* and Raymond Moore's *Home Style Teaching*, have sparked the burgeoning popularity of home schooling. Last year a conference on home education at Stanford University attracted over 500 people.

Why would anybody want to undertake the difficult task of educating offspring at home?

Some parents, appalled at the lack of discipline and the quality of education in public schools and unable to afford a private school, choose home schooling as a second choice.

Others, mostly fundamentalist parents, but also a small number of Catholic parents, want to foster their own religious beliefs. They fear that rubbing academic shoulders with other pupils may corrupt their children. They are convinced that relativistic ethics and a philosophy of secular humanism prevail in the public school environment.

Still others are opposed to all forms of institutional learning. In their view, schools bind students into a mental straitjacket, stifle creativity, and gear classroom teaching to the lowest common denominator. They believe that optimal learning occurs in a one-to-one parent-child relationship.

But how many parents, even when aided by home-school guidance and curriculum materials, have the time, patience, training, or competence of the professional teacher? Parents who are strong in one subject may be weak in another or may stress one study to the detriment of another. Worse still, a myopic view of history, literature, or social studies may be fostered on children by parents who give only their own side of everything.

Are parents who shelter children from contact with their peers really working in their best interests? Cannot parents offset threats to their family value system by home instruction, fidelity to church practice, and by conducting themselves as commendable models? Children who are well-grounded in their beliefs are seldom shaken by bumping into others who believe differently. To imprison children in the cocoons of their homes and churches, pretending they will never have to deal with other believers is to cripple them for living in a pluralistic society. Such overprotection tends to breed suspicion and prejudice.

This is not to deny the fact that an overstress on pluralism in America has led at times to a confused homogenization, where no significant values can win the support of any majority and cynicism and relativism hold sway.

I sympathize with parents who desire the best education for their children and feel the schools have let them down. The answer, however, lies not in withdrawing offspring from school but in working with other concerned citizens, educators, and civil officials to improve the caliber of our schools.

Those parents who are upset about the moral climate of a school or who fear that a child's faith is endangered should speak out and become directly involved in school affairs. Schools belong to the people. Educators are accountable.

The rough-and-tumble of school life and the social interaction which takes place at school more truly reflects life as-it-is and better prepares pupils for living in the outside world than does the sheltered learning climate of home tutoring.

One-on-one home schooling may have some advantages, but it behooves parents to think twice before undertaking this staggering commitment of time, energy, and patience. As I see it, the cons outweigh the pros.

Parents Have Rights in Classroom
(*The Providence Visitor*, March 7, 1985)

Parents who are devoutly religious believe God gave Moses the Ten Commandments, not the Ten Suggestions, or 1,000 Alternatives. So when parents kick about teachers subjecting their children "to classroom talk about dangerous topics" (see "Meddling with values of the classroom," a *Providence Journal* editorial) what really riles them is the way teachers spread out moral solutions to these "dangerous topics" in smorgasbord or supermarket style: "Here, children, is what people say and do; pick and choose whatever lifestyle or 'modus agendi' you like."

The implied ethical relativism of this approach raises parental hackles because it parades under the banner of value neutrality, while actually promoting a doctrine of moral subjectivism—values being equated with personal preference, with likes and dislikes, and the teacher's job being restricted to expounding the various options open to students.

But no teacher can ever be morally neutral. He or she can play any role they want—a mediator, a clarifier, a resource person, a facilitator of classroom discussion—but the moment a teacher faces the class he or she betrays their value-bias by the inflection and tone of voice, by gestures and comportment, and by selection of textbooks and reading material. Far better for a teacher to tell students at the outset where he or she stands on a particular moral issue.

The morally neutral school is likewise a fiction. The "hidden curriculum" —how school officials wield their authority, what teachers expect from students, strict or lax standards of conduct, the impact of peer pressure, the teachers as good or bad role models—this web of intangibles blanket the student and help shape his or her value system.

The individual uses value judgments to organize and give meaning to life. The school ought to help students make such judgments intelligently. But Christians believe the capacity to make these judgments intelligently presupposes a knowledge of God, and a knowledge of man's relations to God—to Whom he has obligations and from Whom he has rights that transcend the scope and power of civil society.

In short, value judgments require a point of reference. If this point of reference does not transcend man's world, it is world-centered and man becomes the "measure of all things." Ethical Culturists and Secular Humanists look upon morality as being wholly man-made and see no need of bringing God into the picture when inculcating values. The state, attempting to be neutral, likewise rules out any appeal to God. For example, a public-school teacher can teach students that it is wrong to steal or murder, but that teacher cannot, without violating the Establishment Clause of the Constitution, teach his or her students to refrain from stealing because God has proscribed it.

Religiously conservative parents argue, however, that if the state may not, because of religious liberty guarantees, teach a particular positive religious belief, then it should not use the weight of its tax-supported educational institutions to push the subjectivist and relativistic ethics of Secular Humanism upon school children. They consider value formation without a religious foundation as a kind of educational brainwashing and British educator Sir Walter Moberly states, "If indoctrination is bad, this sort of subtle conditioning and preconscious habituation is surely worse."

Behind parental concern over "dangerous topics" lies the deeper issue of who should control the child's education, the family or professional educators who act as agents of the state.

So far the courts have equated neutrality with secularity and have rejected charges of parents who allege that certain school programs are biased against traditional morality and offend their religious beliefs. Thwarted there, conservatively religious parents have now turned to raising the question of whether, under compulsory school laws, educators can impose upon students, courses in value inculcation or discuss "dangerous topics" without prior informed consent of their parents. Parents who consider abortion to be murder and who judge premarital sex and open marriage to be wrong, are reluctant to allow their children to engage in classroom discussion where these topics are exposed in "you make your own choice" fashion.

The Biblical Solomon, with all his wisdom, would be frustrated in finding a viable accommodation of the rights of parents and the rights of the state in this area of value education. But Americans have much to build on. All citizens agree on certain basic values: fairness, equality, tolerance, courtesy, honesty, truthfulness, responsible citizenship, as well as the values and rights expressed in the U.S. Constitution. These are "safe" topics. As for those "dangerous topics," parents who voice their concern about how, when, and where they should be treated are not trying to "run the school" but are expressing citizen interest in how their schools are run. Secretary of Education, William J. Bennett, agreeing with parents, has voiced support of federal Department of Education regulations that give parents more control over controversial topics taught in public schools.

(2)
The Law

Law: The Magic Mirror
(Talk delivered on Law Day to the Rhode Island Supreme Court, May 2, 1977)

Today is the propitious time to rhapsodize about the law of the land. All men of good will cherish, honor, and love the law. Indeed, even men of bad will pay tribute to the power of the law. Before he was shot to death, the gangster turned-philosopher, Dennis "Danny" Raimondi, co-authored a book, *I Was a Victim of the FBI*, and dedicated it "... to the law. With the law," he said, "we have society, without it we have a jungle."

Danny was right. The beasts of the jungle obey only one law, the law of tooth and fang: kill or be killed; eat or be eaten in the wild, might makes right; survival of the fittest is the only rule, and the weak are victimized by the strong.

Animals are not troubled over questions of justice. They have no law; they follow instinct. For law is an ordinance of reason enacted for the common good, and animals lack that marvelous gift of reason which makes man, in the words of Shakespeare, "a little less than the angels."

Law is the basis of civilization and thus the gateway to culture. The arts and the sciences cannot advance to fruitful maturity without peace and order. Indeed, the degree to which the law is obeyed is a good index for judging the quality and character of a nation's civilization and culture. The very existence of the barbarian, the outlaw, and the criminal are an affront to the reign of law. To advance, or even to maintain civilization, the reign of law must be continually extended. Look at history. Every great civilization has been inextricably governed by a legal code. The better and more progressive the legal code, and the degree of respect the people have for it, then the greater the civilization. America itself was born aspiring to be the just society. The men who wrote its Constitution put justice even before domestic tranquility on their list of priorities for this "More Perfect Union."

Citizens are so convinced of the magical power of law that whenever society is faced with any problem—pollution, drugs, abuse of campaign funds, racial injustice, sex discrimination, exploitation of children, or a hundred other troubles which plague society—the cry goes up "Pass a law." Perhaps that accounts for the popularity of the comic cartoon carried by many newspapers, "There Oughta Be a Law."

The laws of a nation crystallize the principles, standards, and ideals which motivate citizens. What a country values becomes clear by the laws it enacts. The great jurist, Oliver Wendell Holmes, speaks of "the law, wherein, as in a magic mirror, we see reflected not only our own lives, but the lives of all men that have been."

When people argue over what kind of laws they want, they are really arguing over what kind of people they want to be. We fought a Civil War over slavery—at one time tolerated, indeed, protected by the Constitution. Spartan law encouraged infanticide by allowing sickly infants to be exposed to the elements. On the score of racial purity, Nazi law herded Jews to the gas chamber. Communist law represses religion on the basis of Marxist ideology. Laws do, indeed, reflect the character of a people.

When Americans propose and debate laws concerning pollution, civil rights, nuclear energy, abortion, prostitution, pornography, etc., they are claiming a right to the control of the physical, the intellectual and moral environment in which they live. They are talking about what they prize or value, about the principles, standards, and kind of behavior they consider crucial for living the "good life." What is at stake in this dialogue is the very heart of America—the whole tone of society, the very contours of future American culture.

Laws not only reflect old cultural values; they create new ones. Because they allocate values authoritatively, laws do more than limit deviant behavior; they teach what the culture considers right behavior. What the nation's law allows, therefore, is as important as what it prohibits in creating the norms of society.

It was my privilege to serve on the Commission on the Jurisprudence of the Future inspired by former Chief Justice Thomas Roberts. While the Commission can boast of few concrete accomplishments, my experience as a member served to convince me of the truth of Justice Felix Frankfurter's remark that: "Law is one of the shaping forces of society."

Indeed, is it not true that the development of individual consciences also follows the movement of societal norms? Except for rare individuals who hear the beat of different drummers, or who insist on hearing no one at all, consciences are formed in the community and reflect its values. Most of our ideas, as English literary giant Dr. Samuel Johnson wisely observed, are "not propagated by reason but caught by contagion." The kinds of norms expressed in law, therefore, become critically important even for the formation of individual consciences.

Generally, I am opposed to the use of punitive sanction to control certain kinds of behavior, not only on the grounds that it is seldom effective and risks endangering civil liberties, but because I believe that human conduct is better regulated by non-legal institutions: the home, the school, the church, the family, the peer group, the cultural pressure of society, public opinion, or even the innate decency of the individual. State-enforced morality is not morality at all, because when the state forces its citizens to perform certain acts, it succeeds not in promoting virtue but in transforming citizens into pawns and puppets. For example, widespread social disapproval of drunkenness, illicit gambling, or the use of tobacco and marijuana is often a more powerful force than trying to control them by rigid laws.

Pope John XXIII in his encyclical "Peace on Earth" expresses the same opinion. He says: "In moving individuals to seek the common good through fulfillment of their duties, civil law must appeal primarily to the consciences of individual citizens. Where civil authority uses as its only, or its chief means, either threat or fear of punishment or promises of rewards, it cannot move men to promote the common good of all. Even if it does so move them, this would be altogether opposed to their dignity as men endowed with reason and free will."

At the same time, we must not forget that the "law is a pedagogue." It teaches and proclaims a public moral standard, and this is weakened when laws are changed in the direction of greater laxity. This is scarcely a conclusive argument against any and all change in law, but it indicates that a certain conservatism in regard to the law is also a part of civil wisdom. The law is, in a sense, the voice of society's conscience.

That is why I am against striking from the books those moral laws prohibiting homosexuality, the use of drugs like heroin, prostitution, pornography, etc. The law deters more by virtue of the moral climate which it absorbs and preserves than by the punishment which it enacts and imposes. When you change, or remove, from the books, laws dealing with public morality, it is all too often taken by many as a change in morality itself. Some people argue that if a certain kind of behavior is not illegal, it is, therefore, not immoral. They confuse legality with morality.

The law's concern with interior virtue must necessarily be indirect; its goal is the creation of a climate where the individual personality and the virtues which are adornments of that personality can freely develop. The law can no more compel someone to be good, to be internally virtuous, than it can compel the rising or the setting of the sun. It can, indeed, compel me to respect the rights of others; it is quite incapable of regulating my interior attitude towards others. It can secure freedom; it cannot make me use it wisely or responsibly. It can regulate marriage but cannot make partners love or forgive each other. It can force me to give my neighbor his due, but it cannot compel me to love him. As the English proverb puts it: "In a thousand pounds of law, there is not an ounce of love." What there is in law, however, is the power to create a wholesome environment in which love can grow and virtue flourish. Law does not justify morality; it takes morality for granted.

And the morality which our laws take for granted, indeed, the very cultural pattern of our democratic society is rooted in the Hebrew-Christian religious heritage. Within that tradition we have certain great ethical ideals which we all share—ideals of liberty and social justice, ideals of the love of persons and the sacredness of personality that gave rise to the idea of personal rights and equality of opportunity. These values are shared by Protestants, Catholics, and Jews. We seldom acknowledge their origin. Indeed, we do not sufficiently appreciate them until we go and live in another country where there is no such heritage.

Even the agnostic or atheist in America, though he would be the last to admit it, is parasitic for his ethics upon the religious heritage which permeates our institutions. You will find a small band of the intelligentsia in America who think they have an autonomous ethic. Actually, they have cribbed it from the Judeo-Christian tradition. Of course, a river cannot flow indefinitely after being cut off from its source. So also, the farther a country gets away from its religious roots, the less moral vitality will inspire and permeate its laws.

If America has an ideology, that ideology can be summed up in the words "freedom under God." The moral force in this slogan became a blazing passion and a revolutionary force which inspired a democracy of worth based on the authority of God, as set forth in the Declaration of Independence.

The very existence of a democracy like ours calls for a relatively high level of virtue in its citizens. The civil law aims at enforcing only that degree of good conduct that is necessary for the well-being of society. It demands only the minimum. It does not define the full duty of any citizen in any situation. It prohibits socially intolerable conduct, but it does not prescribe what society regards as optimum or even desirable conduct.

Indeed, the major difference between a democratic and an authoritarian society is that democracy leaves the maximum range of freedom for individual action. In an authoritarian society, on the other hand, the law undertakes to prescribe in detail what the government regards as desirable conduct, thus imposing real obligations with respect to a much wider area and leaving a much smaller degree of choice to the individual.

Educator Robert M. Hutchins puts it well when he says, "In a democracy every person is, in a very real sense, a king, and it is the duty of kings to care about truth and justice and virtue." Indeed, this idea of social responsibility has meaning only in a democratic society; and, correspondingly, a democratic society is viable only when the ideal of social responsibility animates most of the citizens. It is fundamentally wrong for any citizen to take the position that he need not be concerned for the social consequences of his actions, because government will restrain him if his actions are improper or anti-social. Democracy simply won't work on this basis. Democratic processes require that citizens generally obey the law voluntarily and recognize an obligation of social responsibility most of the time regardless of the policeman on the corner.

In short, the survival of democratic society depends upon the exercise of self-control, not upon coercion. Our forefathers warned us that a nation like ours cannot be free unless its citizens freely and willingly set bounds upon their own actions.

Still, we would be living in a veritable paradise if everybody observed the law because it was right and reasonable to do so. That is why the law needs a big stick: obey or be clapped in the hoosegow or be socked with a fine. Without sanction, law is a farce. But the one and only motive to which sanction appeals is fear; and fear loses its deterrent power when cunning and craftiness make it easier to escape penalty. The most successful criminals, the white-collar variety, are neither stupid nor ignorant. Just as they employ skillful techniques in committing crime, so they can, with the help of modern inventions, more easily elude detection and pursuit, or if caught, can, through legal expertise, evade imprisonment.

Former Attorney General Ramsey Clark tells us that courts and police actually have little impact on lawbreakers. The odds are 4 to 1 that a crime will not result in arrest, 50 to 1 it will not result in conviction, and 200 to 1 it will not result in a jail term.

No, we must look to religion, education, and the family if conformity to, and respect for, the law is to be secured. Conduct which is socially desirable is dependent upon good character, and good character is determined far more by the home, the church, and the school than by the police, the law, or the judge.

Alexis de Tocqueville noted many years ago that, "while the law permits Americans to do what they please, religion prevents them from conceiving, and forbids them to commit, what is rash and unjust," and he concluded that Americans hold religion "to be indispensable to the maintenance of republican institutions."

The phrase carved in stone on the Supreme Court building in Washington, D.C., reads: "Equal Justice Under Law." That means the law is no respecter of persons. But is this so? As far back as the third century B.C., the Roman philosopher Plotinus observed: "The law for rich and poor is not the same." And centuries later Irish poet Oliver Goldsmith said: "Laws grind the poor, and rich men rule the law." Does civil justice exist only for the 20% who can afford lawyers? What about our vaunted concern for the helpless, the wretched, the feebleminded, the ex-convict, the handicapped, the "teeming masses" as historian Carl Sandburg calls them?

Few will deny that the rich have more advantages before the law than the poor. Take our tax laws. President Carter recently said that "the current tax structure is a national disgrace." The working man says "Amen" to this stricture. Indeed, every wage earner, threatened by inflation and locked in an economic bind, is outraged when his daily newspaper informs him that a big conglomerate or a millionaire pays little or no taxes. He wonders if the system of justice has been contrived by the upper crust to take care of its own.

St. Paul (1 Timothy I, 8) reminds us: "The law is good, if a man use it lawfully." The trouble is that there are too many in our society who do not use the law lawfully but who exploit it for their own advantage. Much of the most dangerous corruption of our times is entirely legal. The law itself may be used to reap enormous rewards at public expense, as through loopholes, subsidies, write-offs, or manipulation of the tax structure. A giant corporation, exploiting a weakness in the law, can carry away more booty than all the street bandits, prostitutes, pushers, and kindred bad types put together. The little favors and graft of minor officials are trivial in comparison to the special-interest legislation of such large dimensions. As the old English rhyme has it:

> *The law locks up both man and woman*
> *Who steals the goose from off the common?*
> *Yet turns the greater felon loose*
> *Who steals the common from the goose.*

Still nobody can fault us for not trying to give the poor a fair shake. The Legal Aid Society has been with us a long time, and the poor have been aided more recently by the Rhode Island Legal Services. I am privileged to serve on its Board of Directors. I suppose if every lawyer in Rhode Island took five additional cases for indigent people per year, the need for Legal Services would be eliminated. Since this professional benevolence is lacking, Legal Services takes up the slack; it provides legal counsel for the have-nots in our midst.

The procedure of the courts works unfairly on anyone who is unable, either effectively to assert legal rights on his own behalf or to employ a lawyer for that purpose. The poor are in this category. Legal Services tries to remedy this unfairness. In doing so, it reduces (hopefully) that sense of despair and feeling of inadequacy that characterizes the lives of the poor. In short, society says to the poor through Legal Services: "You may have nothing, but you count for something in this land." It secures them in the knowledge that they, like every other citizen, will get an even break before the law.

There is more than a grain of truth in the remark of Irish novelist George Bernard Shaw that: "Every profession is a conspiracy against the laity." The unlettered poor, mystified by the gobbledygook known as "legalese", feel especially lost in trying to thread their way through the inflated, involved and obscure verbiage of the law. Any normal person, unless he is an inveterate crossword puzzle addict, would be somewhat put-off when he hears such statements as: "The plaintiff has a right to the *fructus naturales* of the land and any *emblements*." And who are those bizarre sounding fellows lawyers speak of: the promisor and promisee, lessor and lessee, mortgagor and mortgagee? When I first heard the word testatrix, I thought it referred to what at one time was quaintly called a "private part."

Here's a witty anecdote I ran across in the *Rotarian Magazine*: A lawyer appearing in a case asked the witness: "Now, Mr. James, did you or did you not, on the date in question or at any other time, previously or subsequently, say, or even intimate, to the defendant or anyone else, whether friend or acquaintance or in fact a stranger, that the statement imputed to you, whether just or unjust, and denied by the plaintiff, was a matter of no consequence or otherwise? Answer! Did you or did you not?"

The witness pondered for a little while and then said: "Did I or did I not *what?*"

British judge Lord James Atkins, describing the incomprehensibility of legal jargon, states: "The layman's impression of law is too often that it is the product of a black art, administered as a mystery, which none but the initiates need hope to understand."

But lest you accuse me of judging the legal profession unfairly, I confess that we educators take refuge in a pedagoguery equally baffling to the layman and specifically designed to obfuscate the clearest issues.

God of Justice and right, the verse maker tells us that:

> *A bumper of good liquor*
> *Will end a contest quicker*
> *Than justice, judge, or vicar*

Would that this were so. But many contests end up in the courts and so we need judges who are well-versed, as Shakespeare says, "in those nice sharp quillets of the law." Tonight, we honor Superior Court Judge John McKiernan whose wisdom, skill, and integrity as a judge reflects credit upon himself, his family, and his country. Indeed, the gifts which your vocation requires of you and the works you do as makers and judgers of the law are so close to those of God Himself as to give them some shadow, however faint, of the divine Majesty itself. You are the wielders, in varying degrees, of sovereignty. You interpret and apply, you bind under and loose from, the civil law which is the codification of our society as descended from the natural law the Creator implanted in the innermost hearts of men.

You attain your offices by duly prescribed appointment; you are answerable to those who designate you and the people they represent. But your sovereignty is still of God; there is no true authority which is not divine, no trust which is not sacred, no stewardship which is not answerable ultimately to God.

Our forefathers, the authors of our basic law, understood that a truly humane civilization dedicated to respect for the rights of man must have a government of laws, not of men—of objective, constitutional statutes, not subjective, arbitrary impulses, however high-minded, however immediately beneficial. It is this government of laws that we honor at this 1977 Law Day Celebration.

There Oughta Be a Law
(Talk delivered at New England Conference on Crime and Delinquency, September 20, 1973)

If you read the comic section of the newspaper, you have probably run across a cartoon by Whipple and Borth entitled "There Oughta Be a Law." The cartoonists humorously portray an outrageous situation in which good and honest people are so taken advantage of that readers agree "There Oughta Be a Law" against such flagrant exploitation or breach of good taste.

The popularity of the cartoon provides ample evidence that many citizens, civic leaders, even lawmakers, are convinced that passing a law is an effective way to curb vice, influence public policy, or introduce social change. When society wants to check pollution, control the use of drugs, prevent the abuse of campaign funds, defend civil rights, promote interracial justice, or implement a hundred-and-one other policies relating to the common good, the cry goes up "Pass a law."

Actually, many laws are not effective, in the simple sense that they do not achieve the desired effect. Most polluters, drug users, or easy riders on campaign funds are neither caught nor deterred by the numerous laws. One example will have to stand for all the thousands that could be given: The Corrupt Practices Act prohibits any individual from donating more than $5,000 to any one national, political campaign committee. But as the Republicans set up 46 such committees and the Democrats 97, corporate officers make contributions that vastly exceed the $5,000 limit.

True, a good part of the laws passed were not meant to be implemented, at least not systematically and effectively. Passing these laws is part of the make-believe or theatre of politics in which politicians try to placate two (or more) opposing camps by giving one the law (saying in effect, "You see, I took care of it") and the other camp, more or less, the freedom they desired to continue to pursue the activities which violate the law. Thus, we have laws against gambling which are very sporadically enforced throughout most American metropolitan centers, but which allow the moralistic parts of the community to feel they had their day and which, at the same time, permit the gambler to gamble. Similarly, tough but rarely enforced laws against pollution both please the ecology movement and fail to deter most polluters.

Am I implying that laws are generally ineffective and, perhaps even unnecessary, that it would be better to appeal to the good will and virtue of citizens than to the sanctions of law, and that we should develop a sense of personal responsibility in citizens rather than rely on fear of punishment? Pope John XXIII seems to think so. In his encyclical *Peace on Earth*, he offers some basic norms for rule enforcement and censure in civil society. He says:

> *In moving individuals to seek the common good through fulfillment of their duties, civil authority must appeal, primarily, to the conscience of individual citizens. Where civil authority uses as its only, or its chief means, either threats or fear of punishment or promises of rewards, it cannot effectively move men to promote the common good of all. Even if it do so move them, this would be altogether opposed to their dignity as men endowed with reason and free will.*

This is a beautiful thought and it exemplifies in a striking fashion Pope John's optimism and faith in human nature. There appears, however, to be just one slight flaw in the Pontiff's recommendation. It simply won't work—at least not in our country. In the United States, we seem faced with an attitude toward law which indicates that a great deal more must be made of "fear of punishment" and actual censure than the Holy Father indicates as appropriate. In other words, in our country the appeal to conscience just does not seem to get very far.

It is interesting to speculate why this attitude has arisen among Americans—that laws need not be taken seriously unless and until the lawmaker demonstrates that he "means business." Is it endemic to democratic people everywhere as a result of majorities at times insisting on laws that a minority considers unreasonable and even, unjust? Perhaps it comes from the observation that laws in a democracy can be contradictory. For example, one Southern state until recently prohibited liquor but at the same time raised money for schools (of all things) by taxing (illegal) liquor sales. Whatever the cause, there are clear indications that in our American culture, it is difficult, if not impossible, to enforce civil laws merely by an appeal to conscience. Fear of punishment and actual censure seem necessary for the lawmaker to show that he "means business."

Thomas Aquinas and his mentor, Aristotle, would agree. These philosophers insist that punishment, "shaking the big stick," is an essential ingredient of good law. Indeed, in explaining why the state is of moral as well as material benefit to its members, Aquinas long ago pointed out that if a situation arises in which a father is physically incapable of disciplining his rebellious sons, he can, in an organized society, appeal to the guardians of public order. Aquinas is not referring simply to the fact that these public officers will restore order in a disordered situation, important as that fact is. He is also referring to the influence of such restoration on the young men in question. He is saying, in more modern language, that juvenile delinquents will not only be deterred from crime by the threat of police action but also will be morally improved. Forced obedience, the hypothesis runs, will in time generate voluntary obedience and will develop the virtue of obedience.

You may very well ask "Is this true?" Can moral virtue be developed by means of coercion, through compelled conformity, by putting fear of punishment in the hearts of those who would flaunt the law?

Experience tells us it can. If virtue is developed by repeated actions—and on a natural level it is so developed—then repeated acts of obedience to authority, even if the original reason is ignoble, should make it continually easier to obey and should make it seem even more natural to obey. These repeated acts, even if originally forced, should, in short, develop the virtue of obedience in those who through self-will, faulty home training, or conditioning, are lacking in that virtue.

Does not this thesis run contrary to the wisdom of the maxim "You can't legislate morality?" Yes and no. To say you can't force people to be virtuous is at best a half-truth. Every country has a multitude of laws that quite effectively prohibit evil deeds and encourage, or even command, good deeds. Far from believing that "You can't legislate morality" those who support such social legislation as the Fair Employment Practices Act or Fair Housing or Civil Rights or school integration laws, maintain that legislation is one of the forms of education and that social legislation will produce better men as well as better situations. It is certainly true that law is a matter of reason before it is a matter of will, that it issues primarily from the reason of a legislator and is a form of explanation to those to whom it applies of what they should do in order to achieve the common good. Robert M. Hutchins stresses this educative function of law when he says, "The importance of law is not that it is coercive but that it is pedagogical. The way to begin the rule of law, therefore, is to begin it and to rely on its educational force."

On the level of civil authority, the theory that we can legislate morality seems to have a large amount of justification. When they were first proposed, laws regulating child labor, safety conditions in dangerous occupations, minimum wages, and other such things, were opposed as placing impossible burdens on the economy. They were at first obeyed only because of the legal sanctions attached to disobedience. Yet no one would today even suggest a return to the conditions existing before such legislation.

There may be many reasons for such a changed attitude towards the rights of working people; one of them would clearly seem to be that the business world followed the legal directives, found that the economy somehow survived under these directives, got used to working in such conditions, and gradually came to accept the situation as normal and right. Such a development constitutes real progress for the virtue of justice and that development can largely be put down to the influence of social legislation. Experience would indicate that, at least in this meaning, you *can* legislate virtue.

Certainly, most societies take the possibility for granted and attempt to legislate virtue. The Church insists on her members obeying ecclesiastical law, not only for the sake of the law but also for the sake of the members. That law is designed to make better men as well as to get certain things done. Parents lay down certain rules for their children to obey primarily in order to develop a sense of responsibility in the children, to help them to grow up and reach the condition in which they may run their own lives without further rules from their parents. The basic idea is not just to get the dishes done or the grass cut or even to get the children off the street and out of harm's way at a reasonable hour, though these results are not unimportant. The basic idea is that repetition of these actions, even though there is a certain amount of coercion involved, is designed to lead to a greater degree of maturity and to a heightened sense of responsibility in the children. And it is a pretty general experience that responsibility developed during childhood and adolescence will carry over into adult life.

But is this the way to develop responsibility in the first place? Does it work? Sometimes it does and sometimes it doesn't. Certainly, to let people of any age do exactly as they please is an open invitation both to social chaos and to the deterioration of character; it is not good for any of us to be answerable to no one but ourselves. Yet it is also possible to make discipline so strict and coercion so severe as to invite rebellion. The fictional Captain Bligh was interested in developing strict and unquestioning obedience in his crew; the way in which he went about it produced mutiny on the *Bounty* instead. Parents who are unreasonably strict have driven their children to leave home and as a gesture of defiance to live as they know their parents would not wish them to. Youngsters become hippies, take drugs, smoke pot, and join communes, not only as a result of parental ultra-permissiveness but also as a reaction to extreme rigidity.

Even so; the fact that coercion ordinarily reaches a point, varying with the individual person, at which it produces rebellion, does not invalidate the claim that moral value *can* be developed by the repeated performance of good acts. What it means is that prudence must be exercised in applying sanctions and that the natural human inclination to exercise the freedom of choice cannot be entirely ignored. It is this delicate balance that must be maintained in every attempt to develop moral virtue in children and in the efforts of legislators to make laws which would enforce virtue in citizens. If a law is rushed through or remains on the books against the beliefs of most people, then no punishment or fear of arrest is likely to make it work. It is much better, both for the enforcement of a single law and for the viability of the total legal fabric, to have fewer laws, well supported and backed up, than a myriad that do not have the consensus of the people.

This much is quite clear: Even in a pluralist society like ours, there is a public morality that the law can and does enforce. Indeed, without commonly held moral convictions, the community would degenerate to the level of imprisoned criminals who are held together only by the walls that surround them. But the law should not impose a standard of virtue so high that it is unrealistic to expect the majority of men to observe it. The prohibition of all sale of alcoholic beverages during the 1920s was, no doubt, a "noble experiment"—or so it seemed to President Herbert Hoover—but it failed miserably. The prohibition laws were not obeyed because they asked more than the people thought it reasonable to ask or were willing to give. To escape Mr. Bumble's judgment that "the law is an ass," therefore, legislators are well advised to aim at enforcing only that degree of good conduct that is necessary for the peace, good order, and well-being of society.

British statesman Edmund Burke once remarked that "it is no small part of civil wisdom to know how much of an evil ought to be tolerated. The law may, because it must, tolerate some evils in the realm of moral conduct. If prohibition of a vice is likely to work greater harm to the community than toleration, or if a prohibition is such that it cannot be enforced, or if it invades privacy and freedom, of if it brings the law into disrepute, then lawmakers will prudently refrain from imposing it by statute."

This kind of reasoning seems to support those who want to strike from the books, scores of laws against crimes that are difficult to detect, hard to punish, or which infringe on human freedom—such as those laws banning homosexual liaisons between consenting adults, fornication, the use of marijuana, prostitution where no other crime is involved, and drunkenness among pedestrians, the source of more than half of the arrests made in the United States—and focus our resources on those laws we can really make effective.

There is much to be said in favor of such argumentation, as the Subcommittee on Crime of the Rhode Island Committee for the Jurisprudence of the Future recently pointed out. In my opinion, however, it is not wise to capitulate at once to every demand for more "liberal" laws. Initially, at least, the presumption favors retention of the existing law and the burden of proof falls on those who advocate change, not on those who oppose it. Law, after all, has an important educational function: it proclaims a public moral standard, and this is weakened when laws are changed in the direction of greater laxity. This is not a conclusive argument against any and all change in the law, but it indicates that a certain conservatism in regard to the law is also a part of civil wisdom. When you change, or remove from the books, laws dealing with public morality, it is all too often taken by many as a change in morality itself. Some people argue that if a thing is not illegal, it is, therefore, not immoral. They confuse legality with morality.

Actually, it is almost impossible in an organized society to conceive of so-called victimless crimes or private acts which might not, in some circumstances, harm others in one way or another. Just as low standards in personal hygiene can endanger public health, so low standards in private morals can endanger public welfare. It seems to me misleading, therefore, to try to draw any theoretical line beyond which the law may not trespass. All human activity, however private, can legitimately be the law's business.

Having said this, it is only reasonable to acknowledge that the law can only go so far. It cannot take everything into account; indeed, human activity does not legitimately become the law's business until it begins to affect other persons and thus to impinge upon a public concern. Not only that; even though an action is harmful in some way to the community, it should not be made a subject of legislation unless it is, or threatens to become, substantially harmful. Not every minor social evil justifies legal regulation or prohibition. We should not think a law is desirable merely because it enforces a moral principle.

No matter what the situation may be in more repressive societies, the very existence of a democracy like ours calls for a free and voluntary observance of the law by the majority of citizens. The civil law in our country aims at enforcing only that degree of good conduct that is necessary for the peace, good order and well-being of society. It demands only the minimum. It does not define the full duty of any citizen in any situation. It prohibits socially intolerable conduct and prescribes the minimum that is obligatory in situations where affirmative action is legally required. But the law does not prescribe what society regards as optimum or even desirable conduct. That is why it is fundamentally wrong for any citizen to take the position that he need not be concerned for the social consequences of his actions because government will restrain him if his actions are criminal or anti-social. Democracy simply won't work on this basis. Democratic processes require that citizens generally obey the law voluntarily and recognize an obligation of social responsibility most of the time, regardless of the policeman on the corner. In short, the survival of a democratic society depends upon the exercise of self-control, not coercion.

Here is where the home, church, and school are so important. The crime problem in America is above all a moral problem, not a social or economic or racial or psychiatric or legal problem. Conduct which is socially desirable is dependent upon good character, and good character is determined far more by the home, the church, and the school than by the police, the law, the psychiatrist, the judge, or even the undesirable neighborhood in which a person may have been raised. In short, religion, education, and the family are the agencies we must support and rely upon if we truly want to develop law-abiding citizens.

Please Don't Kill The Lawyers
(*The Providence Visitor*, December 30, 1999)

It's sad but true that obloquy and abuse have always been the lot of the lawyer. Americans wear blinders when they judge lawyers. On the scale of ill repute, the lawyer rates the same status as the carpetbagger. All lawyers, belittlers assert, are rogues and cheats.

The law schools are churning out lawyers *ad infinitum*. This increase in density, however, has not been accompanied by a proportionate increase in mass affection. Plainly, lawyers, once described by Alexis de Tocqueville as "the American aristocracy," have an image problem. This may well be, because the put-upon public have been conned into believing that "every profession," as Irish wit George Bernard Shaw wryly remarks, "is a conspiracy against the laity."

Lawyers deserve to be flayed for their sins. Their maleficence is reprehensible. There are lawyers who steal from estates and trust funds; who feed on the infirm, the orphan, the mentally incompetent, and the divorced; who hide behind collection agencies, credit bureaus, and sheriff's sales; who angle to get themselves attached to the money teat of the probate court as special "guardians"; who chase ambulances, split fees, and bribe public officials; who engage in pettifoggery, barratry, champerty, and maintenance; who appeal to greed by hawking their expertise via television, radio, and the press; and who are lazy and/or inept. No wonder that legal malpractice suits have proliferated steadily in the past 20 years!

The Bar Association is hard-put to police adequately the seamy side of the profession. The courts add to the problem because, too frequently, they are overprotective of lawyers, indulging in what the *Columbia Law Review* has called "the fraternal concern of the judiciary for members of the practicing bar."

While most lawyers are professionals of unimpeachable integrity, shysters often given law a bad name. Sleazy character begets sleazy conduct. While legal ethical codes are in effect, it is nigh unto impossible to weed out all the sleaze balls and ethical barbarians.

The *Rhode Island Bar Journal* (May 1994), quotes U.S. Supreme Court Justice William Brennan's indictment of the villainous lawyer: "There is no profession, save perhaps the ministry, in which the highest morality is more necessary than that of the law. There is, in fact, no vocation in life where moral character counts for so much or where it is subjected to a more crucial test by citizen and public than is that of the members of the bar. The reputation of the profession is tarnished not so much by the flagrant violators, by those attorneys who by unconscionable conduct tip the delicate balance in which trust and confidence in a lawyer's action hang; not by malefactions which are criminal, but rather, from those in the twilight of low morality."

Sue. Sue. Sue. American society is madly litigious. This is not so surprising, for ours is a society built on individualism, competition, and success. Our law system is adversarial. Law schools train their students more for conflict than for the gentler arts of reconciliation and accommodation. There are just so many laws, so many lawyers, and so many legislative bodies which are lawyer-dominated! That is not the healthiest state in a democracy that prizes diversity.

Lawyers are smart. They have to be. Competition is keen. To get ahead, they must be well versed in what Shakespeare calls "those nice sharp quillets of the law." But pride and arrogance lurk in the path of the erudite and proficient. Nothing irks the *hoi polloi* more than a lawyer's know-it-all, supercilious manner. Yet, there is little doubt that law schools succeed more than graduate schools and seminaries in teaching their clientele how to think.

Does the national good suffer harm because the law profession attracts too large a percentage of gifted American youth? Harvard's *quondam* president, Derek C. Bok thinks so. And bishops worry that bright young Catholic men, who at one time chose the priesthood and brotherhood, now go into law. In days past, many talented women entered religious life. Today they flock to the law schools. One happy result of this "the ladies are raising the standards of the profession."

In 1710, Rev. Cotton Mather of Massachusetts admonished the bar in these words: "A lawyer should be a scholar, but Sirs, when you are called upon to be wise, the main intention is that you may be wise to do good… A lawyer that is a knave betrays the liberties of the people."

Lawyers may not win first place in popularity contests, but they are indispensable. For an individual who finds himself a victim of fraud, or threat, or brutality, or injustice, there can be no more heart-warming experience than the assuring word of a good lawyer. Our democracy is a nation of laws, not men; and citizens have faith that, in the long run, justice will prevail.

Lawyering and altruism go hand in hand. While he is entitled to a comfortable livelihood, the lawyer is not a tradesman, nor a businessman whose main objective is making money. Rather, he is a professional who plies his craft in a spirit of public service. Herein lies his dignity.

Lawyers are held in high esteem by the Catholic Church. Theologically, lawyers are shadows, however faint, of the majesty of the Divine Lawgiver. As makers and judgers of the law, they partake in varying degrees of sovereignty. They interpret, apply, bind under, and loose from the positive civil law—which is the codification of our society as God has given us to achieve it—as it derived from the natural law which the Creator implanted in the innermost hearts of men.

The authority lawyers wield belongs so intimately to God that French Bishop Jacques Bossuet went so far as to call those who administer the law "men like unto God."

For the believer, law can be a spiritual calling to loving service of God and neighbor. When a lawyer approaches his work as a vocation, he sees his client not as a mere commodity, but as a human being, often in pain and emotional turmoil, who has come to him for help. He serves his God by serving his neighbor.

When William Bentley Ball, eminent First Amendment scholar and pro-life advocate, was asked what his faith meant to him in the practice of law, he answered: "In all my years of practice, my Catholic faith has been a teacher and an inspiration, especially in one important area of law, an area to which I can best pin the label, 'the sacredness of human life.'"

What Is Legal Is Not Always Moral
(*The Evening Times* (Pawtucket, R.I.), February 18, 1981)

United States Senator J. William Fulbright once asked, "How do we deal with those who ... offend the spirit of the law, but do not violate the letter? What of the men outside government who suborn those inside it.... Why is it that, among so many influential people, morality has become identical with legality"?

The law's reach is necessarily limited. Much of the most subversive corruption of our times is entirely legal. The law itself may be used to reap enormous rewards at public expense, as through subsidies, loopholes, dodges, or an unconscionable juggling of the tax structure.

A giant corporation, exploiting a weakness in the law, can carry away more booty than all the street bandits, hookers, pushers, and kindred bad types put together. The little favors and graft of minor officials are trivial in comparison to the gigantic profits reaped by big business whose lawyers, well versed "In those nice sharp quillets of the law," work within legal boundaries but outside the scope of ethical principles. As an old English rhyme puts it:

> *The law locks up both man and woman*
> *Who steals the goose from off the common?*
> *Yet turns the greater felon loose*
> *Who steals the common from the goose.*

Inside knowledge of future government projects—bridge and road building, public schools and housing, civic centers, and other large undertakings—tempts those in the "know" to exploit their information. Many years ago, Boss Plunkitt of Tammany Hall wrote of "honest graft," and summarized his autobiography in these succinct words: "I seen my opportunities and I took 'em."

The pecuniary stakes in public works are enormous, and the political party in the driver's seat has the power to hand out the plums. Even if political leaders are unusually enlightened, the very nature of the system, based on rewarding political loyalty, tends to corrupt civil administration.

A politician may be above bribery, but he got where he is, not by competitive examination or professional qualification; he had to be nominated and elected to his public post. This is an expensive and complicated ordeal, and, in the process, he becomes beholden to his loyal cronies, financial backers, and the voters who elected him—often in that order. The obligations and commitments he made while campaigning fall due the moment he is sworn in.

Some contend that abuses involving manipulation of the law for private profit—legal but unethical—are an inevitable part of the democratic system. That's the way to get things done. It's in the American tradition for an elected official to take care of his own, look out for his constituents and reward his backers. "To the victor, belongs the spoils."

There are very few matters of large moment, it is argued, that can be accomplished without harming or benefitting, pleasing or offending, one group more than another. If needed housing, roads, bridges, parks etc., can be built only at the cost of lining pockets exorbitantly, then better to tolerate this abuse than endure stagnation and stalemate and end-up with none of these benefits.

Of course, there are alternatives. Loopholes can be closed, laws can be modified, practices which rip off the taxpayer can be abolished. Everybody agrees that promoting general welfare programs ought not to be abandoned simply because they attract unscrupulous profiteers. Still, every effort should be made to curb the rascals.

The law's concern with interior virtue must necessarily be indirect; its goal is the creation of a climate where the individual personality and the virtues which are adornments of that personality can freely develop.

The law can no more compel someone to be good, to be internally virtuous, than it can compel the rising or the setting of the sun. It can, indeed, compel me to respect the right of others; it is quite incapable of regulating my interior attitude towards others. It can secure freedom; it cannot make me use it wisely or responsibly. It can regulate marriage but it cannot make partners love or forgive each other. It can force me to give my neighbor his due, but it cannot compel me to love him.

As an old proverb expresses it: "In a thousand pounds of law, there is not an ounce of love." What there is in law, however, is the power to create a wholesome environment in which love can grow and virtue flourish. Law does not justify morality; it takes morality for granted.

The survival of freedom in a democratic society depends upon the exercise of self-control not upon coercion. Our forefathers warned us that Americans can only be truly free when citizens willingly set bounds upon their own behavior regardless of the policeman on the corner.

The anthropologist, Ruth Benedict, once proposed the thesis that the United States was ceasing to be a "guilt culture"—one in which control of conduct is self-imposed by means of conscience—and was becoming instead a "shame culture"—one in which control is externally imposed by means of public humiliation or punishment, as in some Eastern cultures.

In short, there is a growing shift in the techniques Americans use to develop and enforce honesty. When dishonesty is rampant, it becomes easy to live with a bad conscience; so external rather than internal methods of control prevail.

To protect itself from unconscionable citizens, government must then create a repressive Brave New World, Big-Brother-is-watching atmosphere; it must generate a climate of fear. Indeed, when people refuse to apply the internal brake of conscience, government applies the external brake of public shame, fines, and imprisonment. The ambit of freedom is thus gradually restricted, and morality becomes identical with legality. May Americans never reach this parlous state.

Screening Those Future Judges
(*The Providence Journal*, Wednesday, November 30, 1983)

Judicial work saps energy and vitality to such a degree that candidates being interviewed for positions in Rhode Island courts were asked before all else if they were healthy enough to stand the gaff.

In appointing judges, boo-boos are not unheard of. That's why counselor William A. Curran, chairman of Governor J. Joseph Garrahy's screening commission, started the interviewing by asking candidates if they had ever been arrested or censured by the Supreme Court Disciplinary Committee, and if they had paid their federal, state, and municipal taxes.

Thirty-six lawyers (some of them judges seeking a higher court) were screened by the Garrahy Commission. They ranged in age from 34 to 65; four were women; 32 were men. Some opted for more than one court: Family, 19; District, 26; Superior, 16.

The 15-member commission is made up of lawyers and lay people of assorted backgrounds. Lawyers tended to grill on points of law, legal expertise, and trial experience. (Almost 50 percent of the candidates were not practicing-law). Lay people often delved into personal and family life, community and humanitarian service, and the motivation of applicants.

The best way to place qualified judges on the bench is to find beforehand those lawyers who have all the desirable qualities. The idiosyncrasies and inadequacies of a candidate, once appointed to a judgeship, can create a lot of injustice.

The screening of candidates unearthed one great truth; the most important attributes of judges are not objective but subjective, i.e., primarily personal, not capable of being quantified or scientifically measured.

The discharge of justice requires a high standard of mental and moral alertness. Yet Samuel Rosenman, former president of the New York Bar Association, declares: "In far too many instances, the benches of our courts in the United States are occupied by mediocrities—men of small talent, undistinguished in performance, technically deficient, and inept."

The qualities of a good judge are integrity, knowledge of the law, courteousness, compassion, calmness, concentration, fairness, patience, industriousness, decisiveness, zeal for truth, level-headedness, and efficiency—characteristics which go into what is called "judicial temperament." To find such paragons of intellectual and moral virtue is not easy.

The judge is an awesome figure. He bears all the heady trappings of power. Garbed in a robe, he can expect the court to rise when he enters, and his entry sonorously announced. He presides behind an imposing desk on a raised platform bedecked with flags. He is absolute master of his courtroom, far beyond the imaginings of the most lordly corporate executive. The action of his courts may vitally affect the life, property, and happiness of any citizen subject to its jurisdiction.

U.S. Supreme Court Justice Felix Frankfurter, asked if a lawyer becomes any different when he puts on a gown, answered, "If he is any good, he does."

The public sees judges as endowed with a special mystique and thus shows deference, even reverence, to them. This, in turn, makes every phase of a judge's visible behavior an object of public concern. The judge is "always on stage." A judicial career and a scandalous life simply do not mix.

But it is not only scandal which must be avoided, but immoderate and imprudent conduct—playing too hard, drinking to much, dressing in an excessive high style, betting at the $50 window at the racetrack.

Moreover, partisan political activity is forbidden to judges, as the commission's queries revealed.

Non-political activity is a gray area. Should a judge resign memberships in country clubs? Should he abstain from participation in community drives? Should he forego memberships on academic, charitable, and religious boards?

Those questions are generally answered in the negative, but there are twilight zones. Discretion at all times is the key to a judge's conduct, e.g., he is privileged to play golf, but he should not do it with litigants or with lawyers who appear frequently before him. The life of a judge is a lonely one, especially since he is not permitted anything that could impugn his motives in the least.

It is impossible to reduce intangible qualities to a tangible scale, but judges' salaries are very tangible. In Rhode Island they are grossly below what they should be. Because this creates problems in recruiting candidates of the highest caliber, the screening commission has petitioned Governor Garrahy to make raising judicial salaries one of his top priorities.

Lawyers may get rich, but judges never. As it now stands, most candidates stepping up to the bench take a reduction in income. Consequently, many lawyers delay seeking judicial appointments until their children are educated or after obtaining added revenue from inheritance or investments. If they happen to be legislators or move up form the attorney general's office, their salary may be several thousand dollars above other candidates who have no government service. Inequities like this ought to be righted.

The state needs younger judges with the ability and capacity for hard work. Citizens should be keen to pay them their true worth.

Cops Can Only Do So Much
(*The Providence Journal-Bulletin*, Tuesday, September 25, 1990)

The public expects the moon of the police. The myth of the supercop—a fanciful fiction dreamed up by movie and television scribes—is largely at fault.

Exposing the sham of the super cop and instructing the would-be cop in the routine duties of the working officer is one of the primary goals of the police academy.

Perhaps wishfully, the public pictures the policeman as the master of multiple roles. They are supposed to be familiar with, and help enforce, a staggering 30,000 local, state, and federal laws. They are expected to embody the compassionate qualities of a religious leader, nurse, social worker, Boy Scout, psychologist, parent, and friend—but they must also be ready to galvanize themselves into an instant commander, disciplinarian, military genius, marksman, and karate expert. The complexities of the job would overwhelm a superman. A policeman's education and training simply do not fit them for the chores the public thrusts on them. They may be pardoned if they fail.

Police work is a high-stress occupation. Acute and prolonged stress multiplies personal problems. Cynicism, alcoholism, drug abuse, mental, physical, and psychosomatic ailments, family discord, divorce, and suicide are too often the tragic byproducts of a super stressful career; their incidence in the police force is double that of the populace at large.

Danger augments stress and a cop constantly lives with danger. Besides a 1 in 8 chance of being assaulted during the year, the policeman faces one chance in 22 of being injured and one chance in 3500 of being killed; all in addition to the daily chance of being cursed and defamed by breakers of big and little laws. Indeed, cops find it hard to relax. They have to be on the job 24 hours a day—off and on-duty—giving them little opportunity to recharge their emotional batteries. The marital relationship often becomes a casualty, especially in the early years when the officer is adjusting to a strange and often hostile environment.

Job pressure may be so severe and persistent that the luckless policeman ends up completely frazzled—"a burned-out Samaritan." Burnout begets many evils, none of which worsens police performance so much as a jaundiced cynicism. This frame of mind usually peaks after 3 to 7 years of service and moderates slowly thereafter as the officer matures professionally and becomes more adept at coping with the vexations of the job.

In some quarters cops are hated. But for the most part, citizens view guardians of the law with a mixture of fear and admiration. Fear, because the approach of the policeman induces a spasm of panic in most people, a feeling against which the awareness of innocence provides no adequate protection. Admiration, because the police are posted on the perimeters of order and justice. They are society's security blanket, sparing the rest of the populace direct confrontations with the forces of darkness and evil. Still, people mistrust cops, reasoning, illogically, that those who do society's dirty work must inevitably dirty themselves in the process. While 70 percent of the people polled say they respect the police, and while the ambition of one out of five youngsters is to become a cop, the constabulary calling still rates low in national esteem; it ranks 54th in status along with playground directors and railroad conductors among 90 occupations. This may account for the condescension sometimes shown police by the better-educated and higher-incomed.

Like most people, policemen are involved in a love-hate affair with the administration of justice; they distrust lawyers, including judges, but they have an invincible faith in "The Law." They often think criminals are let-off and let-out too easily. They become confused when society encourages lotteries and legalized betting; they must arrest prostitutes, but society tolerates pornography and commercialized sex; they must jail shoplifters while thieves who embezzle millions get off with a slap on the wrist; and they must crack down on drug dealers when the country is awash on tranquilizers and pep pills. The duty to enforce archaic and incompatible laws complicates their job.

Indeed, a discrepancy exists between what people expect the police to do and what the police are permitted to do under law. In the present drug crisis, for instance, citizens urge police to be more aggressive, yet they worry whether constitutional rights will be endangered by tactics like neighborhood sweeps, no-knock searches, automobile stops, reverse stings, and property seizures. The fear always exists that if the police are given more discretion, the closer the nation will come to being a police state.

American police operate on the cutting edge of swiftly changing social conditions—increased personal mobility and rootlessness, an epidemic of drug abuse, the poverty of the underclass, the massing of people in inner-cities, a mood of mindless hedonism, and the dissolution of family and religious disciplines. Society itself has been unsuccessful in coping with these changes, and the police, who are of one cloth with the society they serve, can only do what society mandates.

By many measures, the policeman's lot today would seem to be a happy one. They are better paid, better educated, and more professional than their predecessors. Indeed, before long, recruits will have to have a college diploma, and a cop's non-crime duties (now consuming two-thirds of his time) will be assigned to parapolice personnel.

But not all is copacetic. As improved performance came in, something fundamental seems to have gone out. Not so long ago, policemen looked on their profession as a calling. But as cops begin to embrace the idea that theirs is just another job, as they consider themselves to be less special, as their pride and group identity diminish, then the romance, the glory, and the commitment will go out of the job. And, in the long run, the public will be the loser.

(3)
Politics

Politics and the Common Good
(*The Providence Journal*, December 17, 1981)

Throwing their hats into the ring, candidates aspiring to local and state offices are testing the political atmosphere to judge what kind of chance they will have at the polls next November. Political orators who usually declare their dedication to "justice" and "right" now seem to be adopting a "hard-headed" or so-called "realistic" attitude in their discussion of public issues.

I refer to the increasing tendency for political exchanges to be "political" in the meanest, narrowest sense. In accordance with this tendency, public questions are almost immediately reduced to an inquiry about who has the votes, or how many he can muster. This, we submit, is not merely "realism"—or, if it is, it is the kind of realism shown by Joseph Stalin when he asked at Yalta, "How many divisions has the pope?"

This anecdote reveals Stalin's ignorance in the very area where he was presumably the expert: that of power. For divisions are not the only source of power, nor always the strongest or most lasting.

But what has all this to do with the political situation in our community or in our nation? Simply, that more and more citizens seem to believe that power—votes, pressures, interests—is the only political reality. More and more of us seem to believe that Fourth of July oratory about democracy is all very well, but what really pays off in terms of getting anything done is being able to deliver the goods, i.e., the votes, or the letters, or telegrams, or the organized protests, or the fund-raising dinners. If you can deliver, then you get your way; if you can't deliver, then the other group gets its way.

All this is not to deny the role of simple power in the life of our democracy, nor to sigh for a more ideal world. We do not deplore the hard political, or any sort, of facts of life. Our intention is merely to reaffirm our belief in some political facts other than the undeniable "hard" ones. In brief, we believe that in the functioning of a democracy too, there are stronger things than divisions.

Every thinker who has directed his attention to the dangers and potentialities of democracy has seen that such a society cannot be simply an arena where conflicting ideas and opposing groups fight to the death for dominance. Such a notion conjures up a jungle scene, not the image of a united people governing themselves according to their expressed and cherished principles of life.

There is, then, as modern political theorists Jacques Maritain, John Courtney Murray, and Walter Lippmann have pointed out, at the core of every true democracy a body of truths held in common. As we move out from the center of this core of belief, we find less and less perfect agreement, and in almost every particular case there may be differences within a larger area of agreement. But there is one article of our democratic belief about which there should be no dispute: that the crucial consideration in all our political activity shall be the furtherance of the common good.

The conscious dedication of a democratic people to the pursuit of the common good means a rejection of sheer majoritarianism; it means a rejection of the "open contest" notion and a kind of Fable-of-the-Bees belief that the common good will be served mechanically and automatically by the clash of competing self-interests.

But is it unrealistic to expect people in a democracy or anywhere else to conduct themselves with such largeness of vision, such unselfishness? We think not. It is unrealistic to expect all of the people to transcend their selfishness all of the time. And when they do not, then we have learned that reliance on the competition among divergent views, on majority rule, furnishes the most practical avenue of decision, and the best guarantee against irrevocable tyranny. Yet even so, it is by no means unrealistic to expect that men in a democracy will at least seek to be guided by this concept of the common good, and that the concept itself will be a meaningful one.

Consciousness of the requirements of the common good will not, of course, lead us all into instant and total agreement. There will be disagreements and conflicts in the working out of our many difficult problems. But some reflections on the common good may save us from a few of our most troublesome errors. Perhaps we will be able to remember that the existence of a "right" does not make any particular political consequence an inevitability. There are innumerable "rights" held by the people and groups of a state. These "rights" often overlap; certainly, they affect one another; sometimes they conflict with one another.

Often those who are fighting for a "right" ask, rhetorically (because they are really not asking) and bitterly: "Can injustice ever contribute to the common good?" Now the terms of such a question are not proper, since to limit the exercise of a right is not ipso facto unjust, but to accept the improper terms, the question is sometimes easily answered in a way that might surprise the askers: Yes, it may well be that the common good, the well-being of the body politic as a whole, positively demands the limitation, the deferral, even the denial, of the exercise of a certain "right."

On the other hand, however, a minority's "rights" are in no way diminished by the fact of its being a minority. The common good may demand that a minority's "right" be recognized even against the conviction of the majority.

As we said, the invocation of the principle of the common good will not mean the end of all political discord. But it seems that arguments based on this idea are likely to be more profitable than mere group conflicts.

Agreeing that we will debate only ways of working out the good which every citizen desires for the nation, and not for his group, might remove some of the bitterness and resentment which deface much of our public discussion today. It might permit us to escape from the view of political activity as a struggle between ins and outs, rich and poor, political parties, religious groups, ethnic and racial groups, or any other category that divides us.

The first loyalty of everyone in a democracy is to the common good, then, not to friends, neighbors, co-religionists, or co-workers. "Our own," in other words, is all of us.

Challenge of Getting Out the Vote
(*The Providence Journal*, October 29, 1986)

The very existence of democracy depends on universal suffrage. Without the vote of the people, political freedom collapses. Political liberty is guaranteed only when the will of the individual citizen actually determines the will of the government.

Winston Churchill once said, "At the bottom of all the tributes paid to democracy is the little man, walking into the little booth to cast his vote—no amount of rhetoric can possibly diminish the overwhelming importance of this act."

In the face of this evident truth, why do so many citizens withdraw from politics or refuse to vote? One inflexible law governs politics: The greater the number of people who refuse to vote or become involved, the greater the influence exercised by those who remain.

When the rank-and-file citizen stays away from the polls, he automatically increases the clout of the fat cats, the rich "angels," the lobbyists, the big contributors, the $1,000 clubs, the vested interests, and the political action committees (PACs). By abandoning the field of battle, the average voter leaves the political wars to be fought only by powerful interest groups.

The percentage of Americans voting has declined in every presidential election since 1960. State, local, and congressional elections do not manifest so clear a pattern, but the overall trend has also been down. This is happening at a time when the American electorate is called upon to vote on more issues than ever before—ecological proposals, abortion, housing proposals, etc.

The history of the 20th century has been marked by the steady expansion of the franchise—woman suffrage, lowering of the voting age, abolition of the poll tax, passage of voting-rights laws—and yet the challenge to get the people to the polls remains.

Some maintain that people don't bother to vote when they are satisfied with things as they are—Americans never had it so good. Others claim the decline in voting is due to the growing disaffection of the have-nots and to the individual's feeling that his vote doesn't count for much, and that it has little impact upon government decisions.

Evidently, all citizens do not exert equal influence on the outcome of elections. Politicians have always preached that a citizen can augment his electoral influence by participating in political activity. Tammany's

George Washington Plunkitt started his political career by reporting to ward and district leaders that he controlled a bloc of votes—relatives, friends and acquaintances—that he could deliver on election day.

Again, since no politician can win without highly expensive mass-media exposure, the wealthy person who votes and contributes money to a candidate is in a position to have a greater effect upon the outcome of an election than a citizen who merely votes but gives no financial help. Big contributions probably have influenced more voters than any other single factor in political campaigns. U.S. Senator David Boren of Oklahoma states that "In close races, there is an overwhelming correlation between candidates with the most money and winning the election." Because this is so, most Americans favor laws limiting the PACs and the total amount of campaign expenditures.

Apparently, Franklin D. Roosevelt's assertion that "inside the polling booth every American man and woman stands as the equal of every other American man and woman" needs interpretation.

Surveys reveal that few voters have an intelligent understanding of issues or candidates. Some vote out of loyalty to a political party—a loyalty often transmitted almost genetically from generation to generation. Others cast their ballot, not for altruistic reasons, but purely on the basis of self-interest—"what's in it for me." Still others are one-issue voters—abortion, nuclear weaponry, etc. The most important factor determining a voter's preference, a recent *New York Times* poll discloses, is the candidate's character, experience, and integrity.

Whatever reasons Americans have for voting is less important than the fact that they have the right to do so. Refusal to exercise that right is, in a sense, a betrayal of the political freedom fought for by our forefathers.

Too many citizens are alienated from the political process. They feel helpless to influence the course of political events; they say, "It doesn't make any difference who wins; they're all crooks." By lumping all candidates together as equally bad, they absolve themselves from their obligations to vote.

But nonvoting is as much a political act as voting—a negative act. It demonstrates lack of confidence in democratic government. By refraining from exercising their franchise, citizens who complain about inequities in society and in the present system of elections and campaign financing lose the best means they have for eliminating those inequities. Without a show of all hands to decide which leaders and policies shall govern the community, the course of the ship of state becomes set by a few.

Spoils System and Political Cronyism
(*The Providence Journal Bulletin*, Saturday, August 9, 1986)

When businessman and gubernatorial candidate Bruce G. Sundlun blasted Governor Edward DiPrete for filling state offices with "Cranston cronies"—at last count, 32—he pinpointed a perennial political problem: How much does an elected official owe his supporters? Isn't it a law of political life for party leaders to take care of their own, look out for loyal followers, and reward their backers? Senator William L. Marcy's dictum of 1832 still holds sway: "To the victor belong the spoils."

Out-of-office Democrats vehemently denounce Republicans for paying off supporters with plum jobs. But returned to power, Democrats give tit-for-tat. Despite public attacks on each other's use of patronage, both parties would be uncomfortable working under any other system.

No ordeal is so expensive and complicated as getting elected. A candidate flounders without the help of supporters. Coping with "the agony and ignominy of raising money" is also a big headache. No matter how valiantly he tries to keep freedom of action, the office seeker, in the course of campaigning, becomes beholden to friends, financial backers, and trusted voters—often in that order. Obligations and commitments made on the hustings fall due the moment an elected official is sworn in. Death and taxes are no more inexorable than the quid pro quo of politics.

In the public mind, patronage is often linked to the shadowy, illegitimate side of government. But the practice of repaying political service with government jobs is credited with at least opening public posts to the common man and rescuing civil service from dominance by an elitist cadre. The record shows, however, that it also leads to inefficiency, corruption, and partisan favoritism.

Georgia governor Lester Maddox once said, "If you want to put politics first, then patronage is necessary. If you want to put government and efficiency first, it isn't."

A century ago, Americans got fed up with patronage's wasteful turnover of federal personnel, so they pressured legislators into creating the U.S. Civil Service Commission. States laggardly followed suit. Rhode Island enacted civil service laws—the so-called Merit System—in 1939.

That merit and ability should have priority over party affiliation is now accepted doctrine. Competitive open examinations largely determine competency for many government jobs. But heads of state and minor officials still control the distribution of numerous other choice positions.

The harshness of the spoils system becomes evident when long-term employees are fired just before pension eligibility. But discharged incumbents grudgingly accept such vae victis—ruthlessness as a hard fact of political life. Axing opponents is standard procedure. Governor DiPrete surprises friends and foes alike when he benignly keeps Democrats in office instead of bouncing them.

Cronyism is defined as partiality to associates—evidenced in the appointing of political hangers-on to office without due regard to their qualifications. But there is no cronyism, politicians insist, when qualified party faithful are chosen for jobs over non-party members.

American politics operates in a way that makes patronage a necessary and legitimate extension of the power of elected officials. Politicians use issues to get in; they use patronage to stay in. That public official who is inept at manipulating patronage is a poor administrator. Indeed, party control over patronage often stands as a reliable index of party discipline and party strength.

Defenders of clientelism (bestowing favors on henchmen) contend it is more humane than meritocracy, because individuals are rewarded not solely on merit, but for years of service or personal loyalty. The major hazard, however, is not that patronage builds personal empires or private fortunes, but that it encourages mediocrity and tempts public officials to compromise public interest for private gain or to sacrifice larger communal interest for pork-barrel wants of particular constituencies.

Without rewards, political power languishes. To consolidate their position, even lower-strata political leaders need to have a say in assigning the lesser favors. Rewards might be non-material, like being singled out in a crowd by the governor, or getting appointed to an unsalaried post, or to an executive commission; or more tangible, like franchises, legal fees, architect's commissions, contractor's jobs, transportation posts, judgeships, etc. Receiving favors binds citizens closer to government; it also obligates them to politicians, thereby diminishing their independence and objectivity.

Nothing makes voters lose confidence in political leaders, and eventually in government itself, than the conviction that politicians work chiefly for themselves and their followers rather than for the people at large.

Reformers who would change society—ways large and small—will learn more by studying the patronage network than from any political rhetoric. Strangely, patronage reveals that cooperation, not conflict, plays a greater role in political life. Indeed, the spoils system can be used either to foster social progress or preserve the *status quo*. Politics gets a bad name, however, because history conditions Americans to connect patronage with partisanship and corruption. Citizens suspect that in the long run the spoils system is dysfunctional, unhealthy, and demeaning to public service.

Politics and Ethics in an Imperfect World
(*The Cowl*, November 13, 1986)

Americans are proud of the high ethical principles that motivated the founders of our nation. But they wonder if those principles always inspire U.S. foreign and domestic policy or have, in fact, been betrayed. Before implementing policy, do government officials first ask, "Does this action jibe with our ethical ideals?" There is a tendency in America to separate practical politics from moral principles. We are told, for instance, that traditional consequences of right and wrong are null and void in the amoral jungle which characterizes international relations.

Inured to political corruption by spy movies and daily scandals, Americans don't get too wrought up over the fact that agencies like the CIA and FBI occasionally use immoral means to achieve morally good objectives. We vindicate our behavior by claiming: "Our enemies do it, why shouldn't we?" So our political leaders, finally scrupulous about their personal conduct, often subscribe to what is probably the most persistent of all moral illusions: the ends-and-means error.

Knavish means, it is argued, are all right, provided that they achieve a politically good end. A specific good end—good politically, good morally—is set forth; then it is asserted that morally reprehensible means are justified because the end in view is so good.

Is this Machiavellian stratagem ultimately impractical, counter-productive, and self-defeating, or does it work? Work or not, it perverts political action, for when bad means are used to achieve a good end, almost inevitably the means become the end and the end becomes merely a means.

Take two examples, one non-controversial, because it's a dead one: the anti-Communism of Adolf Hitler. Anti-Communism is good—morally and politically. But Hitler's means? Could anyone justify them? Those means (illegal suppressions, kangaroo courts, concentration camps) became in time an end themselves; anti-Communism, which won support for Hitler, became merely a means to achieve power for the Nazi politicians.

A controversial example: to combat Communism and protect American commercial interests (a good end), the U.S. supports despotic right-wing governments. A retired foreign service officer remarks that he is not surprised when people in Central America seek assistance from the U.S.S.R. "After all, they perceive, and rightly so, that the governments that are oppressing them are supported by the U.S." So they go to the only other superpower around, to "avoid American imperialism" and to be sustained by an ideology that effectively explains "their colonial oppression."

A crucial distinction must be made, at this point, between two principles of morality which seem akin and are often confused. The one, a good end does not justify evil means; the other, the proposition that under certain circumstances, when action is imperative, one has to choose the lesser of two evils, or, to put it another way, in politics one cannot be paralyzed by perfectionism.

Politics is the art of the possible, not the science of the ideal. Politicians seldom have a choice between black and white. Sometimes their choice is between two shades of gray; rarely, if ever, is there a clear choice between the wholly right and the wholly wrong—between good and evil. Neophyte politicians learn early that making political decisions involves almost a constant round of choosing lesser evils.

Prudence may require the toleration of a measure of evil in order to prevent something worse, or to save the limited good. The principle of double effect is here involved. It is the good effect, limited though it may be, which is willed and desired, not the evil which must be tolerated. Prudence may dictate a decision to let the cockle grow with the wheat, and not to over-drive the flock lest all fall by the wayside.

Jeane J. Kirkpatrick, former ambassador to the United Nations, now suggests that the U.S. can't do everything everywhere, but has to choose between what can and what cannot be done. In the imperfect world in which we live, in political life, one has to be satisfied with limited goals, possible goals.

When one set of goals is reached, there is an opportunity to move ahead in the direction of the ideal. But an all-or-nothing demand usually ends up with the nothing triumphant.

Avowedly optimistic, Americans like to think that moral ideals can be translated into political objectives with one magnificent sweep. They abhor settling for limited goals and wonder why abstract absolutes—truth, justice, peace—cannot be transformed into concrete political realities.

This is impossible for two reasons: (1) we live in an imperfect world of imperfect people (theologians contend that Original Sin remains a constant factor in all political considerations); (2) of its very nature, the political order must be relative. It admits only of the politically possible—what, given such-and-such circumstances, can be done; not what ideally should be done. Ideal circumstances practically never exist.

The fact that politics involves compromise and choices involving lesser evils and limited goals is no excuse for adopting a "to-hell-with-politics" aloofness. The person who is too good for politics is too good for his fellow man—and considerably more pure than anyone on this earth has a right to be.

Public Service and Ethics in Government
(*Rhode Island Medical Journal*, August 1976)

No individual in these United States can hold himself aloof from government. We are all deeply involved in it and are affected by its processes, whether we realize it or not. If you are a student or teacher, an employer or an employee, if you get a ticket for parking or speeding, if you fill out an income tax blank, you are involved with government. Every time you see policemen or firemen in operation, or see a school, you are watching government in action. I cannot think of any human activity in our modern society where the impact of government is not felt. Government is all around you. It fairly cries for conscientious, honest, reliable, and efficient workers. Unfortunately, far too many people are indifferent to government or are merely critical of its operation. They, themselves, do not want to get involved.

That is why college students should seriously consider becoming involved in government as a possible career choice. With their particular combination of talents and training, college graduates should be able to qualify as competent officials or employees. Indeed, in a very real sense, government service is a "calling" to service to your fellow man, and Dr. Albert Schweitzer, famed medical missionary and theologian, once said: "I don't know what your destiny will be, but one thing I know: The only ones among you who will be really happy are those who have sought and found how to serve."

Good government is absolutely essential for the peace and order of our land. Someone has to do it. Someone has to shoulder responsibility for running our country. Chaos results if there is no one governing.

The Lord Jesus Christ bears witness to the importance of government and government service. He said: "Whose is the coin of tribute?... Render unto Caesar the things that are Caesar's." He went so far as to choose a government official, one of the despised tax collectors, as the apostle who become St. Matthew. He, himself, ate with the so-called Publicans, while others scorned to associate with those who were identified in government service.

So, my message to you is simple and straightforward: Government service is a high and noble calling. But if you enter it for unsound reasons: the security of civil service, the fringe benefits, or because you think the pay scale generous, then you are bound to be disappointed. No honest person ever got rich from serving government. Indeed, even the obvious rewards are balanced by hidden burdens. Frustration, ignored achievement, bureaucratic in-fighting, overwork, thoughtless superiors, jealous co-workers, insensitive legislatures, a sometimes hostile press, an often unsympathetic public—these are the lot of public servants everywhere to some degree.

Today, as never before, there is a premium on good government. The efficient running of a nation or state depends upon the quality of the key men or women in each area of policy decision and operations. Even inadequate laws or regulations administered by skilled and sensitive public servants can often do more to decrease suffering or increase happiness than the best of laws carried out by incompetent, mediocre, and unimaginative officials.

We cannot legislate mediocrity out of existence. And mediocrity in government is an expensive luxury. In federal, state, and local government, it is a shackle on progress. The long-run cost is a pall of defeatism, narrow-mindedness, pettiness, and a focus on what has happened, not on what can happen. But for this nation, in this period of history, mediocrity is not merely expensive; it could be lethal. Indeed, government is like an iceberg. Only its top is visible. The quality of the operation of government depends on the people who actively work beneath the surface, as it were, in the day-to-day operation of it.

We Americans have always boasted that ours is a government of laws and not of men. It is clear, however, that our laws will be no better than the men who will enact and administer them. I hesitate to use the word "bureaucrat," because of its pejorative connotation; it raises emotional hackles. No alert young man or woman would ever want to become a "bureaucrat." That is because we still go by Webster's old definition of a bureaucrat as an "official of a bureau, especially one pursuing a narrow and arbitrary routine." But time has passed this definition by. This nation, this state, this community—all owe an incalculable debt to its good bureaucrats. There cannot be good government in a complex society without a good bureaucracy.

Unfortunately, the creation of a good bureaucracy, which is merely another way of labeling professionalism in public affairs, has not been a natural by-product of our own history. Unlike some countries, Great Britain, for example, we have not been able to establish traditions and prestige symbols of public or civil service which would attract the ablest of our young people—or if they are outstanding, they do not stay long in government service. This constant turnover of competent, top-drawer personnel points up the fact that public service presents a tarnished image to the cream of the rising generation; otherwise it would stand at the top of the catalog of careers to which bright young men and women are attracted.

Excellence of brains and talent is as necessary at every level of public service as it is in private enterprise. The challenge of making American democracy work, and for "work" you may substitute "survive," falls no less on the city mayor or manager than on a senator or a secretary of state, on a planner in the smallest city or a zoning official in the smallest town, and on a state voting official no less than on drafters of treaties and molders of foreign policy.

But who will deny that Vice President Agnew's double-dealings, Watergate, and other shenanigans by public officials have placed government service under a smog of suspicion and cynicism? Exposures of unsavory trickery in government contracts, bribery of officials, and other forms of financial corruption have caused loss of respect for government service. Sixty years ago Boss Plunkitt of Tammany Hall wrote of "honest graft," and summarized his autobiography in the wonderfully succinct observation: "I seen my opportunities and I took 'em." Inside knowledge of future official action—the location of a bridge or new highway, or the construction of a public building—offers the "opportunities" that Plunkitt and his many imitators exploit. When you think of the modern American city, with its mobile population, bridge and road building, public schools, public housing, civic centers, and other large undertakings, the pecuniary stakes are enormous—and the political machine is the focus of power to distribute the plums. Indeed, even if the party in power is unusually enlightened, the very nature of the system—based on rewarding political loyalty and seniority—tends to corrupt civil administration. Those areas of government service which come under the patronage system are most open to abuse. In the past, we have had more than our share of "five percenters" and other influence peddlers, and their sordid activity has contributed to the low esteem in which government service is held.

But the dishonesty of public servants reflects not only upon the quality of their personal morality but also upon the general level of morality prevailing in the United States. In a democracy where public officials move from private life into public office and back again, there is a carry-over of influence and of attitude and, certainly, a reflection in public office of the general level of morality held to or sustained in private life. Standards observed and accepted by the people will be reflected in some measure in the conduct of the officials of the country.

In this time of rapid change, people are paralyzed by a neurosis of bewilderment concerning values and their application in daily living; they are lacking a refined sense of right and wrong. A moral relativism seems to have replaced the moral certitudes of the past. "Who am I to say what's right and wrong?" is a remark one often hears. A new code of American ethics seems to be evolving in which absolute standards give way to an "it depends" mentality. Would you fake an insurance claim? "It depends on the amount," says a motorist. Would you return a lost wallet? "It depends who owned it," says the store clerk. It is wrong to cheat in school? "It depends," says the student. Would you take a bribe or graft? "It depends," says a government official, "on whether it is an accepted practice."

It is significant that, in almost every case in which an accused public official has attempted to defend himself, he has argued that his actions were fully within the bounds of accepted practices in the business world or the professional group to which he belonged. Vice President Spiro Agnew said he was innocent because he went along with the system; the fictional Frank Serpico, in a movie by that name, got nowhere in his many attempts to buck the system. People in the system go along because "that's the way you get things done," or because "no government official can live in the style expected of him on the salary they pay him."

Moreover, it is worth noting that the law's reach is necessarily limited, and much of the most dangerous and destructive corruption of our times is entirely legal. The law itself may be used to reap enormous rewards at public expense, as through subsidies, write-offs, or manipulation of the tax structure. The time, fees, and favors of minor officials are trivial in comparison to the special-interest legislation of such large dimensions. As the old English rhyme has it:

> *The law locks up both man and woman*
> *Who steals the goose from off the Common,*
> *Yet turns the greater felon loose*
> *Who steals the Common from the goose.*

Perhaps the transcending malady of our day is the plague of compromise-with-principle. It produces the equivocal man—a strange creation who stalks the land in growing numbers. For the equivocal man, integrity becomes a word of relative meanings. Things that his forebears would never have condoned come easier to rationalize and explain away. Codes of personal conduct become "anything goes" so long as you can get away with it. This deterioration boils out into open sores when "payola" schemes are brought to light, government officials are indicted for frauds, and general crime statistics soar. In such an atmosphere, the no-compromise-with-evil spirit of our forefathers grows dimmer.

A quarter of a century ago, the anthropologist Ruth Benedict speculated that the United States was ceasing to be a "guilt culture" (one in which control of wrongdoing is self-imposed by means of conscience) and becoming instead a "shame culture" (one in which it is externally imposed by means of public humiliation or punishment, as in various Eastern cultures). In other words, there seems to be a shift of some kind in the approved technique by which American society enforces honesty. Apparently, when dishonesty is prevalent, it becomes much easier to live with a bad conscience; so external techniques of control, rather than internal ones, have to take over. The government, to protect itself, has to take prompt action; it has to create an atmosphere showing that Big Brother is alert, that Uncle Sam cares, and that government is watching. When citizens lack internal controls, government usually steps in and establishes careful external controls over citizens and lets them know that if they violate them, they will be publicly shamed and thrown in jail. Morality, then, becomes enforced from the outside rather than springing from the inside—from conscience. Freedom becomes thereby restricted.

Corruption in high places is not new. Moses admonished the judges of Israel not to be respecters of persons in judgment but to hear "the small as well as the great." He said, "A gift blindeth the wise and perverteth the words of the righteous." Later, the Lord, speaking through the prophet Micah, denounces the house of Israel because "the heads thereof judge for reward, and the priests thereof teach for hire, and the prophets thereof divine for money." But corruption in government, wherever found—in the higher or lower echelon—discourages youth from seeking jobs in public service.

History has shown that a nation will preserve those virtues and values that it honors. The individual, likewise, preserves and honors the values to which he is committed. If you enter government service, you will have the privilege of helping to shape and mold the policy and destiny of the state and nation. According to the extent of the authority of your office, you will thereby be afforded the opportunity of putting into effect your own sense of values, of influencing the moral tone of government, and of forming the mind and will of the people.

American philosopher-poet Ralph Waldo Emerson has said that what we are speaks louder than what we say. This thought has special meaning in public office, for it is true that we leave the imprint of what we are upon everything we do. Government can only preserve the values and virtues that we honor. Just as the honest businessman can no more justify cheating by saying, "This is business," the honest government employee, regardless of the scope of his responsibility, cannot deprive the government of honest ethical service simply by saying, "This is the inevitable way our government works." If the moral level of public service is low, there is an obligation on the part of every government official to transform it by eliminating whatever pushes man toward evil and by doing away with those conditions which encourage or make it easier for him to respond by actions which are morally objectionable and wrong.

When one is trying to encourage people to enter government service, there is a tendency to speak more frequently about the prestige and rewards which may be attached to the office rather than its inherent burdens and responsibilities. The responsibility aspects of public office should remind the student of history of the remarks of Claudius, a great Roman emperor, who in appointing public officials would say: "Do not thank me, for I do you no favor but call upon you to share with me the burdens of government, and it is I who thank you, if you fulfill your duty well." Claudius thereby gave clear expression to the thought, and indeed to the ideal, that public office is not merely an honor to be cherished but a trust to be faithfully discharged. May you think of government service in this fashion.

The Kind of Leadership We Deserve
(*The Providence Journal-Bulletin*, November 15, 1986)

It's a good time now, with the hullabaloo of electioneering behind us, to re-examine the quality and purpose of political leadership and the standards by which the citizenry may judge them.

Americans have always harbored a great mistrust of government in general and politicians in particular. Yet we have never hesitated to use the tools of government to expand and develop opportunity and to protect liberty and freedom of action.

How well we use the tools of government depends upon the people we elect to public office everywhere. It is they who finally decide if organized society shall meet the needs of the "public domain." In a very real sense, the politicians run the country.

While citizens often mistrust elected officials, at times justifiably, their failure to see the importance of elective leadership and the manner by which it assumes its responsibilities can have unfortunate consequences.

Ours is not a panic-stricken nation. Nor are we on the verge of decline and collapse. Evidence is accumulating, however, that in our politics we have seemingly lost the way.

We are besieged by armies of would-be office holders, many of whom believe the object of political life ends with the election itself. The idea nowadays is to possess and hold office. Governing is a mere corollary.

Electioneering, therefore, is constant and chronic. No sooner is a person elected to an important post than we begin debate as to who should succeed him. Candidates spend months, even years, running for public office. As a result, they and government are continually distracted from the task of governing.

In the first instance, we are governed by people who necessarily spend most of their energies getting themselves elected, selling themselves like merchandise, and who are apt to devote their time that is not expended in that effort to exercising power for its own value.

We have allowed officials at every level to preoccupy themselves with the form of government, as distinguished from its substance. Through television, we are engulfed by the high-flown, synthetic rhetoric of politicians whose words are seldom translated into equivalent deeds. Again and again we elect to office people whose concept of administering government is to dash about giving speeches, glad-handing, and being hail-fellow-well-met. Creative government suffers.

Public officials appear to be caught up in the most superficial day-to-day events—events which spark interest precisely because they have just happened. Consequently, we are aroused by passing events, if not overwhelmed by them. Deep-seated problems continue—festering and unresolved poverty, pollution, the economy, housing, etc.

Legal and social scholar Charles Reich and civil rights lawyer Burke Marshall contend that "What we really have to confront is the fact that we are governed by people who do not know what they are doing, who lack the knowledge and time to understand how a society works, what it needs, what means might be taken to ensure survival."

So citizens are compelled to raise anew the questions of who should exercise public trust. What kind of people do we want running our cities, our state, the nation? What values should men and women bring to public life? Do we want or need saintly or charismatic leaders? Or should we elect persons of doctrine, of principle, and of purpose? Who are the people who dream the dreams and see the vision of a better country and a better world?

It is self-evident that the politician should be a person of character; that he or she be honest; that his or her private life can withstand the glare of public scrutiny. We need not, moreover, engage in the age-old debate of whether officials' first obligation is to their constituency or the community. They have an obligation to both.

In 1952, Democratic presidential candidate Adlai Stevenson said, "It is the governing that is the acid, final test." Therein lies the first rule, to wit: people should be elected to public office who are intent upon the very process of governing itself. Governor Thomas Dewey of New York once said, "The people did not elect me their governor to cut ribbons at fairs, to open highways, and to give speeches. I was primarily elected to administer the state of government."

Citizens must demand of those seeking office an absolute willingness to concentrate on the substance, the administration, and the business of government; otherwise, statecraft degenerates into a "politics of triviality."

Admittedly, it is hard to tell what a person will do, once in office. In measuring his or her intent, we should ask, "Does this candidate have a program?" Does he have a set of reachable, worthwhile goals?"

John F. Kennedy observed, "We get the kind of political leadership, be it good or bad, that we demand and deserve." Or, as poet Ogden Nash puts it:

Wherever decent intelligent people get together
They talk about politicians as about bad weather,

*But they are always too decent to go into politics
themselves and too intelligent even to go to the polls,
So I hope the kind of politicians they get will have no
mercy on their pocketbooks or souls.*

Public Behavior of Private Officials
(*The Cowl*, February 7, 1990)

At one time, Massachusetts Congressman Barney Frank's misdeed with a male prostitute would have evoked outcries of righteous indignation rather than encouraging applause and cheers as he paraded in Fall River—"We're all for you Barney . . . Hang in there, Barney." This favorable reaction heralds a change in the public's attitude toward so-called sexual deviance.

It also raises some serious questions. When should the private life of public officials become the matter of public concern? When may public officials claim that their private lives are none of the public's business? Former Massachusetts senator Edward Brooke, while in the throes of a divorce, complained that the public had no right to intrude into "every bureau drawer, every clothes closet, every item in my checkbook, every intimate detail in my personal life."

In the past, members of Congress usually connived at the sexual improprieties of their colleagues, and, even when they did not, the press rarely reported them. But since the summer of 1976, the public has been treated to an orgy of sex exposés of political leaders. Some episodes involved misuse of public funds and conflict of interest; others involved abuse of office and violations of the law.

When misbehavior was not illegal, the official sometimes argued that it was caused not by lack of integrity, but by weakness, bad judgment, or naiveté, and should not distract voters from more substantial issues of government or from the politician's history of accomplishment. Thus citizens are left to judge whether their leader's misdeed lessens his effectiveness or interferes with his duties, or whether in the long run, his political achievements redeem—or out-weigh—his sexual misconduct or homosexual lifestyle.

In some cultures, moral expectations about a leader's conduct may differ gently from what Americans look for. Speaking of politics in Indonesia, J. D. Legge observes that its first president Sukarno's "massive preoccupation with sex was a matter of admiration rather than disapproval—a demonstration, perhaps, of Sukarno's continuing virility and thus of his political potency as well."

But in America, individual virtue has always been considered crucial in maintaining responsive and legitimate government. Voters expect their political leaders to observe higher standards of personal morality than expressed in the least common denominator of society's standards. It is impossible to isolate effects of character from those of law and government structure, and society has always supported sanctions against the misbehavior of leaders.

Officials, by the example of their own private lives, can have an effect for good or ill on the way citizens conduct their personal lives. Public figures who deal courageously with personal difficulties—wayward offspring, crumbling marriages, alcoholism, drug addiction, breast cancer, or death of a loved one—not only excite admiration but invite imitation.

In 1987, Barney Frank came out of the gay closet. He was still re-elected despite his public declaration of homosexuality. But, in 1964, when Walter Jenkins, an aide to President Johnson, was charged with homosexual activity in the men's room of a Washington YMCA, the incident received wide publicity and Jenkins promptly resigned.

Frank is now undecided about running for a sixth congressional term. His decision will hinge on the public's reaction—whether voters consider his sexual preferences to be no one else's business and whether the Democratic Party feels he is too great a risk or liability.

There is a moral ambiguity in the Frank case. Acts of fornication, adultery, and homosexuality are commonly classed as acts of private morality which do not directly affect an individual's ability to do a job. At the same time, they indirectly undermine citizens' confidence in elected officials, run counter to traditional morality, and increase the possibility of blackmail. The controversy over the alleged use of marijuana and other drugs by members of the White House staff illustrates the interplay between legal, moral, and political considerations in this area.

Not long ago, the courts upheld the dismissal of a homosexual public employee because he publicly pursued an "activist role in implementing his unconventional beliefs." On the other hand, they reinstated a fired employee because he did not "openly flaunt" his homosexuality. Yet some cities and states have enacted laws guaranteeing rights of job protection to homosexuals. Again, most states have abolished sodomy statutes, and where they still exist, they are rarely enforced.

All this adds up to a greater legal toleration of homosexuality. Notwithstanding, the thesis "it's his own private business" is basically spurious. A strictly private morality is impossible, if that term signifies personal behavior having no effect on the general society. Just as low standards in personal hygiene can endanger public health, so low standards in private morals can endanger public welfare. All behavior, especially the conduct of political leaders, contributes to the creation of a moral climate in which children are raised and in which citizens carry out their daily life and business.

No Cure for Bureaucracy
(*The Providence Sunday Journal*, August 8, 1993)

The Providence City Council a while back chided Mayor Vincent A. Cianci Jr. for appointing a political crony to a mid-level administrative post it deemed superfluous.

Overstaffing, which leads to a bloated bureaucracy, weakens an organization to the point of unmanageability. Alexis de Tocqueville, more than 150 years ago, alerted Americans to this. "What is to be feared," he wrote, "is not a perverse individual, and not a maddened mob—it is a bureaucratic tyranny for which no one person would stand responsible."

Big government, with its network of departments, its overlapping jurisdictions, its duplication of services, its gobbledygook regulations, its endless red tape, and its tendency to pass the buck, especially irritates and frustrates citizens. The 1984 Grace Commission Report reveals that almost every echelon of the federal government is guilty of padding its personnel. The fact that private industry can perform the same non-combat tasks as the military with one-third the number of workers only confirms what civilians already suspect.

A Rhode Island politician candidly acknowledged that forty percent of all state jobs could be abolished without risking loss of service. Cities, bankrupted by a mushrooming bureaucracy, now farm out many services to the private sector. School systems and institutions of higher learning are prime examples of bureaucracy unchecked. Administrators, enlarging their fiefdoms, add new departments, endow minor functionaries with highfalutin titles, and up the ratio of chiefs to Indians. Unions, too, have waxed big and fat, and with their Big Brother mentality, have shown little compunction about saddling employers with drones, drudges, and featherbedders.

Churches, alarmed by dwindling flocks, a shortage of vocations, and a secularized social climate, are seeking solutions in bureaucratic activism. Talk replaces apostolic action. Committees, conferences, seminars, and protracted conventions serve to give the impression that churches are really coping with a decentralized society.

Ralph Waldo Emerson said, "Once we had wooden chalices and golden priests; now we have golden chalices and wooden priests." An institution thrives on ardor and conviction. As its assets grow and its bureaucracy expands, the ardor wanes. The organization gets bigger; the spirit thins out.

Jolly Pope John XXIII was asked how many people were working at the Vatican. He quipped, "About half." A Vatican worker posed this question: "Holy Father, what should we do if Jesus Christ suddenly appears in our midst?" The roly-poly pontiff replied, "Look busy."

"Looking busy," twiddling thumbs, shuffling papers, juggling figures, pushing buttons, and meetings, meetings, and more meetings are what bureaucrats do best. But who is responsible? In government bureaucracies, it is hard to find the single person who is clearly identified with any significant decision of public policy. Because there is no clear allotment of personal authority, there is no allotment of personal responsibility; and personal responsibility is what has made America progress so rapidly.

But good governmental bureaucracy does exist. It signifies recruitment to public service based not on nepotism, cronyism, or political favoritism but on formal qualifications (diplomas, university degrees, examinations). It implies stability and continuity—a career, a life's work. It includes, moreover, a system of promotion based on seniority and achievement.

This kind of professionalism in public affairs has not marked American history. Unlike some countries—Britain, for example—the United States has never been successful in establishing traditions and prestige associated with government service—symbols of public and civil service that would attract the ablest of youth. And, if they are outstanding, American public servants do not tend to stay long in that sector. A big reason for this constant turnover of competent, top-drawer personnel lies in the tarnished image that public service presents to the cream of the rising generation.

But who has the cure for the ponderous inertia of entrenched bureaucracy? King Solomon himself would be stumped at determining the number of hands required to complete any given governmental task. Bureaucratic enlargement feeds on itself—more people involved, more internal correspondence, more staff meetings, more levels of authority, and more offices to be consulted before anyone can decide anything. The bureaucratic coating around government seems to grow thicker and thicker; and citizens feel more alienated from the seats of power.

The overstaffing in government is insoluble, because as the administrative structure grows, so does the number of persons who have a stake in it and an interest in its perpetuation. Wholesale firing is out the question. It would hurt a host of innocent people who are not at fault for being employed where they are not really needed. Nor are these people without means of self-defense, for their numbers are such that, in themselves, they constitute an appreciable electoral force, and the very politicians who got them their jobs would fight for their retention.

Historian George F. Kennan, former U.S. ambassador to the Soviet Union, believes that, even though burgeoning bureaucratic growth saps the strength of a nation, no cure is possible. Even if it were, the application of the cure would be more painful than the disease. We must learn, he says, "to see the governmental apparatus as largely helpless in the throes of this bureaucratic elephantiasis, and handicapped, accordingly, in its ability to be to the ordinary citizen all that government, in normal conditions, could and should be."

(4)
Ethics and Morals

Be Smart: Be Good: Be Wise
(*The Providence Sunday Journal*, January 30, 1994)

"Be good, sweet maid, and let who can be clever," sings the poet. But nowadays, a girl, to be good, needs to be clever. Not that a high I.Q. or a degree in higher education produces a higher type of moral behavior.

> *There was a young lady from Kent*
> *Who said she knew what it meant*
> *When men took her to dine,*
> *Gave her cocktails and wine;*
> *She knew what it meant*
> *But she went.*

Knowing the Golden Rule is no guarantee that a person will "do unto others." The philanthropist who bestowed twenty million dollars upon Harvard Business School to establish a program in ethics was beguiled by the hope that teaching morals will prevent immoral conduct—insider trading scandals, shady business deals, etc.

But the dissemination of knowledge does not ensure its transformation into moral wisdom. Between theory and practice, between the understanding of a principle and its application, between intention and execution, yawns a wide gap. Lurking in this gap are pride, prejudice, bad example, dissolute lifestyle, ignorance, and a host of disordered emotions—all of which make living righteously rather difficult.

Philosopher Mortimer Adler and educator Robert Hutchins adamantly insisted that students will never be made good by university instruction alone. This cannot be done; first, because the university, in the limited time at its disposal, cannot cope with the impact of the rest of society, especially peer pressure and the media of mass communication.

Second, the university must fail because of the nature of the task: The moral virtues are habits, and habits are formed by acts. "We can have no assurance," says Hutchins, "that courses in elementary, intermediate, and advanced goodness will be followed by good acts."

And third, the very nature of the student makes this objective unattainable. To be good involves being practically wise or prudent, and this requires more experience and reflection than is characteristic of most college students.

Furthermore, because man is animal as well as rational, true morality without religion is unlikely. The practice of virtue, now or in the future, cannot be guaranteed merely by the demonstration of its reasonableness. Humans, simply because they are humans, are unlikely to find within themselves the power that can bring the good life to pass.

Cardinal Newman eloquently voices this same idea: "Quarry the granite rock with razors, or moor the vessel with a thread of silk; then may you hope with such keen and delicate instruments as human knowledge and human reason to contend against those giants, the passion and the pride of man."

Not books and syllogisms but home training and daily do-gooding keep people on the straight and narrow. Prudence, practice, and persistence produce probity. Experience in virtuous living generates a moral expertise that can never be gotten from tomes or classroom. How often one meets people who may not be adept in explaining the ins and outs of the Ten Commandments but who are exemplary in living them. On the other hand, history abounds with examples of the famous who were mental giants but moral pygmies. Aristotle observes that the bright may be more effectively vicious than the stupid. A sharp mind can devise more ingenious ways of committing evil.

Nevertheless, if character is "caught, not taught," and if college cannot provide all the life experiences required for the full flowering of the moral virtues, it can do something. Harvard's Derek Bok states: "Ethics courses cannot turn scoundrels into virtuous human beings, but they can teach students to be more rigorous in their thinking about moral dilemmas, and they can counteract the moral relativism that leads students to believe that morality is merely a matter of opinion beyond reasoned arguments."

Moreover, the whole texture of a Catholic college and the campus atmosphere ought to encourage honorable conduct. Examples of upright living are provided by the faculty. Opportunities to participate in the devotional and sacramental life of the Church abound. The playing field, the classroom, and social and extracurricular functions afford occasions for practicing virtue. Most of all, the mental habituation acquired in the study of sacred theology should induce students to apply this wisdom to their own personal lives.

Finally, no student can get very far in learning without an orderly life. Study, writing, and research mix poorly with carousing, wenching, and winebibbing. Booze and books are incompatible companions, contrary to Oliver Goldsmith's quatrain:

> *Let schoolmasters puzzle their brain*
> *With grammar and nonsense and learning;*
> *Good liquor, I stoutly maintain,*
> *Gives genius a better discerning.*

Aquinas notes that the emotional agitation and bodily disturbances generated by lust, gluttony, insobriety, and anger are deadly foes of learning. They bind and blind the mind, absorb and exhaust attention, and focus on sensual pleasures to the disregard of intellectual delights. The unbridled life of the libertine and the disciplined regimen of the scholar are antipodes apart. Disordered living can only result in haphazard learning. Scholarship demands wholehearted commitment.

The Evanescence of Honor
(*The Cowl*, November 5, 1986)

The concept of honor is extolled in literature, iterated or reiterated in classrooms, and praised in public halls. Yet just recently a highly respected institution of higher learning dropped its honor system, leaving only a handful of American colleges with honor codes.

Does this reflect the moral breakdown of our times? In a recent survey of 1,000 high-school students, seventy percent said they saw nothing wrong in cheating, corroborating the old saw that in the "honor system," teachers have the honor and students the system.

Has the notion of honor itself become just a bit archaic? In order to flourish, honor needs a congenial climate, something like the age of chivalry or the postbellum South. While every epoch has high-principled persons who live by honor, it seems to flourish best where a homogeneity of values prevails. The founders of this nation, for instance, pledged their lives, their fortunes, and their "sacred honor" in support of the Declaration of Independence.

Leaders of the American Revolution, differing vastly in background, saw eye to eye in what they regarded as the components of virtue. Aristocrats and commoners, plantation owners and city dwellers, members of diverse churches and varying professions, all agreed upon the code of conduct that should guide one's life. Principle held primacy over expediency, veracity over mendacity, the immaterial over the material. Religion rated highly in our forefathers' personal and political philosophy.

"Confirm your soul in self-control," the hymn to America commanded. "A good name is better than riches," children were taught. "Honor is more precious than life," was an apothegm repeated in textbooks.

An elite group in society based their behavior on the principle of *noblesse oblige*, an elite sometimes of blood and wealth, but more frequently of character, refinement, and education. The fact that the "many" were often not conscious of such obligations served to make these obligations all the more binding on the elite.

Can honor survive in American society? With our pluralistic values, the gulf between our various specialized educations, our deep rut of materialism, and our veneration for the common man, American democracy would seem to have effectively destroyed the historic buttresses of the old idea of honor.

Good riddance, some say. The walls, which made honor the preserve of an elite, deserved to be pulled down. Now we can develop a new democratic code. The rising generations of an egalitarian society can help create a new kind of chivalry, a twentieth-century code of the nobility of the common man. At some happy, future date, everyone with a Social Security number will automatically evolve into the knightly gentleman or lady of honor.

Utopian? Perhaps. But it is a bit humiliating to have to admit that our democratic world cannot retain the best values of the societies it replaces.

If this ideal of honor is ever again to replace the lynx-eyed proctor in our examination halls, we shall have to lay a solid foundation for its democratic acceptance by the students of our time. Somewhere we must find democratic substitutes for the aristocratic ideas that were once its underpinning.

First, students need to have a common ground plan of values. The dignity of the individual person is a good starting point, but it will not be enough for them to hear speeches about this dignity at commencement exercises. Very early in their careers as students they will need to be taught the reasons which validate that dignity: their common relationship as children of God, the fearful responsibilities of free will, the meaning of sin, and the relationship of obedience, truth, and justice to questions of personal integrity.

Second, we must face the fact that many students view college as a kind of placement office that opens doors to the big bucks of business and industry. In this context, a student may regard cheating in exams in much the same way as he expects to regard business practices that give him an edge over rivals in a highly competitive society. He will argue that if everyone is doing it, it can't be wrong. Democratic society has a duty to show its youth that questions of personal morality are not determined by majority vote.

Finally, youth must be convinced that the modern world desperately needs a new kind of elite—not an aristocracy of blood, money, power, brains, or breeding, but an elite of men and women of good will everywhere in this world. We might think of this elite as a natural, moral community with no frontiers, no color bars, no language barriers. As a purely human being, it would be no substitute for religion, and yet it might serve as a propaedeutic to the love of God. As its circle widens, it will strengthen the democratic ideals that helped produce it.

The revived interest in character training in our schools is an encouraging sign that honor may yet return to its esteemed role in the life of civilized people.

Has Greed Come to Define the New American Spirit?
(*The Providence Visitor*, August 11, 2005)

"Financier J. P. Morgan once remarked, "Diogenes would have been hard put to find an honest man in Wall Street." The indictment of five promising, bright, young Wall Street professionals charged with using confidential information for personal profit lends credence to Morgan's observation. These neophytes on the fast track of the stock exchange could be the latest casualties of the American worship of the Bitch Goddess Success.

Stealing, with or without *finesse*, has dogged mankind from time immemorial. However, in the select and hectic atmosphere of buying and selling stocks, stealing has been elevated to the nth degree of sophistication. Indeed, the Wall Street *milieu* is so complicated, and techniques so refined, that the thief is rarely detected by ordinary people. Strangely, the thief finds it difficult to recognize himself for what he is. One stock trader complains, "It's more difficult to know what is right than it is to do it."

Only those who know their ethics and their way around the competitive jungle of commerce are able to recognize the offender and the offense.

One defendant, a young lawyer-turned-arbitrager, insists he did not know what he was doing was wrong. At times, wrongdoing can result more from a lack of a clear ethical code than from malice forethought. Yet when did ignorance ever excuse? The law does not punish or exempt because of motivation. Innocent motives, along with other considerations, may influence the degree of punishment but not the punishability of an act.

What about the value systems of these young men? Did their schools let them down? Law school dean Murray L. Schwartz bemoans the fact that most law faculty members are skeptics. Liberal ideology and notions of academic restraint tend "to preclude deliberate efforts to affect moral standards or values of law students," he said.

Educators argue that students are not born *de novo* from the forehead of a college or graduate school. They batten on the *ethos* of society at large and the special nurturing of family, television, school, church, or synagogue.

Schools can encourage students to reform and redirect habits and dispositions in the light of moral vision. To the extent that the *alma mater* fails to supply that moral vision, she ill-equips her graduates to withstand temptations of the *agora* and establish an order of priorities.

The major defendant, with degrees in law and graduate business, is not even interested in money, says his father. This characterizes many "yuppies" today. It marks a modification in the traditional search for success. While middle-class Americans still measure success in terms of riches, fame, and power (P. T. Barnum, after making a fortune, lectured frankly on "The Art of Money-Getting"), ambitious young careerists today are dedicated workaholics. They pour their energies into, and derive their deepest satisfactions from, their work. Executive recruiter Richard Cox says, "It's the thrill of the chase, keeping the scorecard, the feeling of having influence, being in the "know" and with the in-crowd, that counts most with the new breed."

Acutely status-conscious, the young professional revels in the corporate gamesmanship of the Big Apple and other big cities. Money and material possessions are prized as symbols of success and as a means of pursuing a lifestyle commensurate to his standing. He prefers to be envied more than respected. Acquisitiveness yields top place to vanity.

That these young men were probably naïve, that profiting from confidential inside information of coming mergers has long been a custom on Wall Street, that pressures of the marketplace can be overpowering—these facts might explain, if not excuse, the alleged misconduct of these talented young men whose very future is at stake.

Citizens become alarmed when reading about instances of base behavior in gifted youths of high promise. They fear it presages a shift in the moral standards that undergird society.

Traditionally, Americans view life as an adventure in achievement. Success involves attaining certain standards and obeying certain rules. These rules and standards are not devised by men; they may be thought of as devised by God or as inherent in the nature of things. Knowledge of these standards of right and wrong is easy to come by. The difficulty lies in applying standards to complex problems and ambiguous situations. It requires an instinct for virtue obtained only through practice.

The difference between the good and successful man who achieves these standards and the bad and unsuccessful man who does not is mainly a matter of moral effort and an exercise of willpower. Any good-willed person can reach an adequate standard of honesty, industry, decency, and consideration for others if he tries.

Americans have been raised on this philosophy of personal responsibility and concern for the community. Today, this system of ethical idealism is being challenged by a philosophy of radical individualism and an overweening preoccupation with self-fulfillment.

Honor and Cheating
(*The Providence Journal*, December 9, 1987)

"The sense of honor is of so fine and delicate a nature, that it is only to be met within minds which are naturally noble, or in such as have been cultivated by good examples, or a refined education."— Addison, *The Guardian*, No. 161.

The concept of honor is extolled in literature, iterated and reiterated in classrooms, and praised in public halls. Schools adopt honor creeds, print them in handbooks, or immortalize them in bronze. Everyone likes to be thought of as an honorable person. No one would admit to being unworthy of the trust and respect of his fellow man. And yet all but a few colleges and universities have abandoned the honor system.

Has honor today lost its meaning? Is it nothing but an archaic notion? Classroom cheating is now so widespread, it has become socially acceptable. In a recent survey of 1,000 college students and 25,000 high school students, over seventy percent declared they saw nothing wrong in cheating.

What causes cheating anyway? Poor classroom morale? Slovenly teaching? Sloppy proctoring? Or is it just plain laziness, fear, and a general low moral tone in the student body at large. Some feel it results inevitably from the overuse of objective examinations that overemphasize the regurgitation of facts rather than the ability to think logically and coherently.

But what is the mentality behind cheating, aside from the moral considerations that are obvious, serious, and of utmost importance in analyzing this problem? Why do students believe they have to cheat? What psychology motivates the cheater?

Two facets of personality are disclosed in cheating. First, in turning to others for academic salvation, the cheater asserts that they are proficient, competent, and able in comparison to himself, who is ignorant, inept, and inefficient. The cheater perceives himself as stupid while others are knowledgeable.

Second, the cheater betrays a perfectionist tendency. He says in action, if not in words, that he feels himself measured against standards which are, at best, unrealistic and overly strict, even though his classmates are measured by the same standards.

Contrary to what students think, the worst consequence of cheating is not "getting caught." Whether apprehended or not, the cheating student has "got caught" in a far more significant sense. He has got caught in cheating himself.

Nothing is quite so damaging to self-respect as a pessimistic estimation of one's self, and that is precisely what the cheater has.

His cheating testifies to his desire to be and to have the skills of another. It marks a defeat in his battle for personal dignity and integrity.

Moreover, the cheater displays a lack of self-confidence, and self-confidence is as necessary to pass exams as it is to win ballgames. The cheater believes he must be totally prepared in order to be competent at all. Short of having memorized his material word for word, he feels that he will most certainly fail. Any reliance on self to rephrase, interpret, or select from the given materials, or deviate from them in any way, is already to admit defeat.

The self-confidence that comes from being at least relatively prepared is totally lacking in the cheater. The more the cheater cheats, the more the habit patterns of self-distrust are reinforced, and all the more does self-contempt effectively block an accurate perception of the academic situation.

Indeed, disciplinary action only reinforces the cheater's conception of himself as hopelessly incompetent; it doubles the dearth or self-assurance and self-esteem that provoked cheating in the first place. The cheater loses the opportunity to take a chance on himself, and the punishment inflicted confirms his conviction of his own inferiority. The naïve notion that cheating is necessarily the path to a high or passing grade stays unchallenged; the overestimation of others, as against oneself, remains intact.

Nor does the cheater ever get the opportunity to know himself and to feel his own particular strengths and weaknesses. As a result, his self-reliance is undermined, and his sense of personal responsibility never develops as it should. That is why it is difficult for the cheater to reform. He is irresponsibly infantile. He lacks the courage and the confidence characteristic of the adult who has stretched his mind and knows its tensile strength.

Even if he lacks ability in a particular discipline, the cheater never discovers it; hence he never discovers his abilities either. The pleasure that grows as skill develops, and the satisfaction that comes from vigorous mental exercise, are something the cheater never experiences. He cannot take pride in his forte because he has never permitted himself to discover it. He believes that a student is totally defined by his grades, and failure in a course means failure as a person. Moreover, he cheats himself out of a helpful lesson in humility, which permits one, in turn, to accept personal ineptitude with equanimity and personal failings with tolerance.

Finally, the practical problem of "having to pass" remains unmet and unsolved. The cheater erroneously believes that the only solution to the problem of passing a course centers on a single alternative—cheating or not cheating—when the problem might be more efficiently, more safely, and more successfully solved by many other possible alternatives. For instance, he could ask for suggestions regarding improvement, do extra work, develop better study habits, and seek further instruction and suggestions from the instructor. All these methods are certainly better alternatives to cheating, and they allow a student to maintain his dignity, integrity, and self-respect.

Ethics in Business ... The Good & The Bad
(The Pawtucket Evening Times, May 20, 1990)

The businessman has helped raise the Western world to undreamed-of standards of living. In spite of this, he has never been esteemed highly. Countries have bowed down in adulation before a Genghis Khan or a Napoleon—the slaughterers and egoists of history—but those economic adventurers who upgraded the lot of the common man have been repaid for their pains with ingratitude and vilification.

The well-publicized troubles of top brass like Bert Lance and Bill Miller serve to confirm the public's low opinion of business magnates and offset any Rotary Club kind of effort to build up a more favorable image.

[Polls by] Gallup, Louis Harris, and Roper inform us that almost half the country's citizens believe businessmen have lower standards of honesty than Americans in general—even though the moguls of industry, the public feels, ought to be more delicately attuned to violations of the moral code than ordinary citizens.

Still, anybody who tries to apply universal principles of morality to concrete cases—cases enveloped in a maze of unpredictable circumstances and modifying variables—knows how tough it can be. Not only have ethical problems of businessmen become more complex in an increasingly complex society, but laws and customs varying from nation to nation, combined with conflicting regulations within our own country's governmental structure, have muddied ethical waters and ensnared unwary executives.

Most ethical problems in business require no more than a new application of well-established moral principles. For example, the traditional teaching on rights and obligations with respect to secret information can be applied more or less directly to today's business problems of industrial espionage and pirating of competitors' employees.

But more complicated problems yield an answer only after a grubby digging for relevant facts and a toilsome ferreting out of the ethical principles at issue. The businessman, contending at times with unscrupulous competitors, must hew to the line while dealing with all kinds of people in involved situations. The answers he seeks emerge not in colors of black and white but blue into shadings of gray. A simple choice between that which is wholly right and that which is wholly wrong is seldom given.

On occasion, a manager engaging in a perfectly moral transaction may have to tolerate a measure of evil. He does this reluctantly to prevent something worse, or to save a limited good. Cockle is let grow with the wheat.

But a judgment of this nature calls for know-how in discerning when and under what conditions one is allowed to perform an act that has at least two effects, one good and one bad. Here's where an understanding and mastery of that useful ethical principle known as the "principle of double effect" is necessary.

While the Golden Rule can be an effective guide in simple situations, more intricate issues force a manager to tread his way with care. Who should be hired, for instance, when two unemployed persons apply for the same job? The more qualified? The minority member? The one with more dependents? The more productive? Who deserves preference when there is a conflict of interests between one worker and ten others in the same department? The unraveling of such ethical puzzles takes a good head even more than a good heart.

Industrial managers today are boxed between two roles: What is expected of them in order to turn a profit, and what their duty is as ethical and patriotic citizens. To cite two examples: The United States has curtailed its trade with the East Germans in an effort to force them to let their citizens emigrate freely. At the same time, the West Germans, in whose behalf this cold war is waged, are trading furiously with their East German neighbors. Is it morally permissible for an American-owned corporation with plants in France (the French government feels there is nothing unethical about selling to East Germany) to use its foreign subsidiary to get around these restrictive measures? It's legal. Is it moral?

Another example: The Foreign Corrupt Practices Act prohibits payment to foreign government officials to obtain or retain business. This practice of greasing the palm of overseas officials is justified on the plea "When in Rome, do as the Romans do." By forbidding such conduct, Uncle Sam makes it clear that morality is not a matter of where you are or what the other fellow's ethics may be.

Still, the official acting as sales agent does, in fact, perform some valuable services in helping a firm discover the people who have decision-making powers in that overseas government. Acting as middleman, he helps the firm conform to various local trade regulations and smooths the way through an artificially imposed bureaucratic labyrinth. Is it a fee for service or bribery? Should it be illegal but moral?

Again, is there not a point at which a bribe is given unwillingly, and so becomes extortion, thus excusing the person who yields to the demand for a payoff? It would be reassuring to see moralists analyze some cases of commercial and industrial bribery.

A. A. Berle Jr. suggested that we might create a corporate conscience by developing keepers of it. We need men, he said, who will advise managers and question their corporate decisions, as did the lords spiritual for the kings of olden times, and he fearlessly nominated professors and journalists for the task. But what gain would there be for other citizens in entrusting the safekeeping of business ethics to professors instead of to businessmen themselves? Would this not merely substitute one elite for another? In the long run, each businessman must define what his own course of action should be when he faces moral dilemmas. His ethical system and philosophy of life were surely forged long ago by family, church, school, and associates. Without a developing sophistication in his ethical thinking, however, the businessman will be hampered in trying to cope with, foresee, sort out, comprehend, and evaluate the multitudinous, complex contingencies of modern industrial life. What is basically at stake is the survival of the kind of economy under which America has grown to greatness, the free enterprise system.

Here We Are—Rationalizing Sin
(The Providence Journal Bulletin, July 9, 1994)

If the eighties deserve to be called "The Me Decade" because of overweening concentration on self, then the nineties merit the title "The Who, Me? Age" because of the renunciation of personal responsibility. Today, nobody is willing to take the blame. While "the Devil made me do it" kind of excuse has been discarded along with belief in Hell, the guilty are now more worried about escaping consequences than in owning up to their misdeeds.

The legal maneuvering of Tonya Harding, Jane Alpert, Lorena Bobbitt, Michael Jackson, and the Menendez brothers demonstrates, in striking fashion, the techniques of self-exculpation. That distinctively human tendency to transfer blame, to rationalize sins, to pass the buck, to justify unworthy conduct, has become a standard defense mechanism for the American populace. The philosophy of excuse supplants the philosophy of personal responsibility.

Indeed, a transgressor may react to his moral failings in four ways.

First, he can confess humbly and contritely, "I did wrong." Then the resolution is made, "But I will do right," followed by the effort, painful and often laborious, to reform conduct and refine character. This is the way of personal responsibility.

Second, a malefactor may declare, "I did wrong, but I don't care." Such moral insensitivity characterizes the ethical barbarian, the sociopath, the infantile adult, the maliciously irresponsible. Miscreants of this ilk are a menace to society and to themselves. They fill our correctional institutions.

Third, an evildoer may confess, "I did wrong, but I cannot help it. I am forced to act the way I do; I cannot act otherwise." This profession of irresponsibility rests on the premise that man is not master of his own conduct, rather, he is the victim, the plaything of forces over which he has no control. He is at the mercy of his heredity and environment.

Thus man, once defined as a rational, freely acting, and choosing agent, is reduced to his complexes, structures of the psyche, family background, slum influences, earlier experiences, archetypes.

This conception of human nature makes autonomy illusory. In the sexual realm, it means that fornication, adultery, and sodomy never result from a deliberate choice of free will; rather, they emanate from a person's biological-psychological makeup, his glandular irregularities, his nervous tensions, his libido, his subconscious impulses.

For more than a generation, this doctrine of irresponsibility has been undermining the moral, legal, individual, and social responsibilities upon which the stability of society rests. Nobody is at fault. The alcoholic is diseased, tyrants like Hitler are explained away in terms of their adolescent frustrations; criminals are sick, like the insane; delinquents were made that way by parents or the public.

America has degenerated, says Charles J. Sykes, author of *A Nation of Victims*, into an hysterical, screaming, finger-pointing nation of spoiled brats where no one is held accountable for his or her own actions because everyone is a victim of something, whether it is racism, sexism, toxic parents, patriarchy, weightism, lookism, *ad nauseam*.

Verily, our legislation, our courts, and our social theory must make allowance for the inadequate and the unfortunate, but never at the expense of individual responsibility. Political, social, economic, and other moral disasters simply do not just happen. They are not the result of blind fate or chance. They are caused by human beings. Responsibility should be the universal norm; everything else, the challenged exception. Responsibility is the basis of free self-government, and free self-government is the basis of American greatness.

But there is a fourth way of reacting to one's wrongdoing. A lawbreaker might say, "What I did may appear to many people to be wrong, but actually, it is not wrong but virtuous." So he interprets, rationalizes his misconduct so that his vices become virtues, and wrong becomes right.

Whatever he does is done from the most sincere and reasonable motives, he says. Thus payoffs, kickbacks, padded expense accounts, price rigging, extramarital sex, cheating on exams, on work and contracts, stock and investment frauds, bribery, exaction of campaign contributions in return for promised or implied favors, and a host of other evils are justified on the plea that "if you don't take the bribe or payoff, someone else will," or "that's how politics works," or "it's an accepted business practice," or "everyone has his price and is out to get his," or "look out for number one, because no one else will," or "so long as you love, anything goes."

By a transvaluation of values, the stigma is placed on those who refuse to subscribe to this inverted scale of values. Violators of the moral law are thereby afforded the means of endless self-justification. They portray themselves as protesters against puritan ethics, as virtuosos of sexual self-expression, as realists in a world of misguided idealists. But these moral iconoclasts who parade under the banner of personal liberation are, in reality, trying to escape the burden of personal responsibility.

A lot of moral jiggery-pokery is justified in the name of sincerity and good intentions. The person who does not live by the rules is tempted to change the rules to suit the way he lives. The inevitable result of this contorted thinking is that the good is defined by what serves the whims of the individual.

The history and achievements of America stand as a monument to the personal responsibility of free citizens. American society, with its system of rewards and punishments, with its laws and police force, can gauge its progress according to the measure of individual commitment to responsibility.

If our future is to be worthy of our past, we need to reaffirm the sense of individual obligation, to make clear the foundation on which personal responsibility rests, to determine the causes of its decay, and to seek the means by which it can be revived.

Pensions and Milking the System—
Legal, Yes, But Is It Moral?
(The Providence Visitor, December 7, 1995)

Abusers of the state pension system defend themselves by arguing that their actions were legal and within the bounds of accepted practice.

The question of morality does not seem to enter their minds. The system exists to be exploited. One does not buck the system; one goes along with it.

Quondam senator Fulbright once asked, "How do you deal with those who offend the spirit of the law, but do not violate the letter? Why is it that for so many influential people, morality has become identical with legality?"

The law's reach is necessarily limited. Much of today's corruption is entirely legal. The law itself may be used to reap enormous rewards at public expense, as through loopholes, subsidies, dodges, or an unconscionable juggling of the tax structure.

Some contend that abuses involving manipulation of the law for private profit—legal but unethical—are an inevitable part of the democratic system. It's in the American tradition for public officials to take care of their own and look out for themselves. Anyway, the conduct of public servants merely reflects the general level of morality prevailing in society.

J. Peter Grace, chairman of the bipartisan study on government cost control, pinpoints the ways the welfare state apparatus is worked for all it can bear—a hundred-billion-dollar underground economy, a bloated bureaucracy, income-tax fraud, welfare deadbeats, sloppy management, inept bookkeeping, negligible accountability, resistance to centralization, double-dipping, retirement, pension and sick-leave abuses, military overspending, cost overruns, costly but ineffective antipoverty programs, special-interest legislation—all taken out of the hides of median-income families.

Trying to justify these practices, people say, "Everybody bends the rules and exploits the system, so it can't be wrong." But the thesis that personal morality is determined by majority vote would horrify the founders of this nation. Leaders of the American Revolution differed vastly in background, but they all saw eye to eye with respect to the code of conduct that should guide one's life. Principle held primacy over expediency, veracity over mendacity, the immaterial over the material.

Religion figured highly in our forefathers' personal and political philosophy. "Confirm your soul in self-control," the hymn to America commanded. "A good name is better than riches," children were taught. "Honor is more precious than life," ran the apothegm in textbooks.

Perhaps the super-organized society in which we live mitigates the culpability of those who take undue advantage of the state pension system. To the extent that obligations to individuals are replaced by obligations to governments, corporations, or institutions, the sense of obligation itself loses much of its force and urgency. Obligations to individuals make an impact on our emotions; obligations to institutions or to impersonal public authority do not. A man who would resent the suggestion that he might pick his neighbor's pocket will think nothing of diddling the income tax, or customs, or bending the state pension rules. What is there to cause any compunction? Nobody suffers any loss, nobody is upset, the total damage to the individual citizen is infinitesimal.

But if "everybody-is-doing-it" becomes the operational norm in America, democracy will have to close shop and put up a sign: "Out of business."

The very existence of a government like ours calls for a relatively high level of virtue in its citizens. The civil law aims at enforcing only that degree of good conduct that is necessary for the peace, good order, and well-being of society. It demands only the minimum. It does not define the full duty of any citizen in any situation. The law does not prescribe what society regards as optimum or even desirable conduct.

Robert M. Hutchins stated, "In a democracy, every person is, in a very real sense, a king, and it is the duty of kings to care about truth and justice and virtue." This idea of social responsibility has meaning only in a democratic society, and correspondingly, a democratic society is viable only when the ideal of social responsibility animates most of its citizens.

Americans, our forefathers warned us, can only be free when citizens willingly set bounds upon their own behavior regardless of the policeman on the corner.

Anthropologist Ruth Benedict observed that the United States was ceasing to be a "guilt culture"—one in which control of conduct is self-imposed by means of conscience—and was becoming instead a "shame culture"—one in which control is externally imposed by means of public humiliation or punishment, as in some Eastern cultures.

In short, there is a growing shift in the techniques Americans use to develop and enforce honesty. When dishonesty is rampant, it becomes easy to live with a bad conscience; so external rather than internal methods of control prevail.

To protect itself from unconscionable citizens, government must then create a repressive brave new world, a Big-Brother-is-watching atmosphere. It must generate a climate of fear. Indeed, when people refuse to apply the internal brake of conscience, government applies the external brake of public shame and penalties. The ambit of freedom is thus gradually restricted, and morality becomes identical with legality.

"Right to Privacy" Pushes Aside Common Sense
(*The Providence Visitor*, November 20, 2003)

The U.S. Supreme Court's June 26 decision (*Lawrence v. Texas*) throwing out a state law that banned homosexual sodomy was based in part on the so-called "right to privacy." This dubious right was the lynchpin in the infamous *Roe v. Wade* abortion decision.

Everybody prizes privacy, but the putative "right to privacy" was fabricated from a sun shadow. Former justice William O. Douglas, in *Griswold v. Connecticut*, claimed that he had "discovered" this "right to privacy" in the "emanations" from the "penumbra" mystically hidden in the Third and Fourth Amendments to the Constitution and between the Ninth and Tenth Amendments.

Webster's New Collegiate Dictionary defines "penumbra" as "the shaded region around the dark central portion of a sunspot." This cloudy shadow ended up being a crucial basis for the *Roe* decision.

Former chief justice Warren Burger adamantly insisted that "good governments have always regulated sexual behavior." Indeed, social critic Peregrine Worsthorne asserts: "It is impossible to conceive of a private act which might not, in some circumstances, harm others. Just as low standards in personal hygiene can endanger public health, so low standards in private morals can endanger public welfare. It is misleading, therefore, to try to draw any theoretical line beyond which the law may not trespass. All human activity, however private, can legitimately be the law's business."

Actually, a strictly "private morality" is impossible, if that term signifies personal behavior having no effect on the general society. All moral behavior contributes to the creation of a moral climate (the prevalence or non-prevalence of drug use, adultery, public pornographic displays that have a powerful influence on the young, the bored, the insecure, and the unhappy). In the "detribalized" society of Marshall McLuhan, the mass media cause new customs to permeate the entire culture with great rapidity. Only the most extreme social atomist thinks in terms of "private" morality.

Private behavior has more tangible social effects as well. Only a few years ago, sophisticated moralists could explain that the taboo against fornication was no longer valid because modern technology had obviated its greatest dangers—venereal disease and pregnancy. Now venereal disease has spread like wildfire, a spiraling, unwanted pregnancy rate has multiplied abortions, and AIDS has decimated nations.

Among "liberated" adults the belief is spreading that mature, free people can and perhaps ought to engage in what were formerly called "sexual aberrations" and that healthy individuals will feel neither guilt nor resentment. Yet for many persons, this apparently adds an additional layer of guilt at not being sufficiently "free" not to feel guilty. Meanwhile the new permissiveness, besides affecting the general moral climate, has measurable social effects in terms of divorces, emotional disturbances, and troubled children—all of which are concealed behind the rhetorical "right to privacy" plea.

Ethicists question the wisdom of capitulating to every demand for more "liberal" laws. There have been few societies in the history of the world that have not maintained, through law, official moral attitudes. Proponents of the new freedom will not acknowledge that a society that is officially agnostic about "private morality" is an experiment whose outcome can by no means be assumed as benign.

In the past, although far from ideal, the least unsatisfactory strategy was the maintenance of rather strict laws governing personal morality, which were somewhat laxly enforced—a situation allowing for a measure of personal freedom, but also for the control of dangerously pathological behavior. Many states that retained sodomy laws rarely enforced them. The existing law deterred more by the moral virtue that it absorbed and preserved than by the punishment that it enacted and imposed.

"The law is a pedagogue." It teaches and proclaims a public moral standard. This is scarcely an argument against any change in the law, but it indicates that a certain conservatism in regard to law is part of civil wisdom. The law is, in a sense, the voice of society's conscience.

When laws dealing with morality—homosexuality, heroin use, prostitution, pornography, etc.—are removed from the books, it is too often taken by many as a change in morality itself. People assume that if behavior is not unlawful, it is therefore not immoral. Legality is confused with morality.

(5)
Religion and the Modern World

What Is Religion?
(*The Providence Visitor*, June 30, 1994)

Christianity is essentially a religion. It follows, therefore, that our faith is not a social system or a political creed, nor does it exist to supply a solid basis for society, to give a sense of security to the property holder, or to strengthen the hands of the police.

It is not the Church's role to form a party of law and order in the state, or necessarily to influence public opinion on the side of the ruling power, or again to promote the culture of any race or nationality.

Still less is Christianity a system of economics, or an instrument of enriching people or keeping them rich.

What may seem more surprising, it is not even a school of morals, except in a secondary sense. This fact is sometimes lost sight of by writers who judge the true religion externally by the temporal blessings it has brought mankind rather than by the true test of its internal life.

What, then, is the place of morality in the Christian system? For most people, morality is the really important thing in religion. For them, religion means to keep from violence, stealing, and all injury to their fellow man, to be chaste, honest, conjugally faithful, respectful, and, finally, to carry out what are called the "duties of one's state in life."

This conception is widespread, and yet it is possible to do all these things without being a Christian at all. That is what we are told by honest unbelievers—"Why go to church? We do all these things."

Now quite obviously Christian faith includes a true system of morals, and we could not imagine a good Catholic who did not try to carry out the moral teaching of the Church. But we repeat, Christianity is not a mere system of morals; it is a religion.

It is quite possible to have either of these things existing without the other. For example, in heathen religions, the moral element is almost entirely absent. The gods of Olympus were grossly immoral, and pagan cults were frequently stained with vice. So also there are systems of morality apart from religion. They may have a faulty foundation, it is true, but they exist, such as stoicism and Buddhism. Religion and morality are not the same thing.

What is religion? In its essence, religion is the means by which man is brought into contact with the unseen. In this sense, man is sometimes called a religious animal, for it is only he who concerns himself with the unseen world at all.

Those who are in no way concerned with the whence, why, and whither of life are either humans who have become so brutalized as to be scarcely distinguished from the beasts themselves, or those who are so wrapped up in their immediate environment as practically to be living their lives in an artificial setting. These are modern pagans. They live as if there were no God.

The two essential elements of religion, then, are a system of doctrine that solves the problem connected with the unseen world and a practical discipline establishing relations between man and the unseen God.

Thus, religion is distinguished from superstition, which rests on no coherent system of doctrine, and from philosophy, which tries to solve the problems of existence by personal reflection alone. Religion is based on tradition and revelation.

What many persons cannot grasp about religion, then, is that its essential function is not in teaching men how to behave in relation to each other but rather in establishing true relations between man and God. And since all religion is based on the idea that in the unseen world there are beings superior to man, it follows that worship is primarily an act of homage rendered to a superior according to the rules of a fixed code, like those governing the social relations among men themselves.

The one conclusion to which all this leads is that the real test as to whether or not a religion is true is not what uses it may have rendered mankind. These are secondary. It goes without saying that the true religion will be of service to humanity because it is true; but all the same, utility and social value are not the true end of religion. The only question to be asked in regard to a religion claiming to be true is this: "Does it bring man into right relation with Almighty God?"

What Christianity came to proclaim was the Kingdom of God and nothing else. Our Blessed Lord came to proclaim the gospel of divine love, to set up a new relationship between man and God. Everything else is subordinate to this. All his ascetical teaching and all his doctrine of renunciation and self-sacrifice are no more than conditions or means by which the love of God may become effective in our souls. To love God is the great commandment, and the second is like unto this—love thy neighbor.

Any so-called humanitarian work whose object, whether direct or indirect, is not to bring souls to Almighty God, any type of philanthropy that promotes the idea that it is possible to be happy without God, is alien to the spirit of Christianity. That Christian serves God best who devotes his energies to those works which, while relieving man's bodily ills, will glorify God and his love for mankind.

What Can God and Religion Do for Me?
(*The Cowl*, March 23, 1988)

"I want religion for what I can get out of it." That sentence summarizes the way many Americans prostitute religion for purely temporal and selfish reasons.

To such persons, religion is not something absolute and transcendent and independent, something primarily concerned with the adoration of Almighty God. Instead, religion is seen as something that benefits government, acting as a bulwark of our national ideals, or as a help to peace of mind.

I do not refer to those who dismiss religion as an antiquated fable or a set of medieval dogmas that are incomprehensible to the modern world. No, I have in mind those who profess to be religious, but whose religion is a shallow humanitarianism.

Followers of this fashionable cult boast, not of the truth of their religion, but of its value. They approve the social welfare work of Christ. They praise His work in relieving the ills of mankind, especially its physical ailments. Did he not cure the man sick of the palsy, the centurion's servant, the woman with the bloody flux?

These same persons, however, find enigmatic and almost meaningless the concept of Christ to be adored. They regard as archaic Oriental jargon the words of St. Paul in which he speaks of Christ "... who is the blessed and only sovereign, the King of Kings and Lord of Lords; who also has immortality and dwells in light inaccessible, whom no man has seen or can see, to whom be honor and everlasting dominion" (1 Timothy 6:15-16).

Today we are living in an era where man is considered King of Kings. The brotherhood of man has replaced the fatherhood of God. The humanitarians have robbed Christ of his divinity: such a belief, in their estimation, is nothing more than idle medieval speculation, and adoration derived from it is only a ritual mumbo-jumbo which is a throwback to primitive tribal customs. They want only that type of religion which concentrates on man.

Indeed, since Vatican II, there has been confusion about what the Church should be doing. Some say: "Your preaching is not relevant. You're not talking about social issues —poverty, discrimination, nuclear war, crime, etc." But what could be more relevant than our destiny—why we are here, where we are going? That is what the Church preaches. The

Church addresses itself to what is ultimate: to what we are in our deepest being—heirs to a kingdom.

Of course, the Church must expend herself in service to mankind, but this must be placed in its proper priority. It is a consequence—a consequence of the first thing the Church preaches, which is Jesus Christ. He is our ultimate destiny. If the Church forgets to preach this, then the Church is damned, the Church is lost. The Church then makes itself merely another agency for political or social change.

What would happen if the best social engineering, the best technology, the most equitable economic system we can devise came into being and then we discovered there was nothing in us beyond that? A few years ago, a Swedish columnist wrote an article: "Why the Swedes Are Sad." At that time, Sweden had, and may still have, the most advanced welfare system of any nation in the world. He explained that the Swedes are sad because the whole sense of religion has been lost in the pursuit of technology, in the pursuit of human wisdom. They have forgotten that "man does not live on bread alone."

The genuine Christian asks, "What can I do for God?" Not, "What can God do for me?" We abhor a person who makes friends "for what he can get out of them"; such a test of value is just as reprehensible when applied to friendship with God.

Much of the writing about religion today, the peace-of-mind variety, redefines faith and its central themes, making religion not an end in itself but merely a means to an end. Readers are offered techniques for making God do man's will, instead of man doing God's will. Thus religion becomes egocentric; the selfish impulses of man are sanctified and material success is glorified as a sovereign good and as evidence of virtue. God, in this view, is looked upon as a public utility.

Christ did not parade as a peddler of wonder-working psychological tricks, nor did He come in order to cure mankind's physical or emotional corns. The ebbing of ulcers and the routing of neuroses are nowhere in the Gospel specified as the goal of Christianity, or even as concomitants of it. They lie in the field of medicine, physical or mental.

Indeed, the Lord did not hesitate to voice hard sayings, calculated to disturb humans to the roots of their being. Nor did he substitute pap for principle in order to stop their drift away from Him. He made them face ultimate reality, promising them persecution and tears for their commitment to it, but a transcendent reward after the darkness and agony that, in life, would often be the lot of His followers.

We are living in an age of anxiety, and people are hungering for the courage and mental security which only faith can give; but now as always, the Church must preach Christ and Him crucified. Jacques Maritain sums it up (*The Range of Reason*): "Neither Christianity nor the Church has a mission to make people happy; their business is to teach the truth of the Gospel—not merely to bring about justice and freedom in political society, but to give mankind salvation and eternal life.

How Religiously Mature Are You?
(The Providence Visitor, March 31, 1983)

St. Paul tells us that we should be able to give "reason for the faith that is in us." Yet few Catholics today, even the college-bred, can explain or defend their beliefs intelligently.

This sad state cries out for a study of apologetics. Pope John Paul II urged the youth of Rome to take up this study "especially in our day when religious convictions are apt to be so lacking in depth."

Syllogisms rarely convince tempted, troubled human beings. Nevertheless, like Thomas Aquinas, we must respect people's intelligence and the vital way they make up their minds. The idea is not to prove non-Catholics wrong and we right, but to offer bread to the hungry, for our faith fulfills the highest aspirations of the human heart.

Apologetics can be scientific—we present the chain of reasoning by which the Church established her claim to speak uniquely in the name of Christ, putting emphasis on the objective value of the arguments themselves, regardless of whether they would persuade the individual. And apologetics can be practical—we select those proofs adapted to the needs of living people.

God makes converts, but He uses people to plant the seed, because as St. Paul says, "Faith comes through hearing." The apologist must not only know the case for Catholicism but must know equally the person he hopes to convince; otherwise, he may "win an argument but lose a soul."

Apologetics is much needed in a society that regards religion subjectively, as a matter of sentiment or emotion. Atheism is unfashionable, but people who believe in God often have little grasp of why they believe and know even less about God's true nature. Some show profound respect for Christ but have the haziest idea of his divinity.

American Catholics have one chief heresy to contend with: man-centered religion: "What's in it for me?" Religion, for many, is "good" only to the degree that it enables man to overcome his anxieties and inferiority complexes, provides a crutch in time of trouble, and insures happiness—happiness being defined in terms of "peace of mind," financial success, emotional comfort, and psychological reassurance. Man indicates the terms of his own salvation.

Apologetically, it would be easier to cope with outright disbelief than with a watered-down version of Christianity, a picking and choosing of doctrines that appear comforting and consoling. A recent poll, for instance, revealed that ninety-four percent thought of God as a loving Father, but only thirty percent believed in Hell.

Disbelief in Hell, and in the possibility of going there, shifts the frame of reference within which Americans view religion. If one is sure he is not punished for a bad life, why work so hard to merit a happy life after death?

When the human situation is no longer defined within the framework of traditional beliefs, emphasis becomes placed in social service rather than on man's need to be reconciled to God, and the only role left to the Church is to teach people "how to live better everyday with all other people."

Religion, as interpreted, becomes an instrument of society instead of an institution transcending all that is secular because it is centered on God. Americans do, indeed, still believe in God, but as Oscar Wilde cynically remarked, "Man has made God in his own image and likeness."

Enemies of the Church, e.g., Paul Blanshard, depicted her as a ruthlessly authoritarian society, rigidly controlling the thought, speech, and actions of her members. Intransigent, hieratic, and monolithic, this alien institution, they contended, is both un-American and antidemocratic.

Attacks, nowadays, are more subtle. Catholicism, foes declare, is not only psychologically injurious but also useless or socially harmful. Her doctrines are a part of an amalgam of oppressive social and political concepts. Her insistence on mortification, patience, forgiveness, et cetera is associated with an outmoded, pietistic, and inward-looking vision of Christianity, a Christianity that is ill-equipped to deal with the great issues of war and peace, of nuclear disarmament, and of starvation on a worldwide scale.

Apologetics arms the Catholic with ammunition to refute these charges. A more difficult task will be to persuade the profligate who reject the Church because of her teaching on sex and marriage. Remember the woman at the well? She posed a theological problem to the Lord when her real problem was a moral one—namely, her five husbands. As G. K. Chesterton observed, "Christianity has not been tried and found wanting; it has been found hard and not tried."

As always, the life exposition of the message of Christ is the strongest argument for the Catholic faith. Actions speak louder than words. People know what they want when they see it before their very eyes in the life of another person. The joy, the tranquility, the invulnerable happiness that should be the rightful heritage of every good Catholic is, in itself, the most telling case for Catholicism.

Yves Congar, O.P., explains, "What a terrible danger to live childishly, never to outgrow a magical conception of God and the sacraments!" Many Catholics, wise in worldly wisdom, remain religiously immature. They go through life with the same superficial, religious knowledge they acquired as children, making little effort to deepen understanding of their religion. Apparently, in their scale of important life values, the faith does not rank highly.

Yet the Vatican Council's *Pastoral Constitution on the Church in the Modern World* states: "The remedy for unbelief is to be sought in the proper presentation and defense of the Church's teaching as well as in the integral life of the Church and her members ... This result is achieved by the witness of a living and mature faith."

Intellect Still Has Its Place
(*The Providence Visitor*, December 30, 1993)

If the Gospel story of the three Wise Men means anything, it means that Christianity began by attracting the best brains of the house, and ever since that day, learning has had its place of honor in the Church. Sooner or later really learned people find their way to religion. Only the fool curls his lips and scoffs; the wise man bends his knees and prays.

History attests that through the centuries the torch of true knowledge has illuminated the cross like a holy candle. It is only false science that has been a firebrand seeking to char and consume the cross. Religion and learning, after all, are twin sons of the same God.

In the early Church, there was room for the unlettered shepherds who tended their sheep, and for the Wise Men who held the sheepskin of learning. So even today the Church attracts the very simple and the very smart: the simple who sense the truth, and the sagacious who reason to it.

Obviously, not all bright people are Catholics. Faith is still a gift. People are not irreligious only because they are ignorant. Just reading a few books in favor of divinity will not lead atheists to embrace the faith. Religion is more than a thing to be known, it is a personality to be embraced and lived and loved.

Jesus Christ, who is truth itself, could not convince the Pharisees; they were intellectually confounded by his knowledge so that, after one encounter, no man dared question him again—but still they did not believe. Christ told those who watched the resurrection of Lazarus that some of them would not believe, even though they saw a daily resurrection from the dead. Intellectual knowledge is not the "one thing necessary": not all Ph.D.'s are saints, nor are the ignorant demons. Indeed, a certain type of education may simply turn a student from stupid egotist into a clever egoist, and of the two, the former has a better chance of salvation.

Many people today are ignorant, full of prejudice and misinformation about the faith. It is regrettable that they have had no opportunity for instruction, for acquiring knowledge of the truth. But though God can be discovered by study, instruction, and reading, these alone will not bring one to God. There must also be a willingness to accept the truth personally, that is, in all its implications.

This good-will factor is so important that it seems probable there is no such thing as intellectual atheism. Reason is on God's side, not the

Devil's, and to deny God is absolute is to affirm a competing absolute. But if there is no intellectual atheism, there can be, and is, an atheism of the will, a deliberate rejection of God. That is why the psalmist places atheism not in the head but in the heart: "The fool has said in his heart, there is no God."

It is easy to find truth; it is hard to face it, and harder still to follow it. Higher education is geared to what it calls "extending the frontiers of truth," and sometimes this ideal is prized and used to excuse academicians from acting on old truths already discovered. The discovery of the size of a distant star creates no moral obligation; but the old truths about the nature and destiny of man can be a reproach to the way one lives.

There are, indeed, some who do not come to the truth because they do not know it; but there are many more who do not come because of their present behavior. It is not the way they think but the way they live that constitutes the obstacle to union with the Spirit. It is not the creed that keeps most people away from Christ and his Mystical Body; it is the commandments.

How many apostate Catholics actually thought their way out of the Church? A few may have given up the Catholic's "sign of the cross" for the agnostic's shrug of the shoulders, but not because they had genuine grounds for disbelief. Some stopped answering Sunday church bells, not for lack of faith in the Nicene Creed, but because of a nice, warm bed. The mattress was more appealing than the Mass, God interfered with golf, or they could not abide pulpit talk about money, or the Church's teaching about sex and marriage was too hard to take. Whatever it was, you'll find it was not thought or learning or concentrated brainpower that made them walk on the other side of the street from the Church. G. K. Chesterton summed it up succinctly: "Christianity has not been tried and found wanting; it has been found hard and not tried."

Do Jews Belong in the Ecumenical Movement?
(*The Providence Visitor*, March 5, 1971)

Note: Reverend Joseph I. Lennon, O.P., Vice President for Community Affairs at Providence College, spoke Monday night on the topic "Do Jews Belong in the Ecumenical Movement?" at the Tifereth Israel Synagogue, New Bedford, Massachusetts. Father Lennon's talk was the second lecture in the Ziskind Memorial Lecture Series, which was instituted in memory of the late Rabbi Bernard Ziskind and his wife because of their work in the cause of brotherhood. The theme of the lecture series is "Brotherhood Through Knowledge." The following are excerpts from Father Lennon's talk.

Christian curiosity about Judaism is growing. Pope Paul VI has urged Catholics to know more about the Jewish roots of their own faith. Yet it has been stated by both Jewish and Christian leaders that they do not see any place for Jews in the present ecumenical effort if its aim is the unity of all separated Christians. But this definition of ecumenism, which would have to exclude Jews, is not the only valid one. The term *ecumenism* expresses today something else, over and above its primary meaning. It has come to signify a method, a way of life more than a goal, an attitude toward one's fellow man. It stands for the wish for men to acknowledge and to accept those different from themselves as their neighbor, to establish communication with them, to enter with them into a personal relationship.

Ecumenism thus understood aims at breaking down the barrier of hostility and indifference that has for so long prevented Christians and Jews from knowing each other as they really are. The Christian should try to understand that what the Jew values above all is his own separate Jewish identity, even when this is not related to any explicitly religious belief.

In the ecumenical meeting with the Jews, says Pope Paul VI, a conversation is initiated where each partner makes the effort to understand the other as he is, or ideally wants to be, each formed by his own faith, tradition, social and religious milieu. The aim is to establish a new intimate relationship that has not existed before and that enriches both Jew and Christian, because each is allowed to enter the spiritual domain of the other and to understand how he looks at and defines himself with regard to God, the world, and his ultimate destiny. If ecumenism in the larger sense can mean all this—the total opening of oneself in trust and confidence to the man of another faith, with respect for his otherness and an acceptance of the fact that he has the right to define himself according to his own allegiance—if the Christian can make up his mind that the Jew, by contact and confrontation with him, will be confirmed, not shaken, in his own Jewishness, then ecumenism can and must include the Jew.

But many Jews, by reason of past history, are suspicious of Catholics. They question the honesty of Catholic motivation. Conditioned by historical experience, they have developed a fearful mentality which sees a potential missionary in every Catholic and a hidden strategy of proselytism in every conversation across religious lines. Indeed, when Catholics extend their hand to Jews for dialogue, there are some Jews who do not know whether to shake it or slap it away. One rabbi publicly dismissed interfaith relations as "a farce," warning that dialogue is a veiled attempt to convert Jews. He complained "Why don't they let us alone" when invited by Christians to participate in theological exchanges.

Regarding the ecumenical exchange, the Union of American Hebrew Congregations made its position quite clear in an important resolution which states that "the new directions of American interreligious life, and specifically the call from our Christian brethren for closer community and dialogue, offer fresh opportunities for the strengthening of these relations. We urge the expansion and deepening of the programs of our national Commission on Interfaith Activities and summon our congregations more intensively to enter into dialogue with our Christian compatriots, even into these areas which touch on matters of faith."

Dialogue between Catholics and Jews should be a vehicle for strengthening religious self-knowledge and personal faith, as well as being the means for clarifying the theological basis for any Jewish-Catholic cooperative social endeavor. Is it not incongruous to suppose that there can be interreligious social action without a seeking for the theological foundations undergirding and motivating that action? Were that really possible, American religious involvement in things mundane would be no different from the interest or involvement of any secular (and in some instances atheistic) group's effort.

For example, when Jews and Protestants disagree profoundly with Catholics on such issues as abortion, divorce, and sterilization legislation, at the heart of the issue lies a fundamental difference in the theological view each takes toward the nature of life. Catholics, Jews, and Protestants may not be able to harmonize those differences, but they must never be afraid first to discuss the reasons for their differences and then to act politically as their religious consciences dictate. If religious pluralism cannot withstand the ensuing political dispute, then it isn't worth very much anyway.

It is unfortunate that too often today, the nonreligious and the irreligious Jew represents himself as a spokesman for both Jewry and Judaism. In keeping with the ecumenical spirit, Catholics should seek contact with those who represent Jewish tradition as well as Jewish liberalism and should try to engage in dialogue with those who feel that religion has something to say on the great moral and universal issues of the day.

Sound Doctrine Lacking in Uplift Literature
(*The Providence Visitor*, May 13, 1982)

When Norman Vincent Peale wrote his best-selling *The Power of Positive Thinking* in 1952, he attempted to "demonstrate that you do not need to be defeated by anything, that you can have peace of mind, improved health, and a never-ceasing flow of energy."

That remains the basic objective on the current profusion of books offering advice on how to cope with the problems of daily living—a new variety of self-help manuals, secular, pseudo-religious, and quasi-Christian in nature. These personality booster-uppers abound in the racks of supermarket checkout counters, in doctor's offices, newsstands, and bookstores.

The secular self-help books eschew religion and the supernatural and concentrate completely on this world. Concocted of diluted versions of William James, some popularized Freudianism, and echoes of Coué's "Every day, in every way, I am getting better and better," (which swept through the country in the twenties), these mental bucker-uppers preach a sophisticated selfishness, viz., always look out for Number One; outlaw self-denial; banish guilt, worry, and depression; don't look for social approval and don't try to change society; do only those things that make you feel good about yourself; being happy is only a state of mind; don't let other people or events upset you; squeeze as much pleasure as you can out of each moment.

Authors of these books syncretize a large number of psychological approaches arranging from Gestalt and bioenergetics to parapsychology and self-hypnosis. In a culture where eighty to ninety percent of sickness is judged to be psychosomatic, these books expose readers to a variety of mind-body disciplines such as Tai Chi, Aikido, Feldenkrais exercises, sensory expansion, yoga, energy awareness, and centering. All these methods purport to help practitioners get in touch with their inner selves and actualize their dormant potential.

Apparently, "The Me Decade" of the seventies and "The Narcissist Society" of the eighties have surged into the nineties. This genre of secular uplift literature extols an unabashed and unalloyed egoism largely devoid of altruistic motivation.

The Western world is experiencing a real hunger for fresh ways of experiencing reality. Turning from traditional Christianity, a growing number look to religions of the East and other sources of spiritual inspiration.

A perusal of he pseudo-religious inspirational book unveils a mishmash of cults from animism to Zoroastrianism. Quotes from such diverse notables as Andy Rooney and Pierre Teilhard de Chardin, Rebecca West and Mae West, and Dolly Parton and Roseanne stud its pages. Messages from Mahatma Gandhi, Mother Teresa, and Billy Graham abound. Reincarnation, Zen meditation, Eastern cults, the feminist deity Sophia, and witchcraft form part of the literary mélange, while the flowery and saccharine prose of pantheist Kahlil Gibran (God is all and all is God) provides sop to the sentimental. A revisionist form of Rosicrucianism (tap the power of the universe) has become quite popular, and New Ageism (with its romantic "natural is beautiful; embrace Mother Earth") seems to appeal to women of the better-educated sort.

These pseudo-religious treatises, which place all religions on an equal footing, offer a take-what-you-like kind of religiosity. Designed chiefly for the walking wounded rather than the mentally sick, their purpose is to shore up the shaky and comfort the insecure. Devotees of this eclectic religion usually spurn asceticism, are attracted to exotic rituals and weird doctrines, and pine for a heaven on earth.

There is a great deal of neo-paganism and religious quackery in the pseudo-religious literature. It embraces earth worship, the Goddess (whoever she may be), witches, pyramids, sex-magic, theosophy, fairies, crystals, dolphins, tarot, spiritism, flotation tanks, Transcendental Meditation, eastern religions with gurus, energy in the universe, aliens, crop circles, circle dancing, deep breathing, rebirthing, American Indian lore, cairn building, healing hands, and numberless esoteric therapies.

Former Dominican Matthew Fox, who has devised something he called Creation Spirituality, says, "The idea of private salvation is utterly obsolete ... the cosmic Christ can be both female and male, heterosexual and homosexual ... There is a need to recover the sense of both lust and chastity as powers and therefore virtues within all people."

Then we have the quasi-Christian inspirational books. They are in a class by themselves. Writers assure readers that "they can have all this and heaven too." Cast within the framework of traditional Christianity, these publications, fabricated out of shreds of Protestant theology and biblical aphorisms, are short on doctrine and long on Pollyanna philosophy. Striving for mass appeal, authors tend to trim or degut theological truth and tout an it-makes-no-difference-what-you-believe latitudinarianism.

The bulk of this quasi-Christian self-help literary genre is man-centered rather than God-centered. Prayer is taught as something magical, a technique for making God do man's will rather than vice versa. The emphasis is on this earth, the payoff being a "chicken-in-the-pot" here and now rather than a "pie-in-the-sky-by-and-by." Under the guise of altruism, it sanctifies the selfish impulses of human nature, glorifies material prosperity, and assures the reader that anyone can become a cockeyed optimist if he will only use a little religion and a few psychiatric principles.

In short, much of this so-called Christian inspirational literature confuses the Gospel of Christ with the gospel of worldly success. In doing so, it influences, misleads, and often disillusions sick, maladjusted unhappy, or ill-instructed people, obscuring from them the stern realities of the Christian message.

Under beguiling titles, these books offer, in glib, huckstering language, easy comforts and easy solutions to problems and mysteries that sometimes have no comforts or solutions at all. They promise a cheap "happiness" in lieu of the joy that Christianity can offer, sometimes in the midst of suffering. The awesome sense of confrontation with God is gone. The fear of God, which is awe, has been dispelled. The meaning of worship is nullified and forgotten.

Christians believe that God is to be worshipped because He is God. Contrarily, these publications, which sanctify man's selfish impulses, debase Christianity and make it a means to other and lesser ends that by its nature it cannot be. Father Gerald Vann, O.P., wisely declares, "Mindless optimism, a refusal to face the facts, is a sentimental illusion, distinct from Christian hope."

Christianity (and Judaism too) teaches not that man has sought out God but that God has sought out man. The hope of salvation lies in the fact that man loves God, not that God loves man. Christianity is not a discovery or a technique. The curing of corns, the ebbing of ulcers, and the routing of fatigue, depression, and anxiety are nowhere specified in the Gospels as the goal of Christianity. These nostrums lie in the field of medicine, physical or mental.

Christianity is first and foremost a revelation. Its history is not of what man has done for God but of what God has done for man. The Judeo-Christian religious experience, instead of being an escape or a ready solution to daily problems, is instead the awesome recognition of God's intrusion into man's life, with foundation-shaking implications. Someone has said, justly, "Christianity is too astounding for anybody to have made up." Yes, it can be joyous, comforting, hope-giving, and life-renewing, but its biblical historicity must be understood as the mighty acts of God, and its worship, sacraments, and obedience must be comprehended as man's privilege of response to God's initiative.

The remedies preferred in the quasi-Christian self-improvement handbooks can become, some experts think, a positive hazard in the delicate marginal areas of mental health and religion. Sick and sinking people will commit themselves to any waterlogged life preserver, with possible disastrous results, when psychiatric counsel is needed. Of late, the Church has been developing psychiatrically trained pastoral counselors who know how to recognize the problems that the priest must refer to the realm of the therapist.

Actually, many of these purportedly Christian manuals are noting but shallow revivals of Pelagianism, although the heresy of Pelagianism had a certain integrity and dignity (with a genuine impact on theology) missing from these doctrineless up-by-your-own-bootstraps tracts.

The crucial question is this: Where in all the morass of quasi-Christian peace-of-mind handbooks are the great historic central themes, subjects, and words of Christianity through the ages? Where are the considerations of the Trinity, Incarnation, Mystical Body, atonement, covenant, redemption, salvation, sin, judgment, worship, sacrament, sacrifice, communion, primacy, and the idea of the Holy?

Hunger demands a feeding. The present generation bears witness to a growing hunger among book-buying people bent on finding answers to the ageless questions that have plagued mankind. The danger accompanying such a religious hunger is that charlatans will come forward with the offer of ersatz foods that either lack value or, worse, will leave residual poisons in the system. Religious pitchmen take the natural craving for peace of mind and the good life and reduce these to the lowest denominations of social acceptance, business success, self-confidence, and emotional equilibrium.

Caveat emptor! The reader must be on guard against being duped by unscrupulous purveyors of psychological flummery and religious claptrap. Mental assurance and emotional comfort may be offshoots of valid religion; they can never be its sole objective. Peddlers of psychological gimmicks and rags of doctrine who distort the Christian message for the tawdry gain of a spurious peace of mind are Judases to the cause of Christ.

Religion Possesses Revolutionary Spirit
(*The Providence Visitor*, March 7, 2002)

Christianity is essentially revolutionary, and no follower of Christ can be content with the status quo, according to Dominican Father Joseph L. Lennon, speaking May 7 at the Rhode Island Conservative Union Annual Awards Dinner at the Marriott Inn, Providence. The following is a condensed version of the text of his speech on "Religion and the Revolutionary Spirit":

There is a serious polarization within the Protestant and Roman Catholic churches in South America and South Africa caused by a conflict of fundamental attitudes. Some Christians feel that the Church "should not involve itself in politics," while others view the situation more extremely, perceiving the Church as having abandoned the Gospel in favor of preaching Communism, violence, and racial hatred.

Because of this polarization of attitudes in the Church, I intend to talk about religion and the revolutionary spirit.

Let me state at once that any attempt to encompass the ideal of the modern revolutionary spirit in a single phrase is difficult and dangerous.

Nevertheless, as a working description, we may say that the modern revolutionary is concerned not merely with the factors of man's material existence but also, and in fact primarily, with man's moral condition. What the modern revolutionary wants is a transformation not only of man's environment but of man himself.

To illustrate this point, let me quickly cite two "isms": anarchism and Marxism. In anarchism, one senses at once a strong note of moral indignation. The anarchist's hatred of the state stems from the conviction that man has been corrupted and abased by government and authority. Property he regards as another form of slavery. The anarchist feels that government and property bring out the worst in man, that life under these conditions makes man selfish, rapacious, unjust, and cruel. All forms of compulsion must be accordingly abolished in order that the spirit of antagonism may die and that out of the free, creative activity of the people themselves, a new "spirit of voluntary cooperation may be born.

Marx also shows a thorough disgust with the whole existing order of things. For Marx, the revolution was never merely a question of economic rehabilitation. If he speaks principally of economic development, it is simply the lever that is to overturn the "whole superstructure of juridical and political institutions as well as religious, philosophical, and other ideas."

The outlook of Marx is integral; he is fighting not merely for a new economic system but for a new conception of society and a new view of life.

The idea of a "mass change in human nature" haunts Communist thought. It is the necessary presupposition of the Communist visions of the classless society. Communists believe that under a socialist regime, greed, selfishness, laziness, injustice, and oppression will disappear. Finally, one day, man's psychological makeup and ethical outlook will have become so far transformed that no compulsion of any form will be necessary and the state (i.e., the dictatorship of the proletariat) will be able to "wither away."

Why, then, promote revolution if it is bound to come anyway? Marx replies: "The revolution does not simply happen; it must be made. Philosophers have only interpreted the world in various ways; our task is to change it."

How is it to be changed? By violence, of course. Marx asserts in his work *The Poverty of Philosophy* that the violent revolutionary appeal is necessary, not merely as a means of overcoming the resistance of the vested interests, but also to effect a psychological alteration of man himself.

The Marxist revolutionary movement, as I have described it, considers religion a rival that must be wiped out or neutralized. Why? Not merely because organized religion defends the status quo and supports the entrenched establishment (the "opium of the people" accusation) but because the revolution will have its best chance of success if men can be inspired to give all they've got for its achievement—if they can be made to feel that without its accomplishment life is not worth living.

Religion, the revolutionaries are convinced, distracts men from the revolutionary all-or-nothing outlook, for it teaches that all is not lost if the new order is not achieved. Both the revolutionary cause and religion demand total consecration, and man cannot serve two masters. The Marxist regards Christianity not just as a superstitious survival but as false science. It is a rival understanding of the nature of men and of the laws of human society.

Moreover, religion is, by its very nature, "other-worldly." Christ said, "My kingdom is not of this world" (John 18:38). Even when it is actively concerned in the promotion of social well-being, the Church's crusade is tempered by the consideration that the final end and the meaning of human existence is to be found in another life. It is this "other-worldly" character that the materialistic Marxist hates.

Church leaders, in a manner and measure different from the revolutionaries, but with no less emphasis, have excoriated current economic injustice. With prophetical indignation, they have castigated the moral disintegration they have seen in the modern world. They agree with the anarchists that a spirit of cooperation and a sense of solidarity have been lacking; that men have grown cynically self-centered; that justice and charity have not flourished in the world.

When the revolutionary declares that if we are going to change things socially for the better, then we will have to have the birth of a new spirit, his plea is strangely like the Christian appeal. Was this not precisely what Vatican Council II called for: a renewal or rebirth of the spirit?

In this sense, Christianity is essentially revolutionary. No follower of Christ can ever be content with the status quo. Indeed, fired by love of neighbor, a Christian can never be satisfied with his environment.

It is true, of course, that the thrust of the Gospel message is otherworldly, but this other-worldliness can never be an excuse for avoiding present responsibilities. The hope for perfect brotherhood must express itself not only in striving for greater love but in seeking to bring about needed reforms in social conditions. Indeed, there can be no genuine renewal of mind and heart without concern for social reform.

Having said this much, let me also say that it is a misunderstanding of the Church's nature to accuse it of infidelity to the Gospel because of its failure to solve the great issues of our day. Christ did not provide a panacea for the problems of society. His followers have no special title to the human wisdom necessary to solve the great problems of the world.

To corroborate this view, I appeal to the life of Christ Himself. Is it irreverent to suggest that Jesus Christ enjoyed no special competence in solving complex social problems? We know He was deeply concerned with the injustice He saw, but did He evidence any special skills in formulating administrative techniques that might have ameliorated the inequities of the Roman tax systems or put an end to the economic conditions that made slavery necessary?

Clergy who speak of salvation only in terms of solving the problems of the social order and who ignore the supernatural dimension of religion are speaking for only half a God. There are limits to what political programs can accomplish. Their effectiveness is generally confined to correcting major economic and social injustices. Is it being trite to observe that the problems of society go much deeper? Prejudice, violence, selfishness, fear, ignorance, and oppression are all grounded in the basic predicament of man. The cause of that predicament is theological, not sociological. The judgment of God on sinful men and their societies cannot be wished away.

The idealism that would do away violence, prejudice, fear, and oppression without reconciling men to God is doomed to failure. Churchmen who serve an idealism that discounts this reality are doing a double disservice. The first disservice is to the Church, by diluting its message. The second disservice is to society, by letting it build great expectations it cannot fulfill. Disappointment and increased bitterness must result.

I have been trying to steer a middle course in this talk between those who would relegate the Church to the sacristy and those who demand that it be a social prophet of unfailing wisdom. I feel it is important to realize that the whole of Christianity does not stand or fall on the Church's contributions to particular social problem. The Lord must be worshipped, and the Gospel preached, no matter what happens in the Middle East, South America, South Africa, or in our urban ghettos. The Church cannot become so identified with a particular cause that its success would justify complacency or its failure apostasy.

There is danger of a sellout to secular interests only when the Church rejects its role as the conscience of those it serves. If it is silent when the world proclaims its own message of salvation through human progress, it betrays Him who alone is the Way. If it encourages men in the belief of a world made perfect through human effort alone, it trades Jerusalem for a tower of Babel. If, in the excitement of helping men live, it forgets to tell them how to die, it abandons Him who is the Resurrection and the Life. Its involvement in the affairs of men can never deliver it from its divine commission to remind men that they stand under God's judgment, that without the grace of God they cannot be saved.

Religion, Secularism, and American Polity
(*The Providence Visitor*, April 15, 1998)

Is America a Christian nation? The Founding Fathers of this country thought it was. James Madison believed that "the duty to obey the Creator takes precedence over the duties owed to civil society." Even Jefferson's "wall of separation" was not envisioned as an end in itself but as a means toward achieving religious freedom. The Establishment Clause was executed to prohibit the federal government from foisting a national religion upon the populace, not to prevent cooperation and interaction between church and state, not to make religion inconsequential, devoid of influence in public affairs.

In six U.S. Supreme Court cases, it was affirmed that America is "Christian," if not in the practice of many citizens, then certainly in its origins and foundation. "We are a Christian people," stated the high court in 1931, "according to one another the equal right of religious freedom and acknowledging with reverence the duty of obedience to the will of God." Our ancestors reverenced religion as a wholesome influence on both private and public morality.

But the friendliness and accommodation to the role of spiritual belief in American life have now turned sharply in legal thinking to hostility toward, and restraint of, religion. Under the aegis of secularism, religion has been forced into a small area of interest and action in the affairs of citizens, with a consequent critical shrinkage of Christian consciousness. The unofficially privileged place that organized religion has traditionally enjoyed in American life has been eroded, often with active judicial effort toward that end.

To corroborate this charge, let me cite a few instances. A federal judge orders a mayor to withdraw a pronouncement of a city's day of prayer against youth violence. A school principal is fired for permitting the reading of a morning prayer over a school's public-address system. Invocations before public-school graduations are forbidden. One wonders if these are sensible expressions of the separation of church and state or deliberate attempts to downgrade religion.

In modern society, the state finds ways of aiding institutions which, even though private, are deemed worthy of survival—hospitals, medical schools, zoos, symphony orchestras, and groups that provide contraceptive and abortion services; yet churches and religious schools almost alone are deprived of such aid, despite the fact that countries—Canada,

Australia, and the Netherlands, for example—have maintained such aid programs for many years without serious ill effect.

What concrete harm can possibly come to the body politic as a result of such aid? This beneficent kind of church-state entanglement contributes to the commonwealth and neither interferes with the full exercise of religion nor deprives churches or religious schools of their independence. Is the separationist clause endangered when a private-school pupil is permitted to use a public-school bus to get to class? Some people may, indeed, object to the use of their taxes for purposes of which they do not approve or in which they do not believe. But given the immense size and complexity of the federal budget, virtually any taxpayer could discover numerous uses of tax money of which he or she morally disapproves.

Who shapes the minds of Americans today? A heterogeneous coterie of journalists, commentators, novelists, liberal professors, actors, jet-set idols, movie and television producers, and especially judges. Under the guise of neutrality, the courts have adopted secularism as their philosophy, understanding secularism first in the narrower sense of rejection of institutional religion and then in the broader sense of making no claim to being guided by the teaching of the historical religions. Not only do public figures now find it unnecessary to claim religious affiliation; in society at large, a professed secularist stance enjoys a prestige equal to that of religious belief.

By the standards of secularism, a man may be a saint in his private life, if he so wishes, but he must keep God and religion out of all that are not strictly his private affairs. Secularism does not compel a person to deny the existence of God; it just asks him to ignore God while engaged in anything of a public nature. It says that for the sake of the community, in which there are different religious viewpoints, harmony can be achieved by silence about spiritual and moral matters. So secularists constantly inveigh against the Religious Right, the Moral Majority, the Christian Coalition, or any organization that attempts to bring religious value to bear on public issues.

Some U.S. Supreme Court justices look upon religion as divisive, as a prejudice, as a bias, and therefore inadmissible in law. For them, the churches are natural enemies of freedom. Justices Hugo Black, Felix Frankfurter, and Chief Justice Warren Burger feared "political division along religious lines," while Justice William O. Douglas regarded organized religion in general and the Catholic Church in particular as actual or potential dangers to the Republic.

Is this, asks social critic Professor James Hitchcock, "an even-handed application of some principle of neutrality so much as it is the enshrining in law of a particular philosophy?"

In an ecumenical age like this, ought disagreement along religious lines be held in peculiar horror? Political divisions along the lines of race, national background, economic status, and gender are more divisive than religious divisions. "It remains unproven," states Hitchcock, "that religious division constitutes a uniquely dangerous threat to political stability and, if it is, that it is of such magnitude as to require systematic vigilance by the courts against it."

Leo Pfeffer, a separationist lawyer, who is convinced that sincere Catholics cannot be good Americans, maintains that all religions, partly as a result of court decisions, are fated to become irresistibly secularized. The slow, gradual process of privatizing religion has resulted, Pfeffer avers, in the courts, having enshrined secular humanism as an official creed.

How then shall we describe the secular mentality? With emphasis on the imperial self and the multiplication of rights, there is no common faith, no common body of principles, no common moral and intellectual discipline, no common culture.

The secular pluralist's view of society bases itself on the double premise that there is no such thing as truth, and that this premise (itself a truth?) guarantees civil peace and prosperity among various pressure groups in society. With values like truth, the moral good, and the political bonum commune steadily relativized and whittled down, what is left is a social and ideological free-for-all hedonism.

Without a consensus of values, how shall Americans work with a common purpose and toward a common goal? This is the dilemma secularism has created. The Christian finds himself in an almost alien world, where Christ the Eternal must surreptitiously gain a hearing in the counsels of a society that was once called Christian.

The secularist approach can give only a partial and misleading solution to the problems of society, for man is not merely a political, social, sexual, or economic unit. Secularism obscures the truth of this higher dignity and purpose. That is why we must go beyond politics, beyond economics, beyond sociology, beyond psychology to theology, for it is only in their theological setting that man, society, the sciences that serve mankind, and the woes that beset it can be properly understood.

As we approach the new millennium, the words of General MacArthur at the surrender of Japan deserve to be seared into the mind of every American:

"The problem basically is theological and involves a spiritual recrudescence and improvement of human character that will synchronize with our almost matchless advance in science, art, literature, and all material and cultural developments of the past 2,000 years. It must be of the spirit if we are to save the flesh."

The Devil Is Thriving in American Society
(*The Cowl*, April 10, 1990)

The ritual slayings at a ranch in Matamoros, Texas, the growing fascination with witchcraft, the founding of the First Satanist Church in San Francisco with its cannibalistic rites, Black Masses, and the inevitable nude altar-girl (or rather girl-altar)—all seem to herald a revival of Devil worship.

Many people view Satan as simply a personification of evil, a figure of speech, a prosopopoeia. Freud, with dogmatic sureness, states: "The Devil is nothing but the incarnation of repressed anal impulses." Theologian Karl Barth defines Satan as "confusion and nothingness" the absolute opposite of creation.

The media often portray the Devil as a bogeyman; a horned or cloven-hoofed monster; an innocuous, clownlike, long-tailed, red-tighted figment; a sinister, stylishly dressed rogue, attractive and charming, but all the more dangerous for that. Yet Jesuit Karl Rahner warns against the untheological levity that regards Satan and his cohort as a band of "hobgoblins knocking about the world."

The Devil is "the father of lies" (a deceiver) and reputedly his cleverest deception is persuading people he does not exist. For Jews and Christians, Satan and other demons are real persons, fallen angels permanently in rebellion against God, intelligent, cunning and spiteful spirits who revel in harming and seducing humans.

Sacred Scripture is full of references to the Devil. To explain away Satan is to explain away a good deal of the Old and New Testaments, giving psychological interpretations to Christ's exorcisms and otherwise distorting the record. Demythologizers of Satan claim that in talking about demons, Jesus merely accommodated himself to the language of his hearers, a language devoid of words to describe psychic phenomena.

The Prince of Darkness can take human form (some saw Hitler as Satan incarnate), but he can also cloak himself under the guise of corporate personalities and institutions. This idea of a general obsession, occult and invisible, or of a collective, political, and social possession, helps explain more easily the rarity of individual diabolic possessions in contemporary society.

In this view, Satan no longer appears as a personage, an isolated figure, but rather as an essence insinuating itself craftily into the structures of certain nations or corporations, corrupting them with the sin of pride.

How else account for the monstrous evil that spawned the genocides of the Armenians, Ukrainians, Jews, and Cambodians?

In spite of the present fascination with the Devil, Catholics and liberal Protestants are today downgrading his influence. The Roman Ritual still retains the rite of exorcism, but it is rarely used. The Church has dropped the minor order of exorcist, and few dioceses keep a record of diabolical possession.

Sorcerers have always boasted of employing secret tricks (incantations, divinations, spells, sacrifices, amulets, philters, charms, etc.) to bend the Devil to their will, to manipulate him to use his unearthly power for their selfish purposes. Seeking the protection of Satan, the Matamoros drug-smuggling ring propitiated him by human sacrifice. "Black witches" use black magic to invoke the Devil; "white witches—a non-diabolical cult that traces its origins to prehistoric times—practice ancient cabala. Before subsiding into Vatican-imposed silence, Dominican friar Matthew Fox demanded (in a full-page New York Times ad) that White Witchcraft be included in ecumenism. Augustine compares Satan to a chained dog, ferocious and menacing, but he can bite only those who rashly come within the compass of the chain.

Amid the mixture of folly and error, of what is grotesque and absurd, the diabolic note threads its way through the Judeo-Christian tradition. The Devil is a power of the world insofar as he turns man against God and tempts man to evil. What matters most to Americans believers and nonbelievers is the impact of Satanism on the common good. Devil worship may be dismissed as a bad joke, but human sacrifice and other abominations are no joking matter.

The young are mesmerized by the occult. It is up to parents, clergy, and educators to inculcate that sense of personal responsibility which prevents youth from ever saying "The Devil made me do it."

(6)
Catholicism and the Catholic Church

Call Me Catholic *First*
(*The Providence Journal*, September 21, 1992)

In the flap over Bishop Gelineau's pastoral advice to Catholic politicians about abortion, a state senator remarked: "I may be a Catholic, but I am an American first."

This utterance was meant to be an expression of patriotism, but actually the senator suffered a double misunderstanding. He did not, first of all, understand what it is to be a Catholic. But—and this may be more serious for the community—he did not fully understand what it is to be an American. For it is the very essence of being an American that it always comes second.

Don't get me wrong: Certainly, loyalty to one's country transcends any tribal claim or rival political claim. But a man can be loyal to his country only being loyal to himself. An American is a Jew, a Protestant, a Catholic, or an unbeliever. We do not ask him, as a citizen, to be—or to act like—anything but what he is. If I am a Catholic, I believe certain things; I know I have obligations to God, to myself, and to my fellow man. The obligations come first with me. It is with the understanding that they come first—or, in other words, by agreement that I can act in accordance with my conscience—that I have the privileges of American citizenship.

The state does not ask me to believe what I know to be false, or to act in a way I believe to be wrong before God. It takes me as I am, with my faith, my beliefs, convictions, and sense of moral obligations. Another man may have another faith, other beliefs, convictions, a different sense of obligations. These things come first with him. In our country, the state does not pretend to make a judgment between us. It takes us as we are and is content to come second in our lives. The senator who said, "I may be a Catholic, but I am an American first," missed not one point, but two.

Thomas Aquinas avers that the state has no right to the whole man, only to the part by which he is a citizen. In other activities, man is free, master of himself, his time, his association and his interests.

Paul Blanshard questioned whether Catholicism was compatible with

American democracy. The question itself betrays a misunderstanding of democracy. If there is a question, it should be: Is democracy compatible with Catholicism (or any other widely held belief of our people)? The answer of course is yes. But in its Blanshardian form the very question must be rejected by every American who places demands of conscience first.

American citizens are not asked to subordinate their religion to politics, or to divest themselves of religion whenever they act in a political way. Politics should conform to religion, not religion to politics. Otherwise, political law would be above the religious, which is the same as saying that man is above God.

The Catholic who is a politician believes in certain truths. Some truths he accepts because he is rationally convinced of them: the tenets of natural law, for instance, or the concept of man as a rational animal capable of grasping truth and being responsible to God for his acts, or the idea of the family as the basic unit of society. Other truths the Catholic politician believes because God is good and has given him the gift of faith—the Incarnation, the Resurrection, the divine origin of the Church, the doctrine of the Mystical Body, the role of Mary in the redemption of mankind.

In the first case, the Catholic politician's beliefs are based on human wisdom and refer to those things with which, as a citizen, he is primarily concerned. In the second case, his beliefs are reached through divine wisdom and refer to supernatural realities and mysteries. The Catholic politician will not try to force acceptance of these supernatural beliefs upon others by any means—and especially not by political means. He will not try to do the work of the Holy Spirit with a ballot. But in the first case—pertaining to those beliefs that derive from natural wisdom, from study, human insight and experience—he will certainly try to give voice to them as a Catholic politician.

For most believers, the theological argument against abortion is decisive. For others seeking truth, the natural law argument, philosophers believe, is quite persuasive. Much of the abortion debate today is ambiguous and inconclusive because it consists of nothing more than assertions and counter-assertions. The Catholic politician has an obligation to articulate the moral argument against abortion, using the findings of biological science, history, the tenets of religious traditions, and research concerning the nature of right, personhood's privacy, responsibility, and the role of the state in protecting life. Whenever a living sense of connection between reason and morality is absent, public moral argument degenerates into petty name calling—cacophony—shouting past one another. In such circumstances, even disagreements become difficult to define, for disagreement implies some mutual understanding of the points of reference for debate.

The Catholic politician who says, "Abortion is wrong, but people ought to have the right to choose," is copping out on his obligation to educate his constituency and to right what is wrong. The claim of freedom to choose is plausible only when the range of choices does not include socially, morally, or legally inadmissible acts. Abraham Lincoln, in debating Stephen Douglas, exclaimed, "No man has the right to choose to do evil." The question is not whether abortion is a choice, but whether it is an evil choice.

Ultimately, the abortion question will be resolved only when a moral consensus of the community is attained. This consensus will be arrived at only through a long process of inquiry, debate, and compromise. Since direct and unqualified appeals to Scripture, Church law, or religious doctrine have no place in civil discourse, appeals to the natural-law tradition of the nation ought to carry weight with an educated citizenry.

If moral consensus is ever reached simply by counting noses—a majoritarian notion of public morality—then political leaders are obliged to subject the credentials of such a consensus to constant critical examination, rational testing, and to an evaluation of its effect on political order and the common good.

Catholic Identity and the Second Vatican Council
(Speech at Salva Regina College, February 7, 1978)

This talk is part of the 150th anniversary celebration of St. Mary's Parish, Newport. Anniversaries are a cause of jubilation. The Book of Leviticus (15:8-11) tells us why we should rejoice. The Lord said, "And thou shall sanctify the fiftieth year ... for it is the year of jubilee." So the Israelites took God at his word. The fiftieth year was set aside as a time to reaffirm Jewish identity—a time to live it up in song and mirth and celebration; a time, moreover, to thank God for leading the chosen people into the Promised Land. Sadness was to be banished; joy was to prevail. Debts were blotted out; enemies were reconciled. A happy spirit of peace on earth, good will towards men filled the hearts of all.

This explains why St. Mary's has good reason to rejoice for the 150 years devoted to the worship of God. But isn't it ironical that we celebrate this anniversary at the very time when the Church itself seems to be coming apart at the seams. Good Pope John XXIII opened the window to let in some fresh air; instead he let in a hurricane. Whichever way we look, the Catholic world we know seems to be turned upside down. The pope is derided for being hopelessly out of date, heresy parades under the guise of theological speculation, Canon Law is hooted as Pharisaic legalism, conscience is appealed to, as if it were formed in a vacuum apart from the teaching guidance of the Church. On every side, we see the Church in crisis, in revolt, in upheaval. The prophets of doom proclaim this as her last agony and Catholics ask in bewilderment, "What is the Church coming to?" Some outside the Church ask the same question. Malcolm Muggeridge, neither Catholic nor Christian, but well-known for his penetrating, if not always fair, criticism of the contemporary scene, has this to say:

> *The historian, looking back on our century, would be astonished that the Roman Catholic Church, having witnessed the ruinous consequences to its Protestant rivals of compounding with contemporary trends, should now seem to be following a like course ...*
>
> *The Roman Catholic Church is the only remaining, as it has been far and away the strongest, bastion of Christianity. If it is now (as seems to be the case) in the process of succumbing to the siren voices of material and fleshly well-being wafted across the Atlantic, then the game is finally up. ...*

> *A light will have gone out which will have illuminated all our lives, shone through art and literature of a long civilization, and served to hold at bay, if only fitfully and inadequately, the wild appetites to gorge and dominate which afflict all our hearts.*

We should all be quite clear that nothing of the sort is happening. The Church is engaged in an often agonizing effort to understand itself better and to cut away what is superfluous, but only so that the world may know her for what she is: the fair bride of Christ, the mystery of God's dealing with men, the great sacramental reality of Christ's abiding presence on this earth, the new Israel and the heir of the promises made to Abraham and to David. The Vatican Council was not trying to "de-supernaturalize" religion; it was seeking the means to present the living reality of the mercy of God in such a way that somehow, someday, all men will know their home is in the Mystical Body of Jesus Christ.

The Church, as Cardinal Newman said, is not a paper Church; it is not a theory that men have tried to make real. It is, on the contrary, a reality that men must try to understand. Without this effort, we will not be properly equipped to be a Christian in the world. As Pope Paul VI said in his encyclical *Ecclesiam Suam*: "The Church needs to reflect on herself. She needs to feel the throb of her own life. She must learn to know herself better, if she wishes to live her own proper vocation and to offer to the world her message of brotherhood and salvation."

Fifty years ago, I was an altar boy at St. Pius Church, Providence. At Christmastime, the curate gave the altar boys a little automatic pencil with a legend stamped on the barrel. The legend read: "I bear the title, Catholic, most honored name on earth!" The pencil is long since lost and gone, and so is the triumphalism it epitomized. Yet, at the time, it did not seem either outrageous or pathetic. It meant you stood for something and were proud of it. For when I was growing up, Catholics did not doubt that the Church was the Rock of Peter; that it was the truth, and had the truth; and that those outside, although they might have the greatest good will and sincerity, were, nonetheless, wandering in darkness.

We must have vexed our non-Catholic brethren, because we comported ourselves as if we owned the very ground we walked on, since that ground was paid for in full by the fallen blood of Jesus Christ. Our heads were held high, our manner was serene and confident. We behaved like the elect of God, for we were ever conscious of the gift of faith which lifted us above the motley ragtag of sects and schisms.

But this old view, we have come to see, was narrowminded and tinged with a religiously monopolistic outlook, a view not completely consonant with the full message of Christ. But instead of trying to modify and clarify this viewpoint, critics of the Church, or should I say "detractors," have gone to the grotesque extreme of rejecting her claim of speaking with the voice of Christ, and have even denied that she is the prolongation in time of the life and work of our Divine Master.

Indeed, the Church we love has become a public whipping boy. She is assailed for being corrupt, authoritarian, bureaucratic, rigid, irrelevant, and one ex-priest, out-judasing Judas from the rostrum of a Catholic college campus, screeches that the "institutional" Church—pope, cardinals, bishops, priests, and laity—can all "go to Hell."

In the context of this revolutionary situation, the question arises, "Why bother being a Catholic?" The answer to this question is crucial for every parishioner of St. Mary's and every Catholic. It strikes at the very core of your life. Who are you? Do you want to be the kind of person and parishioner you have been for the past fifty years? Should you change your style and teach your children to conduct themselves according to standards different from those you have followed?

This is a decision intimately personal—a decision that affects your very identity as a Catholic. That identity governs your reactions to life itself. Why? Because it has to do with such questions as: What does God want of me? What is my role in the mission of the Church? What values should I live by and promote in my family and in society?

Perhaps the question: "Why bother being a Catholic?" has to be answered by each person on his own terms. And since few of us command expert knowledge in the areas directly at issue—not being for the most part ecclesiologists, biblical scholars, dogmatic, moral, sacramental or what-have-you kinds of theologians—that means that we have to answer the question out of our own experience, our experience as men and as believers. What I shall have to say represents that sort of response. It does not claim to be backed up by any expertise in theology or philosophy, nor does it draw particularly on the fields of education and psychology where I claim a professional competence.

The first point I want to make is that this question is a fundamentally important one, for it has to do with personal identity. None of us is "just a man or woman." We are all particular kinds of persons—and the kind of man we are, or who we are, is defined by a number of specific qualities. Such qualities, for example, are sex, age, family status (father, husband, etc.), race, nationality, language, profession, social position and so on.

Among other qualities or aspects of personal identity, religion looms very large if we understand religion to encompass that aspect of our identity that has to do with such ultimate questions as the existence of God, His communication with man, the foundation of a Church, as well as ethical convictions about good and evil, the sort of life a man should live and the values society should promote. Therefore, the answer to the question "Why bother being a Catholic?" is profoundly important because it touches the very core of our being and determines the values we chase after in our pursuit of happiness.

Secondly, I would argue that the choice is not between being a Catholic and being simply fully a human, or even between being a Catholic and being fully a Christian. The choice is not between some sort of narrow identity (Catholic) and a completely open-ended or un-differentiated or universal human identity. All are particular kinds of men, and if we cease to be Catholics, we will inevitably become some other particular kind of person in respect to our views on the fundamental questions to which Catholicism gives us answers.

Obviously, we cannot enter into any analysis of this. But the general point is that one does not liberate himself from questions as to the ultimate meaning of the world and of life by ceasing to be a Catholic. To give answers to these questions, or to refuse to give them, is to take a position that excludes other possibilities. Being "completely open" is not, in my opinion, a meaningful alternative to being a Catholic.

My next general point is that it is quite possible that one might arrive at the position that it is not worthwhile being a Catholic anymore merely as a result of drift rather than deliberate choice. In a period of upheaval such as the present—one that tends to muddle things previously thought settled, and to discredit one's earlier beliefs and self-image—the very temper of the times might cause one to lose interest, to grow slack, not to care so much anymore. Hence a man might wake up some morning to find that, for all intents and purposes, he really wasn't what he used to be, that he had become a different person religiously without ever consciously deciding to be different. Then the question "Why bother being a Catholic?" would be "irrelevant" because it wouldn't really apply any longer.

But should questions like this be settled by drift? Drifting in these matters is really slipping into the unexamined life by slow and easy stages, and Socrates said, "The unexamined life is not worth living." The religious aspect of one's identity is usually given by tradition and upbringing, but unlike some other aspects (such as sex or race) it can be changed by conscious choice. And it is so important an aspect that, it seems to me, it should be changed by deliberate choice if it is going to be changed at all.

Drifting is, of course, much easier than taking thought and making choices about who we are and who we want to be. It requires a crisis of some sort to jar us into this painful kind of personal choice. (Consider, by way of analogy, the sort of situations that cause people to decide to change their nationality.) As a general thing I do not think the human personality can stand crisis choices much of the time. But if crises do confront us—and each man must decide for himself—then they do, and we must make the best of it.

Religious crises, however, tend to focus our thinking along lines which, although they are inevitable, strike me as unhealthy, or at least as very apt to take a direction that easily becomes unhealthy. This result follows from the fact that we find ourselves centering our attention upon ourselves. Instead of focusing on the object of our faith, we find ourselves attending more and more to our subjective reactions. We begin asking: Do I really believe in God? Is my act of faith "authentic?" Am I being "honest" in telling myself that I accept the wafer at Communion as embodying Christ really present? Do I experience a feeling of "true community" at Mass? Are not my prayers mere pretense? Am I not using faith as a crutch? Should I not be more "mature" in confronting my doubts? Is not my whole religion a "churchy" refuge, an excuse for my failure to go out into the "secular city" and fight against the evils of the system?

One cannot avoid questions like these at the present. And if a person does not pose them to himself, there are many around us who draw our attention to them insistently. But while we must confront them, it is, in my opinion, profoundly unchristian to dwell on them exclusively or to raise them to the level of the first priority and continuous concern. It is unchristian because it makes the self the principal object of our religious consciousness. This is the worst form of idolatry; for it is God and the things of God that demand the attention and devotion of the religious person, not the honesty of his or her own motives or the quality of his or her own feelings.

Neither is it the way to arrive at firmness of faith, solidarity of commitment, or purity of intention always to be cross-examining ourselves as to our assurance that we possess them. Indeed, deliberate self-analysis of a mental state is the surest way to destroy the mental state that is the object of analysis. How many fewer happy marriages would we have if all husbands and wives constantly interrogated themselves and each other with such "hard questions" as: Do we really have a happy marriage? Are you sure you wouldn't be better off with someone else? Do you honestly mean it when you say I am beautiful? Is our love authentic and fully human?

This is not to deny that much of the general ferment in the Catholic Church is due to a change in perspective. Since the Council, the Church is in process of moving toward a larger understanding, and practical recognition, of the rights and prerogatives of individual freedom and initiative. It is moving from a morality of conformity to one of creative responsibility.

The individual person has, to be sure, always had a central place in Catholic thought. It is the individual person who is created and loved by God and called to eternal life. But although the importance of the individual in the eyes of God has always been recognized, one's vocation as an individual in this life and in relation to temporal structures has not been equally appreciated. One's role was thought to be that of conforming to the will of God as manifested in the given structures of nature and society. Individual initiative and responsibility were played down in favor of obedience and submission.

The Second Vatican Council, however, has taken a new tack. Without elaborating a wholly new philosophy, indeed without being explicitly aware of all the implications of its new stance, it has accepted from contemporary culture the idea of human intelligence as fundamentally creative. The norm for human behavior is not the world as it is, but as intelligent love can make it; not conformity but social reconstruction, both inside and outside the Church, is the order of the day. Man's responsibility extends to the very shape of society; he is called to be a reformer. And since the passage from one state of affairs to another requires the intervention of critical intelligence and individual initiative, the individual person has newly come into his own.

This is what lies behind the new personalism and worldliness manifested in the decrees of Vatican II. This is also why so much stress has been placed upon the need for dialogue between the various elements within the Church and between the Church herself and the world.

Man is viewed as involved in a process of creative interaction with the world, a process which in the measure it is illuminated by human intelligence can give rise to genuinely new and ever more satisfactory meanings. Henceforth, doing the will of God is inseparable from the intelligent re-making of prevailing institutions.

The effect of the new spirit in the Church on all this would be hard to overestimate. It has switched the outlook and activity on the parish level and has practically turned the seminaries upside down. For it must be remembered that what is going on in the Catholic Church today is not simply the imposition of a new orientation from on high; this new spirit is not simply the result of a new set of rules. It results, rather, from a new experiential grasp by all levels of the Church, but especially by the younger elements within it, of the inadequacy of the former stance in the contemporary world. What Vatican II did was to recognize in principle this inadequacy and to sanction the search for new forms.

It is one thing, however, simply to reject old patterns and styles; it is quite another to find a viable way of getting along without them. It is easy enough to say that isolation is "out" and involvement, intellectual and practical, is "in"; that religious formation, and parochial life can no longer be conceived simply in terms of conformity but must allow full scope for individual initiative and responsibility. But it is not so easy to see what all this means in practice. The difficulty here is the one of devising a new and positive concept of Catholic life and service.

This, indeed, is the dilemma confronting the Catholic Church today. The sweeping rejection of widespread and fixed patterns as essential to Catholic life and practice, with little experience to go on of something else that religion might mean, is resulting for many in the adoption of an individualistic humanism as the only alternative. The extreme of objectivism is being replaced by an extreme subjectivism. What is needed is some way of moving beyond both these extremes, a way of achieving genuine communal solidarity without subordinating individual persons to structures, and a way of achieving a genuine personalism (with its respect for the creative initiative of individuals) without the dissolution of community.

Community in the Church is being conceived in more dynamic terms than heretofore, less as a state and more as a process. Vatican II has dropped the notion of the Church as a perfect society and reemphasized its scriptural description as the pilgrim people of God. The unity of this people does not consist in their dedication or adherence to a common structure, but in their faithful service to a Lord Who is beyond all structures. They come together to celebrate His name Who is the unifying focus of the whole order of persons, in Whose love they are united to one another as persons, and Whose service consists in the intelligent remaking of the world in His image (which is that of personal community).

What is new here is that the notion of creative intelligence is being introduced explicitly into the context of community life and is itself being interpreted in communal and processive terms. The intelligent thing to do in a given situation (i.e., what God expects of us as intelligent creatures) is no longer that simply which authority prescribes, nor that merely which some individual takes it into his head to do. It is rather that which is intelligently arrived at through a process of dialogue and discussion by the community as a whole. Liturgy and dialogue thus become the two key notions in the new orientation: the celebration together of the common focus of our personal energies, and the continual interaction of those energies for the purpose of improvising an ever more adequate response to the various situations in which the community finds itself.

Catholic life, therefore, no longer means the adoption of a codified system of regulations. It is rather to participate in a common commitment (whose structures and instrumentalities are to be devised—and revised—along the way) to the continual promotion of human community. In this connection, the notion of authority in the Church is being re-interpreted along more scriptural lines. It is being viewed less as a matter of controlling power and more in terms of a service of unity, a kind of catalyst of concord and consensus, that in and through which the members of the community can think their relationship to one another and articulate a common course.

In the context of these changing emphases brought about by the Second Vatican Council, St. Mary's Parish on this 150th anniversary faces its "moment of truth." It stands eyeball to eyeball with its future. What that future will be, I cannot say. I am no prophet. But I do say this: Whatever trials the Catholic Church faces today, she has faced and overcome yesterday; and what made our fathers strong in faith and practice should not find us timid and insecure. We are not Pollyannas, nor are we pessimists; we are simply Christians, with a confidence rooted in the recognition that men and events pass, God and His work endure.

That is why we reserve the right to question the spiritual soundness, the doctrinal integrity, as well as the intellectual acumen of those who perpetually cry havoc or proclaim the spiritual bankruptcy of the Church, and their disillusionment with the Ecumenical Council. The authentic, sober, yet radiant spirit of the Church is more perfectly echoed in the words pronounced by the late Cardinal Feltin of Paris. He said: "We Christians are more optimistic than all others, even though we recognize the vast errors of which human nature is capable. We are not utopians, but we know that grace is stronger than sin."

The same spirit of Christian optimism animated the valiant Pope Pius XI when he thanked God that he lived in times of such trouble and testing, that it was no longer possible for a Christian to be mediocre. This was the spirit of holy Pope John the XXIII, and it is the same spirit that inspires Pope Paul VI and gives him the courage to carry on.

We who believe in the Church in the midst of her present trials feel that because it is the divine ideal it has recuperative power now, as it has been shown to have such power in the past. Christ expected weakness and failure in the Church. He likened it to a field, full of wheat and weeds. There never has been a time, in the long history of the Church, when it did not need reformation and new inspiration. Its history is the story of a long struggle with a weak membership. But, somehow, it has served its purpose.

Indeed, even as a human institution, one cannot feel that the Church is a failure. After all, we can see an effect upon the general life of its members which, far as it falls short of what we desire, is greater than the results effected by any other institution. We forget how great has been this general advance. It has affected our social life as well as our personal life, our national life, our spiritual life. Its influence for the good is incalculable.

Do you want the answer to the question, "Why bother being a Catholic?" Then focus your eyes on the lives of those who lived and died in this parish. They wore their faith like a medal of honor. They were deeply conscious that they were members of the Body of Christ, that this Body is complete only when each of us is playing his part, that we affect each other by what we say and do, that all of us together form his Body, and that we are all, therefore, profoundly interrelated. It is this sense of identity with the Church that we all need to cultivate. Renewal cannot succeed without it. Any parish runs downhill when this identity is lost.

We have enough of "Why doesn't the Church do something" type of Catholic. We need "more of the kind of Catholic who says, "The Church can act only if I act in and through her." Indeed, each one of us should be willing to say, "This is my Church, the Church I love. If it does not accomplish its full mission, I hold myself, in part, responsible. I feel within myself an urgency to make myself, by the way I live and act, a more authentic living witness to Christ and His Church to the world."

With this kind of spirit, St. Mary's, like the Church itself, will forge ahead in the future years. In spite of present upheavals, we shall witness a sunrise, not a sunset; a second spring, not an autumn; a rebirth of fresh life ever springing up anew, because we have unshakeable certitude that "if these works be of man, they will run their course and have their end; if they be of God, no power on earth can overthrow them!"

Why bother being a Catholic? In closing, I can only say again that every person must ask himself, from his own experience whether criticisms against the Church ring true, whether they touch on the validity of the religion he professes. Everybody must confront the present situation—the changes which disturb some people, the dissatisfaction with Church authority, the new approaches and all the rest—in the light of his own experience. Has he personally known in his life in the Church such a degree of crushing authoritarianism, institutional blindness, and spiritual irrelevance that it outweighs other considerations? Can he find a religion that brings him more satisfactorily in touch with the divine, that teaches him better to understand himself, that urges upon him higher ideals, that holds out a more transcendent hope to man and society and offers better promise of correcting its defects as it goes along? If he cannot reply to those questions affirmatively then "Why bother being a Catholic?" is answered for him by St. Peter, when asked: "Lord, to whom shall we go? Thou has the words of everlasting life."

Ignoring the Saints Is a Sad Commentary on Modern Culture
(*The Providence Visitor*, December 3, 1992)

Enter any Catholic bookshop 25 years ago and you would see shelf after shelf devoted to lives of the saints. Today, those same shelves, if you can find a Catholic bookshop, will be filled with books on sociology of religion, on Zen, Catholic feminism, and social issues of the day.

The fact is that the cult of the saints (Our Lady included) is dying from devotional malnutrition. A whole generation of Catholics has grown up never having heard of the great and little saints gracing the Church's calendar. Indeed, the very idea of sanctity—the striving to grow in knowledge and love of God—is itself looked upon as an endeavor championed only by weirdos and zealots.

Don't blame Vatican Council II for consigning God's holy ones to devotional limbo. In no uncertain terms, the council stated that saints have an inside track with the Lord. They provide models of Christian living at its best and are to be prayed to for help we need.

How, then explain the present plight of saintly veneration? Two reasons stand out. First, people today tend to equate mental health with sanctity. Second, ethical and political secularists contend that traditional Christian virtues are at best inward-looking and irrelevant to the real problems of life, and at worst are the reinforcers of an unjust social system.

The past generation has witnessed a strong push to "psychiatrize" religion and to "spiritualize" psychotherapy much to the detriment of what is unique and irreplaceable in both. Not that religion cannot serve a therapeutic end. It sometimes alleviates emotional disturbances more effectively than tranquilizers. So can music. But it is not as medicine that they enrich life. Popular opinion, however, makes it easy to confuse spiritual fulfillment with the secular by-product of emotional equilibrium.

Neurosis is mistakenly viewed as a moral failing—which, in turn, is rooted in spiritual shortcomings. Carl Jung confessed that he never treated a patient over 35 whose problem in the last resort was not "finding a religious outlook on life." But psychological peace of mind is quite different from the biblical peace that "passeth all understanding." Religion need not divorce itself from personal and social welfare, but it ought not be reduced to a device for achieving the goals of morality, politics, or art.

The priestly ministry is a calling in itself, not amateur psychotherapy or social work.

Indeed, mental health is the point of departure for sanctity, not its destination. Nobody can love God if he hates himself. Nobody can attain peace of soul when in conflict of psyche. Nobody can be spiritually whole when psychologically crippled. It is not that religion makes us healthy, wealthy, or wise, that a healthy, wealthy, and wise personality finds channels to express religion. Religion begins where therapy leaves off, or rather, religion works through what health is given us.

Traditionally, saints belong to that group of God-inspired persons who seek perfection, subscribing to the Lord's words: "Be ye perfect, as your heavenly Father is perfect." This call to perfection, of its very nature, demands asceticism.

But penance and mortification are concepts alien to the modern mind. The very idea of saying no to oneself in the interest of something higher is construed as a sure way of producing inhibitions, complexes, hypocrisy, self-deception, and breakdowns. In this perspective, perfection or holiness, with its penitential aspect, becomes a block or burden to the flowering of human nature. People who are attracted to the message of Christ do not want to end up less than human, turned into individuals who are cold, forbidding, and austere with very little that is lovable about them in any ordinary sense of the word. So they embrace Christ's teaching on love and reject his hard sayings about sacrifice and self-denial.

The quest for holiness involves risk. The effort to love and serve God has at times produced crackpots and fanatics; it has also produced saints—saints who practiced mortification without warping their psyches. To suggest that a saintly lifestyle puts a crimp in one's humanity or that saints are less human than sinners is to deny the evidence of history.

The accusation that saintliness is useless or socially harmful has a lengthy history. Humility, patience, and forgiveness are said to be connected with an outmoded, pietistic, and inward-looking vision of Christianity; a Christianity that is ill-equipped to deal with the great issues of war and peace, of nuclear disarmament and starvation on a worldwide scale.

We are told that the Church's concentration on the virtues of the weak—patience, meekness, and long-suffering—has resulted in generations of Catholics who are more interested in themselves than the world in which they live. We are told it has produced Catholics who are timid and irresolute when faced with the challenges of modern life, Catholics who have used their faith to band together so as to hide and defend themselves against the harsh demands of a real world.

German philosopher Friedrich Nietzsche made the same charge, accusing Christians of teaching slave virtues of patience, forgiveness, and respect for others, not because these virtues help humans strive for the good, but because they hobble the strong and make the world safer for the weak.

This misinterprets what Christianity is all about. Verily, Catholics are "other-worldly," for we are wanderers and sojourners, and "here we have no abiding city." Perhaps, for a time, there may be more fun without the four last things. But what is Catholicism without death, judgment, heaven, and hell? Whatever it is, it is not Catholicism.

The modern mentality confuses gentleness and love with weakness and ineffectiveness. But when the chips are down, and harsh reality has to be faced and surmounted, it is the saints of God who are tough, who do not succumb, who ultimately overcome.

Our age may have little time for sanctity, but that is a judgment on our age, not on the saints.

Catholics Obligated to Become a Political Force
(*The Providence Visitor*, July 15, 1999)

All of us are involved in government and politics. Nobody can hold himself aloof from politics because all of us are affected by its processes. If you are a student or teacher, an employer or employee; if you are ticketed for parking or speeding; if you are concerned about housing for the elderly or food for the poor; if you fill out an income tax form, you are in some way involved with government or politics.

Every time you see a policeman or fireman in operation, or see a school, or read about your government using taxpayers' money for roads, housing, bridges, or recreational facilities, you are watching government in action. There is no human activity in our modern society in which the impact of government is not felt. Government is all around you. If a citizen says he doesn't want to get involved in politics, then he doesn't know what he's talking about because he's already involved whether he likes it or not.

Our Lord, Jesus Christ, bears witness to the importance of politics and government when he said, "Whose is the coin of tribute? ... Render unto Caesar the things that are Caesar's." He went so far as to choose a government official, one of the despised tax collectors, as the apostle who became St. Matthew. He himself ate with so-called publicans, i.e., public officials, while others scorned to associate with those who were identified with politics and government.

Catholics should never have qualms about influencing the political situation. Observe how actors and actresses manipulate the media for political purposes. They are active in fundraising for political parties and are frequently advocates for abortion, same-sex marriage, environmentalism, the homosexual agenda, euthanasia, assisted suicide, and a host of other causes. If show people can be politically aggressive in the cultural war now being waged in America, why should Catholics be shrinking violets?

Catholic activity in politics has its roots in the Christian Gospel teaching of justice, love, and service on behalf of our fellow man, especially to those who are in need. This means that Catholics are obligated to speak out in the cause of justice and love. "Evil triumphs when good men do nothing." Injustice flourishes when the citizens keep silent. Silence is not golden; it is yellow. An old Hungarian proverb puts it succinctly: "If you are among robbers and you are silent, you are a robber yourself."

The silent majority, by being silent, lets the vocal minority take over. In fact, the silent majority sat by and saw Jesus crucified. The silent majority permitted the Reign of Terror in the French Revolution. The silent majority watched as Christians were burned at the stake. The silent majority sneered when Patrick Henry pleaded: "Is life so dear, or peace so sweet, as to be purchased at the price of chains and slavery?" The silent majority watched as the street demonstrations in Germany were taken over by a little, unknown paper hanger and corporal named Adolph Hitler.

There are times when every Catholic, according to his conscience, must break silence, get noisy, get informed, get involved, get ready. He must join hands with those of good will, participate in social-action groups, collaborate with other Christian churches that share our scale of values, be active in any organization—whether it be a PTA or political party—that will help promote the cause of social justice.

Today, politicians do not worry about the Catholic vote. In spite of their large numbers, Catholics are considered by candidates for political office as a small, insignificant minority in post-Christian America. A citizenry that tolerates presidential adultery with a shrug, that greets partial-birth abortion with a yawn, and that sympathizes with killing by assisted suicide, holds positions contrary to some of Catholicism's basic beliefs. Catholics must form a counter-culture or lose their chance of shaping the American consensus.

Indeed, Catholics could learn a lesson from their Jewish brethren. Although Jews comprise perhaps two percent of the population, they have more clout than Catholics who number over twenty-five percent. The key difference is that the Jewish vote is a bloc vote. Politicians know this. They understand the power that can be wielded by a small number of voters willing and able to act as a swing vote, ready to turn against politicians who refuse to uphold the values they prize. No politician worries about the vegetarian vote, but he does worry about committed minorities much more than he worries about larger amorphous groups.

When abortion was legalized, American bishops responded to this decision with vehemence: "The Supreme Court has declared that the unborn child is not a person in the terms of the Fourteenth Amendment. We reject this decision. Its orders completely lack judicial force. No one is obliged to obey this civil law."

Never before in the history of the American Church has the leadership of American Catholics proclaimed, "We shall not serve."

It is time for Catholics to exercise their voting muscle. Catholic voters should not be Democrats or Republicans first, or union members or free-traders, or affirmative-action or no-quota folks; they should be, above all, Catholics. Regardless of how much they are in agreement with a candidate over tax, trade, or foreign policy, if that candidate is perceived as hostile to Christian values, he should not get Catholic backing.

The Clerical Line Separating Church and State
(*The Providence Visitor*, March 25, 2004)

By ordering priests to refrain from accepting any partisan political post, Pope John Paul II declared to the world that the Gospel and the Church's social teaching are not tied to any political party, but offer a global perspective, a total vision of the human person and human progress.

This does not mean that the pope is opposed to, or is turning away, from social activism. If he did so, he would be rejecting the prescriptions of the Second Vatican Council. Indeed, in turning its attention from its own juridical structure to a pastoral concern for all mankind, the Church, through its council, demonstrated a willingness to learn from the world as well as speak to the world.

The pope could rightfully be accused of betraying his mission if he proclaimed a Gospel devoid of economic, social, cultural, and political implications. In practice, such a stance would imply complicity with the established order and the *status quo*.

On the other hand, the pope warns against the opposite temptation: to think of a particular political party as indispensable to the fulfillment of the Church's mission. To yield to this temptation is to equate the Christian message with a specific group in society and put the Gospel in a subordinate position to a political platform or philosophy.

Following conciliar advice, bishops have been urging priests to engage in advanced study. With this growing professionalization, priests are found in all kinds of work beyond the ministerial. The Church, however, refuses to identify itself or its clergy with partisan politics or a specific ideology. Instruct and inspire politicians with principles of social justice, Vatican II urges priests, but the realm of politics is more properly the special care and concern of the laity.

In stressing this traditional view, the pope does not intend to send priests back to the sacristy nor restrict them to the role of acting merely as back-room boys or as the Army Supply Corps to the laity. Rather, he is trying to strike a proper balance between the theocentric orientation of man (his vertical dimensions) and his anthropomorphic concerns (his horizontal dimensions).

The Church aims at more than humanizing man; it tries to divinize him. Societal improvement and human betterment are essential objectives, but the ultimate aim is personal salvation. This mission of bringing

God to human beings and human beings to God necessarily entails the task of fashioning a more fraternal and just society here below.

The Incarnation symbolizes engagement with the world, not its renunciation or denunciation. In the process, as Pope John Paul observes, priests should act as symbols of unity rising above narrow affiliations and political factions. It was for this reason, the late Senator John O. Pastore resented the Republican and former Jesuit John McLaughlin when he challenged him for the senatorship.

In this division of labor, the pope has no intention of denying any priest his civil or political rights. He merely acknowledges the different levels on which the religious and political efforts function, in an effort to make this world a better place in which to live.

In this country, a priest's freedom to exercise his civil right to run for public office is less in jeopardy than is the blurring of a distinction which has helped our democratic system function in a way that leaves diverse religious traditions free to work together on the political level without compromise to their theological convictions.

After the death of Representative John Fogarty, I toyed with the idea of running for his seat in Congress. Being a member of a religious order, I sought and received the permission of my superior. As a priest working in the Diocese of Providence, I asked permission from Bishop Russell J. McVinney. He said that he would not stand in my way, but strongly advised against such a step because he feared I would be restricting my priestly ministry and become a less effective witness to Christ.

In view of the pope's disciplinary prescription forbidding priests to hold political office, Bishop McVinney's advice was ahead of its time.

Catholic Intellectuals: The Need of the Church
(*The Providence Visitor*, February 6, 1991)

Providence College can now boast of more Ph.D.'s on its faculty and more graduates with advanced degrees than ever in history.

The public looks up to Ph.D.'s as bona fide intellectuals. But learning and an academic degree do not always go hand in hand. Socrates and Jesus Christ never wrote a book nor ever penned a line, yet what college would not be proud to have them on its faculty?

Still, educators like to think that bearers of college degrees are habituated to revel in affairs of the mind. William James opined that alumni of American colleges represent, in the realm of intellect, an elite class somewhat similar to the aristocracy in older countries. They form a bastion against mediocrity and superficiality. No prouder name, says James, could be adopted by the college-bred than "intellectuals."

But the *hoi polloi* deride intellectuals for being impractical and out-of-touch with reality—eggheads, highbrows, bubbleheads. Bertrand Russell spurned the title, and heaped scorn on the so-called *cognoscenti* whom, he said, "have less intellect than they think they have." And modern Philistines delight in puncturing the pretensions of those intellectuals who claim an enlightened judgment with respect to public and political questions.

Pundit Russell Kirk draws a more valid sketch of the intellectual: "...the thinking man, the philosopher, the true scholar, the person who believes that the life of the mind is more important than the acquisitive instinct."

Love of learning for its own sake, a conviction that reason will prevail, a consuming desire bordering on obsession to get to the root causes of things—these are the keys that unlock an understanding of the intellectual. Democritus declared he would rather discover a single causal connection than win the throne of Persia. Thomas Aquinas became so enraptured with ideas that he would often forget to eat and drink; once his absorption in theological speculation grew so intense, he felt no pain while having his injured leg cauterized. "The present age is in urgent need," states Pope John Paul II, "of a disinterested search for the whole truth about nature, man, and God" (The Apostolic Constitution on Catholic Universities).

Scholars may be experts, but experts are not always scholars. The expert's thinking focuses on the job to be done. The intellectual, before all else, concentrates on understanding. But just as pure science has been a boon to the workaday world, so also the maxims of the classroom soon become the rallying cries of the crowd. Ideas do have consequences.

Because cerebral activity can be so varied, the work of the intellectual defies classification. But Ortega y Gasset excoriates one type of intellectual whose interests are limited and whose outlook is narrow: the specialist, whom he terms "a learned ignoramus—the person who knows more and more about less and less until he knows almost everything about nothing. The specialist, says Ortega, knows his field but knows little else, tending to exaggerate the importance of his own discipline while making it the measure of things utterly foreign to it.

Cardinal Newman equates the authentic intellectual with the truly educated person. Both possess an "enlargement of mind" and a "university of knowledges." The great intellect, observes Newman, "is one that takes a connected view of old and new, past and present, far and near, and which has an insight into the influence of all these on one another; without which there is no whole, and no center. It possesses a knowledge, not only of things, but also of their mutual and true relations."

Catholics deem it sinful to revile or ignore reason, so intellectuals are warmly embraced by the Church. Thomas Aquinas exalted reason to a degree that seemed scandalous and sacrilegious to the reformers who came three hundred years after him. One of the means of Logos in St. John's Gospel is Reason, and Logos is God. So, under penalty of blaspheming God, Catholics dare not be anti-reason and therefore anti-intellectual. Indeed, the highest act of man, the Angelic Doctor avers, is the act of intelligence, and the highest act of intelligence is to know the first cause of all things. Thus, knowledge has an intrinsic value, because knowledge, as enjoyed in the Beatific Vision, is the very end of the Christianized person.

The great battles of the Church against heresies have been at one and the same time battles against the heresy of anti-intellectualism. Luther's voluntarist *fides fiducialis*, with his repudiation of the intellectual elements in the act of faith and his violent description of the intellect as the "Devil's whore," are as much the evidence of his departure from Catholic traditions as any of his theses nailed to the chapel door. In defending supernatural revelation against heresy, the Church at the same time defends natural reason and the primacy of the intellect over the will, the emotions, the instincts, or any of the other faculties to which voluntarism always appeals.

Indeed, the Church deprecates any contempt shown for that "wild, loving intellect of man" of which Cardinal Newman speaks, and decries any cynicism about the slow, sometimes faltering, but patient, persevering processes by which the intellect seeks to wrest some measure of order from the chaos about us.

Presently, the Catholic Church is embroiled in one of the most tumultuous periods of ferment it has experienced in the past thousand years. Perhaps this is the "Catholic moment" about which Richard Neuhaus speaks—a golden opportunity for the Church to make relevant to the contemporary world its traditional wisdom. To do this the Church needs genuine Catholic intellectuals—men and women who have reconciled with themselves the hard disciplines of scholarship and the high exigencies of Christian faith.

Criticism of Pope Shows Ignorance of Church's Mission
(*The Providence Visitor*, December 16, 1999)

John Cornwell's book *Hitler's Pope: The Secret History of Pius XII*—a tendentious interpretation of the life, conduct, and political stratagems of the pontiff—fails for lack of empirical support. This is widely recognized by responsible historical scholars. Pundits in academia and political leaders who value the way Pius XII contributed to the cause of world peace and shielded European Jews from Nazi atrocities have not remained silent as the name of this public-spirited pope is sullied by detractors. Whether he is deemed worthy of beatification is a question left up in the air until investigation is completed and the "Devil's advocate" has his say.

But James Carroll, former Catholic priest and religion editor of *The Boston Globe*, in an *Atlantic Monthly* rave review of the Cornwell book, predicts that "if (Eugenio) Pacelli is to be canonized now, the Church will have sealed its second millennium with a lie." Indeed, Carroll apodictically states that Pius XII's mission in life was the expansion of power: "He put the accumulation and defense of papal power above everything else."

But what is papal power? Is the pope an absolute ruler with an authority that is unconditional and unlimited? Is he subject only to his own will, unrestricted by the laws of God or nature, or by any other legal limitations? Can he exercise authority that is arbitrary and despotic? Decidedly not. The law of God, of nature, and of revealed truth would prevent that from happening.

Sociologist Max Weber defined power as "the chance of a man or a number of men to realize their own will in a social action even against the resistance of others who are participating in the action."

In other words, power is "the ability of an individual or a group to carry out its wishes or policies, and to control, manipulate, or influence the behavior of others, whether they wish to cooperate or not."

Based on this understanding of power, Lord Acton declared that "power tends to corrupt and absolute power corrupts absolutely."

The pope has enormous power. But it is not the power of guns, or planes, or tanks, or marching legions. Remember the Yalta Conference during World War II, when Churchill suggested to Stalin and Roosevelt that that the pope's help ought to be sought in ending the war. Stalin's derisive retort was, "How many divisions does the pope have?"

Two kinds of power exist in the world today: power that operates out of selfish interest, and power that operates out of selfless interest. Each has held sway at times in the world. When selfish power is enthroned, the world is thrown into chaos. Think of Hitler, Stalin, Mussolini, and other monsters of history. When selfless power prevails, the course of history is radically changed. Think of the Savior Jesus Christ, Moses, Mother Teresa and the holy men and women who made the world a better place in which to live.

The prevalent form of power displayed in the world today—between governments, in national and local politics—is the manipulative, coercive, selfish type of power that seeks to get its own way, as Weber says, "even against the resistance of others."

The defining trait of nations is concentrated force, epitomized by nuclear weapons: the power to kill millions. Simone Weil, in her essay on "The Iliad," defined force as that which turns a person into a thing—either a corpse or a slave. She saw the essence of the modern state clearly. It is the ever-expanding threat of force.

The pope's power is moral, not physical. He operates out of love. That's the kind of power displayed by the God-man Jesus Christ, and the pope is the Lord's vicar on earth. What we see on the cross, in the person of Jesus of Nazareth, is the raw power of divine love. God takes love, which the world regards as weakness, and makes it the most powerful force in the world.

Authority in the Church is not domination. The pope conducts himself, not as a master over his servants, but as a brother among his brethren. His power is shown in service, humility, unselfishness, and self-sacrifice. His title is *Servus servorum Dei* ("servant of the servants of God"). This power to serve avoids imperialism, authoritarianism, or paternalism. Like every bishop, the pope has the power to sanctify, teach, and govern, but he is the supreme symbol of service. In his lifestyle, words, and actions, he communicates clearly that his mission in life is to serve and not be served. The model of the papacy is not a powerful earthly monarch but the humble Jesus of the New Testament.

Loving service denies in no way that authority exists in the Church. The New Testament not only supposes or expressly affirms the existence of offices of authority, but also often does so in the context of its pronouncements on the hierarchy of service. But this authority is not defined in the same way as a juridical authority or a temporal power with, as a kind of appendix, a moral obligation to exercise it in a spirit of service.

History discloses that the Church has fared poorly whenever Church leaders have been involved in a conflict with secular powers and have translated their reaction in terms of power against power (Gregory VII's struggle against Emperor Henry IV; during the 13th century, the struggles of bishops and popes against kings; the quarrel between Boniface VIII and Philip the Fair, etc.).

The jurisdictional power which the shepherds of God's people receive from Christ is in conformity with the order which the Lord willed and instituted (at least in its essential lines). But this power exists only within the structure of the fundamental religious relationship of the Gospel, as an organizational element within the life given to men by Christ, for which each is accountable to all the rest, according to the place and measure granted to him.

So there is never simply a relationship of subordination or superiority, as in secular society, but always a loving obedience to Christ, shaping the life of each with all and for all, according to the position which the Lord has given each one in the Body. In this service, fundamentally identical and coextensive with the fact of being a Catholic, some command and others obey; whether as leaders or members of the flock, they are wholly engaged in the service of Christ and their brethren.

Pope, bishops, and priests are indeed in positions of authority, but in a brotherly community of service. "Truly, truly, I say to you, he who is greatest among you shall be your servant" (Matthew 23:10).

Today, when injustice abounds in the form of racism, violence, and economic exploitation, the power of the pope becomes evident in the way he has been an inspirational force in confronting these burning issues. Although the pope obviously cannot solve these problems alone, he acts as a catalyst in raising the world's consciousness about the dignity of human life from the womb to the tomb. John Paul II put the question of power in perspective when he stated: "Keep in mind that the Church's action in earthly matters . . . is always intended to be at the service of man and man at the service of God."

Vocations. A Need to Address the Vocations Crisis
(*The Providence Visitor*, October 15, 1987)

Pope John Paul II speaks frequently and feelingly on the need for vocations, on the worsening crisis in vocations. He carries this message to bishops, priests, religious, parents, and the young.

In his efforts to motivate priests to promote vocations, the pope has tried to enhance their self-image by stressing their unique dignity. Addressing the clergy in Canada during his visit, he asked priests to focus on the sublimeness of their calling to offer the Eucharistic Sacrifice.

The pope also insists upon the priestly commitment to celibacy, which in the opinion of some is a stumbling block for the young who consider a priestly or religious vocation. Through celibacy the priest becomes a man for others, the pope said. He seeks "another fatherhood, and as it were, even another motherhood.... These are children of his spirit, people entrusted to his solicitude by the Good Shepherd.... The heart of the priest, in order that it may be available for his service, must be free. Celibacy is a sign of freedom that exists for the sake of service."

In his 1984 vocation message the pope urged parents to hold up the ideal of a priestly and religious vocation to their children. "You who have given life to new creatures," he said, "know how to cooperate with Him also in helping your children to discover and realize the mission which Christ entrusts to each one of them.... A vocation is a great gift not only for the one who receives it, but also for the parents."

Research discloses that parents who strongly identify with Church communicate this Catholic identification to their children. High esteem for the priestly vocation goes hand in hand with strong Catholic identity. A home imbued with a spirit of faith and respect for the priesthood becomes a natural nursery for priestly vocations; for parents convey to their children by speech and attitude their pride in having one of their offspring become a priest.

Addressing himself to "boys and girls, young and not so young," the pope said: "I would like to meet you one by one, call you by your name, talk to you heart to heart of things extremely important not only for you, but the whole of humanity. I would like to ask each one of you: What will you do with your life? Have you ever thought of committing your life totally to Christ? Do you think there can be anything greater than to bring Jesus to people and people to Jesus?"

Many parishes throughout the world, even in the U.S. and Canada, are experiencing "priestless Sundays."

The pope's pleas are motivated by the severe vocation crisis that threatens to cripple the Church and prevent her from fulfilling the mandate of Christ: "Going therefore teach ye all nations." Many parishes throughout the world, even in the U.S. and Canada, are experiencing "priestless Sundays," that is, a Sunday when no priest is available to offer Mass. In certain areas the Sunday services are not the celebration of the Eucharist but a prayer service and the distribution of Communion by a deacon or eucharistic minister.

Predictions are that the shortage of priests will be twice as severe by the year 2000—only thirteen years ahead. The priesthood in the U.S. and Canada is an aging body. Forty-four percent of U.S. priests are fifty-six or older. It is estimated that by 2000 there will be only half as many priests as there are today, largely because of death, sickness, and retirement, coupled with only sparse recruits in the years ahead.

The total number of priests has been relatively stable in the U.S. and Canada over the last 20 years while the number of Catholics has increased almost twenty percent. The bleakness of the future stems from the limited prospects of new recruits—only two priests will be ordained for the Providence Diocese in 1988—and the substantial prospects of death, incapacitation, and retirement in the present ranks. The total number of seminarians in the U.S. was 48,750 in 1967, 19,348 in 1977, and 11,262 in 1987.

What are the factors that facilitate vocations? You can be sure that important among them are encouragement by a priest.

The National Conference of Catholic Bishops' "Study on Priestly Life and Ministry" asked the question "Are there some particular groups of priests who are less likely to encourage vocations to the priesthood?" The answer is: The young and those with modern values are less likely to encourage young men to become priests, while those who have religious experiences, like their work, and evaluate themselves highly in comparison with other professionals are more likely to encourage vocations. Every priest is in a sense a vocation recruiter.

This answer is in agreement with those psychologists who tell us that in recruiting for any profession the best way to attract candidates is to multiply contacts of prospective candidates with members of the profession who are evidently satisfied, contented, and happy with what they are doing. Every priest is in a sense a vocation recruiter. By what he is and by what he does he repels or attracts youths to the priesthood. He projects an image of what the priestly life is all about. To quote *The Providence Journal-Bulletin* in the article about seminarian Peter John Andrews: "For months Peter wrestled with his image of the priesthood. He thought many priests were somber, unhappy with their choice in life. 'Nobody wants to go into a profession where you're miserable,' he said. But Father Allard seemed different. 'I was always drawn to him because he always had a smile,' Peter says, 'You could tell he liked being a priest, doing what he was doing and yet he was human enough so that it wasn't always the roses.'"

Most vocation experts believe it is important to give young people with even modest interest in a priestly or religious life an opportunity to see it from the inside. This can be done by having prospective candidates spend a weekend in a convent, monastery, rectory, or seminary. Some projects permit youngsters to "shadow" a priest or a nun for a weekend to get a better insight into the priestly or religious life.

The Serra Club's program, commonly known as "Waiting to Be Asked," is another approach. In the front-page *Journal-Bulletin* article "When a man decides to become a priest"—the first of a series—Peter John Andrews, the seminarian, says that becoming a priest seemed out of the question until he was asked point blank whether he ever thought about becoming a priest. Serra executive director John Donahue says that Serra does not gauge the success of the program primarily by the number of eventual entries into seminaries or convents. He sees the principal purpose of their energies as one of raising awareness to the need to call people to the ministry. He adds, too, that the U.S. bishops recently have changed the name of the program to "Called by Name."

At present, there are two images of the priest. In one image, the priest is pictured as being closed in by authority, shut off from the world, working from a forsaken position, weighed down under effete structures. He represents authority, tradition, immobility, perhaps even obscurantism. It is this kind of priest of which Ivan Illich speaks in his article entitled "The Vanishing Clergyman."

In attempting to revise this conception, the pendulum has swung to the other extreme, and there has emerged a new image marked by insecurity, incompetence, instability, perhaps even infidelity. Neither of these images is flattering to the priesthood. Normally, young people gravitate to the image which they value, and which is valued by their set. Bad images evoke no response; for all practical purposes they are "non-images," without life or sense. To the extent that the priesthood is thought of in the light of these two images, there will be a continuing decline in vocations.

Unfortunately, priests today are frequently classified as either liberal or conservative. I hate such categorizing. I've always liked to think of myself, if not as a rip-snorting radical, at least as a kind of reformist, battling against stand-patties and the devotion to outworn traditions. But suddenly, I am forced to realize that some of the most *avant-garde* clergy associate me with those grim-faced canon lawyers portrayed in movies on the Inquisition. Nobody today wants to be branded an ecclesiastical reactionary.

Not many years ago, any priest felt at home almost at once with any priest: They both knew they had the same basic beliefs, the same basic values, the same ideals. They had so much in common from the very start, that they knew for certain they could trust each other. But not now. When one priest meets another priest for the first time, he may wonder: How far left or right is this one?

The overwhelming number of priestly vocations come from a young person identifying with a cleric or a religious.

This much is certain: The most fertile sources of vocations do not come from vocation posters or recruitment campaigns, or from vocation exhibits. Living, breathing, acting priests are more appealing to young people than pictures or descriptions. The overwhelming number of priestly vocations come from a young person identifying with a cleric or religious, either from personal contact in school or in a direct apostolic situation.

I think most priests will admit that God used a human instrument to draw them to Himself. Pope John XXIII said that while yet a boy, his own vocation to the priesthood was awakened by the Christlike example of his parish priest in Bergamo. I, myself, was attracted to the priesthood when I served on the altar at St. Pius Church and got to know the Dominican priests who served that parish. Saint Jane Francis de Chantal once said of Saint Francis de Sales: "When he passed by, it seemed as though Christ Himself were passing by." I know that the attraction theory of vocational recruiting has its critics, but I have yet to see it effectively refuted. The greatest form of flattery a priest can ever hear is when a boy says, "If I ever become a priest, I want to be like Father So-and-So."

There is one thing we can all do about the vocation crisis: Pray, pray often, pray daily for an increase in vocations. Moreover, we should cultivate in ourselves and in our children a *noblesse oblige* concept of our dignity as Catholics. All of us need to become deeply conscious that we are members of the body of Christ, that this body is complete only when each of us is playing his part, that we affect each other by what we say and do, that all of us together form His body, and that we are all therefore profoundly interrelated. It is this sense of identity with the Church that is the seedbed of the priestly calling. Indeed, it is from proper self-respect, from pride in family, pride in faith, and pride in priesthood, that vocations are nourished.

Professor Says Kennedy Needs Brush-up Courses
(*The Providence Visitor*, August 14, 2003)

Bigotry! That is how Representative Patrick Kennedy stigmatized the Church for its stand on same-sex marriage.

By a strange inversion of values, wrong becomes right, bad becomes good, moral becomes immoral. This repackaging of vice as virtue was predicted five years ago by Community College of Rhode Island professor David R. Carlin: "Many people have bought the party line that those who openly disapprove of homosexuality are motived by bigotry. Because bigotry is un-Christian, and since the homosexual movement is said to be in the forefront of the fight against today's 'bigotry,' then it follows that good Christians must support same-sex marriage." This is sloppy logic.

Catholic politicians seem to believe that they can only be elected to office if they do not behave as Catholics, if they do not take their religion seriously. They relegate their religion to a purely private status; they refuse to hold positions at variance with the general liberal consensus. Almost all Catholics who have achieved political prominence in recent years are conspicuous for their legalized support of abortion and varieties of consensual sex.

Did Kennedy expect the pope to remain silent? Should the Church stay in the sacristy and stick to its prayers? Innumerable public figures have been deeply influenced in their political behavior by their private beliefs. Would one expect a black person elected to public office not to oppose racism? Is a Jewish politician required to turn his back on Israel? Are women in public life asked to keep quiet about feminist issues? Homosexual politicians who have "come out of the closet" are militant spokesmen for "gay rights." Why then are Catholics virtually the only social group whose members are denied full acceptance in the political arena unless they, in effect, agree to suppress their professed principles?

Perhaps we can blame Kennedy's late Uncle John. In a speech in Houston before a Protestant ministerial association, President Kennedy contributed massively to the tragic illusion that faith and politics are utterly separate spheres, hermetically sealed off from one another. Never the twain shall meet. The press loved it; many Americans bought it.

Indeed, when a bishop publicly criticizes a Catholic politician for his pro-abortion or same-sex-marriage stand, the elite media quickly "canonizes" the politician in question as a martyr for freedom (notes M. Charles

Bakst's eulogy of Patrick Kennedy in *The Providence Sunday Journal*, August 10) and brands the bishop as a modern-day Torquemada.

The standard rationalization used by Catholic politicians, the ritualistically repeated cliché that "personally, I am opposed to this, but I do not believe we can impose our values on other people"—is as intellectually and morally bankrupt as any position imaginable.

In effect, such politicians are saying that abortion or same-sex marriage is immoral, but the law not only should countenance it, but even support it. How can intelligent people be persuaded by such nonsense? It is thrown out on the assumption that Catholic voters are patently moral idiots who will swallow anything their political leaders choose to toss them. Indeed, it demeans the rank-and-file Church members by regarding them as too stupid, too apathetic, or too preoccupied to understand the issues properly.

Yes, we live in a pluralistic society and should avoid divisiveness, acting with courtesy and constraint toward one another. However, if pluralism means that no groups should ever seek legislation which is unacceptable to other groups, politics would lose its very meaning.

The obvious fact is that every time a piece of legislation is approved by anything less than a unanimous vote, someone's values are being imposed on someone else. Indeed, every court involves a dispute, and the losers feel that they too are being imposed upon. Every appropriation of tax money involves spending someone's taxes for purposes of which that person may not approve.

In reality, modern pluralism in a democratic society is precisely a continuing and unremitting struggle among competing interest groups, which recognize that their respective interests often conflict with one another. What one group gains, another tends to lose, whether in terms of available funds, direction of public policy, or *modus vivendi*.

In one sense, the story of America is the story of the gradual extension and unfolding of pluralism, the full encompassment of diverse groups and hitherto proscribed beliefs and behavior. However, a unifying principle remains at the heart of American society as that society becomes more and more diverse, especially in terms of accepted moral values. That principle, that sense of American identity, has now become a political question: Can a social order survive based on no moral consensus? Can a society be infinitely pluralistic, infinitely tolerant of all points of view? At some point the legitimization of some positions requires the constriction of others.

America means equality. Patrick Kennedy insists that his stand on same-sex marriage is based on his "respect for treating people equally." Does a due regard for equality require moral neutrality? Dr. Robert P. George treats this question in his work *The Clash of Orthodoxies* and concludes that the appeal to neutrality does not apply.

A logical conundrum exists: If the moral judgment that marriage is inherently heterosexual is false, then the reason for recognizing same-sex marriages is that such unions are, as a matter of moral fact, indistinguishable from marriages of the traditional type. If, however, the moral judgment that marriage is inherently heterosexual is true (as codified in the 1996 Defense of Marriage Act), then the dispute against a government that denies equality to gay unions simply cannot be sustained.

George points out that laws forbidding interracial marriages truly were violations of equality, not because they embodied a particular moral view and thus violated the alleged requirement of moral neutrality; rather, they were unjust because they embodied an unsound and false moral view—one that was racist and, as such, immoral. As Professor George states: "A sound law of marriage is not one that aspires to moral neutrality; it is one that is in line with moral truth."

Before calling anyone bigoted, perhaps Patrick Kennedy should return to his alma mater for a brush-up course on law, religion, and morality.

Noble Celibacy Is Never Out of Date
(source and date unknown)

In a sex-obsessed society, celibacy is viewed as an anachronistic practice. Its heyday is over. It is out-of-date. In days past it may have served a useful purpose, but the sexual revolution has made it more obsolete than the Tin Lizzie.

This kind of thinking, however, exemplifies what is known as "historical relativism."

Actually, the good wrought by celibacy in the past might well be augmented in the present because of the dire condition of American society—hedonistic, egoistic, materialistic. A concupiscent culture like ours cries out for men and women devoted to the celibate vocation. Indeed, the modern romantic concept of marriage as the total emotional and physical giving of two persons to each other and to their children dictates that alternative and freer states of life be open to those who choose not to make this kind of commitment.

In fact, the history of marriage in our bourgeois society suggests that celibacy, that is, the single life, ought to be preferred by more persons than is now the case. Politicians, judges, business executives, physicians, and men whose work absorbs their energy and forces them to spend long periods away from home would probably experience fewer frustrations and cause less unhappiness if they chose not to take wives, in the same way that women who chose a career often opt to remain unmarried.

The suburban syndrome of the neglected, frustrated wife and the ignored, disturbed children stems from men who make a marriage commitment and then refuse to honor it. For husbands of this ilk, marriage is chiefly a matter of convenience, whether domestic or sexual.

The man-in-the-street version of the anti-celibacy argument reduces sexuality to the gnawing need of providing physical release from sexual tensions. This diagnosis is based on the belief that people who live without sex become "queer." Out of sheer frustration, old maids, bachelors, and celibates develop typical eccentricities; they turn into narrow, neurotic oddballs. What they really need to straighten them out is a little of "you know what."

This simpleminded line of thought springs from the prevalent American mythology which looks upon wedded bliss as one of the society's few absolutes, no matter how much the institution of marriage is desecrated in practice. Scarcely any movie or novel, whatever its theme, can become popular without a subplot which ends in a happy marriage. A compulsively coupled society such as ours deprecates and ridicules the so-called sexually unfulfilled.

Yet Sigmund Freud, who made sexuality the linchpin of psychoanalytic theory, insisted that culture and civilization can flourish only when enough people sublimate their instinctual impulses. Without some degree of voluntary self-denial and inhibition, humans would not be able to live together and civilization itself would wane. To grow spiritually, mentally, and morally, altruistic individuals often convert their erotic energy into communal love and work. Indeed, when the physical desire for love and unity is sublimated into friendship, charity, and service, then character expands and personality blossoms.

Conversely, a couple's sexual loving relationship is no guarantee of personality growth. Ten thousand orgasms over the course of marriage do not necessarily change a person's psychological makeup. The life lived between and beyond sexual encounters determines not only the couple's sexuality but also their personality enlargement. Man can live with sex or without it, but he can't do without community life and expression. Old maids and bachelors get "that way" not because they sleep alone, but because they cut themselves off from their fellow man and refuse to participate in community life.

Freud was right on target when he observed that the unique human capacity to redirect sexual drive and energy to artistic and altruistic goals has fostered culture, community, and civilization. Celibates are found in every advanced, refined society—usually, as in the case of Hindu Brahmins and Zen Buddhists, in the role of religious leaders. So too, warriors and intellectuals, living in close community and expending high levels of energy in work, have often embraced celibacy.

Prescinding from the theological motives for choosing celibacy, today there are strong practical reasons for the retention of a celebrate life style. For instance, the religiously motivated person who is inspired to serve Christ in the poverty of the ghetto and share its privations and its violence, and the professor and scientist who esteem the pursuit of truth as the supreme vocation—such people are free to give their all without being hampered by the ties of matrimony.

Celibacy, anachronistic? Never. Throughout the ages, celibates have been the glory of the Church in bearing witness to Christ and His message of salvation. Indeed, changes in the traditional concept of the priestly life bolsters rather than weakens the present-day need for clerical celibacy.

A final word: Genital love within the life commitment of marriage is probably the most intense giving possible, with the exception of the sacrifice of life for love of another. But Jesus Christ said that some men become eunuchs for the "sake of the kingdom of heaven"—the end ennobles the act.

The celibate priest gives up an individual spouse in order to love all human beings more intensely and fully. In short, dedicated celibacy, under the aegis of Jesus Christ, is a voluntary giving of self, for the sake of creating a new universal family, a new inclusive relationship to humanity. Such total giving of self will always be "up to date."

(7)
The Right to Life

The God Squad
(The Rhode Island Medical Journal, May 1974)

CASE 1. A baby was admitted to the hospital on the first day of life because of multiple congenital anomalies. On examination the baby was found to have no opening for either the anus or vagina. There was bilateral absent radii with short ("flipper") arms bilaterally. There was a loud murmur. The child had severe congenital heart disease, most probably irremediable (single ventricle). After consultation with the father it was elected to perform no surgery. The infant died 22 hours later.

CASE 2. One aged patient in Boston, crippled by arthritis, deaf, and having lost his sense of taste, prayed to die. He had dropsy resulting from heart and kidney failure. He had been snatched from death repeatedly. He dreaded the large needles used for his daily injections of iron and was weary of being schooled for failing to take all the 17 tablets per day prescribed for him.

These cases illustrate a vexing dilemma confronting modern medicine: Should lives of retarded infants or those with multiple birth defects be prolonged—at a great cost in manpower, money, and anguish—especially if the life that is preserved will almost certainly be one of pain or merely vegetable-like existence? Should we prolong the lingering death of the elderly or continue to sustain that flickering life (a process which has come to be known as "medicated survival") by wonder drugs, machine resuscitation, surgery, or other methods used to prolong the process of dying?

This dilemma of who should live or how long should we sustain the life of the dying was televised to the American public last January when the ABC television network presented a program titled *News Closeup: The Right to Die*. Two extremes were voiced: one was represented by a physician who insisted that everything possible must be done to sustain even minimal life; the other extreme was defended by a woman who explained how she helped her husband cut his wrists when his terminal cancer was worsened. A middle position was also proposed when a physician said: "The closest rule of thumb we have is something expressed by Pope Pius XII to the effect that it was not obligatory to use extraordinary means to keep a hopeless patient alive." In attempting to resolve these dilemmas it may be helpful to expose briefly the traditional ethical teaching regarding life.

The Right to Life

The right to life is the most fundamental among man's rights, for there can be no further rights or duties unless man first exists, unless he is and moves, and has being. From the very nature of man and from his status as a creature, it follows that the right to life is an inalienable right, that it is also a duty, that life is a gift with definite restrictions or responsibilities attached.

Though God by the natural law gives rights to man, these are some rights God cannot give, for by their very nature they are exclusively God's. One of these is the direct dominion (sovereignty, ownership, proprietorship) over the human person, the compound of body and soul. What God gives to man is an indirect dominion of his person (of use and stewardship), but no direct dominion, no right for a human to destroy his person. This direct dominion is so exclusively God's that if he were to give it away, he would abdicate his position as supreme ruler of the universe. In short, God cannot give complete authority over human life to a creature without ceasing to be God.

Therefore, man is obliged to live out his life to the end of its natural span. In a very real sense, God owns both man and his works and has a right to both. The actual performance of these works God has put under man's stewardship, to be guided by man's free will, but the final approval of these works in quantity and quality rests with God alone.

The right to life is a non-renounceable right, not only in the sense that no one may lawfully take it away from a person, but also even the person himself may not give it up. Those who argue for suicide (the taking of one's own life) or for mercy killing (the giving of an easy painless death for one suffering from an incurable or agonizing ailment) or infanticide (the killing of an infant who is severely deformed) do so on the plea that "no injury is done to one who is willing" or who would be willing if he knew what a painful, deformed, or vegetable kind of life he would have to live.

This kind of reasoning, however, takes no account of God's rights or of man's last end or of the value of patience in acquiring merits for the next life. It is a practical denial of God's providence and the fact that God cannot allow a person to be tried beyond his strength. It appeals to sentiment and is based on the untenable principle that "the end justifies the means"—the end being the relieving of suffering, the means being the direct killing of the individual. "Hard cases do not make good law," but it is not unusual for those moved by a mistaken humanitarianism to cite cases of misery, anguish, pain, and suffering which would be relieved by the injection of air in the vein or by a fatal overdose of drugs.

Obligation to Sustain Life

Just as a person cannot directly take life, so also, he is obliged to sustain life by reasonable care. This does not mean he should become a health fanatic, but he must use the ordinary means of keeping healthy. By "ordinary means" I refer to proper food, clothing, and shelter; due moderation in work and exercise; the avoidance of foolish risks and dangers; taking the usual remedies in sickness; seeking and following medical advice when necessary.

Man, however, is not obliged to preserve life and health by extraordinary means, for no one is obliged to do what is practically impossible or disproportionately difficult. A man in moderate circumstances is not obliged to undergo a serious and costly operation, to break up his home and move to another climate, or to adopt some regimen that would prevent him from earning a living and make him a burden to others. Health must be preserved, but not at all costs. Whether a means is extraordinary or not must be judged, not absolutely, but relatively to the person. A form of life tolerable to one man would be quite unbearable to another. Hence a person's subjective attitude must be considered here as well as his social and financial condition.

Doctors must go to all reasonable lengths to keep a man alive, if there is hope. But the distinction between ordinary and extraordinary means is measured humanly rather than scientifically. A treatment may be common medical practice or involve standard hospital equipment, yet for this particular person the cure may be worse than the disease. Unless the patient or his family want it, there is no point in prolonging life regardless of trouble and expense for a few more days of torment or coma. Doctors have legal and professional responsibilities to consider, but neither doctor nor patient has a moral obligation to go beyond ordinary care, especially in terminal cases. It is often better to let nature take its course so that the patient can die in peace.

. . .

Passive Euthanasia

"To let nature take its course" in treating a terminally ill patient is commonly called "passive euthanasia." To administer a fatal dose of some normally beneficent drug would be to commit "active euthanasia." In virtually all Western countries, that act is still legally considered homicide (though juries rarely convict in such cases).

Withholding surgery, cutting off the machines—or avoiding their use at all—is indeed passive euthanasia. It is an ethical decision—not murder or any other crime in any legal code. This is traditional moral teaching. On several occasions Pius XII enunciated the principle that life need not be prolonged by extraordinary means. But Pius insisted, as have most other moralists, that life must be maintained if it is possible to do so—by ordinary means—that is, feeding, usual drug treatment, care, and shelter.

The question in passive euthanasia is: "Who decides to refuse surgery or call off more surgery?" When do you cease to give or increase drug dosage? Who pulls the plug or turns off the machine and when? The patient himself? His family? The physician? Does the doctor have to make the decision alone? One American Medical Association administrator asserts that doctors should have help in formulating a general policy. He proposes a commission of laymen, clergy, lawyers, and physicians.

This desire to share the responsibility is reasonable, but it is unlikely that any commission could write guidelines to cover adequately all situations. In individual cases, of course, doctors consult the patient or his relatives. But the patient may be comatose, and the family is most likely to be heavily influenced by the physician's prognosis. More often than not, it must be a lonely decision made by one or two doctors.

In coming to this decision, conscientious physicians may not even be certain when they have resorted to active or passive euthanasia. With the growth of medical technology and the increasing use of extraordinary measures, the occasions for passive euthanasia are becoming more frequent. The question of whether terminal suffering can be shortened by active or passive means is often highly technical—depending on the type of ailment.

Principle of Double Effect

In seeking to unravel the moral complexities of human decision and for cases where the line in unclear between ordinary and extraordinary means, traditional ethics employs what is known as the "principle of double effect." This principle may be stated in this fashion: One may never directly intend to do what is inherently evil, but one may, for a proportionate reason, perform an act having evil consequences which are not directly desired. Applying this principle, it is possible, for example, for a physician to administer sedating drugs to a terminally sick patient which, although they will alleviate the pain, also will as a consequence shorten the patient's life expectancy. The effect of hastened death is foreseen by those administering the drug, but it is not the reason the drug is administered. Hastened death is an evil that is tolerated, not directly intended, for the patient is not aided because his life is shortened, but because the drug tranquilizes his pain. Earlier death is a consequence of this act; it is not a means toward achieving it.

This simple example of a highly nuanced principle (for the good accomplished must always bear some reasonable proportion to the evil which is tolerated) illustrates what moralists have commonly referred to as "indirect killing." Administration of the same kind of drug in a perhaps significantly larger dosage with the intention of putting the patient into a coma from which he foreseeably will be unable to emerge would exemplify what is meant by the term "direct killing." This act does not, of course, preclude feelings of genuine compassion and empathy for the sufferer; but it differs from the instance of "indirect killing" in that the intent itself of administering the drug is to terminate the life of the patient, and such termination is the means by which the patient will be relieved of his suffering.

The moral distinctions involved in the application of the principle of the double effect are not mere word games. The distinction between direct and indirect killing is important because otherwise you are left with the bizarre conclusion that what you do matters little at all, provided you do it with a sincere, compassionate heart and judge that favorable effects will result from your action. In traditional ethics it is not the motive alone which determines the morality of an act. Otherwise the task of moral evaluation would be left to the conscience of each individual. Personal conscience itself would become the norm of morality.

In the traditional view some acts are good and evil of themselves. Life, for instance, is so precious and valuable that in the words of Pius XII "there is no man, no human authority, no science, no indication—whether medical, eugenic, social, economic, or moral—that can show or give a valid, juridical title for a deliberate or direct disposing of an innocent human life."

Right to Life

Nor can one redefine life itself in order to bring about a change in the value that one places on life. Perhaps we all have a tendency to assign varying degrees of humanness to other human beings. We assign a scaled degree of humanness to those who are most like us—like us in race, color, creed, wholeness of body, age, social status, or whatever else is convenient. We assign non-humanity or sub-humanity to others.

Joseph Fletcher, who teaches medical ethics at the University of Virginia Medical School, redefines life in terms of what he calls "humanhood or personhood"—a state that includes self-awareness, an ability to operate physically and psychologically as a full human being, a sense of futurity. You are not a human being or a person by reason of having human life, states Fletcher. In effect, if you are unable to "produce" as a person, you no longer have the right to be considered one! The terminally ill, the severely deformed infant, the psychologically incompetent, the senile thereby lose their human accreditation card! Fletcher sees no impropriety in actively terminating the lives of such unfortunates, since he has defined them as "non-humans." Active euthanasia is justified according to arbitrary criteria for classifying human life. The grades of humanness may vary: Some unfortunates may be "incapable of meaningful life"; they may be of less value than others because of intelligence (say, an I.Q. of 70); they may not merit life inasmuch as they fail to measure up to standards of "social worthiness or acceptance"; they may not make the grade as human beings insofar as they are unloved, unwelcomed by society, a ward of the state, an expense to the taxpayers, rejected and unwanted because they are a heavy financial burden to their families or the state; or they may not qualify as persons because they are "unable to fend or take care of themselves"; or simply because they do not fit the definition of "persons in the whole sense" (words used by the Supreme Court in defining human beings who are protected by the Constitution).

What is central to this whole question is the equal allocation of a right to life to every human being—the deformed infant, the physically weak and senile, the retarded in intelligence, or those unable to care for themselves. If parents or physicians deny consent for life-saving surgery to a deformed child while a court commands life-saving surgery or a blood transfusion even though parents do not consent, there is an apparent discrepancy here—a double standard affecting the fate of two human beings who cannot participate in the decision.

* * *

Conclusion

In closing, I wish to state that I believe life should be safeguarded and promoted at all levels no matter what its condition. Therefore, the direct taking of innocent life under any conditions is unjust. If we defend human life, we must defend it under all circumstances, whether in a ghetto, among the starving people of Africa, where war victims are concerned, in cases of the deformed and retarded, or in a mother's womb. If you attack innocent human life at any point from its conception to its natural demise, there is absolutely no moral or philosophical reason why it cannot be attacked all along the developmental curve. So far as I know, no one yet has refuted this statement, and this alone should provide reason to pause and reflect on the consequences of actions involving the direct killing of innocent life.

Indeed, the chief duty of a nation is to protect human life in all forms. That is why the Declaration of Independence states "life" first and then adds "liberty and pursuit of happiness." When any human life is devalued and imperiled, all human life is placed in danger. Frankly, I do not want any individual or group or state tinkering with human life, deciding, God-like, who will live and who will die.

Politics and the Pro-life Voter
(*The Providence Visitor*, June 27, 1996)

Not since the days of slavery has American politics confronted issues with moral roots running so deep as those now on the political agenda. This is especially true of pro-life issues—abortion, assisted suicide, and euthanasia. Instinctively, politicians try to evade confronting questions like these because they touch such deep nerves. For instance, Senator John Chafee refused to face the immorality of partial-birth abortion by asserting that it was a medical procedure best left to doctors.

Catholics are avowedly pro-life. Life is a gift of God, subject to his dominion, mankind is its steward, and each person is accountable to God for how he uses life. Human life is created by the glorification of God through the freely willed return of his love. Because man is made in the very image of God (Genesis 1:26-27), the shedding of innocent blood is absolutely forbidden.

The traditional Christian view, like the Jewish, equates abortion, suicide, and euthanasia with murder. The Second Vatican Council reiterated age-old Christian teaching when it declared that "whatever is opposed to life itself such as any type of murder, genocide, abortion, euthanasia, or willful self-destruction . . . all these things and others of their like are infamies indeed."

If Christians value life so highly, why do they not fight back when abortionists, suicide advocates, and euthanasians exploit the ignorance and naïveté of people, encouraging them by means of slogans and euphemisms to sentimentalize and trivialize these profound issues? Religious people are often too passive and confused. They may feel vaguely uneasy about things they see going on around them, but they are unable to analyze what is happening with any depth or acuity. Fearful of being branded "backward," unsophisticated, or enemies of freedom and progress, they have been conditioned to accept every kind of social and moral change, no matter how much they may personally dislike it.

As David Carlin points out in a recent *Commonweal* article, too many Catholics tend to deny or minimize what is happening even when they do not actually endorse it. They read and see and hear that we are in the midst of a cultural war and they nod approvingly when Pope John Paul II condemns the culture of death, but they are not moved to do anything about it. They forget that they belong not to the Church Triumphant nor to the Church Suffering, but to the Church Militant. Mental apathy and spiritual apathy are soul brothers, and so is political apathy.

Abortion, assisted suicide, and euthanasia are not private, sectarian issues but are issues of broadest public morality, that basic morality which is the foundation of a viable society. These abominable acts are attacks against persons, against humanity, and thus demand legal regulation. The charge that, by being unequivocally pro-life, the Catholic Church is seeking to impose its morality on the nation and is violating the First Amendment is never balanced by the charge that other religious and secular organizations which are anti-life are doing the same thing by their vigorous lobbying in Washington and in state houses.

In a democracy like ours, one should never apologize for his pro-life stance, least of all should he be intimidated into silence. Morally committed citizens become rightfully indignant when they are told that they ought not defend their convictions in a pluralist society. May, then, only the morally uncommitted have a voice among us? This spurious argument is nothing but an insidious attempt to disenfranchise those morally concerned voters who feel they are obligated to express their opinions lest our nation descend to a level at which our philosophy of law cannot recognize any natural rights in man.

Any society, if it is to function properly, must have values, indeed, a consensus of values. If these values are not consciously adopted and publicly acknowledged, they will be smuggled in surreptitiously and often unconsciously. The classical doctrine of strict separationism rests on an assumption that the state can and must be neutral. But in practice this is impossible. Values are always in real or potential conflict and the state inevitably favors some values over others.

That is why elected officials and political leaders are so important in a democracy. We form our political opinions and make our political choices, as social critic Michael Novak points out, not in response to party platforms, position statements, campaign promises, and the like, but at a more irrational or emotional level as we react to a candidate's style or image. Our political leaders are more than elected officials; they are, in a sense, embodiments of our values and we identify with them on a symbolic level. In the end, we voters elect a symbol of ourselves, someone we hope will incarnate our values and our aspirations as citizens, and who will be guided by the principles and standards of traditional morality. Politics is ultimately moral, whether or not it aspires to be.

The question, then, is: What kind of political leaders do we want to follow? I, for one, in spite of the so-called seamless garment theory, am unabashedly and whole-heartedly pro-life, and before all else, will cast my vote for a pro-life candidate. "He who shuts his eyes to the cry of the helpless will himself cry for help and not be heard" (Proverbs 21:13).

Catholics Must Maximize Their Voting Power
(*The Providence Visitor*, October 20, 1994)

Editor Michael Brown's front-page article in *The Providence Visitor* about the lobbying effort of the Network of Respect Life Voters (Lifenet) and about former state senator David Carlin's volunteering his time and talent to help organize pro-life voters moved me to stand up and cheer.

The vote gives every Catholic citizen political power, but individual Catholic voters have little power so long as they remain politically isolated. They magnify their voting power only by standing together. Pooling voters produces a "multiplier effect." George Washington Plunkitt of Tammany Hall fame began his political career by announcing to ward leaders that he controlled a bloc of votes he could deliver on election day. Pro-lifers can do the same thing, and, as David Carlin points out, this is what frequently tips the scales in favor of a pro-life candidate.

Catholics never really developed a successful political agenda, at least not one which won in modern times. So far, the fight against abortion has been one of the Church's ignoble failures.

Label any political cause "Catholic" and it is doomed; label it black, Jewish, feminist, ecumenical, or Hispanic and it gains the support of politicians and the media. These other causes gain respect not because they are unpartisan, but because they are better organized, better promoted, and better reinforced. The determination characteristic of civil-rights groups must invade Catholic precincts, and we must learn to use the vote to gain political clout. Abortion should be the cutting edge of modern politics—the issue which separates believers from half-believers from unbelievers. This crusade for life calls for more *chutzpah* than Catholics have displayed in the past.

The moral absolute "Thou shalt not take innocent life" is non-negotiable, not a political chip, not a ploy in the game of political compromise. That is why, for the Catholics, "right to life" ought to be a litmus test for voting. Theologian Germain Grisez maintains that any individual seeking public office who supports the legality, much less the public funding, of abortion manifests character which makes her or him unfit for public office. He says, "every educated person knows that each time an abortion is done, an innocent and defenseless human being is killed. Nobody who is just can condone that, think it legal, or want to entangle all citizens in it by supporting it with public funds."

The actual political choices may not be this clear-cut, and a voter may be forced to choose the lesser evil, but a pro-abortionist is very different in political potential from one opposed to a higher minimum wage, to fair housing, or other social justice issues.

Catholic politicians who say, "I am personally opposed to abortion, but a woman has the legal right to choose," are copping out on their responsibility to fight against the direct killing of defenseless life in the womb. The Church, which gives wide leeway to theologians and the faithful to judge circumstances and issues where they might exercise proper freedom, has never permitted the use of theological opinions where the direct killing of human life is involved. There can be no waffling here. Whatever the political bind for the Catholic officeholder, he has no choice, if he is a convinced Catholic, but to follow the teaching of the Church. If religious convictions were the main reason for undoing racial discrimination, for supporting fair wage, and a host of other social causes, why should the religious convictions of the Catholic politician not be the chief reason for opposing abortion—stigmatized by the Second Vatican Council as an "unspeakable crime"?

Those who actually fight abortion have discovered that there is a genuine ecumenism growing out of the battle to save the unborn. Catholics, Baptists, non-denominational evangelicals, fundamentalists, and members of all and no religion are united in a belief in God and the value of his creatures. This genuine ecumenism will last, and will flourish, because it believes that in the hierarchy of values, human life comes first. As Pope John Paul II states, "The sacredness of life must be protected in whatever circumstances it is found; whether the life endangered is in the womb of a mother in a large city abortion clinic or in the fear-racked body of a poor peasant in Southeast Asia."

Anti-Catholic Bigotry Again
(The Providence Visitor, September 29, 1994)

Anti-Catholic bigotry in Rhode Island reared its ugly head in a letter to Representative Jack Reed by a group of 13 Protestant ministers and six Jewish rabbis.

They informed the congressman that they were "troubled by the action of the Roman Catholic bishops in encouraging members of the Catholic Church to oppose abortion coverage in a national health care reform bill."

I ask these reverend gentleman and lady: Would you deny Catholic bishops their civil right to counsel their flock about the heinousness of killing innocent life in the womb and about their duty to oppose it?

The First Amendment of the American Constitution states that Congress shall make no law prohibiting the free exercise of religion.

Contrary to the spirit of the Free Speech Clause of that amendment, do these reverends want our bishops to shut up, keep quiet, and stand mute in the face of the unjust slaughter of developing unborn life?

No issue in our time symbolizes more the intersection of the sacred with the secular than the direct and deliberate destruction of the unborn child. The right to life is not just one tenet in the American creed; it is the primary and predominant right, the *sine qua non* of all other rights.

According to this creed, the right to life is granted not by the state, not even by parents, but by the Creator himself. Bishops would be derelict in their duty if they contented themselves with an occasional utterance denouncing abortion while otherwise remaining wholly passive.

Perhaps these bewailers of the bishops' exercise of free speech would like to see the Catholic religion relegated to a totally ceremonial function in life, to a purely private affair, deprived of the public vote to influence those moral decisions made through the democratic political process? No way. The moral tone of society for the next quarter-century is being set largely as a result of certain judicial and legislative decisions, and Catholics, like all concerned citizens, deserve a vote in its formation.

Indeed, the bishops, in encouraging Catholics to "oppose abortion coverage in a national health care bill," are only following the example of clergymen like Martin Luther King, Jr. and other members of the Southern Christian Leadership Conference in the civil-rights struggle and the War on Poverty in the early 1960s, or what was done by William Sloan Coffin, Jr. and other members of Clergy and Laity Concerned in the anti-war movement of the later 1960s and early '70s.

Supporting bills and candidates that held promise of enacting their moral concerns, these zealots used their churches as rallying points and sometimes as places of sanctuary for public-spirited citizens who were trying to overcome racial discrimination and poverty or to redirect foreign policy. Why, then, are Catholic bishops charged with overstepping themselves in the exercise of their constitutional right to campaign against abortion? Every civil-rights gain since the Civil War has been achieved, at least partially, by strong religious pressure.

To say that those who oppose abortion are free not to engage in it, while those who approve may do so, simply begs the question, since in effect, Catholics are being asked to countenance the massive taking of human life.

It is ironical that those who accuse the Catholic Church of seeking to impose its morality on the nation never balance that charge with the fact that the Protestant, Jewish, and non-religious anti-life groups which approve abortion are doing the same thing. Indeed, a greater threat would seem to emanate from organizations like the Religious Coalition for Abortion Rights, which lobbies in Washington and claims to represent 23 Protestant and Jewish factions.

If the pro-abortion clerics had attacked Catholic bishops with the humanitarian intent of dialoging about the abortion issue, one could praise their altruism. But to discuss the morality of abortion is the last thing pro-abortionists want to do. Why? Because the question of whether human life is present from the very moment of conception has nothing to do with religion. It happens to be a scientific fact. The question becomes an ethical one only when we ask: How should we regard that human life? The answer to that question is that we should hold it inviolable.

"Why are we horrified," asks New York's Cardinal John O'Connor, "when discarded fetuses are found in the trash? Is it not because we are profoundly convinced that the unborn child is human?" A common tactic of abortion advocates is to deny "personhood" to the womb-entombed child and thus avoid the difficult debate of rights in conflict. If the fetus lacks the credentials for belonging to the human race, then one doesn't have to confute the argument that the right to life is the foremost of all human rights.

In faulting the Catholic episcopate, the anti-life ministers and rabbis state apodictically that opposition to abortion "does not represent the vast majority of American citizens." On the contrary, no poll exists that shows Americans favor unlimited abortion throughout the gestation period. Far from enjoying the sanction of custom, legalized abortion is a shockingly new and radical idea. Only recently have the so-called liberal churches denied the right to life of the gestating child.

How, then, account for the hateful animus of the pro-abortion camp toward those who uphold the inviolability of life from the womb to the tomb? Can it be because the pro-life movement has shouldered the task of protecting helpless preborn life in the midst of a virtual conspiracy to bury it?

In mean-spirited fashion, pro-life promoters are portrayed as vicious fanatics, political troglodytes, and enemies of sexual fulfillment. With pernicious verbal legerdemain, the stigma is placed on those who esteem and protect life, while rectitude is ascribed to those who snuff it out. Abortion thereby becomes elevated, in this transmutation of values, from the status of an odious crime to the height of almost a virtue.

Abortion is not a Catholic issue. Every American who values his or her humanity, regardless of religious beliefs, should take pride in being champions of the innocent, helpless, defenseless, voiceless unborn. Right now, the prospect is dismal. Abortion has become so routine that, as many of its defenders admit, it is simply used as the ultimate method of contraception.

Presently our nation is in the throes of a crisis which is, at bottom, spiritual. Starting with the abortion issue, it is metastasizing swiftly into many areas of morality where Christian values are being jettisoned. Many citizens see abortion as the single overriding moral question of the day. Vatican Council II stands foursquare against the killing of the growing baby in the womb, calling it an "unspeakable crime" and declaring that "no Christian can ever conform to a law that makes abortion legal."

Anti-Catholic sentiment has undoubtedly surfaced because of the abortion controversy, or perhaps it is more accurate to say that abortion has provided a rationale for feelings already there. Roman Catholics are the major minority group against whom it is still respectable to express prejudice and contempt. Apparently, anti-Catholicism—the dirty little secret of our society—is still alive and thriving. The refusal of the small band of non-Catholic Rhode Island clerics to recognize the right of Catholic bishops to speak out on the social issue of abortion lends credence to the existence of what historian Arthur Schlesinger, Sr. labeled the "most deeply rooted of American prejudices."

The Bloodiest War in Human History
(*The Providence Visitor*, letter to the editor, November 7, 2002)

Of the numerous horrible evils in our world today, abortion is the most hideous. The founders of the feminist movement in the United States insisted that abortion is the killing of innocent unborn babies and that it denigrates the sacredness of sex, marriage, family, and human life.

Susan B. Anthony called abortion "child murder," while Elizabeth Cady Stanton described abortion as "infanticide." Victoria Woodhull, the first woman to run for president of the United States, opposed abortion, as did Alice Paul, author of the original Equal Rights Amendment.

Pope John Paul II placed abortion at the base of the "Culture of Death" and branded it "a most abominable crime."

Abortion is not a lifesaving operation. It is a major form of birth control. Preserving the life of the mother, rape, and incest account for only three percent of all abortions in the United States. Abortion is now being used for gender preference and for eliminating the physically defective.

To kill the defenseless unborn as a method of birth control shows the selfishness of our culture. Some people believe motherhood inhibits one's career potential, children are seen as burdens and dependents, not as assets and sources of joy. They weigh parents down, prevent them from owning houses, buying the material goods they think they need, and prevent them from traveling to exotic places. They can never achieve the "good life" with children around. People don't want to give up their time, money, or standard of living to have children.

Abortion is the easy way out. It is also, as one social critic remarks, "the external manifestation of a nation's growing decadence."

Joining with other pro-lifers to fight abortion is especially effective. In unity, there is strength; we are fighting a war, and no war in the history of mankind has been bloodier or more brutal than the attack on preborn human life.

Indeed, in an appeal to Catholics, Pope John Paul II has stressed the necessity of voting for pro-life politicians.

Single-Issue Voting Is OK
(The Providence Visitor, August 27, 1992)

No pro-abortion candidate will get my vote in the coming November elections. I have become a single-issue voter even though I once thought that a person seeking public office should not be elected or defeated on the basis of one issue.

Some Catholic bishops, Chicago cardinal Joseph Bernardin comes to mind, also thought that right-to-life should not be a litmus test for voting. The cardinal proposed the "seamless garment" concept, later known as the "consistent life ethic" test, to evaluate candidates. According to this test, a candidate's total record, not just his stand on abortion, should be taken into account. If he rated highly in his concern for social problems like poverty, minimum wage, racial justice, and so forth, this would offset his pro-abortion stance. Using the "consistent life ethic" norm, a 1988 booklet Just Life rated pro-abortion Senator Ted Kennedy highly but gave low marks to pro-life Congressman Henry Hyde.

But to equate the sanctity of unborn life with less important issues of human living is bad theology and bad politics. The American holocaust of more than 25 million unborn lives is not just one social problem among others.

Single-issue politics is as American as apple pie. No labor union would ever urge members to vote for an anti-union legislator. No black would ever cast a ballot for a Ku Klux Klan candidate. No respectable Jew would ever give his support to a declared anti-Semite. Try telling a farmer, a banker, a factory worker, or a fruit picker that he should not vote his pocketbook or his ethnic interests. No way. Well, for the Catholic convinced that all human life is precious, the inviolability of innocent life in the womb is paramount. It is the greatest moral issue of our time; it dwarfs all other issues.

Indeed, a candidate's character can be measured by his or her stand on abortion. Abortion is the killing of a defenseless unborn human being. To condone it, to legalize it, or to support it with public funds is unconscionable. Theologian Germain Grisez believes that "Any individual seeking public office who supports the legality, much less the public funding of abortion, manifests character which makes him or her unfit for public office." To vote for an avowed pro-abortion candidate is to condone implicitly the killing of innocent life.

If a Catholic, out of a misguided sense of pluralism, makes no effort to combat abortion because other churches permit it, he falls victim to several errors. First, he is guilty of failing to bear witness to the truth. Second, he demonstrates a lack of love in permitting his fellow citizens to remain in error. Third, he reneges on his responsibility to seek justice for the victim of abortion. Fourth, by his inaction, he condones the exclusion of Catholics from active citizenship—a loss to the welfare of the nation. And fifth, he would be taking a position that is not only contrary to the clear teaching of the Church but also contrary to the best interests of society.

Unfortunately, the actual political choices may not be this clear-cut, and the voter may be forced to choose the lesser evil. But a pro-abortion candidate is very different in political potential from one opposed to a higher minimum wage, affirmative action, or capital punishment.

Catholic politicians who waffle in their abortion stance by saying, "I am personally opposed, but . . ." are not deserving of the pro-life vote. But the alternative may be worse. A half a loaf is better than none, and some pro-lifers judge it better to vote for candidates who would limit abortion, as against candidates who approve abortion of the child at all stages of development in the womb.

Catholic activity in politics has its roots in the gospel teaching of justice, love, and service on behalf of our fellow men, especially the innocent and defenseless—the retarded, the handicapped, children, babies, the preborn. "Evil triumphs when good men do nothing." Silence is not golden, it is yellow. Jesus Christ impels Catholics to speak out in the cause of justice and love. Indeed, the nation and the Church flourish when Catholics act like Catholics. Wherever human life is at stake, there is no justification for leaving one's Catholicism in the sanctuary upon entering the voting booth.

The search has always said that once the inherent value of human life is compromised, the door to genocide is opened. So now we see mothers who abort their children because they are not the right sex, because they have Down's Syndrome, because they are handicapped.

America needs the Catholic voice. It is a voice which speaks with 2,000 years of accumulated wisdom and divine guidance. And it is a voice which, protected by the First Amendment and its own authority, has a right to speak.

Our Desacralized Society Can Spawn a Mengele
(*The Providence Sunday Journal*, June 7, 1992)

Ann Landers and Unitarian minister Thomas E. Ahlburn (*The Providence Journal*, May 16) insist that government should keep out of the abortion issue. How wrong they are! The chief duty of a nation is to protect human life in all forms.

The right to life is the most fundamental right, for there can be no further rights or duties unless there is someone there to have them. That is why the Declaration of Independence states "life" first and then adds "liberty and pursuit of happiness." In a democracy, each life, including the unborn, possesses a singular worth. Political leaders have a responsibility to keep alive for future generations the core principle that a democratic society protects all human beings. Any other basis for equality is fragile and sure to break under the demands for special privileges.

A nation that believes human life is unique and precious must defend it under all circumstances, in the ghetto, among the impoverished, the starving victims of wars and plagues, AIDS sufferers, the infirm elderly, in cases of the deformed, the demented, the retarded, the unloved and unwanted, or the preborn in a mother's womb. Attack innocent human life at any point from its conception to its natural demise and there is absolutely no moral or philosophical reason why it cannot be attacked all along the developmental curve.

The crux of the abortion issue is: Does God or man ultimately control life? For most Christians, human life is sacred because it is God's gift, a gift in its origin, a gift in its development, a gift in its ultimate destiny. Given the premise that God alone is the arbiter of human life, other human beings cannot designate which human life counts as "human" and therefore is entitled to protection by society. Given that premise of divine dominion, the benefit of the doubt must be given to every human being that even remotely qualifies as human, contrary to Reverend Ahlburn's contention that the unborn are only probably human.

There is a logic involved when people begin to take arbitrary control of life. Human life is a consistent whole. We cannot misuse one section without endangering the rest. Make human life at any stage cheap and expendable, and all of it is endangered. Place human life under the full control of determination, and anything is possible, anything is permissible. Once the inviolability of human life is removed, all human life is violable. If human beings—parents, doctors, or whoever—are to be in total control of life in the womb, why should not they, or the state also, have the right to get rid of those unwanted human beings who fail to measure up to arbitrary standards of "personhood" or "meaningful existence?"

Society does not accept the Christian premise of human inviolability and of God's dominion over human beings. A secularized society makes it easy for a new kind of Dr. Josef Mengele to do his work. Thus, embryo experimentation, live fetal research, gender-based abortion, sterilization of the feeble-minded, euthanasia of the chronically ill and the senile, medically assisted suicide, and infanticide of the deformed are becoming more and more acceptable in our desacralized "brave new world."

The abortion struggle is ultimately about who is in charge, who shall control human life. Does life in the womb belong to the woman, and to the woman alone, to do with as she pleases? Does the state have a stake in the preborn child? Does human life belong to God alone, and if so are human beings ever justified in usurping God's prerogative of lordship over life at any stage of its development?

Exercising Our Right to Influence Congress
(*The Providence Visitor*, February 19, 1981)

When the pro-lifers asked Senator John Chafee to vote for a constitutional amendment that would overturn the 1973 abortion ruling, he responded (quoted in a *Providence Journal* editorial, January 24) "What you're asking is that your views be imposed on everybody."

I submit that the problem is not whether personal or group views or values can be imposed, but who can work for public enactment of which values. This poses a dilemma. Few would argue, for instance, that Planned Parenthood (a tax-exempt organization) has no right to fight for federal funding of abortion clinics. Yet many argue that tax-exempt religious organizations cannot fight to stop such funding.

Many see no objection to the American Civil Liberties Union and Planned Parenthood going to court to rescind the Hyde Amendment which restricts federal funding of abortions to certain extreme cases such as the life of the mother, yet resent the Moral Majority, the Life Amendment Political Action Committee, and Catholics for Christian Political Action when these groups work for the passage of an amendment to safeguard the lives of the unborn.

Did the founders of our country mean to paralyze religious groups in the formation of public policy in such value-laden areas? Did they plan for a double standard, one for secular groups and one for religious?

Decidedly not. Madison, in the *Federalist Papers*, squarely faced the problem of religious activism and proposed a solution. His principle was that religious individuals and groups had the same rights and privileges, and no others, as any other individuals and associations. "A religious sect might degenerate into a political faction," he observed, "but the variety of sects dispersed over the entire face of it must secure the national councils against any danger from that source."

Catholics believe that ethical and religious values should inform political conscience and so they join hands with other citizens of like moral commitments in an effort to influence the making of public policy. The Second Vatican Council urged the laity to undertake an "apostolate of the social milieu ... the effort to infuse a Christian spirit into the mentality, customs, laws, and structures of the community in which a person lives."

In a pluralist society, nobody has the right to impose his own religious or moral views on other groups through the use of force, coercion, or violence. Obviously, the Rhode Island pro-lifers who visited Senator Chafee's office do not fall into that category, and indeed their conduct falls well within the limits of the primeval American right to protest and object.

But were the tactics of Bishop Gelineau and his pro-life cohorts prudent? Do bus rides to Washington and confrontation of politicians identify the Church in the public mind as a power group? Is it possible that people might be turned from the faith and the visage of the Church as God's kingdom of truth and freedom, justice, and love obscured? Catholics are people of reason as well as people of faith, and they try to win fellow citizens over by the warmth of love and by the Christ-like reasonableness of their message. But when persuasion fails they have the same right as other interest groups to influence Congress.

Here is where the power of the vote comes in. Politicians are the people's representatives. If they fail to reflect in Congress their constituents' voiced consensus, they can be voted out of office. "Hit lists" are reprehensible because they lump all legislators together indiscriminately. But single-issue voting—abortion, nuclear weaponry, racial justice, etc.—is justifiable, unless a person is so bland and neutral that no single issue really matters to him.

The phrase "imposing your views" has a solipsistic connotation, namely, my insight is mine alone and cannot be shared by another, much less by a community. I hope this was not what Senator Chafee meant, because it implies that value judgments are incapable of proof and hence are simply a matter of personal feeling, taste, or preference.

As a consequence, intelligent discussion becomes an exercise in futility, and civility dies with the death of meaningful dialogue. In a pluralist society, people cherish the hope that truth will prevail when, and if, it is subjected to the unbridled competition of the marketplace of ideas. That is why rational argument, even when strongly disagreed with, ought to be treated with respect and should be answered by as clear an intellectual refutation as one can give. The topic of abortion deserves this kind of treatment.

Actually, the question is not simply one of "imposing views or values." What is at stake is the very heart of America, the whole tone of society, the very contours of future American culture. When people argue over what kind of laws they want, they are really arguing over what kind of people they want to be.

Americans fought a Civil War over slavery—at one time tolerated, indeed, protected by the Constitution. Spartan law encouraged infanticide by allowing sickly infants to be exposed to the elements. On the ground of racial purity, Nazi law consigned Jews to the gas chambers. With atheism enshrined in law as the state belief, Communists persecute believers in God. Laws tell us what a country was and is.

When Americans debate laws about abortion, pollution, civil rights, nuclear energy, etc., they are claiming a right to some control over the physical, intellectual, and moral environment in which they live and raise their children. They are talking about what is most dear to them, about the principles, standards, and habits they consider crucial for living the good life. No wonder everybody gets excited about these issues. They are tied up with what life is all about, what makes life worth living.

(8)
The Family

The Family—The Basic Unit of Civilization
(Speech given to the Providence Rotary, December 18, 1984)

I'm here today to praise—to deliver a panegyric on the family. I feel comfortable doing so. After all, I had a mother ... and I had a father ... and 7 brothers and 2 sisters. In fact, I've lived in a family all my life ... first at home and then for the past 44 years, in the religious family of the Dominican Order.

Families are beautiful. Just think of all the precious things you get from your family—things of more value than all the gold in Fort Knox. Just take education: I learned to do all the basic things at home before I ever went to school.

The real tough teaching jobs were left up to my Mom and Dad: things like tying my shoes; not playing with fire; learning my way to the potty; picking up my own toys and socks; not hitting my brother or sister; saying my prayers; standing up to the bully down the block; learning when to be quiet around my father while he worked. In short, I learned to be a dutiful child, a worker, a citizen, a neighbor, a Catholic, an American and—I hope—a civilized human being—all under the tutelage of this marvelous university called the family—and all before I set foot in a school.

The extraordinary thing about all this is that it isn't extra-ordinary at all. It is all very ordinary. But if I asked any five of you here today what you thought of the family, I would likely get five different answers. But most of you would agree that good families produce good citizens. Why? Well, because responsibility is the keynote to citizenship, and there's no better place to learn that than in the home. But irresponsible parents generate irresponsible children, and since the home gets the child first and has him longest, there is no way the state or school can undo parental mistakes.

So the big problem is how to strengthen families. We are—all of us—pretty much what our families have made us. Oh, I am not saying that what you do as a kid explains how you'll turn out as an adult. Perhaps too much emphasis is placed on early conditioning—you know, the delinquent hates his mother or father and so takes it out on society. But the old saw "As the twig is bent, so the tree inclines" is quite true—for personalities as well as trees.

Now as Americans, we believe there are many important values inherent in our way of life. For instance, we believe in the worth of the individual and in national progress. We believe in universal literacy and education as the means of solving social and personal problems. We're optimists. We think if everybody could just read and write, half our problems would vanish: "Open a school—close a jail." We have confidence in man's ability to control and direct his destiny, to rise in the world, to make something of himself.

But how does the child learn these ideas and values? He learns them in only one way: through the family. But note this: His family experience colors his perception. The child sees the American way of life through the eyes of his family; he learns of it through the words his family use, and he absorbs his family's feelings toward his country, his church, and the American way of life. Indeed, the values and disvalues of our democratic society are transmitted in a family version, compounded out of what the family can see of the so-called American way of life, *how* it sees it and how it *wants* to see it.

All this goes into the hopper to form the child's sense of values. It is in the bosom of the family that judgments are formed, conflicts of value are resolved, and choices are made. My friends, I need not tell you that life is varied and complex, infinitely full of responsibilities. Personality development is a constant series of choices. These choices are made according to a person's scale of values, and these values are shaped largely through family living. The Bible says: "Train up a child in the way he should go; and when he is old, he will not depart from it."

A recent study shows how and where children get their ethical concepts—chiefly, of course, from their parents, especially the mother.

Then there is a classical work on the *Origins of Crime* by sociologist Dr. Joan McCord. She claims that the real factors producing a criminal personality are not found in slum housing, in the poverty of the family, or in the child's I.Q.—although you can't discount any of these factors. No, they are primarily found in the relation of father and mother to each other, their acceptance and love of their children, their maintenance of firm but kindly discipline.

These are the points at which the problem of delinquency and crime must be attacked; and I might add that these are the points so frequently neglected by the community, while it spends great sums on social work of many kinds that come too late to do much good. The root of criminal behavior lies in the family, and all the work of social agencies will be merely stopgap unless they work *with* and *in* and *through* the family.

We have to go further than our family courts and jails have been able to reach. We always seem to start at the wrong end of the spectrum. We put a band-aid on the festering sores of society. We build our Supermaxes, halfway houses, and rehabilitation centers and hire social workers, parole officers, and more policemen when we should be doing everything possible to shore up the family.

As I see it, the greatest good parents can confer upon a child is to provide him with an adequate scale of values, a philosophy of life, certain standards and principles which give direction and purpose to life and serve as a basis upon which he can take a stand to work out a solution to the problems of daily living. Now I speak of a philosophy of life rather than of religion because it is possible to find some people who seem to operate according to a satisfactory scale of values without basing it on religion. Humanists do, but I think it makes for a rather shaky foundation.

But it is a family's philosophy of life, its system of beliefs, which help it meet adversity without crashing, that enables it to be brave and steadfast when the going gets tough, that equips the child to make the business of living synonymous with the joy of living. In short, it gives meaning to life and is a vital element in the psychic atmosphere which envelops the child as he is growing up.

Now, as every child matures, he asks himself these questions: Who am I? What am I? What is my particular relation to this society in which I find myself? What is my peculiar place in it? What is my status?

These questions arise early. Parents sometimes sense them before children are able to even formulate them. Social workers recognize the craving of adopted and foster children to learn about their natural parents—who they were, what sort of people they were—regardless of how they were treated or abused by them. Newspapers often contain stories of grown persons trying to find out about parents they never knew. The study of genealogy is a very human and understandable quest. Why else would Presidents Kennedy and Reagan go back to Ireland to look up their ancestors?

What we say of horses can also be said, to some degree, of human beings: "Blood will tell." That reminds me of the highbrow who was seated next to a lowbrow at dinner. The highbrow, trying to put the lowbrow in his place, said, "Breeding is everything." To which the lowbrow responded, "I wouldn't go so far as to say that, but I do admit it's a helluva lot of fun."

Status has been defined as position in society—the standing accorded the individual by his fellows, one's place on a prestige scale. Now one of the most important things which a family does for the child is to give him status. And the family does this by means of two things: It gives him a name and it gives him a social position. Without a name a child is a nobody. And nobody likes to be a "nobody."

Song: "You're Nobody till Somebody Loves You." Well, everybody likes to be a "somebody." By virtue of his family, by virtue of his family name, a person becomes a somebody—that is, an individual with status.

Family names then are important. Names quickly identify the child as a member of a particular group, and since these groups are apt to have a distinctive status, the child is assigned that status. And this is the basis of what is known as "family pride." And family pride gives a child the self-confidence he needs to cope with the problems of life. Speaking of family pride—I remember: a Lennon never lies or cheats or steals.

When we meet a child for the first time we ask, "What's your name, etc.: I'm John Jones." It's not long before persons of minority nationality groups learn that certain names provoke emotional reactions, or prejudices, as it were. In Rhode Island, for instance, such names as Chafee, Vanderbilt, Nicholson, and Brown connote something different than names like Oliveira, Sullivan, Berkovitz, Dobazynski and Spetrini. When you come to think of it, the name Marilyn Monroe is certainly more euphonious than Sadie Glutz—and for the president of our country, Abraham Lincoln sounds a lot better than say, Mortimer Snerd. Every year millions of people change their names. They feel that a new or false name is an effective mask for disguising themselves, and that if they discard their names, in some way, they discard a part of their personality.

But, family status is also connected with the concept of security. To feel safe means to feel at home—providing our own experience at home gave us a feeling of affectionate security. The emotionally mature person is one who feels at home in the world at large. The person who has never learned to feel at home in his childhood home is apt to have trouble later on.

Robert Frost tells us that "Home is the place where, when you have to go there, they have to take you in." But home is more than that: Indeed, the family has a special vocation to be a place where people are loved *not* for what they *do* or what they *have*, but simply because they *are*, a place where the individual is free to be himself, where he expects to find love and acceptance, welcome and solace, happiness and comfort, support and encouragement.

"Be it ever so humble, there is no place like home." Yes, home sweet home is the child's first psychological laboratory. It is there that the child first learns about other people and about himself, and this is sure to color his subsequent interpretations of human nature. His thoughts on the meaning of marriage and how one ought to bring up children, on the place of the father in the home, or the role of the mother, are given shape and substance by what he absorbs in his own home.

But family name and status also have a great deal to do with a person's behavior because they influence how a person conceives himself. Now, how one thinks of himself determines how he reacts to other people. William James used to say that a man had as many selves as there were persons who recognized him and carried an image of him in their minds. The poet John Masefield tells us:

> *Three men went down the road*
> *As down the road went he.*
> *The man they saw, the man he was*
> *The man he wanted to be.*

You know, when a teenager thinks of himself as a reasonable self-controlled human being, he is liable to act like one. But if adults call him a "crazy mixed-up kid," then he may try to live up to their expectations. Expect much and you get much; expect little and you get little.

Incidentally, this is where the Church can be most effective in developing in each person a proper self-respect. All religions teach that the individual is priceless in the sight of God. He has status in God's eyes. Indeed, Christians believe that God, in the person of Jesus Christ, would have become man for him alone, would have suffered and died for him alone, would have opened Heaven and poured down His graces for him alone. The person who realizes this truth understands that he has inherent worth regardless of what his fellow man thinks of him.

My friends, in spite of Dr. Spock and the child psychologists, nobody has yet discovered the best way to strengthen family life. No one can specify with micrometric exactitude the conditions in which children should be raised. Nevertheless, we do have a lot of information on where to make a start. So, if we're going to try to strengthen family life in Rhode Island, then I would suggest that, first of all, we get the facts.

Let's get the facts about needs of families, about efforts to meet them, about social and economic practices that depress families and perpetuate the dependency of parents. Let's document these facts and use them as the basis of fruitful hypotheses. What is the condition of family life in Rhode Island? Are childrearing practices typically American, or are they American Portuguese, American French Canadian, Italo-American, or American Polish? What's the difference between a child born and raised by Sicilian parents on Federal Hill and a youngster reared by Jewish parents on the East Side? How does immigrant status affect family life? What are the handicaps of black families? How can we help Portuguese and Asian families adapt to American conditions? What effect does all this have on the stability of family life? I know there are "lies, damn lies, and statistics," but we need to know more about families in Rhode Island if we hope to improve their condition.

Indeed, what's wrong with mobilizing public opinion? Why not try to make all citizens family-minded? Every citizen who has some influence on the family, no matter how small, should use this influence to strengthen family life. The teacher in the school, the cop on the corner, the grocer in his store, the social worker, the judge, the lawyer, the physician, the businessman, the pharmacist—all should develop "social eyes" to combat the forces threatening wholesome family life, all should be made conscious of the crucial role the family plays in the progress of the community.

It is trite but true that the great battleground for the moral life of America is the family. We may have great schools, dedicated to education, great temples dedicated to the worship of God, great halls of justice dedicated to law and order, but what this country will amount to in the long run depends on what happens to its homes. There is no substitute for home, for parents, for fathers and mothers. In closing, I quote noted inspirational poetess Grace Crowell:

> *So long as there are homes to which men turn at close of day,*
> *So long as there are homes where children are, where families play,*
> *If love and loyalty and faith are found across those sills,*
> *A stricken nation can recover from its gravest ills.*

Pressures Influencing Family Stability
(The Rhode Island Medical Journal, July 1970)

The *Family Is Still the Best Hope of A Better World.* Plato once said: "The state is the family writ large." The state, that is to say, is simply an extension of the family. But that is no longer true in our modern world. Our great complex nation states are not families; they are rather vast agglomerations of families. And in the interaction between family and society there can be a great deal of conflict. It is the family that prepares the future citizens of society, and it is society that sets the requirements and standards for future citizens. So in any society that is in a state of equilibrium, the family and society must have the same goals; they must be working to produce the same kinds of persons, to function in the same kinds of ways. If the family and the society of which it is a part are in conflict with each other, a battle will have to be fought out in which, sooner or later, either the society changes the family, or the family changes the society.

So the family and the society must sooner or later come to terms if there is to be a healthy, stable community. Our American families in the past were quite different from families of today. They were patriarchal. The father was the unchallenged "lord and master." This kind of family did not have flexibility and adaptability. Consequently, under the impact of rapid social change, the patriarchal family on every hand is dead or dying, decaying and disintegrating. But such families were quite suited to the early days of our country. Pioneer families, for instance, did many, many things like baking and cooking all food consumed, repairing shoes and harness, spinning, sewing, knitting and tailoring the family clothing, laundering all clothing and linen by hand. The family was quite self-contained. In addition, the members of the family, almost all of them, worked together in the homestead. A great deal of the education and guidance of the children in social values was provided in the home. Recreation was provided almost entirely in the home or in the homes of a group of neighbors. The social life of the family revolved around the homesteads so that families were the center of the throbbing life of the community.

Today the family has changed radically in this respect. It has lost a great majority of the functions that it discharged for its members, and, insofar as any of these are left, gadgets now perform them for us. Our life has become so mechanized, so labor-saving, as a result of technological advances, that there is little left by way of chores for the children to do about the home. Do you know that ninety percent of all the scientists who ever lived in the history of the world are alive and working today? What they will come up with in the next fifty years baffles the imagination! Already we buy in the stores, for cash, all the things that the family used to make. Therefore, we have to have plenty of cash. In order to earn the cash to buy the gadgets and the other things at the stores, we have to go out and work; and sometimes not only father spends most of time away from the home community, but mother also is out at work all day.

The family no longer provides its own recreation. Moreover, social life has shifted very largely away from the home and from the family as a participation unit. Instead of doing things together, the man goes to his particular recreational group, and the woman goes to her group, the senior-high children to their group, and the junior-high to theirs, and so on, all down the line. The family goes in all directions, and there is not much left that the whole family can do together. Indeed, for many people in our culture today, the home is not much more than a place where you go to eat and sleep. Or, as Robert Frost wrote, "Home is the place where, when you have to go there, they have to take you in."

Not only is it true that the home has been shorn of many of its functions, it has also, again and again, been deprived of its roots. We live in an era of tremendous social mobility. One family in five, we are told, moves to a new home every year.

When you break down this figure into realistic terms, as somebody once said, it means that every day in the United States, twenty-five thousand families, representing about a tenth of a million people, are on the road with all their worldly goods, moving from one home to another.

In this great melting pot in which families are cast together, there is a constant process of mixing, of leveling down, which deprives many families of their uniqueness, of their identity, and moves them into a common mold. Immigrant families just coming over from the Old World try, at first, to hold on to the traditions in which they were raised, and they may succeed in the first generation. But inevitably, in the second generation, as the children go out into the community and to schools, the old values break down, and by the third generation they are almost totally effaced, and these people are merged in the great American mass. This, of course, has its value. It brings unity and solidarity to the community. But this unity is achieved at the cost of the gradual scaling down and loss of identity that goes on all the time.

When the family has been shorn of so many of its functions, the focus of family life shifts to meeting the needs of an essentially emotional nature. The need for emotional security becomes acute in a bewildering, very impersonal world, where everything is shifting, and you don't know what you can be sure about. The need for affection becomes acute in a world when you often feel you have been reduced in terms of identity to little more than a Social Security number. There is the need that somebody should know you as a unique individual, accept you for what you are, and love you for what you are. There is the need to get closer to somebody in some sort of a more real relationship. Where can all these needs be met except in the family?

It is said that in the Middle Ages in Europe, many people, perhaps the majority of people, went from the cradle to the grave and never saw more than one hundred other human faces. When you think of the vast multitudes with which we are mingled and lost in our great cities today, we crave a sense of personal significance in identity and worth. We bring these needs, sharpened and accentuated, to the home, in the hope that there they may be met. But are these needs being met there? Can they be met there? Or are we overburdening marriage with expectations it cannot fulfill? It would be helpful to look at some of the pressures in our culture which have a profound influence on married people—on husbands, wives, parents, children—and which directly, or indirectly, affect family stability and happiness in marriage.

First of all, there is pressure on the American family to get ahead. American social critic Vance Packard has reminded us that we are a nation of status seekers. We are desperate for recognition. We talk about keeping up with the Joneses, but we are not content to keep up with the Joneses, we want to get ahead of the Joneses. And we can do this only by getting more money, because in the United States wealth and status go hand in hand.

The per capita income in the United States is about $4,000. The per capita income in some adjoining Caribbean countries like Jamaica and Trinidad is little more than $200. The per capita income in India is $70. The per capita income in Pakistan and in Haiti is $60. According to Barbara Ware, North Americans, who constitute twenty percent of the world's population, consume about fifty percent of the world's natural resources. And yet, when ratings are made of family problems in the United States, financial problems are nearly always at the top of the list!

This is not to gainsay the fact that poverty is ruinous of wholesome family life. A grinding poverty curses children with a lack of incentive, inadequate motivation, a week value system, and a loss of self-respect and efficiency in those skills required to make fullest use of the resources—

educational, vocational, cultural, and social—which lead to exits from poverty.

It should be evident, however, that we need more than money to help families caught in the grip of poverty. We need to instill in parents the sense of self-respect and esteem for their individual worth, a conviction that they are not victims of impersonal forces, but, with the help of God's grace, can meet adversity and control their future. We need to put incentives into family-aid programs so that people will want to help themselves, will see the benefits of working full or part time, will begin to develop a family pride that roots out an attitude of hopelessness, despair, and powerlessness.

But parents also strive for status through their children. It is a rather well-accepted American axiom that married people should only have children when they want them. But what are a couple's reasons for wanting a child. Do they desire to give a human being the gift of life and of disinterested, unselfish love? Or do they want a child solely as a means to a selfish end—the fulfillment of themselves in fatherhood or motherhood?

Most parents will deny that they want children for their own interests rather than for the child's. They point to the amount of time and attention they devote to their children. But in more cases than is generally realized, parenthood has become a status symbol. A man and woman have a child because of what the child will do for them, not because of what they can do for the child.

Indeed, there is much evidence that parents today regard the child as an extension of themselves, and like their car or their home, a symbol of influence. There child is less a person than a thing. For example, he may be driven to attend college when he has neither the talent nor desire to go. He goes, because his parents do not want their neighbors to think they cannot afford to send him or that he is not intelligent enough, which thus reflects on them. If he does want a college education, they insist on a "name" college, so they can boast about it. When he chooses a career, they will fight against his preferring a job without prestige. They want their children to wear white collars in their work whether they are miserable doing so or not.

Another pressure in modern society is sex. We are immersed in a culture that is preoccupied with and schizophrenic about sex. Modern sexologists, by their overemphasis on sexual pleasure, have pushed family stability into the background. In their view the only purpose of marriage is to mold a clever and cooperative bedmate. If this doesn't work out, head for the divorce courts. So, we have about 400,000 couples every year get out of a marriage, hoping to do better next time. American divorces are twice those in Russia, four times those in Britain, six times those in Canada, and so on. These divorce rates are almost matched by marriage rates, so what we really have is a rapid turnover rate in marriage partners. It has been described as "serial polygamy."

Needless to say, people who enter marriage expecting a Mohammedan heaven, and who feel that they can call it quits whenever the going gets rough, have two strikes on them before they start. Our cultural environment is made up of *Peyton Place* and *Playboy*; of the laboratory of Doctor William H. Masters, with volunteers fornicating and masturbating for science; of Albert Ellis, Eustace Chesser, and those one-theme arty foreign films; of erotic authors Ralph Ginzburg and Henry Miller, of topless waitresses and go-go girls; and the Kinsey charts. Sane and rational voices are asking where we are heading. David Reisman states that sex has been oversold as the promised land, that we have been conned into believing that sex is a solution to all of life's problems. French philosopher Albert Camus wrote of the "congenital inability to see in love anything but the physical." He saw the obsession with sex as drying up daring and creativity.

Others feel that as society becomes more impersonal, as family ties weaken, then many lonely people are looking to sex to fill the vacuums in their lives and provide the warmth and affection they have not be able to obtain in an uncaring world. And so illicit sex is being justified today by the plea that it helps people develop "skills in interpersonal relationship" with another human being, that it "involves" them in the lives of others, that it cannot possibly be wrong for two people who have a "feeling for each other and have rationally considered the consequences."

Dr. Pitirim A. Sorokin once wrote: "Dedication of an individual to the pursuit of sex pleasure means a growth of the sex drive at the expense of the power of other factors determining his total activity, and radically changes the whole system of forces governing human behavior." Sexual dedication in marriage may be at the expense of the family.

If the child and the family structure are going to be salvaged, the rules governing sex will have to be respected. Every society recognizes some restraints in this matter. A glutton of any kind is a poor parent and a poor neighbor. He is too dedicated to his own individual satisfaction. A society enraptured by sex, as is that of India, tends to let the housekeeping go to hell. If the American middle class were to go off on a giant bedroom chase, this would provide quaint material for *The New Yorker* and *Esquire*, but it would scarcely be indicative of the Great Society. As Doctor

Robert Odenwald observes, "Part of love is sex. If we want to love, we will have to keep sex under some control. If we don't, it will be like putting too much whiskey in the drinks—the guests pass out instead of enjoying themselves." Undoubtedly, the practice of the virtue of chastity in a concupiscent society imposes great strain on the individual, but perhaps sexual discipline is the test case for dedication to standards of worth in every domain of existence.

This overemphasis on sex has further repercussions. It forces our young people into early dating, early steady dating, and early marriage. Advertising, entertainment, and fashion are all designed to produce and to exploit sexual tension. Sexually aroused at an early age, and asked to postpone marriage until they become older, teenagers have no recourse but to fill the intervening years with courtship rituals and games that are supposed to be sexy but sexless. Dating is expected to culminate in going steady, and that is the beginning of the end. The dating game hinges on an important exchange: the male wants sexual intimacy and the female wants social commitment. The game involves bartering sex for security amid the sweet and heady agitations of a romantical entanglement. Once the game reaches the going-steady state, the teenager finds himself driven into a corner, and the one way to legitimize his sex play, and assuage the guilt, is to plan marriage. And so he marries early, and perhaps society loses a physician, a scientist, a lawyer, an engineer, for man cannot serve two masters; and since the energy and the scope of interest for any individual are limited, solid preparation for adult life will not be achieved.

It is high time we recognized the obvious fact that teenagers are not adults. They are young people at various stages of development on the way to maturity. Parental guidance, supervision, and control must consequently be geared to their stage of development in areas like dating, drinking, driving, and recreation. Ultra-permissiveness can be ruinous. A child can experience the meaning of secure love only through being dependent on persons who supply authoritative direction for his life. To my way of thinking, few doctrines in recent decades have been more injurious than the one that opposes the exercise of parental authority in the name of freedom and democracy. The eroding of the parent's authority and the repudiation of the children's obligations to obey have seriously contributed to the disintegration of the family and have hindered the character development of the young in crucial aspects.

Perhaps the trouble has come from failure to distinguish between kinds of authority. Absolute, arbitrary, manipulative authority—power over others—is an evil thing; it should have no place in church, state, or family. But responsible authority which derives from devotion to the good is right and necessary, especially in the family—and I might also add "in the school," because I think it will be a sad day for our children when the school abandons the in loco parentis policy and practice.

Adolescence is a time of rapid physical, emotional, intellectual, and spiritual growth. In our society it is the period during which young people must choose their life goals and acquire the solid foundation and formal education in character development that will enable them to advance their goals. Parents do their teenagers a serious disservice when they continue to treat them as irresponsible children, left ignorant of the challenges of life, yet free to explore its most intimate, profound mysteries.

The facts in the case are obvious. Adult success and happiness in a complex, highly industrial society such as our own require years of formal training, together with the development of a sense of responsibility, self-control, and discipline. These can be achieved only by serious application of interest and energy during adolescence. Yet, by a strange lack of logic, our society promotes sexual attitudes and practices among adolescents which hinder the preparation required for adulthood if our civilization is to survive.

But it is silly to bemoan early steady dating without replacing it with something better. It is a psychological truism that you cannot change behavior without modifying the attitudes and conditions functionally related to it. If we believe that early steady dating leads to early marriages (and the incidence of family breakdown in early marriages is extremely high), then to change this pattern we will have to modify current attitudes and practices relating to dating, teenage recreation, study, sex instruction, marriage preparation, parental authority, and so on. After all, going steady in the early teens is not a wayward pattern of behavior invented by the teenagers themselves, but rather the logical and inevitable result of the way parents are rearing their children. At present the practice of steady dating is fulfilling felt needs created by the social system. The practice will be eliminated only to the extent that alternate means of meeting these needs are found. It can be done, but it will take a great deal of effort to change teenage dating patterns. This is the challenge facing parents, schools, PTA's, CYO's, YMCA's, churches, and community organizations. If we don't expand this effort, we shall continue to have a great many premature marriages, with all the difficulties, disadvantages, and family breakdowns they involve.

I am in sympathy with the speaker at a White House Conference on Children who exhorted the delegates: "Let the children be children."

He charged that we are robbing our children of the golden age of childhood—that period in late childhood and early adolescence when they need to be left to themselves, quietly to find the depths of their own nature. Instead of leaving them to themselves, we are pushing them, with all sorts of pressures, into paired relationships, and then wonder why there is a "husband-hunting hysteria" among girls who are about to get out of high school.

There are also pressures brought to bear upon parents. They are numerous; I will mention only two. The first pressure is for parents to give their children all the things they didn't have. In a land of plenty it is very natural that we should want to heap gifts and opportunities on our children, hoping to keep them happy. But thoughtful people today are beginning to wonder whether we have been doing too much for our children and not showing sufficient concern for the rights of adults. How much should we do for our children? How much should we permit and compel them to do for themselves? If children have a right to develop their own individuality, do not parents have a right to the time and opportunity to develop their individuality?

And so we can identify two contrasting philosophies in the literature and discussions about childhood and parenthood. One emphasizes the overwhelming responsibility of parents and society. Children are what we make them. They cannot be more, they dare not be less. Wise and adequate parenthood requires that parents assume the responsibility for child development, creating the necessary opportunities for their children to grow into happy and healthy adults. The government should aid parents whenever it can in performing this most worthwhile work of rearing children. The major responsibility for child development lies with the parents, and then with the larger society—with the city, state, and federal government.

But the opposite point of view is rather critical of this emphasis; it contends that too much concern has been shown for children in our contemporary society, that modern parents tend to pamper rather than discipline, that society gives children too much and expects too little, and that proper child development calls for more emphasis upon child self-help. Adult life, it insists, is grim and hard, and adequate preparation for it dares not partake too much of the soft, the easy, and the effeminate.

A research worker and writer, Roy Helton, has this to say:

> *It is not that we do too much for our children, for we all agree that their health and education are vital responsibilities not yet*

fully discharged, but rather that we do permit them to do too much to us. We allow them to direct our taste and amusement, to control our time, and to determine how we spend our money. They compel us to insist on easy courses for them in their schools, and to badger educational authorities, not for the parental aim of better and more intensive education, but for the adolescent aim of better football teams. In short, they have so far taken over that a growing characteristic of modern life for the past twenty years has been not its youthfulness, but its juvenility. Today we rob youth of their future because we are too tender to deny them anything they now demand. We pity them as we pick their pockets. We do little for our children because we give them too much.

Indeed, some parents try to make their gifts take the place of their own love, comradeship, patience, and understanding. "My father gave me everything," except his time, his interest, and his love."

The other pressure on parents is to be psychologically sophisticated when it comes to child training. Of course, we want parents to be wise, we want them to understand child development, we want them to benefit from all our rich modern treasuries of knowledge. But how we have threatened, warned, castigated, and scared our poor trembling parents into helpless paralysis by presenting them with awful pictures of their children as being as frail and fragile as Dresden china, until they could no longer act like strong self-willed adults any more.

No child wants a walking psychology text for a parent. He wants and needs an average human being, not free from faults and weaknesses, but one who accepts his responsibilities, who is prepared to give love, to go on giving love, and, when the occasion requires it, prepared to administer discipline firmly and decisively. An article in *Harper's Magazine* recently said that in the old days parents used to carry a big stick and go thump, thump. Nowadays parents go dainty, dainty, and carry a big book!

It is quite possible, however, for parents to do everything right "by the book" and still produce poorly adjusted children. It is the quality of the parents' relationship with the child that counts most. Into this quality go such positive elements as affection, warmth, understanding of a child's needs, respect for the "self of the child," and the mother's ability to accommodate herself to her child emotionally.

Another pressure affecting family stability comes from in-laws. It is a serious problem that must be faced by every young married couple. It is time we stopped joking about it. Judson and Mary Landis, in their study of hundreds of marriages, asked married couples what they found to be the greatest problem in starting their marriage. Overwhelmingly, it was "getting along with in-laws."

John L. Thomas, Jesuit sociologist and author of *The American Catholic Family*, made a study of seven thousand divorces in the Archdiocese of Chicago. If anyone still has the delusion that Roman Catholics don't get divorces, let him look at the figures. Father Thomas tried to identify the causes of the divorces and to correlate the cause with the length of marriage. Obviously, the fact is that the break-up of marriage in the first few weeks might not be the same as those which break up a marriage after twenty years. He found that to be true. He discovered that during the first twelve months after the wedding it was the mother-in-law who was responsible for the break-up of marriages more than any other factor. After that her influence gradually disappeared and alcoholism took its place. (Can there be a causal relationship here?)

I am not sure that I would adopt the slogan "Outlaw the in-laws," but there is something seriously wrong in a situation in which the mother, who presumably loves the young people and wants them to be successful, is the one who destroys the marriage—quite unintentionally in most cases, of course. But it isn't always her fault. Sometimes the younger generation is much worse in its attitudes than the older one. Perhaps we need classes for mothers-in-law. We need premarital education for mothers-in-law just as we do for daughters-in-law. It seems to me that this is one of the areas where the Church might be of great help. We cannot afford to face with equanimity—you may think this strange—the verified fact that the happiest marriages are those in which parents on both sides are dead! I do not know a sadder, more melancholy finding in all modern social science than that. It is time we do something about it.

There is also a great pressure in our culture on young married couples to be happily married. Americans are incurable optimists, and they believe that the saying "And they lived happily ever after" begins with wedding bells. Everybody expects a great deal from marriage; and this is fine within reason, but often it is without reason. Marriage was not designed as a mechanism for providing perfect friendship, unalloyed erotic bliss, perpetual romantic love, comprehensive personal fulfillment, continuous lay psychotherapy, or constant fun, fun, fun. It is absurd to expect any human relationship to bring permanent and unmixed happiness. Indeed, continued happiness would be a most sterile and damaging condition to live in. The nature of human life is struggle, and if we cannot accept it that way, we cannot start really living. To all of us, of course, there come experiences of great and supreme happiness. There come also experiences of great sorrow. Life is not like the colored ads, and the partial fulfillments we do genuinely experience from time to time are more often than not the prelude to disappointments and frustrations. We cannot be happy all the time, *C'est la vie.*

In this regard, however, perhaps our married people are more realistic than they are given credit for. In a well-known study in the Detroit area, women were asked what they expected of marriage, what satisfactions their marriage brought them, what they wanted most from their marriage. Note; these women lived in a large industrial area and not in comfortable little suburbs and towns. They were pretty much under the pressure of their communities, and yet these women said that they value marriage in rank order for: 1) companionship, 2) a chance to have children, 3) the understanding and emotional support that they get from this intimate relation, 4) love and affection, 5) financial benefit. In other words, the picture of women as grasping, neurotic, unhappy, discontented, irresponsible creatures is utterly untrue. American wives and mothers today, as in the past, are finding basic satisfaction in the central roles within the family. This, I know, goes contrary to feminist Betty Friedan's thesis in her book *The Feminine Mystique.*

The American father, however, does not show up very well by comparison. He has left the work of parenthood too much to his wife. Psychologists never tire of telling us that over-centration of affection from one parent, and lack of normal family patterns based on the cooperation of both sexes, can scarcely fail to leave young people with serious handicaps in mental hygiene. The idea that children of either sex can get along satisfactorily in a two-sexed world with the patterns furnished them by only one sex is distinctively harmful. They need the patterns of both sexes from infancy onward. They need a father as well as a mother.

While American fathers tend to neglect their children more frequently than mothers, I feel that the customary portrayal of the American father is more fictional than real. The picture of the average American father on television is a combination of Caspar Milquetoast and a laughable kind of creature who always gets the dirty end of the deal from his wife, his youngsters, his neighbors, and everyone else. Husbands are considered in popular literature as being henpecked individuals who live in a matriarchy, leave their homes in the morning, drudge through the day in their offices, and come back only to pick up the crumbs of affection, attention, and companionship for which they are earning their sustenance. This profile, however, simply does not jibe with fact.

Representative studies across the country tell us that domination by women in America has been greatly exaggerated. Men, in general, still control their families, and whenever henpecked husbands do exist, they are not victims of shrewish wives, but of their own inadequacy. They are henpecked because they are incompetent. They do less around the home than men of influence. The more prestige a man has at work, the more money he makes, the higher his status, then the more decisions he makes at home. In other words, the man of competence is as great an influence in his home as he is in the business world outside.

Contrary to popular opinion, psychologists have found that women want their husbands to have greater authority. They want to look to their husbands as the chief element of control and authority in the family. They look to their husbands for opinions and want them to make the basic decisions. Women want to have a voice, but they want to look up to their husbands. Any person who has done any marriage counseling at all recognizes this fact.

Most women want a man they can look up to, respect, and lean on, as the tower of strength, authority, and control within the home. Husbands and wives today are closer now that they both share more of the same education and marry each other through voluntary choice. Fathers today seem to enjoy their children more, since they are closer to them than traditionally was true. Now that fathers are participating in child care and child guidance, and hearing their children's discussion and problems, they are closer to them.

Men have more interest in the family than formerly was true. This is particularly the case in so many of our homes that are electrically and electronically controlled. There is more to interest a man and more things for which a man is needed in the family than formerly was the case. There seems to be conclusive evidence that men today understand women and children better than their own grandfathers did. They are more sensitive, more tender, and more satisfied with the relationship within marriage and the family.

This needs stating, because much of the literature today dwells too much on the negative aspects of married life. Much is wrong with the modern family, but much is also right with it. It is still an important primary group in which love and affection are shared among its members. It is still the most important agency in shaping personality patterns of children. It is still the best hope of a better world.

The challenge of family instability today is so great that it should motivate all persons in all fields to lend their efforts to a study of its causes.

If all the various social institutions which influence the family were organized to promote a more stable family, and if adequate education were provided for family living and parenthood, it would be possible to develop a strong family life in the nation. This is an objective worthy of our best effort.

First, Let Our Children Be Children
(The Providence Journal, February 23, 1979)

The Catholic Church and Planned Parenthood seldom see eye to eye, especially on the issue of abortion. But the pope himself would cheer the suggestion of Planned Parenthood's Cynthia Weisbord (*The Providence Journal*, January 31) that concerned citizens should unite in promoting programs designed to foster wholesome family life and sound sex education.

This is vital because of the age in which we live. Sex is the big hang-up of our times. Americans seem to be off on a giant bedroom chase. Sane and rational voices are asking where it's all heading. A nation obsessed with sex tends to let the housekeeping go to hell.

Sex, sociologist David Reisman tells us, has been oversold as the promised land, and French philosopher Albert Camus derides our congenital inability to see in love anything but the physical. A land that elevates chambering from a pastime to a preoccupation is left, Camus observes, with scant vitality for daring or creative exploits.

Others feel that the view of sex-as-a-cure-all stems from the state of anomie which characterizes our depersonalized society. As strangers multiply, as family ties weaken, lonely people desperately clutch at sex to fill the emptiness in their lives and supply the warmth and affection they have despaired of finding in an uncaring world. Unfortunately, the joy of sex is too frail to support such a heavy emotional burden.

A concupiscent culture imposes strains on youth. Young people are pressured into early dating, early steady-dating, and early marriage. Advertising, entertainment, and fashion are all designed to produce, and then to exploit, sexual tension. Sexually aroused at an early age, and urged to postpone marriage until they become older, teenagers are expected to fill the intervening years with courtship rituals and games that are supposed to be sexy but sexless.

The dating game hinges on an important exchange: The male wants sexual intimacy; the female wants social commitment. (Even living together sans ring implies commitment of some kind.) The game involves bartering sex for security amid the sweet and heady agitations of a romantic entanglement.

Once the game reaches the going-steady stage, teenagers find themselves driven into a corner, and the one way to legitimize their sex play, and assuage guilt, is to plan marriage. And so they marry early and society loses a physician, a nurse, a scientist, a lawyer, a teacher, an engineer. No man can serve two masters, and since the energy and scope of interest for any individual are limited, solid preparation for a worthwhile career is never achieved.

Isn't it time we acknowledged that teenagers are not adults? They're approaching maturity while trying to grapple with problems peculiar to their state of development. At this period of their lives, parental guidance, supervision, and control are essential in the areas of dating, drinking, driving, and recreation.

Ultra-permissiveness can be ruinous. A child can experience the meaning of secure love only through being dependent on parents who supply authoritative direction to his life and who permit freedom according to the ability of the child to handle it.

Paradoxically, at the time when teenagers need it most, parents have reneged on their obligation to exercise control over them. Indeed, nowadays, parents are horrified at the thought of using force or threats to make a child of any age do anything.

Instead of defining limits to behavior, parents mollycoddle and offer little resistance to their offspring's importunate demands. They countenance in their children what they would not tolerate in themselves.

Character-wise, such parental capitulation wreaks havoc on growing boys and girls, for if parents abandon their convictions under pressure from their children, how can they ever expect children to develop backbone enough to uphold standards under pressure from their peers?

No father or mother would ever think of depriving offspring of a balanced physical diet, yet they unwittingly deprive youth of a balanced moral diet. While stuffing their children's bodies with vitamins, minerals, and proteins, parents often starve their consciences by catering to their every whim and by failing to instill elementary principles of decency, law, order, and occasional renunciation.

Adult success in a complex, highly industrial society like ours demands years of formal schooling. Advanced training, however, can be gained only by dint of mental sweat, undivided interest, and undaunted perseverance. This calls for self-control, self-discipline, and personal responsibility during adolescence.

Teenagers need help. Yet by a kind of schizoid logic, adults continue to approve sexual attitudes and practices among youth which hamstring career preparation and produce premarital pregnancies.

But it is silly to decry pre-teen pairing and early steady-dating without offering something better to replace it. Psychologists tell us that behavior cannot be changed unless the attitudes and conditions functionally related to it are also modified.

If early steady-dating leads to early intimacy, out-of-wedlock births (in spite of contraceptive availability), and premature marriages (family crack-ups rise as marital age level drops), then to change this pattern, current attitudes and practices relating to dating, teenage recreation, study, sex instruction, marriage preparation, parental authority, etc., will also have to be amended.

At present the early steady-dating mania is fulfilling felt needs created by the social system. It can only be gotten rid of when alternate and more satisfying means of meeting these needs are found.

This is the Herculean task facing parents, schools, PTA's, CYO's, YMCA's, family movements, churches, and community organizations. Some of these groups are already engaged in programs designed to remedy this situation. It will require the cooperative effort of all concerned.

As a first step, may I suggest that we let our children be children. Let's not rob them of the golden age of childhood—that period in late childhood and early adolescence when they need to be left to themselves, quietly to find the depths of their own nature. Let's avoid pushing them with all sorts of pressures into paired relationships, where they are often kept ignorant of the challenges of life, yet free to explore its most intimate profound mysteries.

Where Lies Parental Responsibility?
(*The Providence Journal-Bulletin*, July 19, 1996)

The ancient Greeks judged parents by the quality of their children, and the proverb "Train up a child in the way he should go; and when he is old he will not depart from it" is part of moral folklore that proclaims we are pretty much what our homes have made us.

But is it fair to fault parents for every child who comes a-cropper? Mothers who smother and overprotect their offspring (momism) were once charged by psychologist Philip Wylie with causing all the ills of society, and when offspring get in trouble today, parents agonize, "What did I do wrong?" But the cliché "There are no problem children, only problem parents" is as fanciful as the belief that children are "imps of Satan."

Are the parents of alleged Unabomber Theodore Kaczynski responsible for his bomb-making and his weird anti-social lifestyle? Were Jack and Jo Ann Hinckley somehow accountable for their son John's attempted assassination of President Reagan? Can the mother of John Youmans (he killed two hunters) be implicated in his crime because she concealed his guilt?

A human being is not a machine that once set rolling in the wrong direction is unable to change its course. Parents set the stage for the drama of their children's lives, but the human organism is an ongoing, changing concern with the motives of the individual its propelling force. Every person follows his own moral imperative. Free will is a fact of experience. Children are undoubtedly miniatures of their parents, but not up to the point where parents can be blamed for what their children do or fail to do.

Before flunking parents for doing a poor job, one has to take into account the innumerable forces affecting children beyond their parents' values, forces hardly subject to parental control—peer-group pressure, movies, television, etc. Aristotle advocated keeping children away from all that is base and violent in music, art, speech, and conduct. Impossible today.

Notwithstanding, who would gainsay that a family's philosophy of life, its scale of values, largely determines a child's future behavior? Research corroborates folk wisdom: "Like father, like son; like mother, like daughter." Studies of sources from which children derive their ethical concepts show a striking correspondence between the moral judgments of the child and those of parents.

But values are transmitted best in the nitty-gritty of daily living. Instruction counts for much, but actions speak louder than words. Parents who wring their hands and whine about being powerless to influence children's behavior are copouts. "Diogenes struck the father when the son swore."

Excuses for poor parenthood abound. For instance, powerful external ambition—which can often be a force for public good—is used to justify parental neglect. This explains why intelligent, successful, ambitious, political, professional, and business people may not be sufficiently dedicated to parenting to transmit appropriate values to their children.

Parents sometimes opt, implicitly or explicitly, for business, professional, or political achievement rather than for committed parenthood. Successful men, research discloses, are often absentee fathers, spending less than 45 minutes a week in conversation and contact with their offspring. Yet ancient wisdom avows that "one father is better than a hundred schoolmasters."

Absentee fathers produce two negative effects: lack of parental supervision and discipline; lack of a sex-role model for sons. One great function fathers normally fulfill is that of developing an appropriate sexual identity in children. All emotionally handicapped offspring have one thing in common; in childhood, they experienced the absence of an accessible parent because of death, divorce, or a time-demanding job.

Parents like to rationalize their absence by saying, "It's not the quantity of time you spend with children, it's the quality." But time is like oxygen; there is a minimum amount that's needed to survive. The price of success in business, politics, or the professions occurs too often at the expense of successful parenthood.

While dedicated service to one's vocation may serve the commonwealth, committed parents deserve to be told that they, too, serve; they foster America's future just as much as citizen who devote all of their time and effort to "getting ahead."

Inept parents have children who, in turn, become inept parents. As divorces multiply, as separations, desertions, and abandonments increase, welfare costs rise, more children become the community's responsibility, and the nation is burdened with growing numbers of psychologically damaged children.

An improved society of better citizens depends largely on the production of better parents. Americans have to realize that the most challenging, creative task they will ever face is to take an infant, guide him through the shoals of childhood and adolescence, and bring him to the maturity of responsible adulthood and citizenship.

Delinquency Is a Product of Our Own Homes
(*The Providence Visitor*, November 28, 2002)

It is true that delinquency, like poverty, is always with us, but the delinquency perpetuated nowadays is horrifying. More than a generation ago, it was a rare day when a man under 20 years of age was on trial for a felony. Now crimes committed by youths against property and persons run the gamut from burglary and auto theft to robbery, rape, and murder.

What can be done?

Punishment seldom works. So, shall we pat the delinquent on the back and say: "You poor fellow. You really shouldn't have slugged that old man in the park just for the fun of it, but we know what you're up against—what with the slums and bad examples and all. You really couldn't help it."

No, in all cases of delinquency, the true working principle should be that the kids can help it—barring, of course, real cases of pathological and compulsive criminality. Most of the young hoodlums choose to be bigshots, to strut and swagger and bully. When they are caught, they may rage with stubborn resentment, but they are also smart enough to make suckers out of the "coddlers" who offer a diet of mawkish sympathy.

The best way to deal with delinquents lies somewhere between punching them and slobbering over them. Firmness plus kindness—that's what the delinquent responds to most. Punishment must have one objective: interior conversion, a change of heart and mental attitude that will voluntarily produce upright conduct and personal responsibility.

Any reform must be based on a solid system of values, and herein lies the problem. The deviant conduct of the young criminal today is characterized by an almost total disregard for the rights and feelings of others. He exhibits the following traits:

- little knowledge of ethical ideals and limited social conscience;
- a selfishness that considers other human beings only insofar as they are means of satisfying oneself;
- emotional shallowness, lack of regret when caught doing wrong, and violent outbursts of temper when blocked from goals of the moment.

Teenage delinquency reflects the confusion of values in American society. That makes it not merely a problem of individual morality, but also a social problem. Every person does wrong of his own free will, and no temptation, however strong, justifies crime. Nevertheless, given adverse circumstances or grave temptation, more than a few people will succumb to evil-doing. It is a truism that social conditions help or hinder the practice of virtue.

It comes as no surprise, then, that the contradictions of American life show up in the behavior of youths.

When money is worshipped as the only criterion of success, then greed will be a motive in teenage crime. When salaciousness is countenanced and glorified in movies, novels, stage shows, and television, then sexual adventurism will be attractive to youths. When we endow with respectability crooks who flaunt their ill-gotten gains by a high style of living, then expect dishonesty in youths. When homes are bereft of love and understanding and when parents place their own selfish interests above the welfare of their offspring, then youths will seek support in the bosom of the gang.

The delinquent has, more often than not, been psychologically cheated out of his right to love, direction, discipline, and the moral leadership in the home that provides him with an adequate scale of values.

We are pretty much what our homes have made us.

Juvenile crime will continue to escalate until parents, teachers, clergy, and other societal agents inculcate in young people those inner sanctions that restrain them when there are no police to hold them back; until young people are taught those ideals of right that rest not on expedience, but on obedience to the laws of the land and the laws of God; until young people embrace a philosophy of life-encompassing values, principles, and standards by which they can achieve a satisfying lifestyle and bring order into their conflicting desires.

(9)
Gender

American Womanhood: An Untapped Source of Power
(Excerpt of a talk delivered at the New England Conference of State Federation of Women's Clubs, September 1962)

The unfolding of the first half of the 20th century has seen women win rights that would have left Aristotle blinking in amazement. And nowhere have the ladies come more completely into their own than here in the United States. While the belles of Turkey and Persia were shedding their time-honored veils, while the better-class women of China were beginning to appear for the first time in public, and the ladies of Spain, Greece, Germany, Italy, and Russia were starting to trickle into even the fighting armies, the women of America were winning for themselves a social and political quality unparalleled in history.

The power of American women is incalculable. They spend about eighty-five cents out of every dollar for consumer goods (and suggest what man should do with the remaining fifteen cents). They own most of the factories, stores, utilities, and natural resources. Eligible women voters outnumber the men by some 4,000,000. They are principally responsible for the education of the young of both sexes.

But how did American women manage to get into such an advantageous position? Well, the first big step in this direction came from the feminist movement. The general theme of the movement, often expressed in shrill feminine shrieks, was that women had been forced by men to occupy an inferior and secondary place in the world. Indeed, the book I mentioned previously, *The Second Sex*, by the French lady Simone de Beauvoir, has the same motif. The feminists claim that although women number half of the world's population, men have so managed to shape tradition, social custom, and education, that the ladies are condemned to an inferior status. They are not free and independent and cannot associate with men in the professional fields. In brief, women have always got a dirty deal and it's about time that somebody stirred up a "new deal for women" revolution. As Catholic author G. K. Chesterton remarked of the feminist movement: "Thousands of women rose up in rebellion and said that they would not be dictated to; then they went out and became stenographers."

But what did the feminists want anyway? Well, they wanted equality ... equal right to vote, equal educational opportunity, equal access to jobs at all levels of the occupational scale, equal right to divorce, the striking out of all sexual differentiation from the law. And what they believed would result from all these freedoms was not so much that they could then cooperate with man in making a better world, but rather that they would take over the job ... because men had made such a botch of governing, of making a living, and of establishing peace and justice.

Well, it has been over a century since the feminists held the first Women's Rights Convention at Seneca Falls, New York, in 1848. Since that time these determined women have chalked up some formidable victories against a sullen male society. Whether these gains can be said to be beneficial in their results can be hotly argued. But it is easy to say, as many have been saying, that the feminist movement has failed. Let us look at some of the gains and see if they have produced the results which the feminists claimed would follow from them.

Women began their bid for social equality by winning the right to vote in 1920. Today the ladies control several million more votes than men. And yet now that they have the right, how often do they use it, and how well informed are they when they do use it? One thing is sure: no clearly defined "women's vote" has emerged. In fact, women consistently fail to exercise their right of suffrage as often as men, in terms of the proportionate representation of both sexes in the population. The women's vote, moreover, is tied to the man's. Married women vote more frequently than unmarried; and career or employed women vote less than do leisured women. Most important of all, however, married women's voting behavior fluctuates with that of their husbands. Usually husband and wife vote together, but while husbands have wives who do not vote, the reverse occurs much less frequently.

Again, contrary to the feminists' hope, the women's vote did not destroy machine politics. It is true that the ladies were the backbone of the prohibition movement—a rather dubious honor. It is true also that social-problem issues such as child labor, slum clearance, prison reform, and pure food and drug measures have consistently interested various women's groups. Nevertheless, there has been no significant variation in the vote because of sex differences, no women's bloc; nor has there been any great change in the political picture because women now vote.

Moreover, if the success of the feminist movement is to be gauged by their battle cry "political equality," we must again say that it has been somewhat of a failure. Oh, they have come a long way since 1924, when Nellie Taylor Ross of Wyoming won the election that made her the country's first lady governor; and when "Ma" Ferguson was installed as the lady governor of Texas in 1925. But they have failed to obtain the political leadership they looked for. Indeed, by and large, the women have gained auxiliary and not key posts within the major political parties. For the most part they perform the routine tasks ... functioning as election clerks and inspectors, helping precinct captains in checking lists of voters, running errands, and knocking on the doors of indifferent voters. The fact is that a large number of American women are cynical, indifferent, or contemptuous over the political gains of their own sex.

When we enter the business world, we find that women have made many gains; but it is hard to assess whether the results have been beneficial or edifying. While it is generally conceded that women own about three-quarters of all wealth in the United States, it must also be conceded that they neither control nor manage the organizations maintaining and producing that wealth. The whole nation can now list over seventeen million women workers, thirty-three percent of the total female population and twenty-nine percent of the entire American labor force. This percentage will probably increase, especially since there is a decreasing prejudice against women on the part of organized labor since they were so widely employed during the last war (i.e., World War II).

The fact remains, however, that home and marriage still constitute the real and ideal state of America's women. Would we have it otherwise! The country would be in a perilous state if it were not so. If you ask why women work, the answer is, that if she is married, she works from felt economic necessity, or to maintain a higher standard of living than would otherwise be possible. If she is unmarried, she tends to regard her job as a stopgap until such a time as she will be married. Surveys taken in our schools and colleges point up the fact that the vast majority of single women do not prepare wholeheartedly for a career. For over seventy percent the occupation "wife" heads up the list of job preferences. That being so, it is safe to say that the career woman is a statistical abnormality. Perhaps that is why so few women seem to find any satisfaction in the work they do—they never thought of it as a life work. Most modern women do, have, or will work outside the home at some time during their lives, but they work discontinuously, and that work is geared in some way to marriage and the family.

But what do women do at work? Well, modern technology's virtual elimination of the strong back, plus the labor demand of the last war, has opened almost every job classification to some women. Today we find the ladies as railroad workers, bank executives, vice presidents, and a host of other executive officers.

Nevertheless, we are forced to say that although new fields have opened up to many women, the majority continue to be employed either in "women's jobs" or in the new fields which pay little and do not confer prestige of a high order. Some of the unions are now backing the ladies' demand of "equal pay for equal work," and governmental legislation has helped the cause, but in many cases, women still are paid less than male coworkers for doing the same job. Pope Pius XII said in 1945: "The Church has always held that women should receive the same pay as men for equal work and output."

Again, while today there is not a very great residue of prejudice against working women as such, still there is a residue of prejudice against the ambitious woman who is qualified by capability to compete with her male job associates. It is women in supervisory and administrative posts who arouse the ire of men and the jealousy of women. How often do you hear men loudly insist, "I wouldn't work for any woman", and how often do you hear women themselves say, "I would rather work for a man any day." In other words, there is a tacit assumption that there is a job ceiling for women; and this was shown even during the national crisis of the last war when little progress was reported in accustoming either men or women to the idea that women should be placed in positions of command over man. Still, there has been great progress in this area.

In the field of education, the picture is not very much different. More than three times as many men receive master's degrees as women; and in acquiring the doctorate the proportion is more than fifteen to one in favor of the man. Moreover, the male college graduate will earn almost twice as much as the working female graduate; and the occupational range of the female graduate will be much narrower, with sixty percent of all working female college graduates becoming schoolteachers.

There has been a great deal of dissatisfaction and acidulous criticism of women's education in the past five years, especially of higher education. They represent two points of view. On the one hand, there is the old feminist cry of sexual discrimination and inequality in educational opportunity. They argue that women's vocational interests are almost as diversified as men's, but women's colleges, and even coeducational high schools, do not afford them equal opportunity for vocational preparation. On the other hand, there are those who claim that education has been completely masculine dominated, that woman has been treated like a man in disguise, that the curriculum has been oriented toward vocational training that is not appropriate for the majority of women, whose career will be marriage and family life. Indeed, so profoundly masculine is our whole tradition of education that at the present time a woman tends to be defeminized in proportion to her level of education. It may have been necessary in the past century for women battling against masculine domination to prove that they were intellectually tough enough to undertake the same studies men did, and certainly the proof was produced. But it is high time for educational institutions to explore and develop a distinctively feminine higher education in terms of woman's nature.

The feminist movement is not dead, nor even moribund, but is still capable of bringing forth old and new prescriptions for women's equality and her place in the modern world. But a different theme is now beginning to appear, taking a middle ground and steering a middle course between these two extremes. Women should stop trying to win a foothold for themselves in a man's world, and instead should turn their attention to fashioning the kind of woman and the kind of man who can work together in a human world, to which both sexes can contribute equally. In other words, women should stay in the home where and when she is needed, but at the same time she should enter into business, politics, and social welfare work when she has both the time and energy.

Women have tremendous power. It is a tragedy that it is so scattered, dispersed, and disorganized. In spite of the fact that thirty-five million women belong to more than two hundred thousand clubs, they have failed to exert their strength in proportion to their numbers. Much more could be done to make women's power felt more forcefully in the areas of politics, civil rights, social-security legislation, housing, health, and kindred fields.

One thing is sure: the old feminist battle cry against women's status as a woman is being heard no longer. The voice of rebellion is silent; and it is silent because it was stupid. It failed to take into consideration the biological, psychological, and physiological differences between men and women and the respective roles they should play in society. The battle of the sexes is a frustrating, wasteful, and foolish struggle, unprofitable to both men and women and to society as a whole. The byword now should be that of cooperation and not war.

The Status of Women in Business and Professions
(Excerpt of a talk delivered at the National Biennial Institute
for Business Educators, June 16, year unknown)

In most pagan societies, womankind has an inferior status. She is the first of the male's chattels and a social cipher. It is the Gospel that ultimately powers the trend to give woman the suffrage, free her from civic disabilities, and allow her to enter careers where she may use her talents for the upbuilding of the common good.

Despite female emancipation, the male still harbors the illusion that woman is the "lesser man." He fosters a stereotype of the female which emphasizes her lower intelligence, emotional instability, and general ineptitude to engage in activity that transcends home economics. Obviously, it is to the advantage of the lordly male to perpetuate this stereotype and to encourage its submissive acceptance among women. In this way the male employs tradition and prejudice to prevent women from encroaching on such typically male preserves as architecture, engineering, business, and politics. One of the great pities of the modern world is that women generally subscribe to the stereotype created for them by the dominant male and thereby hamper their power to contribute significantly to the betterment of the whole human family.

The masculine posture of superiority finds cold comfort in the Church's attitude toward woman's place in society today, even though the Church deplores the philosophy of individualism that atomizes society and tends to eject woman from the home and make her a mere economic competitor of the male.

Christianity has always maintained that male and female share the same destiny and enjoy an absolute equality in personal dignity and value. Because of this shared goal there is no field of human activity which must remain closed to woman; her horizons reach out to the regions of politics, labor, the arts, and sports. Granted that the sublimest mission of woman is motherhood, still her personal perfection can be attained in other ways. Not all women are called to motherhood, neither is it possible for all to find their maximum personal development in the atmosphere of the home. "Woman's place is in the home" is a neat generality that simply does not fit the reality of modern society. It is not a precept of natural or divine law, least of all in an era of social upheaval that tends to debase woman, destroy the family, and endanger the common good of all the world.

Women have made many gains in the business world. Women workers number thirty-four percent of the total female population and comprise about thirty percent of the entire American labor forces.

Modern technology's virtual elimination of the strong back, plus the labor demand of the last war, has opened almost every job classification to women. Nevertheless, although new fields have opened to many women, the majority continue to be employed either in "women's jobs" or in fields which pay little and do not confer prestige of a high order. Many unions have backed the ladies' demand of "equal pay for equal work," and governmental legislation has helped, but in most cases, women still are paid less than their male coworkers for doing the same job. This is an injustice.

Again, while today there is not a very great residue of prejudice against working women as such, still there is a prejudice against the ambitious woman who is qualified by capabilities to compete with her male job associates. It is women in supervisory and administrative posts who arouse the ire of men and the jealousy of women. How often do you hear men loudly insist, "I wouldn't work for any woman"; and how often do you hear women themselves say, "I would rather work for a man any day." In other words, there is a tacit assumption that there is a job ceiling for women; and that is why even during the last war little progress was reported in accustoming either men or women to the idea that women should be placed in positions of command over men.

It is the right and duty of woman to take an active part in the movements of the day. The fate of human relations is at stake everywhere. So far, the male of the race has not distinguished himself in securing the welfare of humanity. It is not impossible that history may yet see women assuming a dominant role in the direction and control of community activity. Today, of course, this is still "a man's world," and it is the urgent mission of women to cooperate with men for the total good of country and society generally.

The Catholic Woman as an Intellectual
(Talk delivered to Delta Alpha Chapter of Delta Epsilon Sigma at Salve Regina College, October 17, 1968)

As president of Delta Epsilon Sigma, it is always a pleasure to install a new chapter of this honor society at a college for women. It helps to lay to rest the old canard that women are non-intellectual or even anti-intellectual. God does not grant the gift of intelligence on the basis of a person's sex. The brainpower of American women is the largest untapped, natural resource in this country. It is up to the colleges to tap this resource. Indeed, if a women's college is best judged by its end product, its alumnae, then Salve Regina succeeds or fails in its mission to the degree that it instills in its graduates a love of learning and a delight in the affairs of the mind.

Perhaps women themselves have contributed to the stereotyped image of woman being mentally inferior to man, of being less concerned and less capable of dealing with ideas. They have neglected to use the intelligence God gave them. They have been brainwashed for so long with the idea that the development of brainpower is a male prerogative that they have come to believe it themselves. Women are convinced that such is the natural order of things. This follows the psychological law that if you continually tell a person that she is born mentally inconsequential, she is likely to become so.

Moreover, since women see that this mental subservience flatters the male vanity and is a sop to the male ego, they become conspirators in continuing the fiction that women are less mentally acute than men. The worldly wise and witty Erasmus once said that "A wise woman is twice a fool." And the poet Tennyson once remarked, "Men hate a learned woman." In the eighteenth century, Doctor John Gregory in a book titled *A Father's Legacy to His Daughters* tells young ladies to "Be every cautious in displaying your good sense ... If you happen to have any learning, keep it a profound secret, especially from men who are apt to look with a jealous and malignant eye on a woman of great parts and cultivated understanding."

Even today you find girls concealing their intelligence in order to preserve their charm for the boys. Psychologists have found that in coeducational schools a girl's grades will start to slip when she begins dating boys. The reason for this is that she does not want to compete with the boys in the classroom and thus cut down on her chances for eligible dates. So she plays it dumb—keeps her mouth shut or merely talks about the weather—and thus the myth of women's mental inferiority is perpetuated.

No one will deny that women think differently than men. But to say that her mind works differently is not to say that she is any less rational than man. Women's intellectual interests are very largely utilitarian and rooted in concrete reality. A woman is not very interested in the causes of things, but rather in their use here and now. That is why she is sometimes accused of being illogical. But she can always reply that logic will not make a pudding or dry a child's tears. It has often been remarked that while a man is asking himself why a child is crying, a woman has already dried its tears and comforted it. It is the duty of college women, especially you honor students, to change the image of women as being thoughtless, scatterbrained, and mentally incompetent.

G. K. Chesterton once remarked that the "most practical preparation for motherhood" is liberal education. If this is true, and I am convinced that it is, can we not say that a woman with few intellectual interests is to some degree unsuited to be a wife and mother? Who will raise up the Salks and Oppenheimers, the Faulkners, Wrights, and Einsteins, if not the women who rock the cradle and begin the child's education with its first building blocks? German philosopher Johann Goethe once wrote that "the eternal feminine leads us upward." But we need women who are both "eternally feminine" and broadly cultivated. In this age of comparative leisure, no intelligent woman need close the door of her mind when she opens the door of her nursery. Motherhood is not antithetical to mental curiosity, nor is it incompatible with intellectual interests.

Our country has never been in more need of intellectual women. The turmoil in the land clearly shows that our democracy is in a state of crisis. In the late 1920s, men thought that democracy was inevitable; now they know it is an achievement that is always precarious. You have a mandate in regard to that achievement. As Christian women, you are actively to see to it that democracy as a natural demand imposed by reason itself is given more perfect expression in political, economic, and social life than it has hitherto had in American history. Not only have you a mandate from your Christian conscience—is there not also being addressed to you by your fellow American citizens an invitation, even an urgent summons? They ask your help in solving the problems of democracy. These problems are, at bottom, religious and moral. You are called upon to use your intelligence to subdue the mounting sea of misunderstanding and prejudice and fear that separates citizen from citizen. People of good will wait for you, ready for collaboration with you on terms of civic equality—ready even to accept the leadership which your Christian principles make you responsible to give—toward the solution of all the problems of American and world democracy. The problems are endless and every one of them is basically a spiritual and moral problem, and not one of them can be solved except by the whole American people.

The intellectual, man or woman, who retires to an ivory tower when society cries out for help is guilty of moral cowardice and cruel indifference. Indeed, when the intellectual withdraws from society he leaves its ultimate direction up to the salesman and the politician, to classes not devoted professionally to the truth. This is very like the abdication of reason in the person, for intellectuals are by definition the people equipped to think. The intellectual is supposed to be able to ask the right questions, search for correct answers, and arrive at sound solutions to complex problems.

In a healthy society it is the intellectual who determines the values the rest of society accepts. It is ultimately the intellectual who forms public opinion, for he or she teaches those who teach the rest of society and in the learned journals he or she informs those who popularize their information and attitudes in the classroom, the popular journals, the editorial columns, and the other media forming public opinion. Similarly, in a healthy society it is the intellectual who makes the ultimate decision on questions of public policy and public morality, and who serves as the critic of society. If the intellectual abdicates, these decisions will be made by those not qualified to make them. Ideas have consequences in the political order. The pursuit of truth has social effects, and while it is not the task of every individual to apply to the practical order the truth he or she finds, intellectuals as a class cannot afford to be indifferent as to how it is applied. If they are indifferent, then they implicitly deny that intellectual activity is socially important, and they can be rightfully stigmatized as being "bubbleheads."

But if our country has need of intellectual women today, the American Catholic Church has even more need of the help of such women. For a brief period following the Second Vatican Council there was a wave of optimism and enthusiasm. People had visions of a world in which religions and perhaps even nations would be united in a reign of concord, cooperation, and prosperity. Such an outlook, somewhat Pollyannish, was born of a blend of naïveté and a general sense of well-being and good will generated by the Council and the personal warmth of Pope John XXIII. With all that has since transpired in the world and in the Church, this naïve optimism has now yielded to nervous fears and pessimistic defeatism. As Catholic intellectuals, you are called upon to diagnose and to help cure the contagious mood of discouragement spread on every side by a host of prophets of despair, who, impatient with the slow results of the Ecumenical Council, now prepare for Götterdämmerung.

Much of this dispirited and fearful defeatism is due to loss of perspective. People always tend to see their times out of focus, and each generation is tempted to believe that nobody before has known the troubles it must endure.

It therefore becomes our duty as Christian intellectuals to intensify in yourselves, and to communicate to your fellow man, a balanced, serene perspective which sees all things in their relation to one another, and above all, to God, evaluating them in the light of eternity as well as of history. Such calm detachment is difficult to achieve, but it is, nonetheless, most necessary. However, though others may fret and frenzy, our intellectuals—and I consider you honor students to be intellectuals—are called to maintain something of the equanimity of the saints, thus preserving us from the extremes of slothful complacency or vituperative despair. Indeed, this is the perennial vocation of the Christian intellectual: to resist the intemperate talk of the brash innovators and the nervous traditionalists; to remain spiritually competent and intellectually calm in the face of change or challenge, the threat of evil, or the seduction of novelty. It is to recapture the spirit of the ancient Jewish teacher Gamaliel, in the face of the new directions and challenging changes of Vatican II—changes which do not touch on the great dogmas of the faith or basic precepts of the Christian moral code, but which disturb those attached to certain secondary corollaries of a social, economic, or personal kind.

How sanely Gamaliel summed up the lessons which religion and reason, hope and human history, should teach us in times of disturbing new ideas and far-reaching changes. Faced with ideas which alarm the traditional concepts of his contemporaries, he said in effect: "If these things be of man, they will run their course and have their end; if they be of God, you will have no power to overthrow them, and had best come to understand them, seeking to discern how much may be good in what at first jars; how much true in what seems novel; how much beautiful in what is unfamiliar; how much in a word is divine plan, though it seem, at first, to be no more than human striving."

The type of education you receive at a Catholic college like Salve Regina should have one great effect: It should help you to achieve the resolute calm and the imperturbable equanimity sometimes so painfully absent from the reactions even of Christians to the events of our times, and always so needed in an age of great fears. As Christian intellectuals you must keep before your eyes the lessons of history. You are reminded that not all places under heaven are battlefields where evil triumphs, or cities of confusion where justice is mocked, and malice, treachery, and violence hold their evil courts. A study of the history of the Church and the lives of the saints provides proper perspective for our present time. The intellectual does not forget the treachery of the Garden of Eden and the courtyard of Peter's betrayal, but he also features for our times the Mount of the Transfiguration and the Garden of the Resurrection.

What are the worries, the grounds for fear in the hearts of those who love the Church? We are told that the defections of priests, nuns, and other religious, the adverse reaction of the laity to the encyclicals on birth control and celibacy, and the open disobedience and criticism of Church authority are indications that the Church is not merely in evolution, but in revolution and dissolution. The Church has had her day, it is asserted. She may have been pertinent in a feudal order, but she is obsolete in the age of democracy. Her power and authority may have been tolerable or intelligible to the sacral civilization of the 13th century, but it is alien and not to be borne in the free atmosphere of the 20th-century secularism. Challenge then her affectations; expose her irrelevancy; undermine her efforts; and annul her influence. The time has come at last to end this dated farce.

Such things are said—they are written and widely read—in this country and abroad. These statements agitate the timid and insecure and shake the unsteady in faith or the unread in history. The Catholic scholar, however, takes down his history books and notes the number of times the collapse of the Catholic Church in the near future has been predicted. There is one patient lesson the Catholic intellectual learns from all the vicissitudes of the Church, namely that we should not be pollyannas or pessimists, but that we should be Christian men and women of a confidence rooted in the recognition that men and events pass, God and His work endure.

The trials of the Church in the past should also teach us that the tensions which plague us now are not new, either in form or in substance, or in the remedies for them, and that what made our fathers strong in faith and in practice should not find us timid. Nothing can happen in our day, nor in the days to come, so calculated to appall, but what the Christian intellectual, glancing at his *Roman Martyrology* or Challoner's *Memories of the Missionary Priests*, or any standard Church history manual, will say: "We've gone through tougher trials than these!"

That is why we reserve the right to question the spiritual soundness, the doctrinal integrity, as well as the intellectual acumen of those who perpetually cry havoc or proclaim the spiritual bankruptcy of the Church, and their disillusionment with the Ecumenical Council. The authentic, sober, yet radiant spirit of the Church is more perfectly echoed in the words pronounced by the late Cardinal Feltin of Paris. He said: "We Christians are more optimistic than all others, even though we recognize the vast errors of which human nature is capable. We are not utopians, but we know that grace is stronger than sin."

That same spirit of Christian optimism animated the valiant Pope Pius XI when he thanked God that he lived in times of such trouble and testing, that it was no longer possible for a Christian to be mediocre. This was the spirit of holy Pope John the XXIII, and it is the same spirit that inspires Pope Paul VI and gives him the courage to carry on. We who believe in the Church in the midst of her present trials feel that because it is the divine ideal it has recuperative power now, as it has been shown to have such power in the past. Christ expected weakness and failure in the Church. He likened it to a field full of wheat and tares. There never has been a time, in the long history of the Church, when it did not need reformation and new inspiration. Its history is the story of a long struggle with a weak membership. But, somehow, it has served its purpose.

Indeed, even as a human institution, one cannot feel that the Church is a failure. After all, we can see an effect upon the general life of its members which, far as it falls short of what we desire, is greater than the results effected by any other institution. We forget how great has been this general advance. It has affected our social life as well as our personal life, our national life, and our spiritual life. Its influence for the good is incalculable.

But if the study of history thus steadies the sight and composes the soul of the Christian intellectual, the study of her faith should confer upon her an even greater boon. It should prompt the Christian intellectual so to perfect her own spiritual life that she may finally come to see the problems of life through the eyes of Christ, and thus achieve, sinner though she be, some share in the majestic dignity, the spiritual liberty and the unafraid poise of the Son of God.

An intellectual attitude such as I have tried to sketch would produce Christian champions in the great war between truth and error now being waged for the conquest of the empires of the mind, champions more given to reason than to wrath; more conspicuous for their share in the patience of God Himself than for the explosive resentments and petty irritations of human beings who, because they are unreasonable, are really less than human.

St. Paul asked that the Christian Gospel be defended in season and out of season. But he admonished His disciples to rebuke when rebuke they must "in all patience and doctrine" (2 Timothy 4:2), two phrases which sum up succinctly the qualities of will and intellect which must become the Christian intellectual.

A generation of genuine Christian intellectuals, mighty in patience and powerful in doctrine, would have neither time nor taste for ill-tempered denunciations, cheap verbal victories, and frenzied argument; they would prefer the persevering, long-suffering work of leavening, quietly and calmly, the world's resistance to the truth; of building with confident determination and God-like magnanimity the enduring walls of the Kingdom of God among the tribes of men. May you honor students at Salve Regina College belong to this generation.

Sex Discrimination and Ordination of Women in the Catholic Church
(*The Cowl*, April 23, 1986)

By standing throughout Mass in protest against females being denied entrance into the priestly calling, Catholic feminists gave a reverse twist to the old criticism of the Church for the way it treats women.

For many years, the Church was castigated by outsiders for exalting women too much. Now women inside its portals, in ironic turnabout, charge the Church with demeaning their sex by limiting their vocational choice.

When Roman law and custom declared women to be chattel of husbands or fathers, the Church proclaimed their dignity and equality with men. When women were debarred from vital posts in society, the Church opened to them careers as doctors, teachers, writers, and administrators.

What now? Can they be priests? No, says the pope, confirming the 1977 Vatican declaration. The ban on priestesses, some think, is not merely disciplinary, but irreversibly doctrinal. It is the will of Christ manifested to his Apostles and carried out by the Church for 2000 years, at a time when female priests functioned in other religions of the world. Christ did not call women. Not even the pope, then, can validly ordain a woman; his laying-on of hands would be null and void.

Notwithstanding, some Catholic women feel they have the "call," argue that a good God would not give the call and then thwart it. But a true "call," officials reply, requires the okay of the Church. Jesus chose those he wanted (Mark 3:13) and said, "You did not choose me, no, I chose you" (John 15:16), and the Church maintains it speaks with the voice of Christ.

While championing the equality of all the baptized (Galatians 3:28), the Church asserts that the roles of men and women are different. One sex is not superior to the other; nor are they the same. Jung and Freud, with psychological acumen, point out that anima and animus in the male and female can be confused only at the risk of psychological and spiritual damage. The sexes are equal but different, says the Church.

What really counts, women are told, is sanctity, not priesthood. Saints, not priests, are the greatest in the kingdom of heaven. So the Church urges women to have zeal for their mission of holiness and be aware of the capital role they play in "the renewal and humanization of society."

Fine, retort Catholic feminists, but since women represent half of the human race, they should have a bigger say in how the Church is run. Scripture and theology, moreover, can offer no insurmountable reasons against ordaining women.

Chauvinist foes of this feminine crusade for Holy Orders fear that women have already been given too much and "now they want to take over the Church."

This is more than a nuns' protest. Its significance can be gauged best in the context of the women's liberation movement. Feminists are persuaded that a worldwide sexual caste system condemns them to an infra-human condition and shunts them to marginal posts in human affairs, and that patriarchal religion legitimates and reinforces the injustices of this system and forces women to become aliens—perennial outsiders in a man's world. The misogynism of the Church fathers and the entire conceptual apparatus of Christian theology, developed in a male-dominated Church, are part of this gigantic putdown of women.

Indeed, for eons, the masculinization of the creator (our Father) has fostered a sexist society and has served to keep authority in the hands of man. The Bible is part of the conspiracy, because the story of the Fall, with Eve portrayed as temptress, convicts the female through her sexuality and contributes to her centuries-old pejorative status and second-class citizenship in the Church.

Nothing short of a revolution of sisterhood, feminists declare, can transform the sexist religion of Western society, its masculine symbols, language, and values. Not surprisingly, leading feminist Gloria Steinem urges sisters to pray to God because "She will hear you."

Catholic feminists cannot be laughed off as fanatical freaks on the lunatic fringe of the faith. Their militant tactics often turn people off, but they are forcing the faithful to take notice. Conscious that the civil-rights cause got nowhere until blacks hit on a strategy of confrontation, feminists have adopted their style.

Does it work? Apparently. Opposition to female priests is decreasing so much, states a recent research report, that if present trends continue, support for ordaining women should reach the fifty percent mark within five years, and in fifteen years will not only be a majority but a consensus position of the American Catholic community.

How will the pope react? Rome is not known to cave in to pressure, and when a 2,000-year tradition is at stake and grave theological and scriptural problems are involved, chances are, the pope won't budge.

In the long run, stand-ins (ups), placard waving, and other flamboyant devices may well be counterproductive, if not completely off-aim. Catholic feminists might fare better switching targets. Some are recommending a revival of the deaconess order which existed in the early Church. A writer suggests (*The Priest*, March 1979) that "before discussing the possibility of women priests, we should discuss possibility of women cardinals."

Historically, ordination was not a prerequisite for the cardinalate (until recently), and a woman—Mother Teresa, for example—would add luster to this male stronghold and lend greater credibility to the Church's determination to exploit women's potential more fully.

The issue of women's rights in the Catholic Church is far from dead.

Role of Women Religious Is Changing
(*The Providence Visitor*, June 28, 1984)

The demonstration of 25 Catholic feminists protesting so-called "unfair treatment of women in the Church" at the Cathedral of SS. Peter and Paul recently raises this question:

Are former sisters Elizabeth Morancy and Arlene Violet, in leaving religious life, reneging on their vows and flouting Church authority, or are they emulating those saints of old who were creatively disobedient?

Paul resisted Peter to his face at the Apostolic Council of Jerusalem; Catherine of Siena, Hildegard of Bingen, Joan of Arc, and many saints of the Middle Ages resisted regulations and commands of their bishops, prelates, and popes.

Church history abounds with examples of courageous wrestling with "Rome"—which in some heroic cases reminds one of the meeting of Jacob with the angel (the bishops are called "angels" in early-Christian tradition): "I will not let thee go, except thou bless me." Without this work of loving obedience in resistance, chances of bringing about changes would be lost and the "orthodox" might never become aware of their deficient Catholicity.

Carolos de Santamaria (*Obedience and Freedom of Catholics*) claims that nonobedience can at times be more heroic than obedience, but only when a "Christian, urged by innermost duty of conscience, disobeys in order to obey a higher power."

The withdrawal of Elizabeth Morancy and Arlene Violet from religious life calls to mind the loss to the Church in the past two centuries of intellectuals (poets, philosophers, scripturists, artists, scientists) whose churchly affiliation was shattered on the crucible of obedience.

Cultural anthropologist Christopher Dawson once compiled the host of prominent ex-priests and ex-religious who, as an elite of European thinkers, stamped the eighteenth and nineteenth centuries intellectually. These persons, who through flight from their vows withdrew obedience, were preceded by those popes of the Middle Ages who immoderately commanded obedience, and in so doing ruined themselves politically and ecclesiastically, like Boniface VIII, who was condemned to Hell by Dante, and whose bull *Unam sanctam* asserted the total political authority of the pope.

The phrase *Roma locuta causa finita* is often improperly extended to include all decisions of the Holy See, even disciplinary ones, whereas, strictly speaking, it refers only to decisions about dogma. Concretely, this means that the Church is constantly widening the area of freedom by revisions of older judgment and rules and is gradually freeing herself from old anxieties (e.g., towards Protestants, still regarded by Gregory XVIII in 1832 as "devilish," but greeted by John Paul II in 1982 as "beloved brethren").

Religious, like others, are products of their times, and the subjectivist spirit of the age has infiltrated religion. Subverting obedience in the Church, this spirit has been wreaking havoc in religious life. Everyone wants to do his own thing. The individual has to get his own way or he won't play. The fact that this attitude assumes the guise of high idealism does not make it any less subjective.

Today, more than ever, the Church is faced with the challenge of expanding freedom of subjects while preventing subjective license. This becomes impossible so long as committed religious interpret personal responsibility as obeying orders only if one happens to agree with them, or reasonableness is identified exclusively with "What I think."

Vatican Council II urged the faithful to grapple with the problems of the world and superiors of the Sisters of Mercy have supported those nuns who embraced a political ministry. This is a turnabout from former practice. The famous *Imitation of Christ* by Thomas à Kempis along with the Philothea, the rule of conduct of a God-fearing life for 500 years, taught flight from the world. ("The monk who from the cloister flees, returneth less the monk doth he.")

A political ministry for envowed religious poses knotty problems. Pope John Paul II noted that the Incarnation symbolizes engagement with the world, not its renunciation or denunciation. But the mission of the Church, he insists, ought never be wedded to a particular political party. Priests and religious should encourage the laity to be politically active, but they themselves ought to act as symbols of unity rising above narrow affiliations and political factions. Behind the Canon Law prohibition lies a bitter church-state history. Whether the American situation justifies exceptions to the rule is something each bishop must decide for himself.

Will Catholics vote against Elizabeth Morancy and Arlene Violet because they consider them deserters of their calling, traitors to their vows, or disloyal malcontents?* The vindictive and narrow-minded will. Others will judge them on their merits and qualifications for office. Catholics have progressed beyond the ghetto consciousness of a clan besieged on all sides by enemies. The Church has never espoused a military interpretation of obedience, nor does she measure loyalty in terms of party line, closed ranks, and yes-man acquiescence.

Before departing, Elizabeth Morancy and Arlene Violet found themselves in the same bind as other religious who have embarked on new, non-traditional apostolates.* While their personal dedication and level of accomplishment evoked public praise and admiration, their efforts in pursuing public service put them at odds with Church officials. This is ironic, because the Church, by definition, is vitally concerned with social and personal change.

The role and status of women religious in this post-ecumenical age has changed and is changing. Conflicting demands often confront the nun of today. She faces the task of creating new roles while supporting what is still useful in the old, all the while trying in the best way possible to fulfill her commitment as a modern servant of an ancient Church.

---

*In 1984 Arlene Violet was elected Rhode Island's attorney general and became the first woman in United States history to be popularly elected to that office. She served two terms from 1985 to 1989. Elizabeth Morancy of Providence, a former Sister of Mercy like Violet, served several terms in the Rhode Island House of Representatives following her initial election in November, 1978.

(10)
Sexuality

Lust Permeates, Grows, Rooted in Our Culture
(*The Providence Visitor*, January 8, 1998)

America is still in the throes of the sex revolution. Indeed, millions have adopted sex as a new religion. The social landscape has become studded with gaudy and erotogenic allurements. From innumerable screens and stages, posters and pages, sex shines forth in larger than life-size images. From countless racks and shelves, from magazines, books, internet, and television, sex is paraded before the eyes. From thousands of loud speakers sex is broadcast in the words and rhythms of popular music. Again, and again, sex is drilled into the minds and ears of Americans, repeating the same refrain, giving the same message: Sex will save you; libido will make you free. "People now seem to have sex on their minds," British journalist Malcolm Muggeridge once said, "which is a peculiar place to have it."

Is this just another phase in American life? Look at the flaming twenties—a time engrossed with sex. But there is a difference between the twenties and the nineties. Youths of the twenties had parents who laid down a definite Christian law; it was something concrete and fairly well defined. Youths of the nineties, however, have parents with only the tattered remnants of the Christian code. The rule of many people today may be summed up in novelist Ernest Hemingway's one-sentence manifesto: "What is moral is what you feel good after, and what is immoral is what you feel bad after."

But sexual immorality is not an isolated phenomenon. It is part and symptom of an age in which morals are held to be both private and relative, in which pleasure is considered a constitutional right, in which self-restraint is seen as the practice of fools and fanatics. The fear of pregnancy, VD, and AIDS has been reduced by medicine and mechanical means, and with the waning of religious influence, skepticism has diminished fear of divine punishment. In short, the Christian ethic, for so long the dominant moral force in the United States, is widely thought to be out of date, and moribund as the third millennium approaches.

This is not to say that many Americans do not still subscribe to the Christian code of sexual ethics. But many more now live by what might be called "permissiveness with affection." Interpreted, this means that: 1) morals are a private affair; 2) being attracted to another justifies premarital sex, and by implication, perhaps, extramarital sex; 3) nothing really is wrong as long as nobody gets hurt.

One trouble with this human-sounding principle is that it is difficult, if not impossible, to know what in the long run will hurt others and what won't. (Not to say anything about what will hurt the individual in respect to his/her immortal soul). In other words, this ethical principle "Nothing really is wrong as long as nobody gets hurt," while it may appear to show a sincere concern for others, is essentially a self-centered and selfish code. The German philosopher Immanuel Kant set down the opposite standard—which is nothing but a variation of the Golden Rule—namely, "Judge your every action as if it were to become a universal principle applicable to all."

Undoubtedly that is a difficult code to live by, and perhaps few try to. But it makes more sense than the advice given by some psychologists. For instance, one counselor tells a boy and girl that they should ask themselves "Will sexual intercourse strengthen or weaken our relationship?" Another says, "Sex is not a moral question. For answers, you don't turn to a body of absolutes. The criterion should not be 'Is it morally right or wrong,' but 'Is it socially feasible, is it personally healthy and rewarding, will it enrich human life?'"

Apparently, the American populace is swallowing this quackery. There is no more pat shibboleth of our time than the idea that what consenting adults do in private is solely their own business. Hogwash! What we do in private has repercussions on ourselves, and what we are and believe has repercussions on others. What we do in our own homes will inevitably affect, not only our own behavior outside them, but what we expect and tolerate in the behavior of others, and what we expect the rulers of our society to tolerate. Changes in family intimacy will not leave unchanged manners and discipline in the wider society. It may not be wise for society to intervene and punish us for what we do in private—although it does interfere if two consenting adults are to be found mistreating their child in their own home—but the idea that what we do in private is not society's concern is nonsense.

What we are faced with today is the denigration of chastity and the condoning, still more, the advocacy of lust. While there is no evidence that sex is a categorical imperative like food and oxygen, and while there is no evidence that voluntary abstention from sex leads to neurosis or emotional disturbance, the media broadcast a contrary propaganda. The celibacy of priests, religious, and single people demonstrates how sexual energies can be sublimated into works of achievement and benefit to others and to themselves. When motivation is strong enough and chastity is esteemed as part of God's design for human happiness, then the problem of control becomes quite soluble.

Theology warns the licentious that lust gives rise to many evils: blindness of intellect in respect to divine things; precipitancy in acting without judgment; want of regard for what befits one's state or person; inconstancy in good; hatred of God as a avenger of lechery; love of this world and its pleasures; and inordinate fear of death.

Lust, no less than other sins, affects our conduct and attitudes to life in ways beyond its own immediate gratification. Our sexual feelings are registers of our whole beings. That is why it is trifling to say that a democratic society, whose role is to foster the common good, ought not to be concerned about the way citizens indulge their sexual proclivities.

The great Dominican theologian Thomas Aquinas shrewdly observes that lust is rightly named a capital sin because carnal pleasure is so attractive to the majority of mankind that man is led into all kinds of disorders in order to gratify his fleshly desires. Which of us will deny it?

American Culture Nurtures Promiscuity
(The Providence Journal, March 4, 1995)

American culture is preoccupied with, and schizophrenic about, sex. Family stability has been the main casualty of this sexual monomania.

Dr. Ruth Westheimer, a so-called sex therapist, encourages teen "recreational sex." The British author of *The Joy of Sex*, Alex Comfort, advises newlyweds that the chief purpose of wedlock is to mold a clever and cooperative bedmate. If the partner does not measure up to expectations, get a divorce. So every year, almost one out of two couples sever the martial knot, hoping to do better next time. The divorce rate is nearly matched by the remarriage rate. The result is a rapid turnover in marriage partners. Sexologists call it "serial polygamy."

Couples who embark on matrimonial seas expecting a Mohammedan heaven, and whose value system allows them to call it quits whenever the going gets rough, have two strikes on them before they start. The current sexual climate does not help. The social milieu is made up of *Playboy*, *Playgirl*, and *Penthouse*; of the laboratory of sex researchers Masters and Johnson, with volunteers fornicating and masturbating for science; of sex-encounter sessions, and those softcore porno-artsy films; of topless waitresses, male strippers, go-go girls, and the Shere Hite sex charts.

Sane and rational voices are asking where we are heading. Sociologist David Reisman claims that sex has been oversold as the Promised Land, that Americans have been conned into believing that sex will solve life's basic problems. French philosopher Camus derided "the congenital inability of youth to see in love anything but the physical." Obsession with sex, Camus claimed, "is drying up daring and creativity."

Experts predict that as society becomes more impersonal, as family ties weaken, there will be many lonely people who look to sex to fill the vacuum in their lives and provide the warmth and affection they have not been able to obtain in an uncaring world. Illicit sex today is recommended on the ground that it enables a couple to develop "skills in interpersonal relations," that it involves them in a "meaningful relationship," that it produces "intimacy" with another human being, and that intercourse cannot be wrong for two people who have a "feeling for each other and have rationally considered the consequences." This autonomous make-your-own-rules view reduces sex to a non-moral, purely personal affair, with the individual becoming the final arbiter of what is right and wrong.

Sociologist Pitrim A. Sorokin states: "A person's single-minded pursuit of sex pleasure results in the growth of the sex drive at the expense of other factors determining his total activity, and radically changes the whole system of forces governing human behavior."

If the family structure is to be salvaged, the rules governing sex have to be respected. Every society recognizes some restraints in sexual matters. A glutton of any kind is a poor parent. He is too dedicated to his own individual satisfaction. A society enraptured by sex tends to let the housekeeping go to hell.

If the American middle class were to go off on a giant bedroom chase, this would offer quaint material for *The New Yorker* and *Esquire*, but it would scarcely be indicative of the Great Society. Dr. Robert Odenwald remarks, "Part of love is sex. If we want to love, we will have to keep sex under some control. If we don't, it will be like putting too much whiskey in the drinks—the guests pass out instead of enjoying themselves."

Undoubtedly, the practice of the virtue of chastity in a concupiscent society imposes great strain on the individual, but perhaps sexual discipline is the test case for dedication to standards of worth in every domain of existence.

But society's engrossment in sex has other repercussions. It forces youth into early dating, early steady-dating, and early marriage. Advertising, entertainment, and fashion are all designed to produce, and then to exploit, sexual tension. Sexually aroused at an early age and asked to postpone marriage until they become older, teenagers have no recourse but to fill the intervening years with courtship rituals and games that are supposed to be sexy but sexless. Dating is expected to culminate in going steady, and that is the starting point on the road to marriage. The dating game in the United States usually hinges on an important exchange. The male wants sexual intimacy and the female wants social commitment. The game often involves bartering sex for security amid the sweet and heady agitations of a romantic entanglement. Once the game reaches the going-steady stage, young people find themselves driven into a corner, and the one way to legitimize their sex play and assuage guilt is to plan marriage.

And so they marry early, and as a consequence, society loses a physician, a scientist, a lawyer, an engineer; for nobody can serve two masters, and since the energy and scope of interest for any individual are limited, solid preparation for a demanding vocation will not be achieved.

A Christian society strives to create a social climate within which it is possible for individuals to control and express their reproductive drive according to patterns of behavior sanctioned by Christian norms. Many sexual practices of secularized American culture run counter to Christian ideals of sexual expression and control. For Christian youth this creates the problem of trying to live their ideals in a social system where accepted practices are non-supportive, if not inimical, to their cherished ideals.

Viagra, Sex, and Spiritual Impotence
(*The Providence Visitor*, July 2, 1998)

American men cherish the ambition—usually more or less secretly—to be great lovers. It's a perfectly legitimate ambition. Legend has it, however, that compared to the European male, homo-Americans are second-rate lovers at best.

Viagra, the magical sex pill, will change all that. It will liberate the male libido, at least for that half of the male population which experiences "erectile dysfunction."

For many reasons, I refuse to consider the sexual instinct the basic instinct of human life. Sex is not the paramount value and the primary factor in human existence. The aspirations of life and the aspirations of the sexual instinct cannot be identified, for man is, before all, a being of intelligence and will, made for knowledge, love, political and social accomplishments, scientific exploration, and artistic creation. When these fundamental aspirations are not normally satisfied, when human vitality, which aspires to a world of value and achievements, is killed, they run the risk of being taken over, absorbed, and utilized by the sexual instinct.

The desperate man, the solitary man, the man without the multiple satisfactions of the senses and of the spirit, falls on the sexual life. Sex, beyond its own specific pleasure, offers the possibility for vicarious satisfaction.

When the modern man, lacking the satisfactions of noble ambitions, devitalized, living without power and prestige, goes through his dull monotonous life without joy or beauty, his existence depends on a fictitious sexual life. His sexual joys are moral joys camouflaged. He seeks to satisfy them, not having the individual and collective force to satisfy his real aspirations. These disguises of aspirations are the opposite of those which Freud indicated. It is not the sexual instinct which becomes satisfied by creative work and political and religious life; the aspirations that go with art, and the political and economic life, satisfy themselves through sensuality.

The balance and equilibrium of the human system is disturbed when an organ is isolated from its function in the whole organism or divorced from its higher purpose. Sex addicts, who are always talking, reading, seeing, thinking, and acting out sex, are like singers who think more about their larynx than about singing. They make that which is subordinate to a higher purpose so all-important that the harmony of life is upset. The well-rounded man, instead of concentrating on what's between his legs, fits that organ into his overall pattern of living.

Worshippers of Priapus, the Greek god of fertility, who dedicate themselves to the pursuit of sexual pleasure, enhance the growth of their sex drive at the expense of the power of other factors determining their total activity. A man's energy is limited. Focus on one thing; withdraw from other things. Aside from any moral considerations, citizens are concerned about how much President Clinton's sexual prowling distracts him from running the country—despite his protestations to the contrary.

We are still in the throes of the so-called sex revolution. Changes in the sex behavior of the populace presuppose a parallel change in religious, moral, and social values. In the past, Christian sexual morality prevailed. Today, the motivational control of the sex drive is enfeebled. The current culture, instead of inhibiting unlawful sex, tends to approve, glorify, and justify wider and more promiscuous sexual freedom, thus propelling the individual toward less and less restrained sex relations.

Sociologist John Kane states: "In almost all sex revolutions, the increase of the motivational power of the sex drive is due mainly to the weakening of the controls of psychosocial factors or values, and the replacement of the inhibitive psychosocial factors or values by those that approve sex passion, sex prowess, and more varied sex relations."

Where does Viagra come in? Well, it can be a boon to mankind. Why? Because traditionally, the sex drive was considered not an unbridled passion, but was judged to be under the control of the rational and separational forces in the total man. From the standpoint of these forces, sex love has always been viewed as the crowning act of an infinitely rich, beautiful, and transfiguring love of man and woman; as one of the greatest joys in human life, and the noblest way of unification into one "we" of the individual "egos" of the lovers; and finally, as the necessary means for the perpetuation of the human race.

Christian sexual morality has not aimed at the suppression of this great value of human life, but at the prevention of its falsification, degradation, and misuse. These aberrations tend to rob sexual love of its blissful joys, and of its vital functions in the life of humanity, while imperceptibly reducing the total man to a mere sex organ.

Christianity and the Sexual Revolution
(*The Providence Journal*, June 3, 1985)

Sex is here to stay, but the sexual moral standards of Christian civilization may not be. That's the thrust of the *Journal* article "Now 24 years old, 'the Pill' is credited with, and blamed for, drastic social change" (May 11, 1985).

Undoubtedly, today's sexual revolution directly challenges Christianity's prohibition of fornication and adultery. Some church thinkers answer the challenge by advocating a "new morality" that is nothing other than a capitulation to the revolution.

Hard and fast rules which bar premarital and extramarital sexual relations under all circumstances are now considered passé. Only one universal guideline prevails: So long as nobody gets hurt, love makes it right. In any relationship, however, one must accept responsibility. So pleas are made for responsible contraception, responsible sterilization, responsible abortion, responsible fornication, and responsible homosexual relations.

Every one of these appeals assumes that the life-giving function of sex is an accidental quality that people are free to suppress whenever it gets in the way of other, more "personal" values.

Leaders in the sexual revolution are intelligent enough to see that when they cancel one of the fundamental principles of Christian morals—namely, the inherent life-giving character of sex—they radically change the whole structure of sexual morality.

"Procreation as the prime function of sex has now receded into anthropological antiquity," the new moralists aver. This divorce between sex and procreation has profound consequences. Traditionally, sex, love, marriage, and children were all one package. Childless couples were looked down on. Extramarital and premarital relationships were condemned. But with the advent of the sexual revolution, all this changed. A new pattern emerged: recreational sex—a kind of prostitution for enjoyment, rather than for financial gain.

Historian and social critic Christopher Lasch points out that sex valued purely for its own sake loses all reference to the future and brings no hope of permanent relationships. Sexual liaisons, including marriage, can then be terminated at pleasure. This means that lovers forfeit the right to be jealous or to insist on fidelity as a condition of erotic union. Hence "open marriage," wife swapping, casual cohabitation, group sex, etc., become justifiable.

This lifestyle repels Christians. They believe God gave man sexual faculties for reproduction. All words, thoughts, and actions related to sex, therefore, ought to be regulated in terms of its primary purpose.

Such as idea can be realized only when relationships between the sexes are patterned in such a way that it is normally possible to live according to this ideal. Hence, regulation of dating and courtship practices, of extra and extramarital relationships, of modesty in dress, speech, and action, of entertainment, advertising, and so on, are all closely related. They directly affect each other; they are mutually supportive and dependent. In short, if the ideal of chastity is to be achieved, Christians must promote the conditions which make its realization possible.

In an environment dosed with aphrodisiacs, the attainment of this ideal becomes remote and unlikely. Yet, "man has never been governed exclusively by his loins," says Richard Lewisohn. Freud recognized that civilization depends for its existence and development upon some restraint of the most urgent sexual drives. He believed the ego had to mediate between the libidinal impulse to private pleasure and the constructive demands of the group. When he was reminded that savages make no such choice, he replied, "That is exactly why they are still savages."

Culture and intellectual development are related to sexual discipline, says British social anthropologist J. D. Unwin, and English Anglican priest and social commentator Vigo A. Demant tells us that "if the sexual behavior of early European man had been as spontaneously unrestricted as that of the natives of Samoa, there would have been no modern Europe."

Sex outside marriage has never been sanctioned by the courts. Some states have repealed, or rarely enforce, laws against fornication and adultery, but this is more because of practical enforcement concerns than from a conviction that sexual freedom is a "constitutional right." Indeed, the U.S. Supreme Court has refused to grant a right of sexual privacy to unmarried persons, even though a few lower courts have interpreted the right of privacy as being broad enough to give constitutional protection to sex between consenting adults.

The enormous stake society has in the cultural transmission process disposes it to favor the mutual, binding commitment on which the marital institution rests. Up to this point, the state has always looked upon the formal family as the foundation of society, the essential element in child development, and the school of public virtue and citizenship. To the extent that the sexual revolution weakens the family bond, it does a disservice to the nation.

Women's Clothes Can Betray Silent Intent
(*The Providence Visitor*, April 24, 2003)

A Hollywood star bares her belly button in a fashionable gown, and other women follow her lead.

This may be the year of the peek-a-boo look in clothing. See-through and topless fashions are showing more and more epidermis. Perhaps a model's navel, bejeweled or not, is more aesthetic, nay, more honest, than falsies or a codpiece.

Nudity or semi-nudity has its place. Only a morbid adolescent could find anything lewd in a delicate Botticelli or a robust Renoir, or in the celebrated Venus de Milo.

However, for some, it must be allowed, even such nudes may be lewd. The whole question is subjective and personal.

Few, we dare say, even think of the Venus as nude; it is simply unique, world-famous, almost commonplace. Italian artist Sandro Botticelli has a distinctive grace that spiritualizes his subjects; Renoir, remarks Maurice Denis, "has no sense of sin," which means, we presume, that his work is wholesome, ordered, and serene.

Chastity, in the traditional view, has absolute norms valid for all times. Modesty, the guardian of chastity, is something relative. Censors get bogged down in plunging necklines, bare midriffs, and mini-skirts because they fail to realize how subjective the whole question is.

Variations of standards and vagaries of judgment make some incidents laughable. American tourists in Europe are scandalized by nude statues in churches while habited nuns think nothing of pointing out these works of art to their pupils. European teachers are shocked by American students abroad who skinny-dip in a nearby pond. A South Pacific island bishop, upbraided because he permits native women to attend Mass without covering their breasts, retorts that what little clothing they wear is more modest than women who use their "finery" to attract men.

As one travels the earth, one sees how variable modesty can be. In China, a woman conceals her foot; in Moslem countries, she hides her face; in Central Africa, to bare the back of the head or buttocks is shameful.

Is there, then, no reasonable decorum in dress? Undoubtedly, but it varies with persons, times, and places. Contemporary faith in the benefits of exercise and sunshine has influenced fashions by lessening traditional inhibitions concerning exposure. Custom also plays a role. Recall the adage: "What is customary does not affect us."

The type of dress itself is less significant for preserving chastity than is the relationship of dress to the type of association between the sexes tolerated in society. To stress the erotic character of current fashion is to miss the point. It is prolonged, unchaperoned relationships between the sexes that endanger chastity, especially in adolescence. Under these conditions, daring types of female dress become provocative.

Popularly approved clothing that draws the eye to erogenous zones may reflect a change in thinking about sex or reveal a degradation of the public sense of propriety. The attitudes and values of a culture are often imaged in its clothing or lack of it. Near nakedness, with whatever decorations of the body attends it, testifies to a different attitude toward illicit sexual intercourse, a greater casualness about it, and more indulgence in it than is the case where clothing reinforces sexual restraint.

The wearer's intention must also be taken into account. A woman who wears a Molokini is usually conscious of its titillating effect. Nudity in a locker room and in a burlesque show vary greatly in purpose. Again, men and women interpret clothing styles differently. When a woman is harassed sexually, a man may say: "The way she dresses, she was asking for it."

Modesty is a universal principle among mankind, even if its complete development awaits the advent of puberty, or even if it is so corrupted that it loses its force with certain people. The amount of clothing has little relation to the degree modesty is practiced. English physician and sexual researcher Havelock Ellis asserts that naked primitive tribes display a modesty more radical than among the civilized because risqué conduct may lead to consequences harmful to the individual and society. "Naked savages," Ellis says, "have to guard their speech, eyes, and gestures more closely, precisely because they are naked, and hence have less freedom in this matter than people who wear clothes."

Pope John Paul II points out that Adam and Eve were naked and not ashamed because they were mutually conscious of the nuptial meaning of their bodies, because the human body, as a sign and sacrament of the human person, is a holy reality. "The feeling of shame," said the pope, "goes with the realization that one's person must not be an object of use on account of the sexual values connected with it." Thus, a man and wife do not experience shame upon being seen naked by one another, because they realize that each values the other as a person and not merely as a thing or object of enjoyment.

Clothing, some contend, actually promotes immodesty rather than modesty. What is concealed excites more than what is revealed. Regarding sex appeal, women's greatest asset has always been man's imagination. Shakespeare's words are pertinent: "Should you be silent and not speak, your dress would betray what life you lead."

Sex, Even Between Spouses, Can Be a Sin
(*The Providence Visitor*, March 4, 2004)

Pope John Paul II is branded a male chauvinist and is charged with being anti-feminist, a spoilsport of sexual fun and games, and an advocate of "a medieval point of view," because of what he had to say about spiritual adultery in one of his talks on marriage.

Actually, he was merely emphasizing by reiteration the traditional ethical principle that an act, good and pleasurable in itself, can be spoiled by a bad intention—in this instance, when a man treats his wife not as an individual in her own right, but solely as a means of selfish gratification, when she is used, as it were, as a kind of faceless vagina. This is the "adultery of the heart" of which the pope speaks, because a man looks at his wife not as a wife but as a whore.

The pope studied Thomism under the Dominican Fathers at the University of St. Thomas, Angelicum, Rome. He is well acquainted with the *Summa Theologica* of the medieval theologian philosopher Thomas Aquinas. In his tract on marriage, Aquinas asks the question (Suppl. Q 49, a. 6): "Can a man sin while enjoying sexual intercourse with his wife?"

Yes, Aquinas answers, if he fails to appreciate her distinct personality. If he uses his wife as he would a harlot, if he ignores her individuality, not loving her as a human being should love, but lusting after her as a rutting animal—such a man has reduced his wife to a thing, a sex object. He has lost all sense of his wife's uniqueness as a human being.

The same holds true for a wife. She sins likewise, if acting like a bitch in heat she makes herself available for one thing, and one thing only: the pleasure of copulation. She would then be loving her spouse the same way that an adulteress loves her paramour. Sex like this, in the absence of intimacy and tenderness, and loving communion, reduces a husband to a human dildo. To thus offer one's body, and at the same time withhold the self, is a wonderful way of showing disdain, dislike, or an overweening preoccupation with one's desires at the expense of another.

The pope is morally sensitive to the fact that human beings are diminished when people are used for pleasure alone—when they are transformed into things or mere objects. The sexual act itself is thereby made into a biological happening—a source of sensations, of extracting one's needs from another body, of exploitation of another human being. Sex thus becomes robbed of its most rewarding and human elements—

loving communication and intimacy and the mutual reinforcement of self-esteem—along with the shelter and security of an emotional bond.

Christianity holds that the human being is so noble that no person should ever be treated merely as a means, but always as an end. The pope seems to feel that this is quite common even in marriage. A recent investigation corroborates his view. One out of five wives reported "feeling used" during sex.

In the Judeo-Christian view, the marital act is both human and animal. When human sentiments and human ideals are ignored in lovemaking, then a human relationship is debased into a mere animal connection.

The pope would stand foursquare with the feminists when they charge *Playboy, Penthouse, Hustler,* and others with demeaning women by portraying them in one dimension only: as sex objects. He would surely be against those bathing-beauty pageants that parade feminine pulchritude as a commodity, and he would look with disfavor on those predatory bars where females are exploited and then discarded like soiled tissue or throwaway cartons.

Why all the commotion anyway?

Pope John Paul is only "popeing" when he speaks against animalizing human nature and speaks up for human dignity wherever in the world it may be endangered or lessened—this time on the marriage couch.

Cohabitation Stance Ignores Original Sin
(*The Providence Visitor*, June 25, 1992)

Couples cohabitate not for erotic but for economic reasons, Monsignor Joseph Champlin tells priests (*Visitor*, June 11).

Baloney! Naïveté like this belittles the effects of original sin, underestimates the power of concupiscence, discounts human frailty, and ignores the proximate occasions of sin.

In days past, it was marriage first, then sex. Now it is sex with or without marriage in the offing. Couplings outside of marriage have escalated to 2.4 million in the United States. The pill and the condom have made casual copulation easier than lifelong commitment to one marital partner.

Cohabitation is endorsed, cheered, indeed, flaunted. Now, fornication parades under the name of self-fulfillment; now "living in sin" is dignified by the phrase "meaningful relationship," now sexual exploration is praised as "doing your own thing."

Monsignor Champlin urges parish priests to show compassion to cohabitants. Yet Archbishop John F. Wheaton firmly believes that couples living together, but remaining unmarried, are really asking the Catholic Church to give "tacit approval" to an immoral lifestyle when they seek a religious wedding ceremony with all the trimmings.

By "using" the Church, cohabitants not only give bad examples, but also make a travesty of Catholic teaching on sex and marriage. A church wedding is desired for social, not religious, reasons. Caring little about the Sacrament of Matrimony, cohabitants try to mollify parents who prefer the ambiance of lighted candles, organ music, and stained-glass windows to a colorless hotel hall, a country club, or a parlor at the residence of a justice of the peace.

Tolerance and understanding of a sinful condition should never be countenanced at the cost of weakening faith and discipline. "Anything goes" has never been a motto of the Catholic Church. To continue to cohabitate up to the very moment the knot is tied is to make a joke of marital rituals. To utter Christian phrases without Christian meaning is hypocrisy. To move through a Christian blessing when the two have not genuinely, personally sought such a lifelong blessing is a charade—empty rites, meaningless liturgy, going-through-the-motions religion.

No one champions slamming the door of God's grace upon any sincere questing soul. If cohabitants are sincerely searching for God's morality after having lived together though unmarried, the solution is relatively simple. The priest exhorts them to separate and leads them into the way of salvation with the words, "Go and sin no more."

But it would be cruel to ever give the impression that "shacking up" is anything but what it is: an immoral mockery of Christian marriage. The Lord was compassionate, but he also drove the money lenders from the temple, chastised Peter, and uttered some "hard sayings."

Reservations About Dispensing Contraceptives to Teens
(*The Cowl*, February 4, 1987)

The *Providence Journal* editorial sympathizing with the National Research Council's strategy for combatting teen pregnancies deserves close scrutiny. Making contraceptives and abortion available to teens through schools and public health clinics at little or no cost, or without requiring parental consent, is a drastic experiment in social engineering that may well encroach on parental prerogatives.

The American family has always cherished its right to be the primary source of moral authority for developing youth. Indeed, a Yankelovich, Skelly and White national poll states that:

"Among parents and teenage children, eight out of ten feel it is up to the parents to educate their own children about birth control. One in ten assigns the responsibility to the schools. Only seven percent believe that teenagers should be able to get this information from a doctor."

Knowledge about contraception won't curb teen pregnancies, asserts John Hopkins professor Dr. Melvin Zelnick. Only three percent of pregnant teenagers he studied said they did not know about contraceptives and where to get them.

Again, the privacy right established by *Roe v. Wade* giving a pregnant female a limited right to elect an abortion is much newer than the more venerable privacy right of parents to raise, control, and teach their children family or faith values. To the extent the public school facilitates youthful behavior which interferes with the parental right to control the upbringing of children, it may incur legal liability toward the parents.

Other questions are pertinent. Suppose a girl enters a school clinic, says she is sexually active, and wants contraceptive devices. Does the clinic have the right to simply provide that device or must further inquiry be made? If further inquiry be made, it will presumably deal with frequency of intercourse, other person(s) involved, signs of venereal disease, whether the child has medical problems or is on medication, and whether emotional or guilt feelings are experienced because of family traditions or personal, religious, or philosophical values.

Does an inquiry of this nature run afoul of the law which forbids administering any test, questionnaire, survey, or examination containing questions about the pupil's or his/her parent's beliefs or practices in sex, family life, morality, and religion, unless the parent is notified in writing about the inquiry and gives written permission?

Also, will instructional materials in school clinics suggest that a minor's sexual conduct is his or her own business, irrespective of parents' concerns, religious beliefs, and legal requirements? Will the girl be told that the fetus she carries is merely a blob of protoplasm, or an unborn child? Will the information dispensed reflect the value system of the health practitioner or will that person be nonjudgmental and value neutral? Will youths be informed that contraceptives, even when carefully used, entail a 13.6 percent risk of pregnancy? If pregnancy ensues, will the child be encouraged to abort so as not to miss class (each year, more than one million teens become pregnant; 400,000 choose abortion), or to put the child up for adoption?

What about school? Does it stand in place of the parent or is it the surrogate of special-interest population-control groups? Is the school accountable in some fashion to parents or is the school just another government agency answerable to only a political union composed of its employees? If a school clinic, advising pupils about contraceptives or abortion, makes a mistake, can the school be sued for medical malpractice?

Fornication is a criminal offense (R.I. Law 11-6-3), and any person over 18 who copulates with another below 16 is subject to a lengthy term in jail (R.I. Law 11-37-7). Are school personnel who abet fornication by dispensing contraceptives laying themselves open to the charge of contributing to the delinquency of a minor?

In the effort to stem teen pregnancies, two rival visions about the role of sex in life determine how one responds to the problem. Those who favor giving teens contraceptives do not get too "het up" about probable promiscuity; continence is not esteemed highly as a value. Indeed, teenage contraceptive sex is praised as "responsible sex."

Subscribers to the Judeo-Christian ethic, however, believe that the only legal, safe, healthy, and moral course for a minor to follow and a school to counsel is to abstain from sexual intercourse. In this view, schools have a civic responsibility to reflect the values of the majority of parents, and to strengthen their pupils' character, not their libido. Handing out contraceptives is much easier than developing an appreciation of sex as more than a momentary titillation. It betrays a quick-fix mentality and an obsession with short-term results.

It's Not a Street of Joy
(*The Providence Journal*, December 24, 1983)

The recent arrest of prostitutes plying their trade out of a so-called "escort service" resurrects the question of decriminalization. Should the three-billion-dollar-a-year prostitution business (most of it non-declared income) be legalized?

The arguments in favor of decriminalization are quite strong.

Some maintain that prostitution laws attempt to foist the moral values of one segment of society on the whole and divert limited public resources that could be better used against graver types of crime.

A 1974 American Bar Association resolution stated that prostitutes should not be stigmatized and punished as criminals while their male clientele were seldom arrested—a double standard. (Fearing that national moral standards might be lowered, the ABA voted against lifting legal bans on prostitution.)

The American Civil Liberties Union speculates that statutes against soliciting may be violations of the right to freedom of speech as guaranteed under the First Amendment.

Hookers themselves contend that prostitution is not only harmless, it is positively humanitarian.

The harlot organization COYOTE (Cast Off Your Old Tired Ethics) thinks strumpets ought to be as highly regarded as nurses or social workers and conducts seminars to improve the prostitute's self-image as a prostitute.

Finally, history proves the uselessness of trying to stamp out the world's oldest profession. All schemes to regulate, zone out, suppress, license, or tolerate prostitution in red-light districts or legalized outlets have failed.

But the case against legalizing prostitution is even more compelling.

Laws may be unequally applied, but legalization would embolden prostitutes to descend on cities like plagues of locusts. Let's not forget the important educational function of law; it proclaims a public moral standard, and this is weakened when laws are changed in favor of greater laxity. Citizens sometimes confuse legality with morality. If an act is not unlawful, they argue, it is therefore not immoral.

Prostitutes say they have the right to earn a living, but what about the rights of passers-by harassed by the more blatant forms of solicitation, or the rights of mothers and daughters accosted by predatory males? Do not parents have the right to raise children in well-ordered, family-oriented neighborhoods?

Prostitution debases feminine dignity. Pimps frequently beat, threaten, cajole, and intimidate their stable of girls, and prostitutes often become hooked on drugs, supporting the habit by robbing their clients. Inevitably, organized crime muscles its way in wherever prostitution thrives.

Healthwise, ninety percent of all professional hustlers contract venereal disease during their career. Indeed, a city's VD rate usually rises or falls in direct proportion to the number of prostitutes living there.

Emotionally, the very act of peddling her body distorts a woman's feelings toward all men and callouses her attitude toward life itself.

Customers are exploited for all the traffic will bear. Men's feelings of loneliness, shame, fear of rejection, and social ineptness are manipulated for money, and in the tawdry transaction, sentiments of self-worth and nobility go down the drain.

But prostitution victimizes youth most of all. Franciscan Friar Bruce Ritter, founder of Covenant House in New York's Times Square, a refuge for runaway and homeless teenagers, has first-hand contact with the ravages of a lifestyle of prostitution. He opposes decriminalization because "without laws, there would be more impetus to open brothels, more girls on the street, more Johns who would no longer be afraid of arrest, and it would be easier for kids with false ID's to work in joints." How can anyone ever call prostitution "a victimless crime?"

Ultimately, the customer is the key to the control of prostitution. No buyers, no sellers. Fines and prison sentences do not solve the problem. The difficult long-range solution lies in strengthening home and family life, in safeguarding public morality, and in eliminating the financial causes of prostitution.

A concerted re-educational rehabilitation program is needed—a program that deals with the purpose and ideals of human existence, provides worthwhile vocational objectives, and pays due deference to the dignity and awesome potential of the human procreative power.

Imbue Teens with a Proper Sense of Sexual Morality
(*The Providence Visitor*, July 25, 2002)

Whatever consenting adults do in privacy is their own business and has no moral, social, or psychological consequences. This type of argument is proffered by those who contend that the individual, the private person, the self, is the one who determines the rightness or wrongness of one's own behavior.

However, the "consenting adult" contention is spurious. The community has a stake in one's interpersonal relations, because it is a fabric woven of such relations. Nobody is permitted to do what he wants with his or her own body. His body, in fact, has a moral right to one's solicitude and protection, but one's body is not one's alone, because the person owes something to the God who created it, to the phylogeny that endowed it, and to the society that arranged for its protection and nourishment.

Indeed, the libertine's preachment about sexual autonomy weakens those social supports which fortify youths' resolve to adhere to the traditional norm of premarital abstinence and contributes to the avalanche of teen pregnancies plaguing the nation—pregnancies often resulting from contraceptive failure.

Polls reveal that the plurality of Americans still subscribe to premarital abstinence as the only foolproof means of preventing unwanted, out-of-wedlock pregnancy. In 1984, the American Medical Association adopted as policy "the need to encourage practical methods of preventing teen pregnancies ... including continence in unmarried individuals." Any program of pregnancy prevention must employ self-restraint as the first weapon.

All human activity, sex in particular, has a moral significance. Let us say a boy and a girl, unmarried, sleep together. Put aside the question: Is it socially acceptable? Other things are more crucial: To what extent is the boy satisfying himself at some ultimate emotional cost to the girl? To what extent is the girl investing more than the boy in the experience? To what extent has the boy, if having been seduced by the girl, been turned into a utensil? There are few sexual acts devoid of questions about the integrity of one's actions and motives.

Political scientist James Q. Wilson argues in his essay "Character, Private Virtue and Public Policy" (*Public Interest*, Fall 1985) that the flood of teen pregnancies results from deterioration of character. Children once were taught that it was wrong to sire or bear illegitimate children. Now, an ethic of self-expression prevails over an ethic of self-control, and out-of-wedlock pregnancy bears no stigma. Personal development, nay, the progress of civilization demands the delay of present satisfactions for the sake of future goals.

What are the restraining forces which operate on the citizens of a civilized society? There are many, but religion remains the most potent. It creates an awareness of sin, and out of this awareness comes a desire to restrain one's appetites and emotions to gain a happiness on earth that leads to happiness in heaven. In this context, self-mastery and personal salvation are closely related.

The Church deprecates the "scoring" mentality that marks much of the current dating scene and works to transform the life of the Id by eliminating sentiments of commitment and covenanted love. The carefree, swinging, single life of casual sex is actually a form of mindless rutting—a caricature of what love is all about.

Perhaps the greatest threat to the stability of sexual morality in America comes not from the Hugh Hefners but from behavioral scientists who are now replacing the Church as the recognized authority in determining what is proper and is not proper sexual behavior. Largely secular in their outlook, these "experts" speak little of the importance of will in human behavior, of religious ideals, of moral training in the early years, of the sanctity of marriage, and of the concept of duty, responsibility, obligation, and sacrifice.

Science deals with what is, not with what ought to be. All the science in the world cannot tell people what they should or should not do. Yet scientists often proffer opinions, based not on an understanding of theology, philosophy, or history, but on statistics, observations, and measurements. In doing so, they reduce sex to a strictly pleasure-seeking, animalistic level or to a temporary euphoria induced by the twitching of nerve endings.

Traditional religion realizes that youth have difficulty in regulating their emotions, appetites, and instincts when left to themselves. Youth, therefore, should not be hurried into encounters with the opposite sex until they have, by dint of fairly rigorous self-discipline and systematic moral education, learned to control their urges.

In short, sound religious and moral training in the early years is a powerful deterrent to the sexual adventurism which leads to teen pregnancies. This fact ought to be exploited by parents, educators, and political leaders.

Preach Abstinence; Youths Need to Hear It
(*The Providence Visitor*, November 14, 2002)

We live in times of sexual anarchy and moral ambiguity. The "sex revolution," with its horrific consequences of spoiled lives, is symptomatic of a meltdown of Christian culture. A permissive, subjective philosophy of "Do your own thing" has replaced the objective ethical values of past generations.

Today's society is saturated with sex. It's the motif in movies, music, and the modern dance. It's accentuated in risqué clothing styles and fashion. It is used to hawk merchandise from automobiles to automatic washers.

Sex screams out from newsstands and magazine racks. Lewd references to it are emblazoned on T-shirts and bumper stickers. It is blatantly vulgarized by graffiti on public walls. It grabs the eye on billboards, tabloids, and television.

St. Augustine's condemnation of ancient Carthage—"a hissing cauldron of lust"—could be applied to the current cultural scene.

Couple this parlous state with the loss of inner restraints and lack of societal support and you can see why it is increasingly difficult for the populace at large and youths in particular to maintain sexual sanity.

Young people find it well-nigh impossible to acquire healthy attitudes toward sex when living in an atmosphere where extramarital sex is not merely tolerated but even encouraged. Society seems to accept youthful dalliances and fornication simply as a fact of life. One hears supposedly responsible adults say, "Everybody's doing it. What does it hurt, really?"

This fatuous remark is made at a time when the AIDS epidemic and other baffling venereal diseases contaminate every echelon of society. In this context, the Catholic critique of libertine lifestyles and the affirmation of monogamous, procreative sex is not only morally justifiable but is being adjudged more and more as a public-health imperative.

One of mankind's age-old shortcomings is that we don't look at the results of our actions. What is the result of premarital sex? How does it affect one's future? How does it affect a future marriage? How does it affect personal relationships? How does it affect one's children?

Young people today assume that irresponsible sex is okay simply because too many parents, schools, clergy, and governmental agencies lack the conviction or determination to guide them responsibly.

Why should youngsters have to find out the hard way—through debilitating STD's, the shock of illegitimacy, marriage-wrecking sexual delusions, emotional scars, and wasted lives—that premarital and extramarital sex and homosexual activity have serious consequences?

The "just say no to sex" concept has been ridiculed as simplistic by those who believe that premarital sex is not in itself wrong. They argue, "Look, they're going to do it anyway, so let's at least teach them how to lessen the risk of disease ad how to use contraception."

A stance like this is a surrender to cowardly defeatism. Acquiescing to the cliché that "they're going to do it anyway" soft-sells the reality of human sexuality and, in effect, lets young people down by not holding before them admittedly difficult yet noble ideals.

Adults often send ambivalent messages to teens. They tell them, more or less, that premature sexual activity is wrong, unwise, perhaps unhealthy, and certainly unadvisable. Then they tell them, in other ways, how they can "lessen the risk."

Teens hear two contradictory messages. They hear an attempt to deter them from being sexually active, then they hear adults giving them preventative information (from which they hear that we are expecting them to become sexually active).

In our current drug campaign, we do not hear advice on how to lessen the risk of serious drug problems. Youths are simply told to "Just say no!" Why do we not challenge them similarly when it comes to sexuality? Those who deride such education as "moralizing" wish to push their own brand of morality on an immature segment of society too inexperienced to defend itself!

The living Lord does not force his law of perfect love on humanity. The Almighty gives mankind a choice. "I have set before you life and death, blessing, and curse. Therefore, choose life that both you and your descendants may live." (Deuteronomy 30:19).

God gives us his Church, his Holy Spirit, his words; he gives the example of holy men and women. Yet, how many today are prepared to put into practice what they believe? How many are willing to recognize the Creator as having authority over their lives? How many are really convinced that God knows what is best for them?

When teens hear a parent, a teacher, a priest, a judge, a law officer, a government official, or anyone else state that saving sex for marriage is the best and safest use of sex, they are hearing the truth—truth based on God's own authority.

Young people can be taught the truth. With patient, loving instruction, youths can be helped to develop an understanding and an appreciation for the ideal of chastity, for the vocation of marriage, for the dignity of parenthood, and for the role of sex in the plan of God.

Will adolescents respond? Yes, they have, and they will. Most juveniles, and even young adults, appreciate frank, clear guidance that enables them to stand up to the strong pressures which lead to disaster.

Teens desperately need this guidance, and they need it from adults who love them and who care deeply for their physical, psychological, and spiritual welfare.

Pope John Paul vs. Ann Landers on Solitary Sex
(*The Cowl*, February 11, 1987)

Pope John Paul II and Ann Landers disagree. The pope says that masturbation is sinful; Ann tells her 20 million readers: "Masturbation provides God-given release of sexual tension and is a lot more moral than going to bed with anybody who happens to be around."

Most sexologists, following Dr. Alfred Kinsey, maintain that ninety percent of all males and thirty-five percent of all females indulge in sexual self-relief. Prevalence of a practice, however, does not make it desirable. Colds and hives are prevalent, but who desires them? The physically harmless may be spiritually or psychologically harmful. Stealing, the physical act, is harmless, but who would claim that it is morally beneficial?

What can one say about behavior that nobody is proud of? How many masturbators are so enslaved to the habit that they feel compelled to gratify themselves against their will (compulsive self-gratification)? Are persons, conditioned to habitual self-stimulation, capable of appreciating sex relations with a feeling of mutuality and all the sublime and rewarding psychological overtones that should, in a human being, accompany such relations? Do masturbators use self-gratification as a consolation? As a substitute? How many practice self-relief symbolically to signify a need for affection?

These are pertinent, valid, and highly important questions to which the physician, clergyman, parent, and counselor need answers.

First of all, the very word self-gratification is misleading. The self can no more gratify its sexual desires by producing an orgasm than the self can satisfy its desire for companionship by talking to itself, or its desire for competition by playing chess with itself. The ego must have an external love object. This point is absolutely fundamental, because sexual desire of its very nature is social; that is to say, the mature impulse is outward-striving.

In self-gratification, the impulse (and this refers especially to inveterate and deliberate self-relief) is anti-social, that is, inverted. This inversion explains why masturbation is as much a social problem as it is a personal one.

But does masturbation quench or inflame sexual drive? Are persons who gratify themselves bothered less with sex? Those who have abandoned the habit say no. When an impulse as powerful as sex is turned in upon itself, with temptation always present, the individual feels less able to cope with it and conflict inevitable arises.

Intercourse requires a partner; nocturnal emissions are regulated by certain psychological and physiological conditions, but self-relief is not. Consciously, a person recognizes that he has a ready means at hand of producing orgasms, so that he is constantly tempted and tormented by an urge to gratify himself.

Orgasm can only give spiritual satisfaction under the right conditions of mutual affection, respect, and lack of inhibition. If intercourse itself does not frequently fulfill these conditions, how can auto-eroticism ever fulfill them? Without spiritual satisfaction, orgasm is fleeting, frustrating, non-fulfilling, for it is not an end in itself, but a means of expressing marital love and affection.

Because of its frequency, self-gratification is hailed as being "normal." But normal and natural are horses of different colors. In view of the nature and purpose of the sex drive, solitary sex is unnatural. While sexual self-gratification can be expected as a transitory and experimental part of the growing-up process, it has never been accepted as a character-building exercise, and has often been looked upon as a sign of arrested development.

In short, self-relief practiced without restraint, or without compunction, is not only morally disordered but denotes a lack of maturity, a withdrawal from reality, an inability to control and sublimate drives (almost all drives must be harnessed to promote well-being of the individual and society), a lack of personal integration, or an unwillingness to appreciate the role of sex in the social context of the family.

In their zeal to dispel ancient, misconstrued, and sometimes absurd notions about sex, secularists promote self-gratification as a desideratum. But masturbation is neither biologically nor physiologically necessary, even in males. Nocturnal emissions, with the lack of inhibition, spontaneity, dream reality, and automatic regulation, are nature's way of relieving sexual tension.

If self-gratification is approved, condoned, and encouraged as laudable conduct, then homoeroticism (homosexual practices) deserves to be accepted. If homoeroticism is to be condemned because having sexual activity with a member of the same sex is against natural law, what about sexual activity without any partner or an imaginary one?

Those who endorse unrestrained, sexual self-gratification as a part of the sexual revolution are turning teleological ethics upside down. When ideals of sexual conduct based on God's natural law are thrown out, sex itself becomes debased. What was once considered a joyful, consecrated, God-given urge to be exercised within the ambit of matrimony is finally reduced to a spiritually meaningless biological function of a mechanical character.

(11)
The Temper of the Times

The 'Geriatric' Divorce
(*The Evening Times*, September 29, 1980)

Nobody knows how many people over 60 are shedding their spouses. Statistics aren't kept. But clergymen, counselors, attorneys, and judges say the numbers are increasing. What was practically unheard of before—couples married 30 or 40 years throwing up their hands and walking away—we're now seeing frequently.

Religious and social restraints that once curbed divorce no longer hold. The stigma is gone. No-fault divorce and "do it yourself" divorce kits attest to the general loosening of the marital bond. Older people look around and see their children and grandchildren dissolving the indissoluble, and God (so it seems) hasn't punished them. For many today, the words, "What God has joined together, let no mand put asunder" express an unrealistic ideal. If the knot can be untied at 30, why not at 60?

Divorce can be contagious. A woman gets a divorce and crows to her bridge club how happy she is to "no longer have to put up with his . . ." The idea snowballs. In a twinkle, other divorces are under way.

Women today are tolerating less. They simply don't put up with the garbage anymore. They fight back against being pushed, shoved, battered, or neglected. In days past, a wife seldom thought of ridding herself of a husband who was alcoholic, unfaithful, abusive, shiftless, or grossly immature. God gave her this special cross to bear. Motherhood inspired her to sacrifice for "the sake of the children." With children grown, an older woman is less ashamed to admit that she made a mistake "after all those years."

But divorce is always harder on the woman. The husband has business contacts, his country club, lodge, and cronies. The wife's life has revolved around family and home. She's dependent on him for income and security, and she knows that, at her age, the chances of getting a job are slim.

A fiftyish wife may despise her husband, but she sticks with him. He's all she's got. Today, nobody expects offspring to care for a mother for the rest of her life, and few women seem capable of adopting an independent lifestyle. Though her relationship with her husband may be hellish, the fear of being left alone is even worse.

History attests that women are more naturally monogamous then men. They play for higher stakes and have much more to lose. Again, as a woman ages, her beauty fades and her marital marketability goes down, while a man's physical appearance bears little relationship to his social acceptability, and he has little difficulty finding companionship.

Cards offering "congratulations on your divorce" sell almost as well as anniversary greetings. Notwithstanding, the junking of vows after thirty years of marriage is a traumatic experience. A primary support system is lost. It's similar to separation brought about by death. Frequently, bereavement symptoms are displayed. A familiar part of one's life has disappeared. The divorced person mourns even while rejoicing.

People over fifty have less resiliency. After divorce, an older person needs time to snap back and adjust to the single state. Hating to be alone, the newly divorced may rush into another marriage, ignoring the adage "Marry in haste, etc."

What accounts for the splurge of geriatric divorce? The empty-nest syndrome? Children often keep incompatible couples together even though they have been emotionally divorced for a long time. When offspring go off on their own, parents no longer see the need for living under the same roof in a kind of uneasy truce.

The last-straw effect? The divorce may be the culmination of a long series of disagreeable events. Having taken the wrangling, sniping, and belittling for thirty years, and with growing resentment at being wrapped in a loveless marriage, a spouse finally says, "I've had it."

The late middle-age doldrums? This malaise hits the man more than the woman. The so-called male climacteric may be at work here. Under pressure at work and at home, he feels weary, listless, and too hemmed in by responsibility. Down in the dumps and with a fear of losing his libido, he may decide on a quick divorce and remarriage to a woman in the wings who better "understands him."

Boredom? For some, marriage becomes a prison. They feel you're in a rut and yearn to try a lifestyle different from anything they've ever experienced. Driven by a vague and restless discontent, they seek other relationships and activities, hoping to find variety and excitement in their declining years. Divorce is looked upon as the last chance for a change.

Retirement can also bring to a head the dissatisfactions that have long plagued a marriage. The stress and strain of too much togetherness can be the final blow. With children and work obligations eliminated, the couple are thrown face to face with each other. Conflicts that were submerged before may begin to surface.

Temper of the times? We live in an age of personal fulfillment and "do your own thing." This spirit infects the old as well as the young. Marriage is not seen as a lifetime commitment. There is a growing unwillingness to risk entrusting one's destiny to another. Gift of self and sacrifice for the sake of another are left out of the marital equation. With loss of the spiritual dimension in marriage, couples decide to stay together only if it is mutually satisfying or "only as long as I'm happy."

Many marriages on the verge of divorce after thirty years can be salvaged. They need to be strengthened rather than dissolved. It's easier to refurbish a house than to tear it down and start over. Counseling could help. But the couple must want it. Society has a stake in successful marriages—both of the old and the young.

Competitive Spirit and the Highway
(*The Providence Journal*, May 11, 1985)

The competitive spirit that permeates America is nowhere more evident than on Downtown Providence's Route 95 when citizens are riding to and from work. Drunken drivers take their toll, but the darting, weaving, death-defying dodgers on the highways take years off one's life.

A recent study shows that the "aggressive or competitive driver is not only responsible for the largest number of accidents but is also guilty of the largest number of traffic violations."

Driving a car is no longer an enjoyable experience. It's a highly competitive sport. The "beat the other guy" spirit carries over into education, into business, and social life. Not surprisingly, it asserts itself on our roads.

Accident studies show that many traffic fatalities occur when one car overtakes or tries to overtake another. Often the competitive spirit drives the person at the wheel to dangerously high speed. He takes a chance, as he often does in sport or business, and, as so frequently happens, gets away with it. Next month, he takes another chance—and another, until one fine day he takes a chance and several innocent people are killed or injured.

After all, hasn't the driver been taught since his earliest days to get ahead of the other fellow? That's the way to win. What's wrong with winning?

Psychiatrist Franz Alexander believes that the harsh rivalry developed by the competitive spirit engenders "a deep-seated hostility that can be of murderous intensity." Our 45,000 traffic deaths annually show how great that intensity can be.

TV's Stunting Impact on Growing Minds
(*The Providence Journal*, April 22, 1986)

The recent front-page headline "Child experts suggest limiting TV" warns against the violence and aggression in some TV programs. Undoubtedly, TV violence desensitizes children. It not only moves them to act out their aggressions but also anesthetizes them to real-life violence.

But what should alarm concerned adults just as much is the boob tube's power to stunt youthful minds. Television is inherently anti-intellectual. It preaches a philosophy of excitement and escapism and has altered the mode of thought and feeling in which children grow up.

American schools were founded on the basis of a typographic culture, as student of media theory Marshall McLuhan called it. Reading used to be the chief way children drew information or enjoyment from society. The movies came along, but one had to make a special trip to a special place to see them; hence there were limits to the role movies could play in a child's life.

Then there was radio—but reconstructing the full drama from sound clues alone required sophistication and imaginative ability; a clever child could identify with the hero's rhetoric, but the hero's actions were too indirectly perceived.

So, children's reveries were fed chiefly through the printed word, at worst through penny dreadfuls, cheap thrillers, etc. But before a child could wallow in derived reverie, he had to learn to read—that is, he had to acquire a certain initial academic competence. Now, he is exposed to television long before he learns to read. So, he can satisfy his need for fantasy and escape without any academic competence whatever.

The TV screen, moreover, is surrounded by familiar household objects, each with its penumbra of responsibilities and associations. To compete with these circumambient stimuli, the television story must be sharply told. So, the viewer is barraged with sensations. Turn on any TV program. Note the stridency of tone, the highly charged emotion, the exaggerated gestures, and the staccato speech. Children addicted to television come to need a high level of effect and impact, a great swiftness of consequence.

In short, TV entices children by presenting a hopped-up fantasy world in which entertainment is the highest value and every problem is neatly solved in thirty minutes. Little wonder that children, on becoming teenagers, develop an appetite for confrontation politics, way-out cults, punk rock, and pot.

Psychologists also speak of television's narcotizing dysfunction, on the assumption that the common good is ill-served by rendering citizens apathetic and inert—wall-eyed vegetables, as it were.

Americans do spend a lot of time "keeping abreast" of the news. But time spent "watching" cuts down on time left for "acting." The viewer comes to mistake knowing about problems of the day for *doing* something about them. His social conscience remains clean. He is informed. But after he has gotten through dinner, after his stint of evening news and favorite programs, he is ready for bed, his energies inadvertently transformed from active participation into passive knowledge.

American cultural critic Neil Postman argues in *Amusing Ourselves to Death* that television has infected our epistemology—the way we arrive at knowledge. In making "entertainment itself the natural format for the representation of experience," television has altered public discourse. "All culture is conversation," and the quality of this conversation depends on the vocabulary and the conditions in which it is held.

For the TV buff, words are no longer something one speaks but something one merely hears; not something he does but something he receives. This development toward an existence without speech inevitably produces the type of person who, because he no longer speaks himself, has nothing more to say; and who, because he only listens, will do no more than listen.

The initial effects of this growing disinclination to use language are manifest: With language becoming cruder and poorer, man himself becomes cruder and poorer. For man's inward life, its richness and subtlety cannot endure without the richness and subtlety of language; man not only expresses himself through his speech, he is also, in a sense, the product of his language.

Television has no coherent ideology; it supports no clear set of beliefs and policies. Its overall impact, however, is to cast doubt on everything; it is a debunker. Businessmen are money-mad power bullies; parents are nincompoops; politicians are crooks; and labor leaders are mobsters. Material aggrandizement and consumerism are the driving forces of TV's heroes, who flourish in a world of cutthroat competition, a world that says nothing about the larger issues of existence.

Parents and educators have the duty of counteracting that world by teaching children to view television not only with irony and reservation but with discernment and criticism.

Technology and Today's Society
(*The Cowl*, April 29, 1987)

Computer technology has become an indispensable tool in every area of life, industry, science, education, government, medicine, and sports. Bob Amato, one-time Providence College track coach, declares: "No Olympic medal will be won in the future without the help of a computer-assisted training program."

A vital adjunct to man's mental operations, the computer now casts its shadow over all human decisions. It is the Aladdin's lamp for acquiring awesome power over the material world, indeed, over human nature itself.

In his book *The Psychiatric Programming of People*, H. L. Newbold asserts: "Man is, for psychological purposes, a computer..." If so, to manipulate him to function in desired directions all one has to do is press the right levers. In effect, this man-is-a-machine concept reduces people to objects to be turned on and off, exploited, used up, replaced, or turned in for a more efficient model.

Undoubtedly, humans are like computers; they have parts, are capable of making things, and are a complex of stimuli and "reactors." And computers are like human beings. That's why they're called "giant brains" and "thinking machines." Their reason, intelligence, and memory exceed man's insofar as they quickly solve problems which ordinarily take hours, days, and weeks to work out.

But remember a computer's purpose is determined by human intelligence, just as the flight of an arrow is determined by the archer.

Moreover, a computer has no life, no entelechy; all of its energy is supplied from without. No matter how intricately designed, the computer lacks self-consciousness. Nor can a computer love or run the gamut of human emotions. In Dostoevsky's novel *The Brothers Karamazov*, Father Zosima epitomizes the humanist critique of a depersonalized society when he says: "Fathers and teachers, I ponder 'What is hell?' I maintain that it is the suffering of being unable to love."

Other differences abound. Man is free; the computer is not. Experts plan and program its activity. "Garbage in, garbage out." Einstein remarked, "Machines cannot create. They answer problems but cannot propose one." Neither can computers refuse to work; they have no will. Nor can they repair themselves—else why do they have engineers supplied with them?

Finally, computers lack humor. Oliver Wendell Holmes tells us: "A little nonsense now and then is relished by the best of men." Only humans can relish the absurd and giggle at the zany non-sequiturs of a Rowan and Martin *Laugh-In* production.

Pop-psych addicts delight in knowing what things like computers stand for—what they symbolize. Machinery, some experts say, "is an alternate to sexual procreation." This idea is borne out by a former bestseller, *Giles Goat-Boy* by John Barth, in which a supercomputer gets pretty sexy with coeds and in fact sires the hero. Other theorizers, however, are not quite sure whether the computer is a father or mother figure, or stands for psychiatrist Jung's "wise old man" in mechanized guise, or represents modern man's ultimate alienation.

Of course, it may well be that a computer is just a computer, even as a cigar, Freud observed, is at times just a cigar.

Will computers usher in a new paradise? Electronic aficionados think so. Just as the plow and the horse collar were basic tools of the agricultural era, the computer will be man's basic tool of the future. A golden age is opening up—an era in which drudgery and scarcity, disease, poverty, and ignorance will be rooted out; and man himself will become a conscious agent in the evolutionary change of his own species.

Futurists hail the computer as a philosopher's stone capable of transforming *homo sapiens* into *homo hominefactus* (man-made man). The human race is on the verge of a new and rapid leap forward sparked chiefly by electronic wizardry. A computer's potentiality is limited only by the finiteness of man's creativity and the natural boundaries of fanciful free association.

But is not such speculation naïvely utopian? French philosopher Gabriel Marcel chides us for believing that man will become nobler and higher and purer as he gains greater power over the physical world. Human nature remains the same. Impulse, blind rage and fits of brutishness are never far off. Indeed, technology threatens mind and spirit. It immerses man's consciousness in the tangible, the visible, and the material and leaves little time for reflection and aesthetic appreciation. G. K. Chesterton remarked: "I would rather sit in a meadow and watch the autos go by than sit in an auto and watch the meadows go by."

Morally neutral, computers can be a boon or a bane. Einstein in his later years was so afraid of having discovered a fundamental weakness in technology—did it not serve good and evil quite indifferently?—that he joked if he could have had his time over again, he would have left science alone and sold papers or cleaned boots.

Such Einsteinian despair cannot be attributed to aging arteries, but to the fact that this scientist humanitarian was aghast at the horrors of atomic warfare. If computers have accomplished nothing else, they have forced man to think of what kind of world he wants to build—a garish, dystopian *Brave New World* of novelist Aldous Huxley or one in which the highest aspirations of the human spirit can be fulfilled.

French philosopher Henri Bergson recommends laughter as a defense against mechanization and automatism. Perhaps we need the raillery of a Charlie Chaplin or Woody Allen to put the excesses of a mechanized society in proper perspective. Freedom-loving Americans despise a dehumanized society and so are leery of technology as an idol of earthly salvation. But if used wisely, the computer can help build a better world for better people.

Homosexual Orientation a Matter of Choice
(*The Providence Visitor*, November 27, 1977)

Irish bishop Michael Browne equates being gay with "being black, or Hispanic, or a man or woman" ("On homosexuality and chastity," *Visitor*, November 6). In doing so, he, along with many bishops, buys the theory that homosexuality is a genetic "given," a biologically determined trait. Gays are born that way; they are not free agents to choose their sex attraction or orientation.

Yet this thesis clashes with the experience of mental-health experts who contend that homosexuality is not an innate, unchangeable instinct. (The putative discovery of the gay gene fizzled.)

Dr. Joseph Nicolosi and Dr. Charles Socarides, colleagues in the National Association of Research and Therapy of Homosexuality, maintain that reparative therapy—treatment and prevention—can be successful. A survey of 285 psychoanalysts, with 1,275 homosexual clients/patients, found that over one-third reported a successful change to heterosexuality and over eighty-five percent reported a vast improvement in their condition.

This finding flies in the face of the American Psychological Association's committee on gay, lesbian, and bisexual issues, which is trying to ban reparative therapy for homosexuals. It also belies the action of the School Board of Provincetown, Massachusetts, which voted to begin teaching kindergarten-to-grade-six pupils about homosexual families and how "someone can romantically love someone of the same sex, if they want to."

Consider the fate of free will in the current debate over homosexuality. Once, in pre-Freudian times, homosexual behavior was considered purely a matter of choice, a preference. Then, during the psychoanalytic era, it began to be seen as a rough composite of choice and family influences. Now, at least among many mental health professionals, a vaguely emerging consensus points toward a complex mixture of genetic and environmental influences with freedom to choose being squeezed out altogether. The free-will factor in the etiology of homosexuality has shrunk to the point of "I can't help being what I am" and vaulted to the point of "I am gay and proud."

Psychiatrist Jeffrey Burke Satinover argues that the social and political forces arrayed around the question of homosexuality happen, at this moment, to be constellated in such a way as to make many people want to find little or no choice involved in it. Indeed, he claims that the homosexuality debate is configuring itself in precisely the reverse way of most debates about the medical basis of human behavior: People usually resist the idea that their behavior is given by unchangeable biological factors. (Feminists decry the adage: "Woman's anatomy is her destiny.") But in the case of homosexuality, many people, through homosexual propaganda and media sympathy, have been persuaded that a gay person's condition and conduct is predetermined and ineluctable.

Free will is the quintessential manifestation of the human spirit. The essential feature of the Christian and Jewish view of reality is that it turns on the question of individual moral choice. Everything depends on our decisions. To imply that a psychological orientation is a stable and fundamental dimension of one's personality cuts off reasonable hope of change and freedom, and is scarcely consistent with traditional Catholic teaching. Personal moral choice provides the clue to the salvation or damnation of the individual and forms the foundation and framework of our democratic society.

Demotion of Grieving Leads to Greater Loss
(*The Providence Visitor*, January 20, 2000)

My sister and sister-in-law died recently. Like myself, they were in their 80s. They lived long and lived well. Though quite ill, they struggled to survive. They clung to life. God implants the instinct to survive in the very marrow of our bones. Euthanasia practitioner Dr. Jack Kevorkian notwithstanding, self-preservation is the law of life.

Pope John Paul II, reflecting on death, states: "Even we elderly people, fond of life, find it hard to resign ourselves to the prospect of making this passage to eternity."

In the great democracy of death, every person is equal. Death levels the high and the low. "You are dust," says the Book of Genesis, "and to dust you shall return." Shakespeare's Cymbeline laments:

> *Golden lads and girls all must,*
> *As chimney-sweepers, come to dust.*

Six feet of earth makes us all of one size—or, as the rhymester puts it: "Don't you laugh when the hearse rolls by ... cause you may be the next to die." An elderly gentleman once observed, "Nobody gets out of this life alive." And a wiseacre remarked, "We have been born into a world where three out of every three people die." Then we have the proverb: "Live every day as though it is your last, and one day you'll be right."

Yet people, especially if they enjoy good health, hate to think of death as inevitable. Most humans prefer to feel exempt. Their attitude is that "the captains and kings depart," but not me.

If the instinct to survive is so natural, it might seem that to accept death would be unnatural. Yet dying is the most natural thing in the world. Death comes inexorably. Even in his agony, when the good Lord prayed, "Let this cup pass from me," he accepted death with the words, "Not my will, but thine be done." And mystic Thomas à Kempis tells us, "If one is not able to die, he is not really able to live."

Yet, although we may be confident that a loved one has gained eternal glory, we are still sad. There is a void, an emptiness that is hard to fill. The Church warns us not to spend bereavement in "vain and unavailing grief," but it takes a strong faith to realize that the death of one who is near and dear is final. And even greater sadness is experienced when one has to dispose of the earthly possessions of the deceased. Four times within the past few years, I have had this duty. I used large plastic bags to contain the things I was discarding.

The items had value, sentimental, for the deceased (when they were alive), but for no one else. One departed brother had saved old Christmas cards, mail, clippings from newspapers and magazines, gold scorecards, favorite poetry, prizes, citations, and a variety of mementos and souvenirs. I filled 12 trash bags with his baggage. As I packed things to be taken out, I thought sadly, "Is this the sum of a person's earthly life? Twelve plastic trash bags full?"

Even if a dead person leaves thing of great value—a Mercedes Benz, a mansion, a yacht—it all amounts to something that "moths and rust consume" (Matthew 6:19). Photographs—what do you do with hundreds of them? Yet, there is no more healthy experience than to dispose of the earthly goods of the deceased. It shores up one's scales of values. It helps one see all things in the light of eternity.

Recall Christ's story of the rich man who had such a bounteous harvest that he had to build extra silos. Then he said to himself, "I have goods in reserve for years to come. Relax! Eat heartily, drink well. Enjoy yourself."

But, warns Christ, "God said to him, 'You fool! This very night your life shall be required of you. To whom will all this piled-up wealth of yours go?'" That is the way it works with the man who grows rich for himself instead of growing rich in the sight of God.

Ours is an acquisitive society. Wealth is a sign of prestige. We are amazed that Bill Gates, Sam Walton, the Sultan of Brunei, the ultra-rich of this world, have accumulated so much money—billions upon billions. And the comfortable middle class often complains about not having enough closet space. At the time of death, I have seen many a stuffed closet, a well-stocked cellar, and a loaded attic. "Naked came I out of my mother's womb and naked shall I return thither." (Job 1:21).

Is it morbid to speak of death and dying? Some people think so. Twenty years ago, anthropologist Geoffrey Garer wrote a much-reprinted article on "the pornography of death." Grief, he alleged, is going underground. People want briefer funeral obsequies—shorter wakes, little or no church services, fewer prayers, and a shielding of relatives from the strain of seeing the casket lowered into the grave. Even those much-scolded death merchants, the undertakers, seem to sense that something has gone awry.

The outward signs of mourning—veils and widow's weeds, black hat and armbands, crepe-hung doorways—have gone the way of the hearse pulled by plumed horses. There is no social censure against going on a cruise or marrying a short time after the death of a spouse.

The clergy and psychologists who have no quarrel with the life-must-continue attitude worry about the unintended effects of the decline in the expression of grief. By saying no to weeping, wailing, waking, and "sitting Shiva," family members may have to mourn covertly, by subterfuge—perhaps in various degrees of depression, perhaps in mad flights of activity, perhaps in the haze of alcohol.

Thanatologists tell us that the social repression of grief goes against the experience of the human race. Mourning is one of the traditional "rites of passage" through which families pay respect to the dead and return to normal living. Perhaps that is why St. Augustine observed that "Funerals are rather the solace of the living than the comfort of the dead."

For the Catholic, resurrection faith tells us not to look for the living among the dead. Our loved ones who die in Christ are to be found with him in the land of the living in the presence of the One who is light and life. The four last things—death, judgment, Heaven, and Hell—are facts of faith for the Catholic.

The death of one who is close forces the individual to face the fact that we are all pilgrims and wayfarers on earth. In meditating on our journey to eternity, perhaps it would be well to keep in mind the words of an ailing Pope John XXIII: "My bags are packed, I am ready to leave."

Drug Control Necessary in a Thrill-Seeking Society
(The Providence Journal-Bulletin, June 8, 1995)

Cocaine hotline founder Dr. Mark S. Gold declares that cocaine is "the drug of the future in cities and on college and high-school campuses," and psychologist H. Stephen Glenn warns parents that children who are never taught to delay gratification for the sake of future goals will be the drug addicts of the future.

"Instant gratification"—this phrase explains why drug addiction has got a stranglehold on so many Americans. The "drug culture" is with us because "getting stoned" makes people feel good. Unless Americans are honest enough to face that fact, the war on drugs will never get very far.

Drugs fire the emotions, exhilarate, produce euphoria, "blow the mind," create a high, transport into a mystical state, beget feelings of gaiety, jocularity, and ecstasy, induce heavenly bliss or sweet oblivion. Short-lived as these beatific effects may be, they are so intensely pleasurable that drug users gladly risk the side effects of horror, panic, psychosis, dread, depression, hostility, aggression, anxiety, paranoia, and brain damage.

Sedatives, euphoriants, hallucinogens—all obtain, in their own peculiar way, their hold on users. Cocaine's superman effects make it especially insidious. Users extol its intense, euphoric rush with its "I can do anything" feelings of tremendous physical and mental prowess.

Drug expert Andrew Weil feels that the failure of Prohibition should have taught this country that the criminal law will not affect drug taking in our society. According to Weil, what we are now doing in the name of stopping the drug problem is in reality the drug problem.

Parents, educators, and legislators are beginning to see that the condition of our culture is part of the problem. We live in a time of great anxiety and profound doubt; life for many Americans is devoid of larger purpose. They seek escape from frustration, boredom, aimlessness, anonymity, anger, and despair. Drugs offer an easy out.

Millions chase after the high—some for excitement, others out of psychic need or physical dependency. Self-styled swingers, effete middle-agers, bored housewives, et al. are persuaded that any thrill-producing activity is in itself worth pursuing. So long as one gets "kicks" out of it—that's what life is all about. For many Americans, morality is, says sociologist of religion Will Herberg, "a fun morality"—a repudiation of traditional morality in favor of a way of life governed by a self-indulgent quest for pleasure.

Purveyors of transporting experience exploit this yen for kicks. The amusement life of the city is one vast emporium for the sale of thrills—from the visceral responses of the roller-coaster ride to the frenzy evoked by hard-rock music. Much of it is harmless.

It's different with drug-produced thrills; they thwart the effort of society to socialize impulse, and to absorb and utilize an individual's desires in the realization of social objectives. Drug thrills allow impulse to run riot, so that the energy which might have been expended for the work of the world goes over the dam unproductively. In a life dominated by thrill seeking, the individual expends energy for the sake of his own personal pleasure; his enjoyment is not related to any larger social wholes. That is why every civilized country in history has outlawed hard drugs.

Drug abuse is inextricably tied in with the larger ethos of American society. In a democracy, the dignity of the individual is understood in terms of a moral universe—a set of expectations of how citizens should live. Until very recently, our American society operated on an ethic of duty, character, hard work, and achievement—that celebrated "Protestant ethic" which is in such bad repute today. Heavy drug users subscribe to a hedonistic ethic.

In the final analysis, a person's attitude toward drugs reflects his attitude toward life. Educators now perceive the drug problem as the creation of an adult culture that is more powerful than any school ethos. A school can teach about drugs, or it can expel or suspend a drug-using student; it cannot convince him or her that it is foolish to take drugs in the first place because it is self-destructive. Young people know that—they just don't care. To educate youth to a consciousness of why they should care demands the all-out cooperative effort of parents, churches, schools, the media, political leaders, and other societal agencies.

Even then, the drug epidemic will continue to flourish until there is a resurrection of the "hard" culture of discipline, restraint, and dedication—until Americans can instill in youth a moral vision where drug taking is seen as unnecessary for living the "good life."

Case of the Narcissistic Philanthropist
(*The Providence Journal-Bulletin*, December 23, 1993)

Volunteerism in America has taken a different tack. The new breed of volunteer now sacrifices himself for his neighbor in need because he hopes to get more than he gives. The result of this is a decided decline in volunteer effort.

Did the biblical Good Samaritan expect to get paid back when he rescued the poor beggar waylaid by robbers? When he doctored his wounds and donkey-hauled him to the inn, did he ask himself, "What's in it for me?" Was he on a self-serving, look-out-for-number-one, ego-tripping, personal-fulfillment kick when he dug down into his purse to care for the victim?

No, the idea of selfless voluntary service is imbedded in the very core of religious doctrine and practice, and from its inception, the United States has been famous as a nation of volunteers.

It took the psychically preening, narcissistic movements of this era, combined with the lunatic fringe of feminism and the philosophy of studiously cultivated selfishness advocated by novelist Ayn Rand, to encourage Americans to turn their backs on their own history and condemn service-above-self as suckers' work.

To flourish, indeed, to survive, volunteerism cannot afford to neglect its theological and philosophical underpinnings. The dynamism that drives a volunteer to help his fellow man derives from his convictions. When a man helps his neighbor only because of selfish, emotional, or even moral considerations, he begins to flag early in the fight.

The poetess Edna St. Vincent Millay charms the listener when she writes, "A man was starving in Capri . . . And [I] knew his hunger as my own." Yet, she talks sentimental rubbish unless her moral idealism is firmly rooted in a philosophy or dogma concerning man and, indeed, death.

It is only a powerful doctrinal consideration that compels a Mother Teresa to pursue the lowliest of the low in the slums of Calcutta, not with poetry, but with exhausting work, seeking them out and swabbing their sores, not in Capri, but as she finds them in the gutters of the teeming alleys of the metropolis—which is more difficult and more rare. She is driven to spend her talent, her energy, herself, by the dynamic that comes from her faith.

She doesn't arise in the morning asking herself what the sensitive moral conscience should say about the problem of the poor in the ghetto. Rather, a consuming dogma makes her seek the image of Christ in every pariah and pest-ridden human flotsam who cries out for help. There is, and must be, a sound doctrinal foundation for the volunteer's good work, or he soon gives up or grows perfunctory in performance.

The human being is so built that he or she is moved to action more by ideas than by codes. It is not enough that one acts out of noblesse oblige, unless those obliged have clear ideas of why noblesse obliges, and of what noblesse is. More is needed than a kind of vague good will; a burning belief in the inestimable value of the individual is also required.

This ambition to serve mankind differs radically from the what-do-I-get-out-of-it kind of commercial philosophy. Why are volunteers in such short supply today? Simply because the religious motivation that galvanized volunteers to action has become progressively weaker under the impact of secularization.

Americans prefer to combine idealistic aspirations with pragmatic justification. Work for an abstract, selfless cause can also bring many satisfactions. Volunteerism contains many generous dollops of *quid pro quo*. Altruism rewards its practitioners. Newcomers learn about their community and meet neighbors; women in various stages of change can develop self-confidence and build résumés for future jobs; persons recuperating from illness can take gradual steps back to complete, healthy functioning; students can experience the roles and atmospheres of careers they are considering; retirees can stay active, feel useful, and share their wisdom; and employed persons can discover emotional satisfactions in helping their fellow man that they could never derive from their jobs.

Enlightened self-interest like this can scarcely be faulted. All these effects, however, while honorable and laudable, should be wholesome concomitants rather than the main objectives of volunteerism. To prevent the "service ideal" from degenerating into shallow ego indulgence or narcissistic self-seeking, the primary motivation should always be anchored in a deep-rooted conviction concerning the nature and destiny of man, and the inherent value of the law of love; otherwise, the desire to serve will be as short-lived as the ephemeral incentive that sparks it.

In his book *Markings*, former UN Secretary General Dag Hammarskjöld noted, "We glide past each other . . . because we never dare to give ourselves." That's what volunteerism is all about: giving oneself. In the words of the ancient Hebrew sage Hillel:

If I am not for myself, who is for me?
But if I am for myself only, what am I?
And if not now—when?

How Far Can Tolerance Go?
(*The Cowl*, February 10, 1988)

Tolerance demands that we be patient and understanding toward those of other faiths, classes, or cultures and free from severity in judging their actions. It follows that, to be tolerant, we must first believe something ourselves. Genuine tolerance is impossible for people who hold no definite convictions.

Yet there are Americans who maintain that nonbelief in objective truth is the *sine qua non* condition for achieving tolerance. If this subjectivist view of tolerance predominates, our nation will be devoured by the fierce convictions of its enemies. This drift toward a flaccid live-and-let-live stance moved Soviet premier Nikita Khrushchev to remark: "We will bury you!"

Our forefathers did not design a constitution based on tolerance and freedom because they believed less than the purveyors of tyranny, but because they believed a great deal more. The cheapest counterfeit of tolerance is the sheer indifference that argues that we want everybody to believe as he pleases because we have no settled beliefs of our own. This type of pseudo-tolerance easily becomes license for evil.

For centuries, racial injustice hid under an easy tolerance that counseled gradualism, i.e., given enough time, humans would stop abusing other humans, naturally.

In promoting tolerance, two extremes are to be avoided: 1) The harsh moralist position that fails to distinguish between sin and sinner—and concludes that since sin has no right to exist, neither does the person in sin. 2) The position that shifts feelings from the individual, who must be tolerated even if in error, to the error itself. Charity toward the sinner ends up condoning the sin; forbearance that thrives on a lack of interest in the difference between right and wrong comes ultimately to embrace the wrong itself.

Again, tolerance may degenerate into acceptance of conditions people ought to find intolerable. Protestant theologian Reinhold Niebuhr asks, "Does not tolerance of a theological position which one knows or believes to be untrue become a betrayal of the truth?" Niebuhr's question suggests that tolerance can parade as intellectual cowardice and evasion—as a weak acceptance of the world as it is.

To be tolerant one must be intolerant. Scientists, for instance, must be tolerant of every reasonable hypothesis, but they must be intolerant of sophistry and sham. A proper intolerance involves a discriminating judgment of ideas, not a rude suppression of persons. Every person ought to have his say, but we are not obligated to provide every nutty notion a permanent pulpit. Not all opinions are of equal worth. Merely having an open mind achieves nothing for, as English Catholic writer G. K. Chesterton points out, the purpose of opening the mind is to close it on something solid.

No one can love justice without hating injustice, nor can anyone promote right by slurring over wrong.

For centuries, racial injustice hid under an easy tolerance that counseled gradualism, i.e., given enough time, humans would stop abusing other humans, naturally. Martin Luther King, Jr. saw through this sophism and served notice that time had run out. No society can be tolerant when injustice prevails, or where freedom and human dignity are at stake.

Pseudo-tolerance, because it is actually indifference, can become a subtle form of superiority that reveals contempt, not respect. Agnostics often pride themselves on being tolerant in matters of religion—but only because they believe religion to be irrelevant. Belief in religious freedom becomes a high-sounding name for contempt of religion.

Again, intolerance often rages in apostates—those who have renounced a demanding religion of strict orthodoxy. They cannot contain the urge to castigate the system they left. Media personality and dissenting Catholic Phil Donahue is one example. Intolerance like this represents an over-revulsion against a severe religious home life and usually involves taking revenge on parents and upbringing. Atheist Madalyn Murray exemplifies how disavowal of faith can become militantly fanatical.

But human beings have such a need to believe in something that even religious skeptics tend to adhere to a belief in nonbelief—and intolerantly cudgel those who do not adopt their nonbelief and the brand of tolerance springing from it. Movie star Henry Fonda remarked: "I didn't tell my daughter [Jane] whom to marry, but I'd have broken her back if she had big eyes for a bigot." Apparently, Henry's tolerance was selective. This reminds one of the Southerner who declared: "If there are two things I can't stand, it's prejudice and niggers."

The acid test of genuine tolerance is one's attitude toward the intolerant. Perhaps Pope John Paul II displayed the highest form of tolerance when he forgave and embraced his attempted assassin. But this was an expression of charity—a virtue as far above tolerance as Heaven is above Earth.

To be deeply committed, yet truly tolerant, is no small task. The secret lies in remembering that the object of tolerance is always the right treatment of persons. Hence tolerance and truth need not be mutually exclusive. We may remain unqualifiedly intolerant of erroneous ideas and actions yet be truly tolerant toward persons we believe to be in error.

Indeed, we are obliged to pursue and profess truth with unflagging zeal, and even try to persuade others by argumentation and appeal to evidence; but we must always respect the good will and dignity of those with whom we disagree.

(12)
Sundry Subjects

George Washington Admonishes Americans of Today
(The Providence Journal, February 22, 1967)

If we Americans today took a hard and careful look at the life of George Washington, we would see that the "Father of our Country" has something to say to us. But we can learn from him only to the extent we are willing to listen to his words and imitate the virtues which made him the great patriot he was.

Washington was a unique character. History hails him as an "indispensable man." No other national hero can be saluted this way. For instance, Julius Caesar and Caesar Augustus reformed the Roman Republic, which had become rotten and inefficient, into a competent and, for generations, beneficent empire. But if they had not done so, perhaps another great Roman would have risen to the challenge and saved the Republic. It was not so at the birth of our nation. As Lafayette wrote, "What American, except George Washington, could have held the Continental Army together for six months?" Indeed, what other man of his moral stature and influence could have been found to lead our jealous and divided colonial forefathers to accept the peace and prospective prosperity of our Constitution?

Let us examine the qualities of character possessed by this First Statesman of our land, because the world is greatly in need of these qualities today. Historians all agree that George Washington, above all else, was a man of integrity. Indeed, no man has ever appeared upon the theater of public action whose integrity was more incorruptible, or whose principles were more perfectly free from the contamination of those selfish and unworthy passions which find their nourishment in the conflicts of party. Having no views which required concealment, his real and avowed motives were the same. A prolific letter writer, his whole correspondence furnishes not a single case from which even an enemy would infer that he was capable, under any circumstances, of stooping to the employment of duplicity. It can be said with complete confidence that our first president's objectives were always upright and his means always pure. I need not illustrate this truth by relating the silly story of the cherry tree.

Washington exhibits the rare example of a politician to whom intrigue was absolutely unknown, and whose professions to foreign governments and to his own countrymen were always sincere. In him was fully exemplified the real distinction which forever exists between wisdom and cunning, and the importance as well as the truth, of the maxim that "honesty is the best policy."

Contrast Washington's integrity with the moral flabbiness of the age in which we live. Never in the history of our country has the practice of fraud been so dignified by constant use and acceptance. Dishonesty from outright crime to sharp legal practices is on the increase. Scarcely a day passes without headlines announcing indictments, convictions, and scandal. Misdeeds uncovered in government, business, labor, entertainment, education, and the family induce an impression of moral hollowness in our most vital institutions.

Novelist Allen Drury in *Advise and Consent* calls this the "age of the shoddy," when the job on the car is half finished, the suit from the cleaners half dirty, and when "Everybody wants his" is the guiding principle. It is the fly-now-pay-later mentality. It's the itch for the fast buck, for the irresponsible pleasure, for the shortcut to power or status. It's the clever dodge, the inside track, the ideal, the gimmick, the angle, the guy we know who'll "fix" it. It is the omnipresent yen to push somebody else out of the way and become the fellow who's got everything.

This is a far cry from the integrity of character lived out in daily affairs by the Father of our Country, yes, and a far cry from that firmness of purpose and loyalty to principle which have been responsible for the progress of these United States. Let us heed the warning of the Irish poet Oliver Goldsmith:

> *Ill fares the land, to hastening ills a prey,*
> *When wealth accumulates and men decay.*

Can it be that we are becoming victims of a refined materialism and a creeping secularism? Today we often hear of the lonely man, the hollow heart, and the faceless crowd. Have the bigness and organization of modern society reduced us to ethical ciphers and irresponsible cogs? It is a rather strange and unwholesome paradox that while we are sending young Americans to Vietnam 10,000 miles from home, to fight, and perhaps to die, in the cause of freedom, here on the home front, we are all too apathetic and lethargic about preserving the very virtues and principles for which we are asking these men to risk their lives. Truly, there is no phenomenon of American life more offensive to the watching world than the spectacle of our leaders and citizenry who preach high and noble purpose, but who practice power politics and use underhanded methods on the plea that it is justified in the name of enlightened self-interest. If we want the nations of the world to respect us for our moral integrity, we cannot "play the saint and be the sinner."

This gradual sapping of our moral fiber has even subtler implication. It touches us all in a way that is difficult to define. Thinking men call it a loss of faith, a clouding of reason, a failure of nerve, a loss of confidence, a failure, in the words of Jesuit editor Thurston Davis, to maintain "our grip on the big idea about ourselves and the world we inhabit."

In short, we are gradually losing our grasp on the meaning and purpose of human life in relation to a real order of objective and transcendent being. Our problem is that we no longer know who or what we are. We no longer collectively see ourselves as a people bound together by common affirmations, common assumptions, and common loyalties to a commonly shared universe of values. We are allowing our vision of the American dream to grow dim, and, as the Scripture says, "Where there is no vision, the people perish."

A common perspective, common principles, common standards, and common ideals sustain and nourish the morale of a nation. George Washington was acutely conscious of this. That is why he labored against the countless local attachments and distinctions among those who supported the cause of the Revolution. And yet he was moved to write sadly to John Hancock, the president of the Second Continental Congress, on December 20, 1776, "I have found it impossible to overcome prejudices."

This was a discouraging situation. Not so discouraging, however, to make Washington refrain from deprecating jealousies among the troops from the difference provinces; not so discouraging to prevent him from pleading for unity in "the noble cause in which we are engaged and which we ought to support with one hand and heart." In his general orders of August 1, 1776, the great American earnestly begged officers and men "to consider the consequences; that they can in no way assist our cruel enemies more effectively than making division among ourselves; that the honor and success of the army, and the safety of our bleeding country, depends upon harmony and good agreement with each other; that the provinces are all united to oppose the common enemy, and all distinctions sink in the name of an American."

Such a plea for unity and loyalty and courage has pertinence today. Just six years ago, Ireland's Frederick H. Boland, then president of the UN General Assembly, remarked that there are "thousands of young intellectuals to whom the idea of freedom means nothing." As a consequence, they exist without purpose and "life itself has become flat, stale, and unprofitable."

How different from the life of George Washington, whose dedication to the mission of freedom moved him to heroic sacrifice! When men deserted; when officers carried over provincial rivalries into personal antagonism; when the Congress and the states were unable or unwilling to supply the armies with a bare minimum of essentials; when provisions were refused to the Continental Armies, only to be sold at a fat profit to the enemy for good British gold; when military disasters piled up one on another; when in the dark days at Valley Forge there was a growing fear that the people might become completely disunited and supine, or even yield to the enemy's peace offer—when facing all these dangers, Washington was dauntless. His courage inspired his officers and men, and his example should inspire our youth of today and all citizens, with a willingness to work and sacrifice for the welfare of their country. At Trenton, Washington saw the Hessians. A man of smaller vision would have seen only the Delaware choked with ice. History records the success of those who have the "guts" to fight for the objectives they esteem, while oblivion is the reward of those who see only the obstacles.

But the "Father of Our Country" was not merely a starry-eyed idealist. He was also a hardheaded, practical soldier. Indeed, he was too wise to believe that patriotism alone would bring about the success of the Revolution. He wrote from Valley Forge in April 1778, "Men may speculate all they will; they may talk of patriotism; they may draw a few examples from ancient history of great achievements performed by its influence; but whosoever builds upon it, as a sufficient basis for conducting this bloody war, will find themselves deceived in the end. We must take the passions of men as nature has given them and those principles as a guide which are generally the rule of action. I do not mean to exclude altogether the idea of patriotism. I know it exists, and I know it has done much in the present contest. But I venture to assert that a great and lasting war can never be supported on this principle alone. It must be aided by a prospect of interest or some reward." And so, Washington struggled to put the army on a "respectable footing," to convince soldiers and civilians that the cost of defeat would be immeasurable and the rewards of freedom sweet and lasting.

If the letters of soldiers are sufficient evidence of their sentiments, fighting men in all wars are preoccupied most of the time with thoughts of food, drink, mud, lice, and sex, rather than with patriotic sentiment and sustained conscious devotion to country. This was true of American Revolutionary soldiers. Nor should this surprise us, since the Revolutionary soldier knew nothing of a national government and was not even too clear about just what his country was. His loyalty and patriotism were in one sense negative: He was against what seemed to him wrong and oppressive. Only falteringly did he come in a positive way to associate American rights with an American nation, and when he did so, the American nation was an abstraction. For in 1776, an American nation might exist as an idea, as an aspiration, but it hardly existed as an actuality.

The situation today should be much different. The United States has now existed for almost two hundred years. Citizens of all ranks should have more than a vague idea of what we are, of what we stand for, of what we are working toward, and of what we aspire to become. America is frequently called a pluralistic society. This pluralism is thought to be a product of our freedom and a source of immense strength. Perhaps it is. But if it signifies divisions on matters vital to our process and survival, it could become a debilitating disease.

Patriotic fervor, as well as proper self-respect, should impel us to imbue our youth with that "pride in country" which motivated George Washington and our illustrious forefathers to instill an appreciation of the American way of life, and to develop an understanding of our American heritage. Civil War historian and novelist Philip Van Doren Stern once said: "The fight for freedom is an endless battle. It's victories are never final; its defeats never permanent. Each generation must defend its heritage, for each seeming conquest gives a rise to new forces that will attempt to substitute fresh means of oppression for the old. There can be no peace in a world of life and growth. Every battle the fathers thought finished will have to be fought anew by their children if they wish to preserve and extend this freedom." Freedom is not a privilege; it is a responsibility.

If, like George Washington, we are devoted to freedom, we will never permit the Democratic Idea to slip away. Indeed, we should be constantly asking ourselves the big questions connected with this Democratic Idea. What are the questions? They are manifold. Some of them may be phrased in this fashion: What is the nature of man? Is there a difference between man and the rest of nature? Is the nature of man spiritual in a unique sense? What is man's destiny? Is it to be found and fulfilled beyond time in "another world"? What is the "sense" of history? Does history have some kind of finality? Or is the notion of "finality" meaningless? What can a man know? Are there varying degrees of knowledge and certitude? Can man's knowledge and love reach realities that are transcendent to the world of matter, space, and time? Is there a God? What is God? Does God have a care for man? Has God entered the world of human history to accomplish a "redemption"? What is meant by "salvation"? What is meant by freedom, justice, order, law, authority, power, peace, virtue, sin, morality, and religion? Are the concepts of human equality and excellence realized best in a democratic society?

George Washington, like every thinking man, asked himself these questions. He found an answer to many of them in Christianity. The principles of his faith served as a foundation upon which he built the edifice of patriotic duty and service to his fellow man. Indeed, he was convinced that the practice of religion and the progress of the new nation would go hand in hand. In his Farewell Address he said, "Of all the dispositions and habits which lead to political prosperity, religion and morality are indispensable supports ... And let us with caution indulge the supposition that morality can be maintained without religion. Whatever may be conceded to the influence of refined education on minds of peculiar structure, reason and experience both forbid us to expect that national morality can prevail in exclusion of religious principle."

Our first president feared what would follow if God were left out of the life of the nation. In this, he had history on his side, for experience verifies that wherever God is ignored, the ethical code seems to resolve itself into several axioms: "Everybody's doing it"; "If I don't, somebody else will"; "You can't do business on Gospel principles"; "I'm not in politics for my health"; "What's in it for me?"; "Do unto others as others would do unto you, but do it first."

These are cynical expressions of a look-out-for-number-one philosophy of life. Yet, if God has no significance in the life of the individual, such cynical self-seeking is quite logical. For if there be no God, and since no God, no soul; and since no soul, no conscience; and since no conscience, no moral responsibility; no accounting here or hereafter; no final rewards or punishments; no blessing upon virtue, and no curse upon vice, then, who or what is to prevent any person from doing anything he can get away with?

As English judge Baron John Moulton once observed "Unless we have sufficient citizens who will obey the unenforceable, we must expect increasing regimentation until our free societies go the way of the dictatorships." We need a code of morals that will work on the street, in business, in dancehalls and theaters, in courthouses and statehouses, in the national Capitol, and in all the relationships of man with man. We need those inner sanctions which will restrain man where there are no laws or police to hold him back. We need to inculcate those ideas of right and justice, which rest, not upon expediency or the latest Gallup Poll, but upon the law of God.

George Washington was not willing to settle for a "lip-service" kind of religion. Even as a schoolboy he inscribed in his copybook, as a maxim for daily living, the following words: "Labor to keep alive in your breast that little spark of celestial fire—conscience."

Truly, this great patriot was a "man of character." Devoid of personal ambition, he loved his country well enough to hold success in serving it an ample recompense for all that he did. He never calculated "How much will this cost me?" and when his country needed sacrifices that no other man could or perhaps would be willing to make, he did not hesitate for a moment. This is virtue in its most exalted form. George Washington serves as an exemplar for all who would follow the advice of President John Kennedy, "Ask not what your country can do for you; ask what you can do for your country."

Is America producing persons of strong character like this today? We are building a defense of steel, ships, planes, guns, atom bombs, and intercontinental missiles. But is this enough? No nation is stronger than its individual citizens.

What we have to fear is not force from without but weakness from within. No one is likely to destroy America but Americans. Our way of life could be destroyed without a shot being fired. Theodore Roosevelt said, "The things that will destroy America are prosperity at any price; peace at any price; safety first, instead of duty first; the love of soft living; and the get-rich-quick theory of life."

That is why we need national heroes like George Washington. These great Americans show us clearly how patriotic ideals can be powerful driving forces in the lives of men. They give an answer to those who would belittle altruism and sneer at love for country as a value embraced only by chumps and simpletons. They demonstrate that it is possible to restore patriotism without the hundred-percent chauvinism of "my country right or wrong," or without the negativism of a spirit of debunking which can find nothing good in what we do. They remind us—and all of us need to be reminded again and again—that political democracy is worth fighting for, and that it has been bought only at the high cost of pain and suffering. Finally, the heroes of our country fire us with the will to respond to the call of a noble ideal, and these great men help, by their example, to instill in youth a devotion to duty.

Could you ever imagine George Washington, when he was asked to assume the leadership of our country, replying to members of Congress, in the jargon of the sick humor of today: "Gentlemen, I am honored. But I do wish you would try someone else. Let's say: General Horatio Gates. I'm just getting things organized at Mount Vernon. Also, you might say, I have already served my time. Against the French, you know."

And what would you think of patriot Nathan Hale, if he had responded in this fashion: "Me, spy on the British? Are you trying to be funny? Do you know what they do with the spies they catch? I'll give you a news flash, chum. They HANG them." No, our heroes would never have subscribed to a "better-Red-than-dead" philosophy. They believed there are values more precious than mere survival. And there is: freedom. Indeed, the words of Nathan Hale are just as inspiring now as when they were first uttered, "I regret that I have but one life to give for my country."

The spirit of George Washington speaks to us across two centuries and tells us, by word and example, that the things which go right in these United States, and the things that go wrong, are not something outside of us. The splendor of America is our splendor. The shame of America is our shame. America is just people, people like you and me.

So we look up to George Washington, and admire his character, and hope that our children will be moved to emulate his virtues, for in trying times like these, the nation needs true patriots.

As the American poet and novelist Josiah Gilbert Holland exhorts:

> *God, give us men the time demands:*
> *Strong minds, great hearts, true faith, and willing hands;*
> *Men, whom the lust of office does not kill,*
> *Men, whom the spoils of office cannot buy,*
> *Men, who possess opinions and will;*
> *Men, who have honor; men who will not lie;*
> *Men, who can stand before a demigod*
> *And damn his treacherous flatteries without winking;*
> *Tall men, sun crowned men, who live above the fog*
> *In public duty and private thinking.*

How to Break Out of Prison
(Talk delivered at the Rhode Island
Adult Correctional Institution, July 1970)

You are gathered here this evening to have an honor conferred upon you. You will receive a diploma, a testimonial to your progress in learning. That diploma is public recognition of the fact that you have worked hard. It is a sign or symbol that you have successfully acquired a certain amount of knowledge and skill.

But perhaps you have made a mistake in trying to acquire knowledge. What will this learning get you? Isn't it true that "the more you know, the worse off you are"? Remember the old saying: "What you don't know won't hurt you." In other words, don't try to learn more and more; it will only make you miserable. Do you recall the quatrain about the joyful dumbbell?

> *See the happy moron*
> *He doesn't give a damn*
> *I wish I were a moron*
> *My God, perhaps I am!*

Perhaps some of you recall the days when Joe Penner was a popular radio comedian. I think it was he who used to sing:

> *It pays to be iggerent*
> *To be dense, to be dumb, to be iggerent*
> *It pays to be iggerent*
> *Just like me.*

Then we have the famous line of the Greek dramatist Sophocles: "The happiest life consists in ignorance." And it was the poet Alexander Pope who said: "Where ignorance is bliss, 'tis folly to be wise." Finally, in the Bible, the Book of Ecclesiastes states: "In much wisdom is much grief; and he who increases knowledge increases sorrow."

Even so, would you, if you had the choice, prefer a joyful lie to harsh truth? Would you, for the sake of a spurious bliss and false peace of mind, choose to live by ignorance and happy illusion than by knowledge and bitter reality? Verily, as the Scripture says: "A gloomy truth is better than a cheerful falsehood."

And that is why I chose as my theme this evening (with all due respect to your warden, Harold Langlois) the topic "How to Break Out of Prison." I am not trying to be humorous or facetious ... for, certainly, that is what education should do: It should help you to escape from the prison of ignorance, of prejudice, of discouragement, and of boredom. It is in this sense that the words of the English poet Richard Lovelace are most true.

> *Stone walls do not a prison make*
> *nor iron bars a cage:*
> *Minds innocent and quiet take*
> *That for an hermitage*
> *If I have freedom in my love,*
> *And in my soul am free*
> *Angels alone, that soar above,*
> *Enjoy such liberty.*

It was with this thought in mind also that French mystic Jeanne Guyon penned these lines:

> *But though my wing is closely bound,*
> *My heart's at liberty;*
> *For prison walls cannot control*
> *The flight, the freedom of the soul.*

Remember the old song: "If I had the wings of an angel, over these prison walls I would fly." Well, in a real sense, learning does give you wings so that you are able to enjoy life more fully, so that you are able to solve your problems more effectively, so that you are able to earn your living more proficiently, and so that you are able to use your time more wisely, whether you are in jail or out of jail. That is why I hope that your learning does not end with the granting of this certificate. My wish for you is that you continue to learn—from books, from people, from your successes and failures, from life itself, and from every little thing you are called upon to do.

As American poet Bayard Taylor says:

> *Learn to live and live to learn*
> *Ignorance like a fire doth burn*
> *Little tasks make large return.*

The purpose of education is to mold mind and character. But when all is said and done, you, and you alone, are going to be responsible for your own character, because you, and you alone, are the cause of your own actions. And that is why we can all be at times our own worst enemy.

How do we know anything about a man's character? Only in one way: by his actions. As a man is, so he acts. You can tell a man's character not merely by what he says, but how he acts in the varying situations of his life. The actions of a man may be of many different kinds, but whatever their aim or objective, they will always reveal character in some way.

But can't a man fool you this way? Can't he merely play a role? Can't his actions become a mask? Can't he play the hypocrite and fake it in such a way that no one would know the difference, behaving so as not to shock his neighbors, acting like other people do, so that he will not appear different—playing Dr. Jekyll and Mr. Hyde.

Yes, he could do this. But not for long. You can't fool all of the people all of the time. So let me state at once: If a person behaves in a certain way only because it is useful or agreeable, or because if he does not act that way he will be inconvenienced, then I say he can't hold that pose continually. The true nature of such a person is bound to leak out sooner or later.

All right, you can tell a man's character by the way he acts. But why does he act? Well, he can act for any one of a hundred thousand reasons; but you can be sure that when he does act he acts for some purpose, aim, objective, or some value. When he acts he always tries to get some good, some satisfaction, or something of value. These values can be put on a scale. Some are higher than others. So the type of character a person has will depend on the scale of values he holds—values which he tries to realize in his life.

But can a man change his character? Well, history and biography—the lives of saints—give examples of astounding and outstanding changes of character. Still, some have said that he can't. Man, they say, is completely determined to act the way he does by reason of his heredity and environment.

Now nobody will deny that heredity and environment have a tremendous influence on you, and upon the formation of character. Your body build, basic intelligence, and temperament—all are a result of inheritance, and all play a part in the development of personality. Your environment, too, is important. When the late Senator Robert Wagner was held up as a living example of American initiative for having risen from the slums of New York to become a senator for his state, he said, "Bosh, think of the thousands who never had a chance to better themselves."

No one will deny that, generally speaking, there is a higher incidence of delinquency in the slums than elsewhere. This still does not, however, take away self-determination. Would you say that Hitler could not help himself—that what he did was merely the product of his adolescent frustrations? Would you say that everyone in this prison is here on a bad rap, and that no one here is responsible for what put him here? No! Man is not merely acted upon by forces over which he has no control. He is free and capable of choosing between right and wrong. He builds his own character. Indeed, if he were not responsible for his own character, if he could not change it—why should we even be talking about such a thing as education and character and personality development. Truly, in regard to character you are the captain of your soul and the master of your fate.

But what about the saying to the effect that you can't change an old dog, "You can't teach an old dog new tricks." That just isn't so. Think of King Solomon. Look what happened to him even in his old age. He certainly changed. Maybe, however, we should discount that instance because he was under powerful feminine influence.

By and large, however, it is true: You can't change an old dog. Why? Because his habits are too settled—he's comfortable in them, they fit him like an old shoe. They are not flexible—which is all for the good, because if his habits are good, why should he want to change them? You form habits in order to act swiftly, promptly, smoothly, and easily in order to attain with pleasure some goal. You gain habits by repeated action, and they make for efficiency. But just as you gain habits by repeated action, so also you can break them only by repeated contrary acts which will make opposite habits. There is a great deal of truth in the saying:

> *Sow a thought*
> *Reap an act*
> *Sow an act*
> *Reap a habit*
> *Sow a habit*
> *Reap a character*
> *Sow a character*
> *Reap a destiny*

That is why the psychologist William James said: "The hell to be endured hereafter is no worse than the hell we make for ourselves in this world by habitually fashioning our characters in the wrong way." Could the young but realize how soon they will become mere walking bundles of habits, they would give more heed to their conduct while in the plastic state. We are spinning our own fates, good or evil, and never to be undone. Every smallest stroke of virtue or vice leaves its never-so-little scar. The drunken Rip Van Winkle excuses himself by saying, "I won't count this one!" Well, he may not count it, and a kind Heaven may not count it; but it is being counted none the less. Down among his nerve cells and fibers the molecules are counting it, registering it, and storing it up to be used against him when the next temptation comes up. Nothing we ever do is, in strict scientific literalness, wiped out.

Of course, this has its good side as well as its bad. As we become permanent drunkards by so many separate drinks, so we become saints in the moral sphere and experts in the practical and scientific spheres by so many separate acts and hours of work. Let no one have any anxiety about the upshot of his education, whatever the line of it may be. If he keeps faithfully busy each hour of the working day, he may safely leave the final result to itself.

Of one thing you can be sure: No habit is endowed with an irresistible virtue or force. If a man wants to get rid of a habit and he is unable to do so, it is not because the habit is irresistible, but because he still clings to the aims and the values that this kind of action realizes. You can't teach an old dog new tricks, then, because he really doesn't want to learn them. He's happy and satisfied with his old tricks. He gets pleasure out of them, and it is too much trouble to change. It all depends on what he wants, then, and how badly he wants it—whether he wants lofty ideals or low ideals. As the writer Dale Carnegie has said:

> *Two men looked out through prison bars*
> *One saw mud; the other stars.*

If you want to change character you've got to change habits, and to change habits you have to change motivations and intentions. These intentions, moreover, must not remain in the realm of the abstract, but must be reduced to action.

Do you recall the saying, half true, half cynical, to the effect that: "The road to Hell is paved with good intentions." Well, perhaps it is—if by good intentions you mean those half-hearted, unformed, and ineffective wishes to be better that come to the most hardened sinners when some satiety or shock of conscience arouse them to a faint fear of the punishments of God or men. But if by good intentions you mean honest resolves to root out faults and lead a better life, resolves that are expressed in concrete action, then the saying should run: "The road to Heaven is paved with good intentions; for it is only by making very many good resolutions—even though one breaks them and remakes them again and again—that anyone can ever accomplish anything worthwhile. We are not angels and cannot move with angelic swiftness and decision. Being men, we must act as men; and it is human to have to make many efforts before we conquer a bad habit and place a good one in its stead.

And since each person can only accomplish those things of which he is capable, the parable of the talents seems to apply here. In the Gospel account, three men were given talents: the first, one talent; the second two; the third, five talents. It was the man with the one talent who failed to use it profitably, and he was cast into outer darkness. Sometimes one wishes that the parable had been differently told, that it had been the man with five talents who failed to use them to the fullest extent and had therefore been condemned; for the Scripture states: "To him whom much is given, much shall be demanded." But our Divine Master Jesus Christ wanted to point out that those who can do only little must do that little, and great is their merit if they do it faithfully; and that what counts most is not so much what one has, but what one does with what one has.

So the cardinal sin is not to use your God-given talents, not to achieve according to your ability, not to realize your potentialities—whether they be great or small. Do what you can with what you have, and waste not your energies in brooding over the past, moaning over the present, or indulging in useless self-pity. The Chinese have a proverb:

> *I wept because I had no shoes*
> *Until I saw a man who had no feet.*

As a courageous physically handicapped person once said to me—and this is a motto we could all profitably adopt:

> *I am only someone,*
> *But I am someone.*
> *I can't do everything,*
> *But I can do something.*
> *That I can't do everything is no reason,*
> *For my not doing what I can.*

This is all that God asks of you; this is all that others should require of you; this is all that you should demand of yourself. Give of what is in you—and if this certificate symbolizes that you have been trying to perfect yourself according to your abilities, then I say congratulations to you, to Mr. Al Morro and to whomever has given you assistance and encouragement to achieve this goal.

Free? In Prison?
(Talk delivered at High School Graduation,
Rhode Island Adult Correctional Institution, 1980)

Ten years ago, I spoke to the men at the ACI. It was the feast of their patron saint, St. Dismas, the thief who was crucified at the right hand of Christ on Calvary, the thief who heard Christ whisper: "This day you will be with me in paradise." I asked one of the prisoners what in prison life he found hardest to take. He was a very sensible young fellow, and intelligent; he answered: "Father, for the most part it's not too bad. They're quite kind to me here: I'm learning a trade; I have friends; I have some time to myself; even the food could be worse. But the one thing I don't have is the one thing I want: I don't have freedom; I'm not free."

The point I want to make is this: There is a part of your life that is utterly free, a part of your life that no state can take from you, no power can force. In that aspect of everyday living you do as you please; in every waking hour you are as free as president or pope, you are as free as I. There is a part of your life no human being can enter, unless you say yes. I mean: your mind, your thoughts.

You see, what I think is not determined by where I am. Just because I am kneeling in church does not mean that my thoughts are fixed on God. So too for you. The state can put you behind bars for stealing; it cannot compel you to believe that stealing is sin. It can put you in total darkness; it cannot extinguish the light in your mind. It can make you say, "I'm sorry"; it cannot make you think it. It can keep you here for a lifetime; it cannot make you like it.

I can talk to you till sundown with all the warmth of my soul; and you can close your mind to every word. Why? Because your mind is your own. God will not force it, and man cannot. There is only one way to destroy that freedom—and that would be to destroy you.

It is a remarkable gift, this power to know, this power to think. Why can it not be taken from you by force? Because it is one of the qualities which make you a human being—which make you so very much like God.

Do you remember the words of Scripture when it describes the sixth day of creation? "And God created man to His own image"—to the image of God He created him, male and female, He created them.

What does this mean? It means that every human being bears a striking likeness to his Lord. It means that, no matter who you are, no matter what your blood, or skin, or accent, you come into this world sharing two of God's precious perfections: You have the power to know, and you have the power to love.

It is the power to know that interests me now. You are like God in that you have intelligence, you have the power to know. Not as a plant knows where the sun is; that is a figure of speech. Not as a dog knows where an enemy lurks; that is a question of seeing and hearing and touching, and tasting, and smelling. No, of all earth's creatures, you alone can think. You alone can put two and two together and get four. You alone can fashion the formula for an H-bomb. Only you can appreciate a sonata, a cantata, or a fugue. Only you can think of God; only you can know God.

So then: You have the power to think; this power makes you somewhat like God; this power no human being can take from you. This is where your freedom lies—you are master of your mind. But the big question, because this is what separates the big people from the little, the women from the girls, the good from the bad, and the wise from the foolish: It all depends upon what is going on inside of you, in that mind of yours that nobody else can touch.

On broad lines, there are two ways you can think. You can, if you wish, make all your thinking center around yourself. You can pity yourself for the pitiful situation you are in. You can blame others—mother, father, relatives, friends, enemies, or society, for what they have done to you or have not done. You can hate with a hatred bitter as bile. You can plot revenge and lick your lips in devilish anticipation of what will happen when you get out. You can think lustful thoughts, all the more frustrating, because you can do so little about them. You can be selfish and brutal and angry; you can be mean and obscene. And all you will achieve is this: You will be small, foolish, ignorant, inhuman, unloved, and unlovable.

Or you can do just the opposite. You can fill your mind with what is true, what is beautiful, and what is good. By reading and thinking, by talking and listening—yes, by praying too—you can open your mind like a ripening bud to truth and beauty and goodness.

Instead of imprisoning your mind, you can let it roam over the world, to Europe, and Asia, and Africa, even to those Communist-controlled lands where men and women are far less fortunate than you, because, unlike you, they have no hope. You can fill your mind with history, with the story of man and what he has done, because this is your story. You can learn how to do things, to make and create. You can grace your mind with art, and music, and literature. You can even think about God; at least, don't close your mind to Him, for He loves you very dearly, and He wants so very much to live in you. Do this, and you will achieve a remarkable change, a transformation; you will be a different person; you will be much wiser, much more mature, much more human, and much more lovable.

And that, I suggest, is what makes this occasion, this graduation, such a striking thing. Had they wanted to, these young men might well have imprisoned their minds as well as their bodies. They could have been content with the little they knew; they could have closed their minds to the outside world, to truth and beauty and goodness; they could have closed their minds to everything except their own small selves. Had they done so, they would this day be tragic men, because they would be men without hope. And a human without hope is not quite human; a man without hope is not quite manly.

But this they have not done. They have used their minds as God intends minds to be used. They have opened their minds—opened them to a little more truth, a little more beauty, and a little more goodness. And so, they are this day a little more divine, because they are a little more like the God who is Truth, who is Beauty, and who is Goodness. And they are a great deal more human because their minds are so much more free. More divine, more human; no wonder their hope is high.

Graduates: I am unbelievably moved by what you have achieved—far more moved than I have ever been at a graduation outside the prison walls. Outside, men are free—so free that most of them resist knowledge. Here, only your mind is free—and you have opened it to knowledge. That is why my hope for your future is so high—high hope that, when you are utterly free, you will use your freedom to know what is true, to love what is good, and to do what is right. God bless you and keep you ever in His care!

The Spirit of Providence College
(*The Cowl*, October 21, 1987)

Whoever dares to gauge the spirit of a college by examining only its physical aspects—a manicured campus, well-kept buildings, adequate playing fields, and excellent equipment—is mistaking the husk for the pith. Things are not of the essence, but persons are.

In days of yore, colleges had no campuses. Students and masters might be found walking in a garden, or strolling through the *agora*, as in ancient Athens, or squatting on straw in the street, as did scholars in medieval Paris. The place meant little, what really mattered was the purpose: students and masters imbued with the desire to enrich their minds with reality, to know being, its inter-relationships, its meanings, and its purposes.

Academic life, upon analysis, is not just a guild with its professional standards, principles of craftsmanship, and rules of procedure. Rather, it resembles a family, with members bound together by a common aim, collaborating, communicating, and provoking minds to a consideration of ideas, while helping one another to attain the end of liberal learning: intellectual excellence.

The sense of kinship is not produced by mere physical proximity; nor is it the camaraderie more appropriate to a locker room, barracks, or camp. More precisely, it is the unceremoniously and unofficially felt solidarity, unforced and unappointed, of those performing mental tasks which bring personal fulfillment and benefit to society; it is the spontaneous readiness for mutual help and joint efforts, and for joint intellectual creations.

This kind of spirit prevails at Providence College. Young in years, this Dominican institution boasts a tradition of learning stretching back 750 years to great minds such as Thomas Aquinas, Antonius, Albert the Great, and Catherine of Siena. Her disdain for mental mediocrity shines forth in the intellectual history of the Dominican Order, an Order, responsible, in no small measure, for the flowering of the medieval universities.

In the classrooms of Providence College, truth is not simply revered; it is deified. Truth is worshipped literally, since all truths are but adumbrations of the First Trust which is God—and the word Veritas, emblazoned on the escutcheon of the Friars Preachers, is also engraved in the heart of every professor.

Students soon learn that the worst enemy of mankind is not the tyrant, nor the merely greedy or lustful person. Rather he is the irrationalist, the enemy of truth, whether he be a philosopher attacking the foundations of metaphysics or a demagogue twisting issues or distorting facts by loaded language and subtle appeals to emotion.

That Providence College graduate who has acquired a genuine love of objective truth, no matter in what domain—scientific, historical, theological or any other—has received a hundredfold return for his tuition. The mind that has escaped the straitjacket of prejudice, superstition and ignorance, the mind that knows the truth about itself, its world and its God, and by knowing the truth has been made free, is itself the highest value a college can confer.

Contemplata aliis tradere ("To hand down to others the fruits of contemplation") is the motto of the Dominican Order. No institution of higher learning could embrace a more noble educational mission.

Ralph Waldo Emerson once said, "The secret of education lies in respecting the pupil." Providence College heeds this advice. How can a college generate loyalty in its clientele when it operates as a soulless machine, geared to run by a set of impersonal rules according to inhuman formulae that make no provision for personal dignity and student individuality? What a garish Brave New World campus it would be, what a nightmarish Orwellian college we would have, if a student was known merely as Number 2011, identification card 433, dining-hall passport 868, cumulative record folder 211, or under M in filing cabinet 32.

Cor ad cor loquitur ("Heart speaks to Heart"), Cardinal John Henry Newman's motto on his coat of arms, implies that contact with the heart must precede contact with the head.

Providence College holds high her "level of expectations" and demands that students give the best that is in them. "What all of us need," says the sage, "is someone to make us do what we are capable of doing." To develop potential to the utmost, the college places students under the tutelage of faculty members who are themselves living examples of intellectual force and refinement. Love for learning is contagious. "If you would be learned," the proverb advises, "attach yourself to the wise."

The distinctive ethos of Providence College is exemplified best in the wedding of faith and reason—a characteristic that sets a Catholic college apart from secular institutions of higher learning. The intellectual offspring of this union of faith and reason is the formed Catholic college scholar, a person able to exert an impact on the whole area of higher culture. As Vatican II points out, the best product of Catholic higher education should be "truly outstanding in learning, ready to shoulder society's heavier burdens, and to witness the faith to the world." (The Declaration on Christian Education, No. 18).

St. Augustine defines society as a group of persons united by agreement about the things they love. No school can thrive if it is a mere dumping ground of diverse interests and activities existing side by side, unrelated to any main purpose. A soul or spirit is needed to unite the parts and breathe into them the core values which undergird the operational procedures of the entire faculty student population.

The *esprit de corps* of Providence College springs from twin values: the faith she professes and the truth she pursues. In this psychic atmosphere flourish those loyal feelings toward *alma mater* which last lifelong, enkindling admiration in the freshman, riveting the affection of the senior, and evoking nostalgia in the alumni.

The Meaning of Being Irish
(*The Evening Times* (Pawtucket), March 17, 1982)

The Bible tells us that everything has its season, so St. Patrick's feast day is a fitting time to talk about the Irish. Nor should such eulogizing be ascribed to Hibernian chauvinism. On March 17th, the Irish tell us there are only two classes of people: those who are Irish and those who wish they were. You have to be Irish to know what it is to be Irish; there is no other way.

Four men were rapping at a bar. A Frenchman was asked: "If you were not what you are, what would you rather be?" He replied: "If I were not French, I'd rather be Scandinavian." The Scandinavian said: "If I were not what I am, I'd rather be English." The Englishman responded: "If I were not English, I'd rather be French." All turned to Pat Casey and asked. "If you were not Irish, what would you rather be?" Casey replied: "I'd be rather ashamed of myself."

No fair man ever begrudged an Irishman's paean for the glories of Irish history, the beauty of colleens, the holiness of Irish saints, the erudition of Irish scholars, or the dear imprisoned sunlight of Irish whiskey. What might rightly be construed as boasting by other nationalities must be regarded as simple understatement when proclaimed by a son of Erin.

One does not become a true Gael simply be reason of forebears who came from the "Auld Sod," or by merely waving a shamrock, blandishing a shillelagh, or exclaiming "Erin go Bragh." No, he must measure up to his Irish heritage.

The heritage is marked by a strong faith in God. It is faith's power to make the weak strong and the timid bold, to inspire courage in the face of hardship, to stand up for the free, the beautiful, the humane, and the spiritual; and the power to fight for human dignity.

For St. Patrick and the Irish, the dignity of man is but a reflection of the glory of His Maker, a mirror, in faces and hearts, of the eternal truth that man is a unique creation, an immortal among mortals. In a world where human life is frequently devalued and human rights are often trampled, the Irish have kept the torch of human dignity and freedom burning in the far-flung lands adopted as their own.

Granted the Irish are not without blemish. The imperfections of human nature are doubtless found less frequently in the Hibernian character, yet it would be a lover's blindness to ignore the fact that Irish, more than any other nationality, are plagued with an envious spirit. Let an

Irishman stick his head above the level of his fellows and he gets hit with a blackthorn.

George Bernard Shaw sneered, "The Irish are fair people; they never speak well of one another." A Gaelic pastor once remarked: "The only time the Irish stand together is when they stand for the Gospel at Sunday Mass." Verily. But the predominance of this fault only proves the Irish are more fully human, for the canker of envy is pandemic among men.

What faults the Irish have are more than offset by their legendary compassion. Let them hear the cry of distress and hearts and hands are quick to lift, console, soothe, or heal. No people are more generous than the Irish in giving their time, effort, and themselves to those in need.

The history of Ireland is threaded with appalling misery, bloodshed, and poverty; and black pages are being recorded in Northern Ireland today. Such long suffering has not, however, turned the Irish into a tribe of crepehangers.

Whoever said "You can't keep a good man down" must have had the Irish in mind. No matter what life brings, the Irish display a never-failing gaiety and sense of humor, an ability to accept the bitter with the sweet, to roll with life's punches, to laugh at its problems, to smile when others cry, and to sing when others sob. Herein lies their attractiveness.

Eire has been called the "land of the soft tongue." But the Blarney Stone is really an excess luxury among a people for whom eloquence is almost second nature. Irish talk is quite picturesque; an Irishman in a Dublin pub was overheard telling a drinking crony, "Don't provoke me or they'll have to dig me out of you."

The Irish are realists. They do not blind themselves to the greed, injustice, and barbarism of the world. But they have the knack of seeing the finger of God in the happenings of life, and so have trust that God's love is always there to draw good out of the evil He permits.

Sad experience has taught the Irish there is poverty, illness, misfortune, crime, and deceit around them. But there is also beauty. For every pain there is pleasure, music, art, or literature. There are fragrancies, sweetnesses, and lovely forms to gladden the heart, and delight the soul. There is love, kindness, comfort, mutual stimulation, jollity, and gay diversion.

Indeed, only those who see God's will in all things can sing the Irish "Te Deum," or hymn of praise to God.

Thanks be to God for the light and the darkness.
Thanks be to God for the hail and the snow.
Thanks be to God for lightning and tempest.
Thanks be to God for weal and for woe.
Thanks be to God when our pockets are empty.
Thanks be to God when again they o'erflow.

Poor Entitled to 'American Dream'
(The Providence Visitor, January 3, 1985)

It may well be true, as a *Journal-Bulletin* editorial recently pointed out, that "Only a little over one-half of the individuals living in poverty in one year are found to be poor in the next."

Still, this does not militate against the existence of a distinct culture of poverty into which the very poor are born and from which they are unlikely to emerge without considerable help.

Poverty is twofold; physical and psychological. The psychological is harder to cure. A kind of internal insufficiency permeates the character of the poor. It makes helplessness a way of life, breeds despair and bitterness, and affects the way they see and think—and the way they do not hope. They are life's "losers."

A Gallup Poll tried to find out what Americans looked forward to in the nineteen-eighties. Those at the bottom of the economic level did not expect to get a better job, have a vacation, or even have enough to eat. They did expect to get sick, lose their jobs; and many predicted World War III. Their pessimism reflected their hopeless existence—shut out, rejected, frightened, discouraged and defeated.

Money is the first, indispensable step in rooting out poverty. But all the money in the world cannot instill a sense of self-respect, an esteem for individual worth, or a conviction that people are not victims of impersonal forces but have the power to meet adversity and control their future. The poor must be educated to see that they are not merely formed by, and react to, their environment but that, in a very real measure, they create their environment.

Incentives must be put into public-welfare programs so that the poor will want to help themselves, will see the benefits of working full or part time, and will begin to realize that they are captains of their soul and masters of their fate. In short, a strategy is called for that rewards personal effort and initiative and roots out an attitude of hopelessness, despair, and powerlessness.

Not long ago, the U.S. Department of Health and Human Services released a study explaining "why poor people are like that." Basic areas were selected: family life, educational opportunity, health care, and consumer practices.

In each category, the poor were deficient. Family life was unstable, the mother assuming major responsibility for homemaking, rearing the children, and earning a living. The very structure of welfare militates against job seeking on the part of the man and prevents normal family living due to "absentee" fathers.

Educationally, poor children lag behind in subject matter, in comprehension, and in breadth of experience—some ghetto kids have never seen a live cow. Parents who themselves never read a book or newspaper cannot inspire offspring to succeed in school. The child's vocabulary is meager; he has never heard a variety of words; he can't communicate. There is simply no incentive for learning.

Health-wise, the poor, while most in need of medical services, get the least. They are less informed about health, get sick more, take fewer preventive measures, and wait longer before seeking medical attention.

In the hospital, the poor, studies disclose, are treated with less care and attention than patients in private rooms, and the clergy visit them less often than affluent parishioners. Moreover, they are fatalists about their health. Early symptoms of illness are often ignored, because "If you're going to get sick, you're going to get sick," and nothing can be done about it.

The poor even get stuck buying goods. They purchase irrationally. The saying "Only the poor pay full price; the rich get discounts and buy in quantity" is quite true. Indeed, the poor's very attitude works against them. They say, "I'll buy a bucket of coal to keep warm today—and worry about tomorrow when tomorrow comes." The practice of "getting by" is much more real than "getting ahead."

The fact that the poor lack shopping skill and often have inferior merchandise fobbed off on them for higher prices accounts for the existence of such organizations as consumer councils and social agencies designed to help the disadvantaged get the most for their money.

The poor are neglected, economist John Kenneth Galbraith tells us, because they are an inarticulate minority. The bishops' letter on the American economy provides a pulpit for the poor.

Enlightened self-interest alone dictates a cure for the poverty problem. Economists estimate that a person who lives on welfare from the age of 17 until the age of 57 costs the public well over $200,000.

Black militancy, civil-rights laws, and a rising crime rate have also created a new urgency to clean up conditions which generate social unrest. Far better to recognize that basic poverty exists than to be forced into acknowledging it by a series of riots, murders, muggings, and violent demonstrations of hostility.

Americans prize democracy as a political system which protects every individual by equitable laws, an economic system whose benefits are enjoyed by every citizen, and a moral system governed by compassion from which none are excluded. The glory of a country like ours is revealed in how we deal with that fifteen percent of our people who are destitute. A democracy must retain its reason for being—a government of the people, by the people, and for the people—all the people.

The answer to poverty lies not only in alleviating deprivation and hardship, but in helping the young escape the self-regenerating cycle of poverty in which their parents have been trapped. A mindset of poverty is handed down from parents to children to the children's children. Breaking that cycle will enable the poor to enter into the mainstream of American life and obtain their portion of "The American Dream."

A Cult of Mediocrity Is a Danger to Be Avoided
(*The Providence Visitor*, August 26, 2004)

There is a monumental stupidity problem facing our technological society. The more complex and industrialized a country becomes, the more will the natural distribution of brains be out of kilter with assortment of jobs that need to be done.

This state of affairs is inevitable, because intelligence among human beings seems to be parceled out in a fairly consistent pattern. Assemble 100 typical Americans. You will find that one or two are brilliant, 29 are quite bright, 46 are average, 20 are fairly dull, and two or three are extremely slow-witted.

While such figures, based on standard Stanford-Binet tests, must be taken with a grain of salt, the general conclusion holds true: Some people are born a lot brighter than others, and will stay that way. No amount of training will convert a weak mind into an intellectual powerhouse.

Until fairly recently, the world had plenty of jobs for people of low intelligence. They could herd sheep, dig ditches, hoist bales, tote loads, draw water, and hew wood. Most of the world's work called for strong backs. Few jobs required sharp minds, and most communities had room for only a few doctors, lawyers, clergymen, and big-scale industrialists.

As a consequence, thousands of bright people lived in frustration because no work equal to their talents was available. Even today, in undeveloped parts of the world, highly gifted people are hauling nets, throwing the shuttle on hand looms, sweeping streets, and winnowing grain with handbaskets.

However, in a world of computers, robots, and cranes, muscle has become almost obsolete. Anything brute strength can lift a machine can lift better. Virtually any task involving repetition of the same motions can be done faster and cheaper by a mechanical or electronic device. The number of chores demanding muscle alone is dwindling every day.

The permanent "de-jobbing" of the slow-witted is different from technological unemployment, in which workers, often bright, are replaced by machines. Because most craftsmen were smart enough to learn a complicated skill in the first place, they are presumably smart enough to be retrained for another occupation high on the skill scale. However, about twenty-two percent of the population—the dull segment—may in many cases never learn to do a useful job.

School dropouts are a case in point. Most leave school not because of economic problems but because they can't keep up with the not-very-demanding work. Eighty percent of dropouts are lagging by at least one grade, and by the end of high school, almost none of them is still in school. A few get jobs pumping gas or washing dishes, but many drift straight from the classroom to the relief rolls or crime.

We apparently have built ourselves into a society out of whack with the natural distribution of brains. We can't find any use for the low achievers in our midst—a situation unjust and miserable to them, and costly and dangerous to the rest of the community. Fifty years ago, James Conant, the Harvard educator, alarmed the nation by calling the plight of the unemployable dropout "social dynamite."

Before we can make a start in coping with this problem, several things must be done.

First, we must re-establish the respectability of all work, even the most menial. A man's self-esteem is intimately connected with the job he does, the pride he takes in doing it, and his ability to see its relation to his own and his community's well-being. No man should be looked down upon because of his job, and no honest work should ever be considered personally degrading.

Second, we'll have to face up to the fact that all men are not created equal. While singing paeans for the American ideal of educational opportunities for all citizens, we blind ourselves to the fact of individual differences. As French observer of America Alexis de Tocqueville observed more than a century ago: "A middle standard is fixed in America for human knowledge. All approach as near to it as they can, some as they rise, others as they descend... The gifts of intellect proceed directly from God, and man cannot prevent their unequal distribution."

The cult of mediocrity is the great danger to be avoided. There is no reason why quality need be sacrificed for quantity. The more conscious we become of the need to emphasize quality in education, the more must we come to grips with the problem of creating jobs for the less talented while persuading them to stay in school long enough to obtain training needed to carry out these jobs. Each young person should be encouraged to strive for excellence in terms of the kind of excellence that is within his or her reach.

Vocational education is a must. In heavily-industrialized America, educating youths, even those who are intellectually challenged, to the fullest extent of their ability, is not a luxury, but sheer necessity. Objective studies about how this can be done are not lacking. Unfortunately, they are often discounted, ignored, or filed away for future reference. Nobody expresses it more poignantly than John W. Gardner, U.S. Secretary of Health, Education and Welfare under Lyndon Johnson:

> *"It is an appalling error to assume that young men and women incapable of the highest standards of intellectual excellence are incapable of any standards whatsoever, and can properly be subjected to shoddy, slovenly and trashy educational fare."*

The Lottery Craze and Lady Luck
(*The Providence Journal*, March 20, 1984)

The chance to make a quick bundle at one big killing in the Massachusetts Megabucks Lottery has created a gambling frenzy bordering on mass hysteria.

The staggering sum of the prize prompts a question which has long intrigued students of gambling: whether players prefer to stake their money on a small probability of winning a large prize, or on a large probability of winning a small prize.

Philosophy professor John Cohen asserts that if players could be quite sure of winning one of two possible prizes, almost everyone would prefer it, provided it was large enough in relation to his money values, however much larger the uncertain prize might be.

The catch is that the prize has to be large enough. For instance, a blue-collar worker might well prefer a big chance of winning $10,000 rather than a very small chance of winning $100,000. Whereas the millionaire might prefer the more uncertain prize because $10,000 means little or nothing to him.

The more money we have, the less we value a given increase. That's why the low-incomed in society are the heavy lottery players. For them, winning makes a big difference. Indeed, concerned lawmakers think of lotteries as a kind of sneaky tax on the poor, even though some of the state gambling money eventually goes back to provide welfare for the impoverished.

A lottery differs from games of chance and from betting on one of several outcomes of an event insofar as it is totally devoid of any element of skill, and prizes are distributed by a randomizing device. But the idea of luck is found in all of them.

Ralph Waldo Emerson tells us, "Shallow men believe in luck... Strong men believe in cause and effect." But the Italian proverb "An ounce of luck is better than a pound of wisdom" disputes this.

Luck has two meanings: one, an unearned advantage, that is, something fortunate befalling a person without any effort on his part; and the other, that what happens is unexpected, against the odds, unpredictable, intrinsically fickle, and capricious.

For the religious person who believes in the governance of all things in the universe by divine Providence, there is no such thing as luck. Or more properly, what appears to be luck to humans actually falls in some way under God's causative power. So early Christian philosopher Lactantius could say, "Ignorance of causes forged the idea of fortune."

People tend to believe they have stores of luck that can be depleted and replenished. If, therefore, one of two players has been winning for a time, he may think he has used up his luck, while his opponent's store has remained intact. Gamblers also talk about "streaks" of winning and losing, and the laws of probability suggest that streaks are indeed real.

High-rollers get the publicity, but casinos, bookies, and lotteries batten on those of low and average income. Few players ever beat the game. Hence the adage "Bookies never cheat, they just wait." Professional gambler Nick the Greek observes that gamblers never get rich but bookies do—slowly—on the sure percentage.

Hope abounds in youth. So does the feeling of being lucky. With increasing age this feeling modulates. Women generally feel luckier than men, but when it comes to the use of lucky charms, numbers, colors, systems, rituals, etc., there are no sex differences.

Neanderthal man gambled, and so does sixty percent of American adults. Yet psychologists say there is no such thing as a gambling instinct. They do concede that the normal (as opposed to the compulsive) gambling impulse is part of the human drive for self-expression. By taking a chance, whether it be an adventure, a daring sport, or simply a bet, we assert our independence and shake our puny fists at Fate.

Moreover, gambling provides an outlet for those locked into humdrum, boring lives. It enables them to cast off temporarily the harsh realities of a cause-and-effect society, and furnishes, as one psychiatrist says, a "form of masturbatory pleasure." While life teaches us there is no such thing as a free lunch, gambling lets people dream of getting something for nothing.

Finally, belief in luck has social value. It allays discontent. If a person makes a fortune merely because he is believed by others to be lucky, and not because he has the right connections or any special merit, then he is safe from green-eyed envy. Someone else might have been lucky.

Similarly, the unsuccessful need not lose face; they are merely unlucky. The proverb "Fools have all the luck" is balm to life's losers. The words "I had bad luck" are more comforting than the words "I deserved it."

There are those who maintain that gambling is a painless way of raising money for churches, service groups, and the state, and so can be truly charitable. But we are only kidding ourselves to pretend that donations which are part of gambling losses are equivalent to self-conscious and purposeful support of worthy causes.

Optimists predict that the lure of gambling will diminish as American life gets fuller. Citizens, finding greater challenge in their jobs, their families, their sports, their reading, and their travels, will no longer have to resort to the artificial excitement of gambling. So that strange and beguiling itch to risk will disappear.

Don't bet on it.

Sports and the Whole Man: First Things First
(*The Cowl*, February 25, 1987)

The NCAA's approval of tougher academic standards for varsity players comes at a time when authorities are beginning to question the worth of contemporary athletics: their emphasis on competition, on performance, on technical excellence, on beating the next guy, and on winning at all costs.

Viewed in the narrowest terms of teaching Americans to keep fit, the sports and physical-education establishment is a bust. The value of exercise is broadcast throughout the land, yet scores of Americans are turned off to their bodies—we are the nation of fans rather than a nation of active sports persons. Even for those who measure up athletically, the results are doubtful. Successful athletes past the age of 40 end up in worse physical shape than their nonathletic counterparts; they put on more weight; they exercise less. And the correlation between success in athletics and success in life is negligible.

In the past, attacks on the established physical culture came from outside the athletic world—from irate college presidents and disgruntled intellectuals. Now, well-known athletes and sportswriters scourge the prevailing sports ethos in books and articles.

Strangely, at the very time when newspaper headlines recount drug escapades of rogue athletes, new approaches to sports are being unveiled and the old Roman ideal of *mens sana in corpore sano*—a sound mind in a sound body—is being resurrected.

One new direction, however, has the potential for doing a lot of harm: the use of psychological techniques, drugs, and hypnosis to improve performance.

The value of the psychological dimension in winning is well known to coaches. The common practice of "psyching up" players before a game is one example. Going a step further, coaches are now using psychological techniques of relaxation with their athletes, and football coaches have developed elaborate psychological profiles that pinpoint the personality of a good player—e.g., a blocker needs aggression, lack of empathy, etc.

Americans look askance at these methods because they smack of a "win at any cost" mentality, seem to take unfair advantage, and introduce mind-control techniques into something that is supposed to be play.

The movement to broaden the perspective of physical education as it is taught in schools and colleges shows promise. In the past, there has been an overriding interest on the technical aspects of the sport, for example, how to swing a bat, how to field, bunt, slide, etc. Now greater emphasis is being placed on teaching physical awareness as it relates to personal functioning. The body is now being used as a vehicle towards the education of the whole person. A coed enrolled in aerobic dancing exclaimed, "I discovered I had a body!" Dance lessons led to lessons in expressive movement. Knowing her body, working on it and with it gradually, became a powerful means of developing health, strength, agility, and grace.

Socrates states, "The purpose of physical exercise and games is the development of the soul." Author Michael Murphy sounds this same theme in his novel *Golf in the Kingdom*: "If we look at life in the largest sense—the return of human life to the divine—then sport is potentially a vehicle for this return because it builds essentially on delight and play, which are at the heart of the universe.... Today, there seems to be so much work involved in sports. Certainly, we need commitment and whole-heartedness in sport, but there need be no forcing things, no work."

The dictionary corroborates Murphy's view. The word "sport" derives from "disport," which originally meant "to carry away from work, to divert from care and make mirth."

If sports are ever to return to their proper role of pastime or amusement, Americans will have to change their attitude. This need not rule out rivalry. Indeed, even the negative elements of games have value. Competition, for instance, exists in life, and it exists to be overcome as people evolve higher values. At the simplest level this means transcending our own competitive drives in the spirit of the "sporting" attitude: the thrill of competing, winning, or losing, embracing an opponent, and the discipline of training.

Such acts can be taken as symbolic of the general struggle to reach beyond ourselves in the direction of a higher life. Right now, though, we have no vocabulary in sports for dealing with those transcendent moments when an athlete seems inspired and lifted beyond the possible into incredible feats.

A big task facing sports researchers is to determine specific psychological qualities and character traits which each sport helps to develop. How do different sports affect different people at different times in their personal development? Which sports last lifelong; which sports develop the will; or what is the role of the mind in particular sports? Is it the mind in the intellectual sense, or is it an instinctive, animal awareness that is actually developed in most sports? Which sports are good for whom, when, and under what conditions?

Conventional sports can be a powerful philosophical searchlight, teaching the player about himself. This knowledge could be consciously used in the development of the whole personality and could become a major focus of sports. Then, instead of being an end in themselves, sports would be back in their rightful place as a means, along with other human activities, to the full development of the person.

Pope John XXIII positioned sports properly in the wider frame of life, when he said: "Truth, justice, love and righteousness, equality, integrity of morals, natural modesty, right care of one's family, and of profession too, of one's good name, honor unsullied—these must not be slighted because of sports, their victories and joys."

Holy 9-Irons!
(*The Cowl*, unknown date)

The Catholic Church claims it has no place for part-time priests. It does. They are called golfers. In the state of Rhode Island, they flourish like mushrooms and account in no small measure for the high standing in which the Catholic clergy is held, even by men who flinch from the sight of a church as much as they would from a water hazard guarding the eighteenth green.

Latins view the golfing priest with unfounded suspicion. I remember a Spanish Dominican, who later became a celebrated provincial in Latin America, answering snappily when I asked him what he had learned from his years of study in the United States: "Americans do not worship God, they worship sports." But there was a guilty look in his eye because, while here, he had become a golf junkie and his handicap was almost down to single figures. Had he stayed in the States for just another couple of years, we might have seen Father Pancho Quixote, O.P., putting on the Master's green jacket long before Seve Ballesteros.

Father Pat Hunt, doyen of the clergy hackers, put the argument for the golfing priest in a few crisp words when someone asked him how he managed to remain so youthful and fit: "The road to heaven is either a rough way or a fairway. I have chosen the fairway."

Bishop Louis Gelineau (a non-golfer), at first suspicious of the time his priests spent on the course, at last saw the light and came to a similarly benign conclusion, though with a useful proviso. "A pastor," he said, "with a handicap below ten is neglecting his parish; over 17 and he's neglecting his golf." That fine episcopal judgment is the golden rule. When observed, both priest and parish prosper. God loves a cheerful golfer.

Father Bob Randall provides telling evidence of how golf helps the apostolate. Having won many tournaments, his name lives for evermore in letters of bright gold in clubhouses here, there, and everywhere. The faithful rejoice. Agnostics recoil. His church is crowded with lapsed golfers hanging on his words like pacifists listening to a Quaker preacher. They look for the power of the Lord that adds fifty yards to a drive. They seek the healing word that cures shanking or putter's twitch. They trust a spiritual authority that gets results in low scores. When they see a priest driving three hundred yards and sinking thirty-foot putts, they know that the grand old faith is doing its stuff. And if it does so well by the shepherd, why not also for his sheep?

Of course, it works both ways. The golfing evangelist's vocation is a testing one. Every time he picks up a club he does battle for his faith. One bad round and the agnostics take heart and the faithful waver. I remember once playing what I thought was a friendly match with a disbelieving fellow golfer. It was only as we teed off that I realized that not just my golf but God was on trial. If my foe won, his doubts would be confirmed. If I won, Augustine, Aquinas, and John Henry Newman might need to be reconsidered.

In the first few holes, the Almighty was clearly preoccupied with more weighty matters. My opponent drilled his shots straight down the fairway, judged his chips to an inch, and sank his putts without a flutter. After six holes, I was five down and drifting steadily into the agnostic ranks myself. Perhaps the five proofs for the existence of God had to be rethought. At last, I raised my eyes to heaven and told the Deity that I might be a bad golfer, but He was a good God and it was high time He proved it. It worked like a charm. My agnostic competitor fell apart, my game pulled around, and I won a whopping victory by a great one-hole margin. He went home to throw away his David Leadbetter instructional video tape and swore he would purchase the *Summa Theologica*.

For the priest golfer such stresses are magnified a hundredfold. He is always in the front line, and the evil spirit will be sniping from close quarters. The wiles of Beelzebub are often met under many guises. A priest, so the story goes, once popped into his country club to play a quick round and was told that a stranger guest was looking for a partner. The priest, a fair player, agreed to fill the bill. When he met his opponent, they exchanged their handicaps, the priest an iffy 16, his opponent, he claimed, about the same. But before they had played nine holes, it was clear that the stranger had been bluffing and was practically a scratch golfer. When they reached the 19th hole the stranger was ebullient, the priest uncommonly silent. "Well, Father," said the stranger, "any time you want a game, I'm your man." "You don't call me, I'll call you," answered the priest, "but tell your parents to come around and see me whenever they want to get married."

Good golfers and priests easily recognize a bad lie.

Where'syoursenseofhumor?
(*Columbia*, February 1965)

A person can survive without food and drink for a relatively long period of time, but no man can live long without humor. The ability to see a joke helps us make the most of this life and merit the most of heaven. Man was made to be happy. When he stays depressed for days on end he harms himself. Indeed, among Americans, laughter is held in such high esteem that a person is deeply offended when he is accused of not having a sense of humor.

Medical investigators recently discovered that lighthearted patients shake off infection much more promptly than "down in the dumps" patients. Moreover, physicians attest to the fact that people who are cheerful resist disease better than do gloomy persons. Apparently, the surly bird catches the germ. Folk wisdom sums up this relation between good humor and health in the rhyme:

> *Care to our coffin adds a nail, no doubt.*
> *And every grin so merry draws one out.*

Again, mirth at the dinner table often adds to the conviviality of this family ritual, or it serves at least to take one's mind off a tasteless meal. And has not the belly laugh always been thought to be an aid to digestion? That is the source of the saying "Laugh and be fat." And so stout people have the reputation for being jolly and fun-loving. Shakespeare acknowledges this truth when he has Julius Caesar say, "Let me have men about me that are fat, sleek-headed men and such as sleep a-nights."

Whether fat men are jolly, and thin men glum, is an arguable point. But nobody will gainsay the beneficent influence of a sense of humor. As the Book of Proverbs says: "A merry heart doeth good like a medicine." In the case of humor, the medicine blesses both him who gives and him who receives.

But humor has other uses. We all need it to keep our balance amid the stresses and strains of daily life. Nobody can possess sound mental health unless he develops the ability to laugh some things off. So long as he can laugh, things are not too bad. No matter how desperate a situation may appear, if a person manages to see some humor in it, something can be salvaged. Indeed, one must not only be able to laugh at the world because it is ridiculous, but he must also be able to laugh at himself (before others do) because he, and every person, is, in some sense, ridiculous.

Humor and emotional stability go hand in hand. The laughing individual is not a brooder. He doesn't take any of his emotions too seriously. Nursing ancient hates, maintaining a hostile silence for those who have wounded his pride, being suspicious of another's motivations, feeling that other people have it in for him—all these make it difficult for a man to be playful. To laugh, a person must be in the mood for laughter. His mind must be free. It ceases to be free for laughter the moment a situation calls up any strong emotion—hate, rage, fear, grief—that is stronger than his enjoyment of seeing something incongruous. The bigot and the hatemonger seldom see the humor in a situation because their prejudice blinds their judgment.

Humor demands perspective, a coign, or angle of vantage. It rests foursquare on an individual's scale of values, his beliefs, and the convictions according to which he judges everything. The man of humor perceives the gap between the real and the ideal, between what is and what ought to be, and between what people say and what people do. Because he has standards for measuring human conduct, he can sift the important from the unimportant and be amused at the foibles and follies of human nature. Humor supplies a person with magic glasses to look at the world and spot the comic and the ironic, the paradoxical and the contradictory, the pretentious and the blundering, and to derive sport therefrom.

Perhaps humor could be defined as the art of not being solemn about little things. It takes the larger view of life upon which good judgment is founded. Hence, the habit of laughter fosters the talent of objective appraisal. With it, a man is better prepared to evaluate things sanely and correctly. Even the most solemn feelings or actions are comic when they are overdone. It is the big man who can laugh at his own pomposities. The paranoid individual, on the other hand, wants to be taken seriously at all times. Happy the person who can appreciate the incongruity of taking himself too seriously! Such a man can laugh off many a jibe and many a barbed thrust at his own pretensions.

But humor also ensures social success. The person who can sense the humorous in any situation is never without friends. As the poet Ella Wheeler Wilcox says in her poem "Solitude":

> *Laugh, and the world laughs with you;*
> *Weep, and you weep alone.*

The lugubrious look and the "woe is me" attitude alienate all but the saints. Who ever invites the moody and broody and gloomy person to his anniversary party? The sad-sack is usually a loner. Popularity contests are invariably won by those who have a keen sense of humor. We do not need a Dale Carnegie to tell us that a smiling face helps to win friends and influence people. English humorist Sir Alan Patrick Herbert expresses it in verse:

> When laughing Ann trips down the street
> The sun comes out as well,
> The town is at her twinkling feet,
> The crier rings his bell,
> The young men leap like little fish,
> Policemen stand and purr,
> While husbands look behind and wish
> That they had married her.

Most people react favorably to a ready smile that is genuinely motivated. They come to despise, however, the phony smirk of the paid entertainer, or the insincere half-grin frozen on the faces of the musical-comedy chorus line. It would be a mistake, moreover, to confuse a silly laugh, or a readiness to laugh on all occasions, regardless of the provocation, with a sense of humor. Such laughing may merely indicate a lack of emotional maturity or may point to a need for self-control and for a more reflective spirit. Thomas Aquinas observes that those who carry humor too far are clowns, while those who never see the humor in anything are stuffed shirts and killjoys.

The great Roman orator Marcus Tullius Cicero advised public speakers to begin by rendering their audiences "well-disposed, attentive, and willing to learn." The easiest and surest way generally used by speakers to make an audience well-disposed is to begin by telling a witty story. More than a good beginning is needed, however. To keep an audience awake, or to break the tension of a solemn address, the skillful orator frequently inserts a humorous anecdote at a strategic point in the middle of his speech. This is sound psychology. Educational researchers state emphatically that learning spiced with humor helps a student grasp a lesson thirty to forty percent faster and retain it forty percent better. This is because we are so built that we tend to forget the unpleasant and remember the pleasant.

Moreover, smart teachers know that humor disarms ill-will. When the emotions are strongly aroused the brain does not function properly.

A pupil who is angry with the teacher is in no condition for learning. But no one can laugh heartily and stay angry for long. The teacher need not be a pedagogical Bob Hope or Martha Raye so long as he or she realizes that humor makes learning more attractive, palatable, or at least tolerable. When pupils laugh heartily at their teacher's jokes, however, the teacher may rightly suspect that it is not because he is clever, but because his pupils are.

Thee is one active ingredient of a working and ubiquitous sense of humor: intelligence. From time immemorial, man has been defined as a rational animal, and a rational animal is a risible animal—a being who laughs. The tickle in humor is mental. That is why no one likes to admit he does not "get the point" of a joke. It implies that he is stupid.

Animals have no sense of humor. They may have a playful disposition and a tendency to mischief which is sometimes laughable to us. But no irrational animal ever really laughs. Genuine laughter involves a grasp of the relationship of ideas, and this requires an intelligence that animals lack. For instance, the successful humorist in telling a joke must call upon judgment, reason, memory, and intelligence. He must have a background of universal knowledge, must be able to use words effectively, and must have a sense of timing. Because it is cerebral, the regular practice of humor cannot fail but to sharpen the mind.

Besides, a high percentage of humor is purely linguistic in nature. To appreciate or indulge in puns, wisecracks, exaggeration, understatement, irony, satire, malapropisms, and the like, one must possess some mastery of the English language. The paradoxes of G. K. Chesterton, the wit of C. S. Lewis, and the satire of George Bernard Shaw are wholly lost on the illiterate. Indeed, the dull or slow-witted would find it difficult to see any humor in the nonsense verse of Lewis Carroll or Edward Lear. This is because humor depends largely upon perception of incongruities, objective evaluation of human foibles, and the ability to recognize and use peculiarities of language construction.

But if humor and intelligence are irrevocably wedded, then faith must be a first cousin. This is as it should be, because the tidings of religion are the tidings of great joy. The very word Gospel means that. The Holy Spirit, moreover, dwells in the Church, and joy is one of His gifts. God dwells in our souls, and God is infinite joy. It is a well-founded opinion that a sense of humor is a gift that God gives to those who serve Him well. St. Teresa was convinced that "a saint who is sad is a sad sort of saint." And on another occasion, she did not hesitate to say, "From silly devotions and sour-faced saints, deliver us, O Lord."

Religion should be limber and light-hearted. Hilaire Belloc, that serious and prolific Catholic author, has left us these immortal lines:

> *Wherever the Catholic sun doth shine,*
> *There's plenty of laughter and good red wine,*
> *At least I've always found it so,*
> *Benedicamus Domino!*

If humor is an appreciation of the incongruous things in life, if it consists in the ability to see the absurdities and inconsistencies in what people say and do, then a Catholic should have this insight more than others. The man of faith views his life and his conduct through the eyes of God and in the light of eternity. His faith shows him the proper relation of all things and their harmony, and whatever preserves that harmony is admirable, and whatever jars with that harmony is laughable. "The fashion of this world passeth away" says St. Paul. And only those who know this can be truly lighthearted.

But the humor of faith would be a fragile vessel if it existed only when "everybody's happy and the goose hangs high." Anyone can retain his sense of humor when everything is hunky-dory. As Paul Dunbar observes:

> *It's easy 'nuff ter titter when de stew is smokin' hot*
> *But it's might hard ter giggle when dey's nuffin in de pot.*

Catholic humor can be found even when things are not "going our way." For instance, when St. Thomas More was climbing the stairs of the scaffold to be beheaded in 1535, he said to the Lieutenant of the Guard, "See me safe up. Coming down I can shift for myself." Then there was the sickly saint, who, when he had the gout, thanked God it wasn't influenza, and when he had influenza thanked God it wasn't the gout.

This is a far cry, however, from a saccharine, Pollyanna attitude towards adversity and suffering. A "grin and bear it" posture can be more unrealistic and out of place than a pose of "I stand bloodied but unbowed." It is the inalienable right of every human being to be glum, depressed, and humorless when troubles pile up, and we are down on our luck. To express it in a parody of poet Rudyard Kipling:

> *If you can smile when things go wrong*
> *And say it doesn't matter,*

If you can laugh off cares, and woe
And trouble makes you fatter,

If you can keep a cheerful face
When all around are blue,

Then have your head examined, bud,
There's something wrong with you.

For one thing I've arrived at:
There are no ands and buts,

A guy that's grinning all the time
Must be completely nuts.

Look at the saints. They show us that it is possible to be cheerful even in the face of suffering. Indeed, it may well be that the Lord, Jesus Christ, fortifies His saints with a keen sense of humor because he demands such great sacrifices from them. St. Aloysius Gonzaga used to ask himself in every varying circumstance of life, "How does this look in the light of eternity?" And if everyone asked himself this question, what an infinity of laughable things he would see, what a wise, kindly, smiling view of life he would acquire. Think of the countless little things during the day that fret and annoy, and that tend to make a person petty and mean and irritable. Would they not evaporate in the light of this question: How does this look in the light of eternity?

It is the wholesome objectivity, the undisturbed equanimity and the cool steadiness which our faith gives us, that is the basis of a Catholic sense of humor. And it is this humor which should help us transform this vale of tears into a mountain of joy, here and hereafter. Perhaps it would be a good idea for all of us to pray every day:

Give me a sense of humor Lord
Give me the grace to see a joke
To get some pleasure out of life
And pass it on to other folk.

Ecclesiastical Jokes Needed
(*The Providence Visitor*, June 16, 1983)

My contention, namely, that humor in the pulpit is a rare phenomenon, needs no proof. If the pews could talk back, they would verify my thesis.

But why this lack? Can it be that preachers cater to a clientele of sad-sacks? Sellers, after all, supply what the buying market demands. Maybe the faithful want all the verities of life served straight: "Gimme Truth on the Rocks! Don't cut it with jest and jollity."

What bunk! The devout are always ready for a laugh. Who could doubt it who ever beheld a portly bishop run a captive audience through his repertoire of ecclesiastical jokes? The nuns—those paragons of propriety—rock the sanctuary with laughter if a retreat master so much as cracks a pun. "A saint who is sad is a sad sort of saint," said St. Teresa.

As for the laity, they smile and chuckle, grin, giggle, and guffaw at a preacher's feeblest jest—even though it would evoke a groan anywhere but in church. But pulpit humor is mostly unconscious—the blooper kind.

One specious way of rationalizing the dearth of wit in preaching is to badmouth humor itself. Denounce it and its outward signs, the smile and the laugh, as minuscule values, trifles that ill-become the lofty aim of announcing the Good News. Indeed, in a world of vanities and idle words, one could argue that sallies of wit bear some faint stigma of moral fault.

For the puritan, laughter has "sin for a father and folly for a mother," while the patrician spurns it for being crassly plebeian. British statesman Lord Chesterfield—though he suffered his ideal of a gentleman sometimes to smile—would not condone laughter; the smile for him had a certain snob value, but laughter had only a mob value, being the mark of merriment of the ill-bred.

Perhaps the British nobleman could not dissociate laughter from the mockery, contempt, and envy that often inspire its grosser forms. But plainly, not every display of humor implies a failure in justice and charity.

Indeed, a happy heart, medical research reveals, raises a person's efficiency level, and the cheerful resist disease better than the gloomy. Hence the adage "The surly bird catches the germ."

The smile and the laugh are not like the hyena's grin. They are distinctively human and have the power to give relief from tension when all other means fail.

American humorist James Thurber phrases it nicely: "After a little of Einstein there ought to be a little Cole Porter, after a talk abut Kierkegaard and Kafka should come imitations of Ed Wynn and W. C. Fields. Humor is counterbalance. Laugher need not be cut out of anything, since it improves everything. The power that created the poodle, the platypus, and people has an integrated sense of both comedy and tragedy."

A novel called *Jesus the Unknown* by T. M. Mathew downgrades laughter by claiming it belittles the dignity of Christ. To quote: "Sometimes He wept, but He never laughed . . . That convulsion of the face which may not be human or even animal, but purely devilish, never distorted this perfect human face."

I gag on that. It dissevers humor from holiness. If Christ did not laugh, you would have to imagine an infant Jesus who never gurgled with delight at His mother's lullaby; a boy Jesus who never shouted with glee while playing with the lads of Nazareth; a divine Teacher who never relaxed His disciples by harmless jokes about the persistence of tax collectors and the vagaries of the weather, or chuckled at Peter's astonishment when he found a stater in the fish's mouth. Verily, "we cannot really love somebody at whom we never laugh."

But my main reason for thinking the Man of Sorrows did not eschew fun and frolic stems from Thomas Aquinas. That portly ascetic of enormous common sense somehow makes room for a little treatise on mirth in his mighty *Summa Theologica*.

For the Angelic Doctor, merriment embraces words and deeds that serve no end beyond the soul's delight. He insists that there is a call for such playfulness on the human scene, just because the soul, like the body, grows weary and needs occasional jollity to renew its ardor.

As a final slap at the killjoys and the unbendingly solemn, Aquinas elevates mirth to a virtue, and accuses the lugubrious of sinning when they cast a pall of gloom over wholesome fun and gay diversion.

Can it be that homilists, engrossed in the sacred, take themselves too seriously? Obviously, life's no joke to the priest who reads its value in the fallen blood of Christ. The good Lord is not an actor in an ancient TV sitcom, and the preacher who plays the pulpit comedian, studding his sermon with quips and wisecracks, demeans himself and his message.

But the Church suffers more from sacerdotal stuffed shirts than from clerical buffoons. Mother Teresa counts a joyful spirit as one of the signs of vocation to her religious institute. She knows a sunny disposition attracts souls, and that the funny bone is one bone which needs jiggling now and again. Conceivably, a dash of the ridiculous could sharpen the laity's conception of the sublime. An aperitif of humor might whet the palate of the faithful for larger portions of the dish of divine truth.